Lecture Notes in Computer Science 3186

Commenced Publication in 1973
Founding and Former Series Editors:
Gerhard Goos, Juris Hartmanis, and Jan van Leeuwen

Zohra Bellahsène   Tova Milo
Michael Rys   Dan Suciu
Rainer Unland (Eds.)

Database and XML Technologies

Second International XML Database Symposium, XSym 2004
Toronto, Canada, August 29-30, 2004
Proceedings

 Springer

Volume Editors

Zohra Bellahsène
LIRMM UMR 5506 CNRS/Université Montpellier II
161 Rue Ada, 34392 Montpellier, France
E-mail: bella@lirmm.fr

Tova Milo
Tel Aviv University, Computer Science Department
Tel Aviv 69978, Israel
E-mail: milo@post.tau.ac.il

Michael Rys
Microsoft Corporation
One Microsoft Way, Redmond, WA 98052, USA
E-mail: mrys@mircosoft.com

Dan Suciu
University of Washington, Computer Science and Engineering
Box 352350, Seattle, WA 98195-2350, USA
E-mail: suciu@cs.washington.edu

Rainer Unland
University of Duisburg-Essen
Institute for Computer Science and Business Informations Systems (ICB)
Practical Computer Science, especially Data
Management Systems and Knowledge Representation
Schützenbahn 70, 45117 Essen, Germany
E-mail: UnlandR@informatik.uni-essen.de

Library of Congress Control Number: 2004110717

CR Subject Classification (1998): H.2, H.3, H.4, D.2, C.2.4

ISSN 0302-9743
ISBN 3-540-22969-8 Springer Berlin Heidelberg New York

Springer is a part of Springer Science+Business Media

springeronline.com

© Springer-Verlag Berlin Heidelberg 2004
Printed in Germany

Typesetting: Camera-ready by author, data conversion by PTP-Berlin, Protago-TeX-Production GmbH
Printed on acid-free paper   SPIN: 11317616   06/3142   5 4 3 2 1 0

Preface

Modern database systems enhance the capabilities of traditional database systems by their ability to handle any kind of data, including text, image, audio, and video. Today, database systems are particularly relevant to the Web, as they can provide input to content generators for Web pages, and can handle queries issued over the Internet.

The eXtensible Markup Language (XML) is used in applications running the gamut from content management through publishing to Web services and e-commerce. It is used as the universal communication language for exchanging music and graphics as well as purchase orders and technical documentation.

As database systems increasingly talk to each other over the Web, there is a fast-growing desire to use XML as the standard exchange format. As a result, many relational database systems can export data as XML documents and import data from XML documents and provide query and update capabilities for XML data. In addition, so called native XML database and integration systems are appearing on the database market, whose claim is to be especially tailored to storing, maintaining, and easily accessing XML documents.

After the huge success of the first XML Database Symposium (XSym 2003) last year in Berlin (already then in conjunction with VLDB) it was decided to establish this symposium as an annual event that is supposed to take place as an integral part of VLDB. The goal of this symposium is to provide a high-quality platform for the presentation and discussion of new research results and system developments. It is targeted at scientists, practitioners, vendors and users of XML and database technologies.

The call-for-papers attracted about 60 submissions from all over the world. After a careful reviewing process, the international program committee accepted 15 high-quality papers of particular relevance and quality. The selected contributions cover a wide range of exciting topics, in particular XQuery processing, searching, ranking, and mapping XML documents, XML constraints checking and correcting, and XML processing. An exciting highlight of the symposium was the keynote by Mary Fernandez from AT&T Research. Her talk *"Building an Extensible XQuery Engine: Experiences with Galax"* was a perfect start for this symposium.

As the editors of this volume, we would like to thank all the program committee members and external reviewers who sacrificed their valuable time to review the papers and helped in putting together a truly convincing program.

We would also like to thank the organizers of VLDB 2004 (and of XSym), especially Iluju Kiringa, and the general chair of VLDB 2004, John Mylopoulos, without whom this symposium would not have been possible. Our special thanks also go to Akmal Chaudhri. He not only was always available when a helping hand was needed but he also did an excellent job with implementing and maintaining the XSym homepage. Finally, we would like to thank Alfred Hofmann from Springer for his friendly cooperation and help in putting this volume together.

Tel Aviv and Orsay, Seattle, Essen, Montpellier, Redmond

July 2004   Tova Milo (Program Committee Co-chair)
                                             Dan Suciu (Program Committee Co-chair)
                                                 Rainer Unland (General Chair)
                                          Zohra Bellahsène (General Co-chair)
                                             Michael Rys (General Co-Chair)

Members of the International Programme Committee

Bernd Amann, CNAM Paris (France)
Sihem Amer-Yahia, AT&T Research (USA)
Michael Benedikt, Bell Labs (USA)
Phil Bernstein, Microsoft Research (USA)
Elisa Bertino, University of Milan (Italy)
Angela Bonifati, CNR (Italy)
Vassilis Christophides, ICS-FORTH & University of Crete (Greece)
Gregory Cobena, Xyleme (France)
Mariano Consens, University of Toronto (Canada)
Alin Deutsch, University of California at San Diego (USA)
Mary Fernandez, AT&T Research (USA)
Dana Florescu, BEA (USA)
Juliana Freire, OGI School of Science and Engineering (USA)
H.V. Jagadish, University of Michigan (USA)
Christoph Koch, Technische Universität Wien (Austria)
Alberto Laender, Universidade Federal de Minas Gerais (Brazil)
Laks Lakshmanan, University of British Columbia (Canada)
Yossi Matias, Tel Aviv University (Israel) and HyperRoll (USA)
Giansalvatore Mecca, Università della Basilicata (Italy)
Hamid Pirahesh, IBM (USA)
Evaggelia Pitoura, University of Ioannina (Greece)
Neoklis (Alkis) Polyzotis, University of California at Santa Cruz (USA)
Philippe Pucheral, INRIA (France)
Elke A. Rundensteiner, Worcester Polytechnic Institute (USA)
Arnaud Sahuguet, Bell Laboratories – Lucent Technologies (USA)
Oded Shmueli, Technion (Israel)
Val Tannen, University of Pennsylvania (USA)
Vasilis Vassalos, New York University (USA)
Stratis Viglas, University of Edinburgh (UK)
Masatoshi Yoshikawa, Nagoya University (Japan)

External Reviewers

Marcelo Arenas
Paolo Atzeni
Attila Barta
Marco Brambilla
Paolo Cappellari
Yi Chen
Valter Crescenzi
Francois Dang-Ngoc
Natasha Drukh
Maged El-Sayed
Vladimir Gapeyev
Georges Gardarin
Ashish Gupta
Vagelis Hristidis
Dao-Dinh Kha
Georgia Koloniari

Juliano Lage
Wei Luo
Marco Mesiti
Flavio Rizzolo
Stefanie Scherzinger
Toshiyuki Shimizu
Bernhard Stegmaier
Hong Su
Liying Sui
Alberto Trombetta
Ling Wang
Nuwee Wiwatwattana
Yu Xu
Lingzhi Zhang
Yifeng Zheng

Table of Contents

XML Processing

Clustering, Indexing, Statistics

Author Index

Building an Extensible XQuery Engine:
Experiences with Galax
(Extended Abstract)

Mary Fernández[1] and Jérôme Siméon[2]

[1] AT&T Labs Research, 180 Park Avenue, Florham Park, NJ 07932, USA
mff@research.att.com
[2] IBM T.J. Watson Research Center, 19 Skyline Drive, Hawthorne, NY 10532, USA
simeon@research.bell-labs.com

Abstract. XQuery 1.0 and its sister language XPath 2.0 have set a fire underneath database vendors and researchers alike. More than thirty commercial and research XQuery implementations are listed on the XML Query working group home page (http://www.w3.org/XML/Query). Most of these implementations are targeted to particular storage systems or application domains.

Galax (http://www.galaxquery.org) is an open-source, general-purpose XQuery engine, designed for maximal extensibility. In this talk, we will discuss Galax's extensibility features and the design trade-offs that we continuously face between extensibility and performance.

For the past four years, we have been actively involved in defining XQuery 1.0 [10], a query language for XML designed to meet the diverse needs of applications that query and exchange XML. XQuery 1.0 and its sister language XPath 2.0 are designed jointly by members of the World-wide Web Consortium's XSLT and XML Query working groups, which includes constituencies such as large database vendors, small middle-ware start-ups, "power" XML-user communities, and industrial research labs. Each constituency has produced several XQuery implementations, which is unprecedented for a language that is (still!) not standardized. A current listing of XQuery implementations is on the XML Query working group home page (http://www.w3.org/XML/Query).

Not surprisingly, each constituency has implemented XQuery with a particular application domain, user base, or existing database architecture in mind. The large database vendors are concerned with implementing XQuery efficiently and compatibly within their relational database architectures. Draper [1] surveys the dual problems of storing XML data in relational storage systems and of publishing relational data in XML, when the relational database is entirely agnostic to XML data. In the same text, Rys [8] considers extended relational architectures that integrate XML data into the underlying data model and the techniques for compiling XQuery to SQL. The solutions described in these surveys are biased towards XML applications that can benefit from the features of mature relational database technologies: storage and indexing of large data

Z. Bellahsène et al. (Eds.): XSym 2004, LNCS 3186, pp. 1–4, 2004.

sources; transactional data access for updates; and high-performance relational query engines.

Other XQuery implementations focus, for example, on the requirements of XML messaging applications, in which XML data is typically accessed in a streaming fashion. The BEA/XQRL streaming XQuery processor [5] is the first complete implementation of XQuery that supports streaming access to XML data. All input and output XML data is represented as a stream of tokens. The content of a token is similar to the content of a SAX event, but is enhanced with types identified during XML Schema validation. In the XQRL query engine, the token streams are accessed by pulling, not pushing, data. Every operator consumes and produces streams of tokens, which permits efficient discarding of data not required by the operator. These two examples of XQuery implementations represent two extrema: The relational engines are tailored to large, persistent, and mutable data sources and the streaming engines are tailored to small, transient, and immutable data sources.

Unlike other XQuery implementations, our implementation, called Galax[6], was not designed with a particular application domain or existing database architecture in mind. Instead, Galax began as a platform for validating the XQuery formal semantics [11]. Validating the language definition required implementing the complete XQuery data model and all phases of the XQuery processing model[1]. Because completeness was a requirement, Galax was designed from the top down, and the resulting architecture, depicted in Figure 1, closely follows the XQuery processing model. The processing model consists of three interdependent phases: (a) XML Schema processing, (b) XML document processing, and (c) XQuery processing. For expediency, we chose the simplest possible implementation strategy for each phase and focused on designing semantically simple and transparent representations of queries, documents, and types that are shared by phases. An important outcome of this strategy is that we were able to apply Galax to production applications that consume and produce large XML documents and that have non-trivial query requirements [9]. In the talk, we will describe the processing model and related implementation issues in detail.

While we worked on getting Galax up and running, myriad research papers on evaluation strategies for XPath and XQuery were popping up. We soon realized that Galax's contribution might not be solutions to the numerous open problems of evaluating XQuery, but instead, Galax could provide a well-designed, open-source environment within which researchers (ourselves included) could explore evaluation strategies, document storage and indexing, interactions between optimizations and more. In such an environment, extensibility is paramount, so our recent work focuses on making Galax extensible in almost every phase.

Currently, Galax provides extensibility features for the phases highlighted in Figure 1. Galax supports user-defined, built-in functions, which can be dynamically loaded into the Galax query engine. We have used this feature to provide built-in support for sending and receiving SOAP messages. The logical rewriting phase is implemented using a generic tree-walking algorithm, into which new

---

[1] The first IPSI XQuery processor [2] was also designed for this purpose.

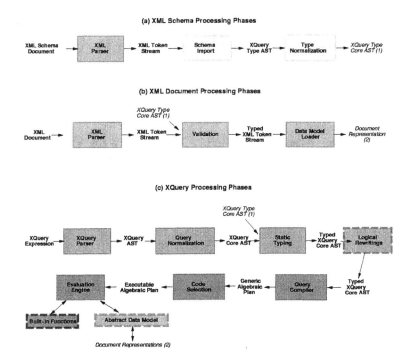

Fig. 1.

rewriting rules can be added declaratively. We have implemented a technique for detecting redundant sorting and duplicate-elimination operators [4] within this framework. Lastly, Galax's abstract data model is implemented for three physical representations of documents: a main-memory tree representation, a secondary storage system that uses Berkeley DB and that is used in a production system [9], and a streaming file representation [7]. All three representations can be accessed simultaneously within a single query, and adding other representations is straightforward.

Interestingly, Galax's architecture has evolved to include features from *both* the classes of implementations that we first described. Like relational engines, Galax now includes a secondary storage system that provides indexes and we are adding physical operators to utilize the storage system. And like streaming engines, Galax includes operators that consume and produce streams of typed XML tokens.

As Galax matures, balancing the requirements of extensibility and versatility with performance raises numerous issues. Our near-term future work focuses on implementing an algebraic query representation, whose efficient evaluation depends on the capabilities of the data representations underlying the abstract data model. In the talk, we will describe the design tensions that we face between extensibility and performance.

References

1. D. Draper, "Mapping Between XML and Relational Data", in *XQuery from the Experts: A Guide to the W3C XML Query Language*, edited by H. Katz, Addison-Wesley, 2003.
2. P. Fankhauser, T. Groh and S. Overhage. "XQuery by the Book: The IPSI XQuery Demonstrator", International Conference on Extending Database Technology (EDBT), 2002: pp 742–744.
3. M. Fernández, N. Onose, and J. Siméon. "Yoo-Hoo! Building a Presence Service with XQuery and WSDL", Demonstration track, SIGMOD Conference 2004: pp 911–912.
4. M. Fernández, J. Hidders, P. Michiels, J. Siméon, and R. Vercammen. Automata for Avoiding Unnecessary Ordering Operations in XPath Implementations, Technical Report 2004-02, University of Antwerp and AT&T Research and IBM Watson, 2004. `http://www.win.ua.ac.be/~adrem/pub/TR2004-02.pdf`.
5. D. Florescu, C. Hillary, D. Kossmann, et al. "The BEA/XQRL Streaming XQuery Processor", VLDB 2003: pp. 997–1008.
6. M. Fernández, J. Siméon et al. "Implementing XQuery 1.0: The Galax Experience", Demonstration track, Proceedings of Conference on Very Large Databases (VLDB), 2003, pp. 1077–1080, `http://www.galaxquery.org`.
7. K. Fisher and R. Gruber, "PADS: Processing Arbitrary Data Streams", Workshop on Management and Processing of Data Streams, 2003, http://www.research.att.com/conf/mpds2003/.
8. M. Rys, "Integrating XQuery and Relational Data", in *XQuery from the Experts: A Guide to the W3C XML Query Language*, edited by H. Katz, Addison-Wesley, 2003.
9. A. Vyas, M. Fernández, and J. Siméon. "The Simplest XML Storage Manager Ever", Workshop on XQuery Implementation, Experience and Perspectives, 2004: pp 37–42.
10. XQuery 1.0: An XML Query Language. W3C Working Draft, May 2003. http://www.w3.org/TR/xquery/.
11. XQuery 1.0 and XPath 2.0 Formal Semantics. W3C Working Draft, May 2003. http://www.w3.org/TR/query-semantics/.
12. XQuery 1.0 and XPath 2.0 Full-Text. W3C Working Draft, July 2004. http://www.w3.org/TR/xquery-full-text/.

A Light but Formal Introduction to XQuery

Jan Hidders, Jan Paredaens, Roel Vercammen*, and Serge Demeyer

University of Antwerp, Middelheimlaan 1, BE-2020 Antwerp, Belgium
{jan.hidders,jan.paredaens,roel.vercammen,serge.demeyer}@ua.ac.be

Abstract. We give a light-weight but formal introduction to XQuery by defining a sublanguage of XQuery. We ignore typing, and don't consider namespaces, comments, programming instructions, and entities. To avoid confusion we call our version LiXQuery (Light XQuery). LiXQuery is fully downwards compatible with XQuery. Its syntax and its semantics are far less complex than that of XQuery, but the typical expressions of XQuery are included in LiXQuery. We claim that LiXQuery is an elegant and simple sublanguage of XQuery that can be used for educational and research purposes. We give the complete syntax and the formal semantics of LiXQuery.

1 Introduction

XQuery is considered to become the standard query language for XML-documents [1,10,7,9]. However, this language is rather complex and its semantics, although well defined (see [3,2,4]), is not easily defined in a precise and concise manner. There seems therefore to be a need for a sublanguage of XQuery that has almost the same expressive power as XQuery and that has an elegant syntax and semantics that can be written down in a few pages. Similar proposals were made for XPath 1.0 [12] and XSLT [6], and have subsequently played important roles in practical and theoretical research [8,11]

Such a language would enable us to investigate more easily certain aspects of XQuery such as the expressive power of certain types of expressions found in XQuery, the expressive power of recursion in XQuery and possible syntactical restrictions that let us control this power, the complexity of deciding equivalence of expressions for purposes such as query optimization, the functional character of XQuery in comparison with functional languages such as LISP and ML, the role of XPath 1.0 and 2.0 in XQuery in terms of expressive power and query optimization, and finally the relationship between XQuery queries and the classical well-understood concept of generic database queries.

The contribution of this paper is the definition of LiXQuery, a sublanguage of XQuery with a relatively simple syntax and semantics that is appropriate both for educational and research purposes. Indeed, we are convinced that LiXQuery has a number of interesting properties, that can be proved formally, and that can be transposed to XQuery.

---

* Roel Vercammen is supported by IWT – Institute for the Encouragement of Innovation by Science and Technology Flanders, grant number 31581.

Z. Bellahsène et al. (Eds.): XSym 2004, LNCS 3186, pp. 5–20, 2004.

Section 2 contains an example of a query in LiXQuery , while section 3 explains the design choices we made. In Section 4 we give the complete syntax and its informal meaning. Section 5 further illustrates LiXQuery with more examples and finally in Section 6 the formal semantics of LiXQuery is given. In the remainder of this paper the reader is assumed to be acquainted with XML and to have some notions about XQuery.

2   Design Choices

We designed LiXQuery with two audiences in mind. First of all, we target researchers investigating the expressive power and the computational complexity of XQuery. From experience, we know that the syntax and semantics in the XQuery standard is unwieldy for proving certain properties, hence we dropped a number of language features which are important for practical purposes but not essential from a theory perspective. The second audience for LiXQuery are teachers. Here as well we learned from experience that the XQuery standard contains features which are important for designing an efficient and practical language, but not essential to understand the typical queries written in XQuery.

Therefore, we choose to omit a number of standard XQuery features. However, to ensure the validity of LiXQuery, we designed it as a proper sublanguage. Specifically, we specified LiXQuery so that all syntactically valid LiXQuery expressions do also satisfy the XQuery syntax. Moreover, the LiXQuery semantics is defined in such a way that the result of a query evaluated using our semantics will be a proper subset of the same query evaluated by XQuery. Of course, the lack of a complete formal semantics for XQuery does not allow us to prove that relation.

The most visible feature we dropped from XQuery are *types* (and consequently *type coercion*). Types are indeed important for certain query optimizations because they enable to catch certain mistakes at compile time. Moreover, type coercion is quite convenient when dealing with semi-structured data, as it allows for shorter expressions. Unfortunately, types –especially type coercions– add lots of complexity to a formal semantic definition of a language. And since types are optional in XQuery anyway, we decided to omit them for our sublanguage.

Secondly, we removed most of the axes of navigation namely the horizontal ones ('following', 'following-sibling', 'preceding', 'preceding-sibling') and half of the vertical ones ('ancestor') preserving only the 'descendant-or-self' and 'child' directions. Indeed, it has been shown formally that all other axes of navigation can be reduced to the ones we preserved, thus from a theory perspective such a simplification makes sense. From an educational perspective, it is sufficient to observe that the extra navigation axes are rarely needed, hence add to the cognitive overhead.

Finally, we omitted primitive functions and primitive data-types, the **order by** clause, namespaces, comments, programming instructions and entities. For these features we argue that they are necessary to specify a full-fledged query language, yet add to much overhead to incorporate them a concise, yet formal semantics.

```
declare function oneLevel($1,$p) {
  element { "part" } {
    attribute { "partId" }{ $p/@partId },
    for $s in $1//part where $s/@partOf=$p/@partId return oneLevel($1,$s)
  }
};

let $list := doc("partList.xml")/partList return
  element { "intList" } {
    for $p in $list//part[empty(@partOf)] return oneLevel($list,$p)
  }
```

Fig. 1. A LiXQuery query

3 An Example

The query in Fig. 1 restructures a list of parts, containing information about their containing parts, to an embedded list of the parts with their subparts [5]. For instance, the document of Fig. 2 will be transformed into that of Fig. 3. The query starts with the definition of the function oneLevel. This is followed by the let-clause that defines the variable $list whose value is the partList element on the file partList.xml. Then a new element is returned with name intList and which has as content the result of the function oneLevel that is called for each part-element $p in the $list element that has no partOf-attribute. The function oneLevel constructs a new part-element, with one attribute. It is named partId and its value is the string of the partId attribute of the element $p (the second parameter of oneLevel). Furthermore the element part has a child-element $s for each of the parts in the first parameter $1 and which is part of $p. For each such an $s the function oneLevel is called recursively. If the file partList.xml contains Fig. 2 the result is shown in Fig. 3.

```
<?xml version ="1.0"?>
<partList>
  <part partId="1"/>          <part partId="2" partOf="1"/>
  <part partId="3" partOf="1"/>   <part partId="4" partOf="3"/>
  <part partId="5"/>          <part partId="6" partOf="5"/>
</partList>
```

Fig. 2. Content of the file partList.xml

```
<intList>
  <part partId="1">
    <part partId="2"/>
    <part partId="3">  <part partId="4"/>  </part>
  </part>
  <part partId="5">  <part partId="6"/>  </part>
</intList>
```

Fig. 3. Result of the query in Fig. 1

4   Syntax and Informal Description of LiXQuery

We first give the syntax and the informal semantics of LiXQuery, and then extend it with some syntactic sugar.

4.1   Basic Syntax

The syntax of LiXQuery is given in Fig. 4 as an abstract syntax, i.e., it assumes that extra brackets and precedence rules are added for disambiguation.

All queries in LiXQuery are syntactically correct in XQuery and their LiX-Query semantics is consistent with their XQuery syntax. Built-in functions for manipulation of basic values are omitted. The non-terminal ⟨*Name*⟩ refers to the set of names $\mathcal{N}$ which we will not describe in detail here except that the names are strings that must start with a letter or "_". The non-terminal ⟨*String*⟩ refers to strings that are enclosed in double quotes such as in "abc" and ⟨*Integer*⟩ refers to integers without quotes such as 100, +100, and -100.[1] Therefore the sets associated with ⟨*Name*⟩, ⟨*String*⟩ and ⟨*Integer*⟩ are pairwise disjoint.

The syntax contains 24 rules. Their informal semantics is mostly straightforward. Some of the rules were illustrated in the introductory example.

The ambiguity between rule [5] and [24] is resolved by giving precedence to [5], and for path expressions we will assume that the operators "/" and "//" (rule [18]) are left associative and are preceded by the filter operation (rule [17]) in priority.

4.2   Informal Semantics

Since we assume that the reader is already somewhat familiar with XQuery we only describe here the semantics of some of the less common expressions.

In rule [5] the built-in functions are declared. The function doc() returns the document node that is the root of the tree that corresponds to the content of the file with the name that was given as its argument, e.g., doc("file.xq") indicates the document root of the content of the file file.xq. The function name() gives the tag name of an element node or the attribute name of an attribute node. The function string() gives the string value of an attribute

---

[1] Integers are the only numeric type that exists in LiXQuery.

[1] ⟨*Query*⟩   → (⟨*FunDef*⟩ ";")* ⟨*Expr*⟩

[2] ⟨*FunDef*⟩   → "declare" "function" ⟨*Name*⟩ "(" (⟨*Var*⟩ ("," ⟨*Var*⟩)*)? ")"
                  "{" ⟨*Expr*⟩ "}"

[3] ⟨*Expr*⟩   → ⟨*Var*⟩ | ⟨*BuiltIn*⟩ | ⟨*IfExpr*⟩ | ⟨*ForExpr*⟩ | ⟨*LetExpr*⟩ | ⟨*Concat*⟩ |
                 ⟨*AndOr*⟩ | ⟨*ValCmp*⟩ | ⟨*NodeCmp*⟩ | ⟨*AddExpr*⟩ | ⟨*MultExpr*⟩ |
                 ⟨*Union*⟩ | ⟨*Step*⟩ | ⟨*Filter*⟩ | ⟨*Path*⟩ | ⟨*Literal*⟩ | ⟨*EmpSeq*⟩ |
                 ⟨*Constr*⟩ | ⟨*TypeSw*⟩ | ⟨*FunCall*⟩

[4] ⟨*Var*⟩   → "$" ⟨*Name*⟩

[5] ⟨*BuiltIn*⟩   → "doc(" ⟨*Expr*⟩ ")" | "name(" ⟨*Expr*⟩ ")" | "string(" ⟨*Expr*⟩ ")" |
                 "xs:integer(" ⟨*Expr*⟩ ")" | "root(" ⟨*Expr*⟩ ")" |
                 "concat(" ⟨*Expr*⟩ ", " ⟨*Expr*⟩ ")" | "true()" | "false()" |
                 "not(" ⟨*Expr*⟩ ")" | "count(" ⟨*Expr*⟩ ")" | "position()" | "last()"

[6] ⟨*IfExpr*⟩   → "if " "(" ⟨*Expr*⟩ ")" "then" ⟨*Expr*⟩ "else" ⟨*Expr*⟩

[7] ⟨*ForExpr*⟩   → "for" ⟨*Var*⟩ ("at" ⟨*Var*⟩)? "in" ⟨*Expr*⟩ "return" ⟨*Expr*⟩

[8] ⟨*LetExpr*⟩   → "let" ⟨*Var*⟩ ":=" ⟨*Expr*⟩ "return" ⟨*Expr*⟩

[9] ⟨*Concat*⟩   → ⟨*Expr*⟩ ", " ⟨*Expr*⟩

[10] ⟨*AndOr*⟩   → ⟨*Expr*⟩ ("and" | "or") ⟨*Expr*⟩

[11] ⟨*ValCmp*⟩   → ⟨*Expr*⟩ ("=" | "<") ⟨*Expr*⟩

[12] ⟨*NodeCmp*⟩   → ⟨*Expr*⟩ ("is" | "<<") ⟨*Expr*⟩

[13] ⟨*AddExpr*⟩   → ⟨*Expr*⟩ ("+" | "-") ⟨*Expr*⟩

[14] ⟨*MultExpr*⟩   → ⟨*Expr*⟩ ("*" | "idiv") ⟨*Expr*⟩

[15] ⟨*Union*⟩   → ⟨*Expr*⟩ "|" ⟨*Expr*⟩

[16] ⟨*Step*⟩   → "." | ".." | ⟨*Name*⟩ | "@" ⟨*Name*⟩ | "*" | "@*" | "text()"

[17] ⟨*Filter*⟩   → ⟨*Expr*⟩ "[" ⟨*Expr*⟩ "]"

[18] ⟨*Path*⟩   → ⟨*Expr*⟩ ("/" | "//") ⟨*Expr*⟩

[19] ⟨*Literal*⟩   → ⟨*String*⟩ | ⟨*Integer*⟩

[20] ⟨*EmpSeq*⟩   → "()"

[21] ⟨*Constr*⟩   → "element" "{" ⟨*Expr*⟩ "}" "{" ⟨*Expr*⟩ "}" |
                 "attribute" "{" ⟨*Expr*⟩ "}" "{" ⟨*Expr*⟩ "}" |
                 "text" "{" ⟨*Expr*⟩ "}" | "document" "{" ⟨*Expr*⟩ "}"

[22] ⟨*TypeSw*⟩   → "typeswitch " "(" ⟨*Expr*⟩ ")" ("case" ⟨*Type*⟩ "return" ⟨*Expr*⟩)+
                 "default" "return" ⟨*Expr*⟩

[23] ⟨*Type*⟩   → "xs:boolean" | "xs:integer" | "xs:string" | "element()" |
                 "attribute()" | "text()" | "document-node()"

[24] ⟨*FunCall*⟩   → ⟨*Name*⟩ "(" (⟨*Expr*⟩ ("," ⟨*Expr*⟩)*)? ")"

Fig. 4. Syntax for LiXQuery queries and expressions

node or text node, and converts integers to strings. The function xs:integer()[2] converts strings to integers. The function root() gives for a node the root of its tree. The function concat() concatenates strings. Rule [11] introduces the comparison operators for basic values. Note that "2 < 10" and ""10" < "2"" both hold. These comparison operators have existential semantics, i.e., they are true for two sequences if there is a basic value in one sequence and a basic value in the other sequence such that the comparison holds between these two basic values. Rule [12] gives the comparison operators for nodes where "is" detects

---

[2] "xs:" indicates a namespace. Although we do not handle namespaces we use them here to be compatible with XQuery.

the equality of nodes and "<<" compares nodes in document order. Rule [15] expresses the union of two node sequences, i.e., it returns a sequence of nodes that contains exactly all the nodes in the operands, contains no duplicates and is sorted in document order. Rule [21] gives the constructors for each type of node. The semantics of "element $\{e_1\}\{e_2\}$" is that an element node with name e_1 and content e_2 is created. The semantics of "attribute $\{e_1\}\{e_2\}$" is that an attribute node with name e_1 and value e_2 is created. The semantics of "text $\{e\}$" is that a text node with value e is created. The semantics of "document $\{e\}$" is that a document node with attributes and content as in e is created. Rules [22] and [23] define the typeswitch-expression that checks whether a value belongs to certain types and for the first type that matches returns a certain value.

4.3   Syntactic Sugar

To allow for a shorter notation of certain very common expressions we introduce the following short-hands.

The Empty Function. The function empty() is assumed to be declared as follows:

```
declare function empty( $sequence ) {  count( $sequence ) = 0  };
```

Quantified Formulas. The expression "some $v in e_1 satisfies e_2" is introduced as a shorthand for "not(empty(for $v in e_1 return if (e_2) then $v else ()))", and "every $v in e_1 satisfies e_2" is introduced as a shorthand for "empty(for $v in e_1 return if (e_2) then () else $v)".

FLWOR Expression. When for- and let-expressions are nested we allow that the intermediate "return" is removed. E.g., "for v_1 in e_1 return let v_2 := e_2 return e_3" may be written as "for v_1 in e_1 let v_2 := e_2 return e_3". Furthermore we allow in for- and let-expressions the shorthand "where e_1 return e_2" for "return if e_1 then e_2 else ()".

Coercion. Let e_1 (or e_2) have the form "string(e)" where the result of e is a sequence containing a single text node or a single attribute node. Then e_1 (or e_2) can be replaced by e in the following expressions: "xs:integer(e_1)", "concat(e_1,e_2)", "$e_1=e_2$", "$e_1<e_2$" and "attribute$\{e_3\}\{e_2\}$".

5   More Examples

In this section we demonstrate the expressive power of LiXQuery.

5.1   Simulating Deep Equality

The first example shows that we can express deep equality of two sequences. This essentially means that we have to check whether two fragments are isomorphic except that we have to take into account that attributes are unordered. For a more formal definition see Definition 9.

```
declare function deepat1($e,$f) {
(: detects whether the attributes of $e are equal in name and value with those of $f :)
  every $ae in $e/@* satisfies
    some $af in $f/@* satisfies
      ( name($ae)=name($af) and string($ae)=string($af) )
  and
  every $af in $f/@* satisfies
    some $ae in $e/@* satisfies
      ( name($ae)=name($af) and string($ae)=string($af) )
};

declare function typetext($e) {
(: verifies whether $e is a textnode :)
  typeswitch ($e) case text() return true() default return false()
};

declare function deepequal($se,$sf) {
(: detects whether $se and $sf are sequences of pairwise deep equal items :)
  if (empty($se) and empty($sf)) then true()
    else
  if (empty($se) or empty($sf)) then false()
    else
  if (typetext($se[1]))
    then if (typetext($sf[1]))
          then ( string($se[1])=string($sf[1]) and
                 deepequal($se[1 < position()], $sf[1 < position()]) )
          else false()
    else if (typetext($sf[1]))
          then false()
          else ( name($se[1])=name($sf[1])  and
                 deepat1($se[1],$sf[1])  and
                 deepequal($se[1]/(*|text()), $sf[1]/(*|text())) and
                 deepequal($se[1 < position()], $sf[1 < position()])
                 )
};
```

5.2   Simulation of Other Axes

We can simulate all the axes that are not already directly supported in the syntax of LiXQuery. To demonstrate this we show here the `following-sibling` and `ancestor` axis.

```
declare function following-sibling($s) {       declare function ancestor($s) {
  (: retrieves all fs's of the nodes in $s :)     (: retrieves all anc's of the nodes in $s :)
  for $node in $s                                 for $node in $s
    for $sib in $node/../*                           for $anc in root($node)//.
    where $sib >> $node                             where some $v in $anc//* satisfies $v is $node
    return $sib                                     return $anc
};                                              };
```

5.3   Simulation of the Full string() Function

In LiXQuery the `string()` function is only defined for integers, attribute nodes and text nodes, but in XQuery it is defined for all items. We can simulate this more general function as follows.

```
declare function concatAll($x) {
(: concatenate all strings in $x :)
  if ( empty( $x ) )
  then ""
  else concat($x[position()=1], concatAll($x[position()>1]))
};
```

```
declare function xqString($x) {
(: simulates full xquery string function :)
  if ( empty( $x ) )
  then ""
  else typeswitch ($x)
        case document-node() return concatAll($x/text())
        case element() return concatAll($x/text())
        default return string($x)
};
```

5.4 Turing Completeness

It is easy to see that the amount of arithmetic and recursion in LiXQuery allows us to express all partial recursive functions over numbers. It is also possible to simulate LISP. For this purpose we represent a LISP list ((b c) d) as shown in Fig. 5. Given this representation we simulation the car, cdr and cons functions:

```
declare function car($x) { $x/*[1] };
declare function cdr($x) { element{ "list" }{ $x/*[1 < position()] } };
declare function cons($x,$y) { element{ "list" }{ $x,$y/* } };
```

Since we can also compare strings and have conditional expressions, it is easy to see that by using recursion we can define all partial recursive functions over LISP lists.

```
<list>
  <list> <atom> b </atom> <atom> c </atom> </list> <atom> d </atom>
</list>
```

Fig. 5. Simulation of the LISP list ((b c) d)

6   Formal Semantics

We now proceed with the formal semantics of LiXQuery.

Definition 1 (Atomic Value). *We assume a set of* booleans $\mathcal{B} = \{\textbf{true}, \textbf{false}\}$*, a set of* strings $\mathcal{S}$ *and a set of* integers $\mathcal{I}$ *that contains integers.*[3]

Furthermore a set of Names $\mathcal{N} \subseteq \mathcal{S}$ *is identified that contains those strings that may be used as tag names [1]. For each of these sets a strict total ordering, written as* <*, is presumed to exist. The set of all atomic values is* $\mathcal{A} = \mathcal{B} \cup \mathcal{S} \cup \mathcal{I}$*.*

We also assume the functions $AtValueToString : \mathcal{A} \to \mathcal{S}$ *which is a function that maps the atomic values to their string representation, and* $StringToInteger : \mathcal{S} \to \mathcal{I}$ *which is partial function that maps strings that represent integers to their integer value.*

Definition 2 (Node). *We assume four countably infinite sets of nodes* $\mathcal{V}^d$*,* $\mathcal{V}^e$*,* $\mathcal{V}^a$ *and* $\mathcal{V}^t$ *which respectively represent the set of* document, element, attribute *and* text *nodes. These sets are pairwise disjoint with each other and with the set of atomic values.*

---

[3] We denote the empty string as "", non-empty strings as for example "123" and the concatenation of two strings s_1 and s_2 as $s_1 \cdot s_2$.

The set of all nodes is denoted as $\mathcal{V}$, i.e., $\mathcal{V} = \mathcal{V}^d \cup \mathcal{V}^e \cup \mathcal{V}^a \cup \mathcal{V}^t$.

Expressions will be evaluated against an *XML store* which contains XML fragments. This store contains the fragments that are created as intermediate results, but also the web documents that are accessed by the expression. Although in practice these documents are materialized in the store when they are accessed for the first time, we will assume here that all documents are in fact already in the store when the expression is evaluated.

Definition 3 (XML Store). *An* XML store *is a 6-tuple $St = (V, E, <, \nu, \sigma, \delta)$ with*

- *V is a finite subset of $\mathcal{V}$; we write V^d for $V \cap \mathcal{V}^d$ (resp. V^e for $V \cap \mathcal{V}^e$, V^a for $V \cap \mathcal{V}^a$, V^t for $V \cap \mathcal{V}^t$);*
- *(V, E) is an acyclic directed graph (with nodes V and directed edges E) where each node has an in-degree of at most one, and hence it is composed of trees; if $(m, n) \in E$ then we say that n is a child of m;[4] we denote by E^* the reflexive transitive closure of E;*
- *$<$ is a strict partial order on V that compares exactly the different children of a common node, hence $((n_1 < n_2) \vee (n_1 = n_2) \vee (n_2 < n_1)) \Leftrightarrow \exists m \in V((m, n_1) \in E \wedge (m, n_2) \in E)$*
- *$\nu : V^e \cup V^a \to \mathcal{N}$ labels the element and attribute nodes with their node name;*
- *$\sigma : V^a \cup V^t \to \mathcal{S}$ labels the attribute and text nodes with their string value;*
- *$\delta : \mathcal{S} \to \mathcal{V}^d$ a partial function that associates with an URI or a file name, a document node. It is called the* document function. *This function represents all the URIs of the Web and all the names of the files, together with the documents they contain. We suppose that all these documents are in the store.*

The following properties have to hold for an XML store:

- *each document node of V^d is the root of a tree;*
- *attribute nodes of V^a and text nodes of V^t do not have any children;*
- *in the $<$ -order attribute children precede the element and text children, i.e. if $n_1 < n_2$ and $n_2 \in V^a$ then $n_1 \in V^a$;*
- *there are no adjacent text children, i.e. if $n_1, n_2 \in V^t$ and $n_1 < n_2$ then there is an $n_3 \in V^e$ with $n_1 < n_3 < n_2$;*
- *for all text nodes n_t of V^t holds $\sigma(n_t) \neq$ "";*
- *all the attribute children of a common node have a different name, i.e. if $(m, n_1), (m, n_2) \in E$ and $n_1, n_2 \in V^a$ then $\nu(n_1) \neq \nu(n_2)$.*

Definition 4 (Union of stores). *Two stores $St = (V, E, <, \nu, \sigma, \delta)$ and $St' = (V', E', <', \nu', \sigma', \delta')$ are disjoint, denoted as $St \cap St' = \emptyset$, iff $V \cap V' = \emptyset$. The definition of the union of two disjoint stores St and St', denoted as $St \cup St'$, is straightforward.*

---

[4] As opposed to the terminology of XQuery, we consider attribute nodes as children of their associated element node. The definitions of parent, descendant and ancestor are straightforward.

Definition 5 (Root of a node). *Given a store St, the root of one of its nodes n, denoted as* root(n) *is the unique root of the tree of n, i.e.* root(n) = r *iff $(r, n) \in E^*$ and for no node $s \neq r$ of St holds $(s, r) \in E^*$.*

Definition 6 (Item). *An* item *of an XML store St is an atomic value in $\mathcal{A}$ or a node in St.*

We denote the empty sequence as $\langle \rangle$, non-empty sequences as for example $\langle 1, 2, 3 \rangle$ and the concatenation of two sequences l_1 and l_2 as $l_1 \circ l_2$. The expression $\langle y_i \in l | \varphi(y, i) \rangle$ with $\varphi(y, i)$ a formula of an item y and position i denotes the subsequence of l that is obtained by selecting from l all items that satisfy $\varphi(y, i)$.

Example 1. The XML store that is represented in Fig. 5 is $St = (V, E, <, \nu, \sigma, \delta)$ and is shown in Fig. 6. The set of nodes $V^e = \{n_1^e, n_2^e, n_3^e, n_5^e, n_7^e\}$, $V^t = \{n_4^t, n_6^t, n_8^t\}$, $V^d = V^a = \emptyset$, $E = \{(n_1^e, n_2^e), (n_1^e, n_7^e), (n_2^e, n_3^e), (n_2^e, n_5^e), (n_3^e, n_4^t), (n_5^e, n_6^t), (n_7^e, n_8^t)\}$, the order relation $<$ is defined by $n_2^e < n_7^e, n_3^e < n_5^e$; furthermore $\nu(n_1^e) = \nu(n_2^e) =$ "list", $\nu(n_3^e) = \nu(n_5^e) = \nu(n_7^e) =$ "atom" and $\sigma(n_4^t) =$ "b", $\sigma(n_6^t) =$ "c", $\sigma(n_8^t) =$ "d".[5]

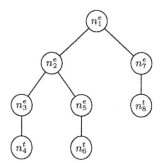

Fig. 6. XML tree of Fig. 5

Definition 7 (Document Order of a Store). A document order $\ll$[6] *of a store St is a total order on V such that*

1. *if $(n_1, n_2) \in E^*$ and $n_1 \neq n_2$ then $n_1 \ll_{St} n_2$;*
2. *if $(n_1, n_2) \in E^*$ and $n_1 < n_3$ then $(n_2 \ll_{St} n_3)$;*
3. *if $(n_1, n_2), (n_1, n_4) \in E^*$ and $n_2 < n_3 < n_4$ then $(n_1, n_3) \in E^*$.*

1. and 2. define the preorder in a tree. 3. say that the nodes of a tree are clustered.

The set of items in a sequence l is denoted as **Set**(l). Given a sequence of nodes l in an XML store St we let **Ord**$_{St}$(l) denote the unique sequence $l' = \langle y_1, \ldots, y_m \rangle$ such that **Set**(l) = **Set**(l') and $y_1 \ll_{St} \ldots \ll_{St} y_m$.

6.1   Evaluation of Expressions

Expressions are evaluated against an environment. Assuming that $\mathcal{X}$ is the set of LiXQuery-expressions this environment is defined as follows.

Definition 8 (Environment). *An* environment *of an XML store St is a tuple $En = (\mathbf{a}, \mathbf{b}, \mathbf{v}, \mathbf{x}, \mathbf{k}, \mathbf{m})$ with*

---

[5] We do not mention here the documents on the Web and on files.

[6] A store can have more than one document order, but we choose a fixed document order here that we denote by $\ll_{St}$.

1. *a partial function* $\mathbf{a} : \mathcal{N} \to \mathcal{N}^*$ *that maps a function name to its formal arguments; it is used in rule [1,2,24];*
2. *a partial function* $\mathbf{b} : \mathcal{N} \to \mathcal{X}$ *that maps a function name to the body of the function; it is also used in rules [1,2,24];*
3. *a partial function* $\mathbf{v} : \mathcal{N} \to (\mathcal{V} \cup \mathcal{A})^*$ *that maps variable names to their values;*
4. $\mathbf{x}$ *which is undefined or an item of St and indicates the context item; it is used in rule [16,17,18];*
5. $\mathbf{k}$ *which is undefined or an integer and gives the position of the context item in the context sequence; it is used in rule [5,17,18];*
6. $\mathbf{m}$ *which is undefined or an integer and gives the size of the context sequence; it is used in rule [5,17,18].*

If En is an environment, n a name and y an item then we let $En[\mathbf{a}(n) \mapsto y]$ ($En[\mathbf{b}(n) \mapsto y]$, $En[\mathbf{v}(n) \mapsto y]$) denote the environment that is equal to En except that the function $\mathbf{a}$ ($\mathbf{b}$, $\mathbf{v}$) maps n to y. Similarly, we let $En[\mathbf{x} \mapsto y]$ ($En[\mathbf{k} \mapsto y]$, $En[\mathbf{m} \mapsto y]$) denote the environment that is equal to En except that $\mathbf{x}$ ($\mathbf{k}$, $\mathbf{n}$) is defined as y if $y \neq \bot$ and undefined otherwise.

We write $St, En \vdash e \Rightarrow (St', v)$ to denote that the evaluation of expression e against the XML store St and environment En of St may result in the new XML store St' and value v of St'.

6.2 Semantic Rules

In what follows we give the reasoning rules that are used to define the semantics of LiXQuery. Each rule consists of a set of premises and a conclusion of the form $St, En \vdash e \Rightarrow (St', v)$. The free variables in the rules are always assumed to be universally quantified. We will use the following notation: v for values, x for items, n for nodes, r for roots, s for strings and names, f for function names, b for booleans , i for integers and e for expressions.

Query (Rules [1] and [2]) A function declaration extends $\mathbf{a}$ and $\mathbf{b}$ and then the last expression is evaluated with these $\mathbf{a}$ and $\mathbf{b}$. Function declarations are allowed to be mutually recursive.

$$\frac{En' = En[\mathbf{a}(f) \mapsto \langle s_1, \ldots s_m \rangle][\mathbf{b}(f) \mapsto e] \qquad St, En' \vdash e' \Rightarrow (St', v)}{St, En \vdash \mathtt{declare\ function}\ f(s_1, \ldots, s_m)\{\ e\ \};\ e' \Rightarrow (St', v)}$$

Variable (Rule [4])

$$\frac{}{St, En \vdash \$s \Rightarrow (St, \mathbf{v}_{En}(s))}$$

Built-in Functions (Rule [5])

$$\frac{St, En \vdash e \Rightarrow (St', \langle s \rangle) \qquad \delta_{St'}(s) = n}{St, En \vdash \mathtt{doc}(e) \Rightarrow (St', n)} \qquad \frac{St, En \vdash e \Rightarrow (St', \langle n \rangle) \qquad n \in \mathcal{V}^e \cup \mathcal{V}^a}{St, En \vdash \mathtt{name}(e) \Rightarrow (St', \langle \nu_{St'}(n) \rangle)}$$

$$\frac{St, En \vdash e \Rightarrow (St', \langle n \rangle) \qquad n \in \mathcal{V}^a \cup \mathcal{V}^t}{St, En \vdash \mathtt{string}(e) \Rightarrow (St', \langle \sigma_{St'}(n) \rangle)}$$

$$\frac{St, En \vdash e \Rightarrow (St', \langle x \rangle) \qquad x \in \mathcal{A} \qquad AtValueToString(x) = s}{St, En \vdash \mathbf{string}(e) \Rightarrow (St', \langle s \rangle)}$$

$$\frac{St, En \vdash e \Rightarrow (St', \langle s \rangle) \qquad s \in \mathcal{S} \qquad StringToInteger(s) = i}{St, En \vdash \mathbf{xs : integer}(e) \Rightarrow (St', \langle i \rangle)}$$

$$\frac{St, En \vdash e \Rightarrow (St', \langle n \rangle) \qquad n \in V_{St'}}{St, En \vdash \mathbf{root}(e) \Rightarrow (St', \langle root(n) \rangle)}$$

$$\frac{St, En \vdash e_1 \Rightarrow (St_1, \langle s_1 \rangle) \qquad s_1 \in \mathcal{S} \qquad St_1, En \vdash e_2 \Rightarrow (St_2, \langle s_2 \rangle) \qquad s_2 \in \mathcal{S}}{St, En \vdash \mathbf{concat}(e_1, e_2) \Rightarrow (St_2, \langle s_1 \cdot s_2 \rangle)}$$

$$\frac{}{St, En \vdash \mathbf{true}() \Rightarrow (St, \langle \mathbf{true} \rangle)} \qquad \frac{}{St, En \vdash \mathbf{false}() \Rightarrow (St, \langle \mathbf{false} \rangle)}$$

$$\frac{St, En \vdash e \Rightarrow (St', \langle b \rangle) \qquad b \in \mathcal{B}}{St, En \vdash \mathbf{not}(e) \Rightarrow (St', \langle \neg b \rangle)} \qquad \frac{St, En \vdash e \Rightarrow (St', \langle x_1, \dots, x_m \rangle)}{St, En \vdash \mathbf{count}(e) \Rightarrow (St', \langle m \rangle)}$$

$$\frac{}{St, En \vdash \mathbf{position}() \Rightarrow (St, \langle k_{En} \rangle)} \qquad \frac{}{St, En \vdash \mathbf{last}() \Rightarrow (St, \langle m_{En} \rangle)}$$

If-expression (Rule [6]). The semantics of the if-expression is given by two inference rules: one for the case the condition evaluates to **true** and one for **false**. Note that in each case only one of the branches is executed.

$$\frac{St, En \vdash e \Rightarrow (St', \langle \mathbf{true} \rangle) \qquad St', En \vdash e_1 \Rightarrow (St_1, v_1)}{St, En \vdash \mathbf{if}\ e\ \mathbf{then}\ e_1\ \mathbf{else}\ e_2 \Rightarrow (St_1, v_1)}$$

$$\frac{St, En \vdash e \Rightarrow (St', \langle \mathbf{false} \rangle) \qquad St', En \vdash e_2 \Rightarrow (St_2, v_2)}{St, En \vdash \mathbf{if}\ e\ \mathbf{then}\ e_1\ \mathbf{else}\ e_2 \Rightarrow (St_2, v_2)}$$

For-expression (Rule [7]) The rule for **for** \$s **at** \$s' **in** e **return** e' specifies that first e is evaluated and then e' for each item in the result of e but with s and s' in the environment bound to the respectively the item in question and its position in the result of e. Finally the results for each item are concatenated to a single sequence.

$$\frac{St, En \vdash e \Rightarrow (St_0, \langle x_1, \dots, x_m \rangle) \qquad St_0, En[\mathbf{v}(s) \mapsto x_1][\mathbf{v}(s') \mapsto 1] \vdash e' \Rightarrow (St_1, v_1)}{\dots \qquad St_{m-1}, En[\mathbf{v}(s) \mapsto x_m][\mathbf{v}(s') \mapsto m] \vdash e' \Rightarrow (St_m, v_m)}$$
$$\overline{St, En \vdash \mathbf{for}\ \$s\ \mathbf{at}\ \$s'\ \mathbf{in}\ e\ \mathbf{return}\ e' \Rightarrow (St_m, v_1 \circ \dots \circ v_m)}$$

Let-expression (Rule [8])

$$\frac{St, En \vdash e \Rightarrow (St', v) \qquad St', En[\mathbf{v}(s) \mapsto v] \vdash e' \Rightarrow (St'', v')}{St, En \vdash \mathbf{let}\ \$s := e\ \mathbf{return}\ e' \Rightarrow (St'', v')}$$

Concatenation (Rule [9])

$$\frac{St, En \vdash e' \Rightarrow (St', v') \qquad St', En \vdash e'' \Rightarrow (St'', v'')}{St, En \vdash e', e'' \Rightarrow (St'', v' \circ v'')}$$

Boolean Operators (Rule [10])

$$\frac{St, En \vdash e' \Rightarrow (St', \langle b' \rangle) \qquad St', En \vdash e'' \Rightarrow (St'', \langle b'' \rangle) \qquad b', b'' \in \mathcal{B}}{St, En \vdash e' \text{ and } e'' \Rightarrow (St'', \langle b' \wedge b'' \rangle) \qquad St, En \vdash e' \text{ or } e'' \Rightarrow (St'', \langle b' \vee b'' \rangle)}$$

Atomic Value Comparisons (Rule [11])

$$\frac{\begin{array}{c} St, En \vdash e' \Rightarrow (St', \langle x'_1, \dots, x'_{m'} \rangle) \\ x'_1, \dots, x'_{m'} \in \mathcal{A} \quad St', En \vdash e'' \Rightarrow (St'', \langle x''_1, \dots, x''_{m''} \rangle) \quad x''_1, \dots, x''_{m''} \in \mathcal{A} \\ b_= \Leftrightarrow \exists_{1 \le i \le m', 1 \le j \le m''}(x'_i = x''_j) \qquad b_< \Leftrightarrow \exists_{1 \le i \le m', 1 \le j \le m''}(x'_i < x''_j) \end{array}}{St, En \vdash e' = e'' \Rightarrow (St'', \langle b_= \rangle) \qquad St, En \vdash e' < e'' \Rightarrow (St'', \langle b_< \rangle)}$$

Node Comparisons (Rule [12])

$$\frac{\begin{array}{c} St, En \vdash e' \Rightarrow (St', \langle n' \rangle) \qquad St', En \vdash e'' \Rightarrow (St'', \langle n'' \rangle) \\ n', n'' \in \mathcal{V} \qquad b_{\text{is}} \Leftrightarrow (n' = n'') \qquad b_{\ll} \Leftrightarrow (n' \ll_{St''} n'') \end{array}}{St, En \vdash e' \text{ is } e'' \Rightarrow (St'', \langle b_{\text{is}} \rangle) \qquad St, En \vdash e' << e'' \Rightarrow (St'', \langle b_{\ll} \rangle)}$$

Additions (Rule [13])

$$\frac{St, En \vdash e' \Rightarrow (St', \langle d' \rangle) \qquad St', En \vdash e'' \Rightarrow (St'', \langle d'' \rangle) \qquad d', d'' \in \mathcal{I}}{St, En \vdash e' + e'' \Rightarrow (St'', \langle d' + d'' \rangle) \qquad St, En \vdash e' - e'' \Rightarrow (St'', \langle d' - d'' \rangle)}$$

Multiplications (Rule [14])

$$\frac{St, En \vdash e' \Rightarrow (St', \langle d' \rangle) \qquad St', En \vdash e'' \Rightarrow (St'', \langle d'' \rangle) \qquad d', d'' \in \mathcal{I}}{St, En \vdash e' * e'' \Rightarrow (St'', \langle d' \times d'' \rangle) \qquad St, En \vdash e' \text{ idiv } e'' \Rightarrow (St'', \langle d'/d'' \rangle)}$$

Union (Rule [15])

$$\frac{St, En \vdash e' \Rightarrow (St', v') \qquad St', En \vdash e'' \Rightarrow (St'', v'') \qquad v', v'' \in \mathcal{V}^*}{St, En \vdash e' \mid e'' \Rightarrow (St'', \mathbf{Ord}_{St''}(\mathbf{Set}(v') \cup \mathbf{Set}(v'')))}$$

Axis Steps (Rule [16]) The semantics of a step consisting of an element name s is that all element children of the context node (indicated in the envorment by $\mathbf{x}$) with name s are returned in document order. The semantics of the step consisting of the wild-card $*$ is the same except that all element children of the context node are returned.

$$\frac{\mathbf{x}_{En} \text{ is defined}}{St, En \vdash . \Rightarrow (St, \langle \mathbf{x}_{En} \rangle)} \qquad \frac{(n, \mathbf{x}_{En}) \in E_{St}}{St, En \vdash .. \Rightarrow (St, \langle n \rangle)} \qquad \frac{\not\exists n(n, \mathbf{x}_{En}) \in E_{St}}{St, En \vdash .. \Rightarrow (St, \langle \rangle)}$$

$$\frac{W = \{n | (\mathbf{x}_{En}, n) \in E_{St} \wedge n \in \mathcal{V}^e \wedge \nu_{St}(n) = s\}}{St, En \vdash s \Rightarrow (St, \mathbf{Ord}_{St}(W))}$$

$$\frac{W = \{n | (\mathbf{x}_{En}, n) \in E_{St} \wedge n \in \mathcal{V}^a \wedge \nu_{St}(n) = s\}}{St, En \vdash @s \Rightarrow (St, \mathbf{Ord}_{St}(W))}$$

$$\frac{W = \{n | (\mathbf{x}_{En}, n) \in E_{St} \wedge n \in \mathcal{V}^e\}}{St, En \vdash * \Rightarrow (St, \mathbf{Ord}_{St}(W))} \qquad \frac{W = \{n | (\mathbf{x}_{En}, n) \in E_{St} \wedge n \in \mathcal{V}^a\}}{St, En \vdash @* \Rightarrow (St, \mathbf{Ord}_{St}(W))}$$

$$W = \{n|(\mathbf{x}_{En}, n) \in E_{St} \wedge n \in \mathcal{V}^t\}$$
$$\overline{St, En \vdash \texttt{text}() \Rightarrow (St, \mathbf{Ord}_{St}(W))}$$

Filter-expression (Rule [17]) The semantics of e' [e''] is that first e' is evaluated, then for each item in the result of e' the expression e'' is evaluated with $\mathbf{x}$ bound to this item, $\mathbf{k}$ to the position of the item in the result of e' and $\mathbf{m}$ to the number of items in the result of e'. The result of e'' is a boolean or an integer, in which case it is converted to **true** if this integer is equal to $\mathbf{k}$ and to **false** otherwise. Finally, the result is the subsequence of the result of e' that contains exactly all items for which e'' evaluated to **true**.

$$St, En \vdash e' \Rightarrow (St_0, \langle x_1, \dots, x_m \rangle)$$
$$En' = En[\mathbf{m} \mapsto m] \qquad St_0, En'[\mathbf{x} \mapsto x_1][\mathbf{k} \mapsto 1] \vdash e'' \Rightarrow (St_1, \langle x'_1 \rangle)$$
$$\dots \qquad St_{m-1}, En'[\mathbf{x} \mapsto x_m][\mathbf{k} \mapsto m] \vdash e'' \Rightarrow (St_m, \langle x'_m \rangle)$$
$$x'_1, \dots, x'_m \in \mathcal{B} \cup \mathcal{I} \qquad v = \langle x_i | (x'_i \in \mathcal{I} \wedge x'_i = i) \vee (x'_i \in \mathcal{B} \wedge x'_i) \rangle$$
$$\overline{St, En \vdash e' [\ e''\ ] \Rightarrow (St_m, v)}$$

Path Expression (Rule [18]) The semantics of $(e' \ / \ e'')$ is as follows. First e' is evaluated. Then for each item in its result we bind in the environment $\mathbf{x}$ to this item, $\mathbf{k}$ to the position of $\mathbf{x}$ in the result of e', and $\mathbf{m}$ to the number of items in the result of e', and with this environment we evaluate e''. The results of all these evaluations are concatenated and finally this sequence is sorted by document order and the duplicates are removed. The result is only defined if all the evaluations of e'' contain only nodes.

$$St, En \vdash e' \Rightarrow (St_0, \langle x_1, \dots, x_m \rangle)$$
$$En' = En[\mathbf{m} \mapsto m] \qquad St_0, En'[\mathbf{x} \mapsto x_1][\mathbf{k} \mapsto 1] \vdash e'' \Rightarrow (St_1, v_1)$$
$$\dots \qquad St_{m-1}, En'[\mathbf{x} \mapsto x_m][\mathbf{k} \mapsto m] \vdash e'' \Rightarrow (St_m, v_m) \qquad v_1, \dots, v_m \in \mathcal{V}^*$$
$$\overline{St, En \vdash e' \ / \ e'' \Rightarrow (St_m, \mathbf{Ord}_{St_m}(\cup_{1 \le i \le m} \mathbf{Set}(v_i)))}$$

$$St, En \vdash e' \Rightarrow (St_0, \langle x_1, \dots, x_m \rangle) \qquad W_1 = \{x \in V_{St_0} | (x_1, x) \in (E_{St_0})^*\}$$
$$\dots \quad W_m = \{x \in V_{St_0} | (x_m, x) \in (E_{St_0})^*\} \qquad \langle x'_1, \dots, x'_{m'} \rangle = \mathbf{Ord}_{St_0}(\cup_{1 \le i \le m} W_i)$$
$$En' = En[\mathbf{m} \mapsto m'] \qquad St_0, En'[\mathbf{x} \mapsto x'_1][\mathbf{k} \mapsto 1] \vdash e'' \Rightarrow (St_1, v_1)$$
$$\dots \quad St_{m'-1}, En'[\mathbf{x} \mapsto x'_{m'}][\mathbf{k} \mapsto m'] \vdash e'' \Rightarrow (St_{m'}, v_{m'}) \qquad v_1, \dots, v_{m'} \in \mathcal{V}^*$$
$$\overline{St, En \vdash e' \ // \ e'' \Rightarrow (St_{m'}, \mathbf{Ord}_{St_{m'}}(\cup_{1 \le i \le m'} \mathbf{Set}(v_i)))}$$

Literal (Rule [19]) The result of a literal is simply a sequence with one element, viz., the atomic value the literal represents.

Empty Sequence (Rule [20])
$$\overline{St, En \vdash () \Rightarrow (St, \langle \rangle)}$$

Constructors (Rule [21]) Before we proceed with the presentation of the rule for the element constructor, we first introduce the notion of *deep equality*. This defines what it means for two nodes in an XML store to represent the same XML fragment.

Definition 9 (Deep Equal). *Given the XML store* $St = (V, E, <, \nu, \sigma, \delta)$ *and two nodes* n_1 *and* n_2 *in* St. n_1 *and* n_2 *are said to be* deep equal, *denoted as* $\mathbf{DpEq}_{St}(n_1, n_2)$, *if* n_1 *and* n_2 *refer to two isomorphic trees, i.e., there is a one-to-one function* $h : C_{n_1} \to C_{n_2}$ *with* $C_{n_i} = \{n | (n_i, n) \in E^*\}$ *for* $i = 1, 2$, such that for each $n, n' \in C_{n_1}$ it holds that (1) if $n \in \mathcal{V}^d$ ($\mathcal{V}^e$, $\mathcal{V}^a$, $\mathcal{V}^t$) then $h(n) \in \mathcal{V}^d$ ($\mathcal{V}^e$, $\mathcal{V}^a$, $\mathcal{V}^t$), (2) if $\nu(n) = s$ then $\nu(h(n)) = s$, (3) if $\sigma(n) = s'$ then $\sigma(h(n)) = s'$, (4) $(n, n') \in E$ iff $(h(n), h(n')) \in E$ and (5) if $n, n' \notin \mathcal{V}^a$ then $n < n'$ iff $h(n) < h(n')$.

The semantics of the element constructor $\texttt{element}\{e'\}\{e''\}$ is the defined as follows. First e' is evaluated and assumed to result in a single legal element name. The e is evaluated and for the result we create a new store St_3 that contains the new element with the result of e' as its name and with contents that are deep-equivalent with the result of e if we compare them item by item. Finally we add St_3 to the original store and return the newly created element node.

$$\frac{\begin{array}{c} St, En \vdash e' \Rightarrow (St_1, \langle s \rangle) \quad s \in \mathcal{N} \quad St_1, En \vdash e'' \Rightarrow (St_2, \langle n_1, \ldots, n_m \rangle) \\ n_1, \ldots, n_m \in \mathcal{V} \quad St_4 = St_2 \cup St_3 \quad n \in V_{St_3} \Rightarrow (r, n) \in E_{St_3}^* \quad r \in \mathcal{V}^e \\ \nu_{St_3}(r) = s \quad \mathbf{Ord}_{St_3}(\{n' | (r, n') \in E_{St_3}\}) = \langle n_1', \ldots, n_m' \rangle \quad \mathbf{DpEq}_{St_4}(n_1, n_1') \\ \cdots \quad \mathbf{DpEq}_{St_4}(n_m, n_m') \quad \forall\, n, n' \in \mathcal{V}((n \ll_{St_2} n') \Rightarrow (n \ll_{St_4} n')) \end{array}}{St, En \vdash \texttt{element}\{e'\}\{e''\} \Rightarrow (St_4, \langle r \rangle)}$$

$$\frac{\begin{array}{c} St, En \vdash e' \Rightarrow (St_1, \langle s \rangle) \\ s \in \mathcal{N} \quad St_1, En \vdash e'' \Rightarrow (St_2, \langle s' \rangle) \quad s' \in \mathcal{S} \quad St_4 = St_2 \cup St_3 \quad V_{St_3} = \{r\} \\ r \in \mathcal{V}^a \quad \nu_{St_3}(r) = s \quad \sigma_{St_3}(r) = s' \quad \forall\, n, n' \in \mathcal{V}((n \ll_{St_2} n') \Rightarrow (n \ll_{St_4} n')) \end{array}}{St, En \vdash \texttt{attribute}\{e'\}\{e''\} \Rightarrow (St_4, \langle r \rangle)}$$

$$\frac{\begin{array}{c} St, En \vdash e \Rightarrow (St_1, \langle s \rangle) \quad s \in \mathcal{S} - \{\text{""}\} \quad St_3 = St_1 \cup St_2 \quad V_{St_2} = \{r\} \\ r \in \mathcal{V}^t \quad \sigma_{St_2}(r) = s \quad \forall\, n, n' \in \mathcal{V}((n \ll_{St_1} n') \Rightarrow (n \ll_{St_3} n')) \end{array}}{St, En \vdash \texttt{text}\{e\} \Rightarrow (St_3, \langle r \rangle)}$$

$$\frac{\begin{array}{c} St, En \vdash e \Rightarrow (St_1, \langle n_1 \rangle) \\ n_1 \in \mathcal{V}^e \quad St_3 = St_1 \cup St_2 \quad n \in V_{St_2} \Rightarrow (r, n) \in E_{St_2}^* \quad r \in \mathcal{V}^d \\ (r, n_2) \in E_{St_2} \quad \mathbf{DpEq}_{St_3}(n_1, n_2) \quad \forall\, n, n' \in \mathcal{V}((n \ll_{St_1} n') \Rightarrow (n \ll_{St_3} n')) \end{array}}{St, En \vdash \texttt{document}\{e\} \Rightarrow (St_3, \langle r \rangle)}$$

Typeswitch-expression (Rules [22] and [23]) Let $[\![\texttt{xs : boolean}]\!] = \mathcal{B}$, $[\![\texttt{xs : integer}]\!] = \mathcal{I}$, $[\![\texttt{xs : string}]\!] = \mathcal{S}$, $[\![\texttt{document-node()}]\!] = \mathcal{V}^d$, $[\![\texttt{attribute()}]\!] = \mathcal{V}^a$, $[\![\texttt{text()}]\!] = \mathcal{V}^t$ and $[\![\texttt{element()}]\!] = \mathcal{V}^e$.

$$\frac{\begin{array}{c} St, En \vdash e \Rightarrow (St_1, \langle x \rangle) \\ (x \in [\![t_j]\!] \vee j = m+1) \quad \forall_{1 \leq i < j}(x \notin [\![t_i]\!]) \quad St_1, En \vdash e_j \Rightarrow (St_2, v) \end{array}}{\begin{array}{c} St, En \vdash \texttt{typeswitch}(e) \texttt{ case } t_1 \texttt{ return } e_1 \ldots \texttt{ case } t_m \texttt{ return } e_m \\ \texttt{default return } e_{m+1} \Rightarrow (St_2, v) \end{array}}$$

Function Call (Rule [24]) The semantics of $f(e_1, \ldots, e_m)$ is that $e_1, \ldots, e_m$ are consecutively evaluated, and then the expression $\mathbf{b}(f)$ is evaluated with the variable names of $\mathbf{a}(f)$ bound to the results of $e_1, \ldots, e_m$.

$$\frac{\begin{array}{c} St, En \vdash e_1 \Rightarrow (St_1, v_1) \\ \cdots \quad St_{m-1}, En \vdash e_m \Rightarrow (St_m, v_m) \quad \mathbf{a}_{En}(f) = \langle s_1, \ldots, s_m \rangle \\ En' = En[\mathbf{v}(s_1) \mapsto v_1] \ldots [\mathbf{v}(s_m) \mapsto v_m][\mathbf{x} \mapsto \bot, \mathbf{k} \mapsto \bot, \mathbf{m} \mapsto \bot] \\ St_m, En' \vdash \mathbf{b}_{En}(f) \Rightarrow (St', v') \end{array}}{St, En \vdash f(e_1, \ldots, e_m) \Rightarrow (St', v')}$$

7 Conclusion

In this paper we have presented a fragment of XQuery called LiXQuery together with a formal and concise but complete description of its semantics that is consistent with the formal semantics of XQuery. We claim that this fragment captures the essence of XQuery as a query language and can therefore be used for educational purposes, e.g., teaching XQuery, and research purposes, e.g., investigating the expressive power of XQuery fragments and query optimization in XQuery implementations.

References

1. XML query (XQuery). http://www.w3.org/XML/Query.
2. XQuery 1.0 and XPath 2.0 data model, W3C working draft 12 november 2003. http://www.w3.org/TR/2003/WD-xpath-datamodel-20031112/.
3. XQuery 1.0 and XPath 2.0 formal semantics, W3C working draft 20 february 2004. http://www.w3.org/TR/2004/WD-xquery-semantics-20040220/.
4. XQuery 1.0 and XPath 2.0 functions and operators, W3C working draft 12 november 2003. http://www.w3.org/TR/2003/WD-xpath-functions-20031112/.
5. XML query use cases, 1.8.4.1. 2003. http://www.w3.org/TR/xquery-use-cases/.
6. G. J. Bex, S. Maneth, and F. Neven. A formal model for an expressive fragment of XSLT. *Information Systems*, 27:21–39, 2002.
7. D. Chamberlin. XQuery: An XML query language, tutorial overview. *IBM Systems Journal*, 41(4), 2002.
8. G. Gottlob, C. Koch, and R. Pichler. Efficient algorithms for processing XPath queries. In *VLDB 2002*, Hong Kong, 2002.
9. J. Harbarth. XQuery 1.0 primer. 2003. http://www.softwareag.com/xml/tools/xquery_primer.pdf.
10. H. Katz, D. Chamberlin, D. Draper, M. Fernández, M. Kay, J. Robie, M. Rys, J. Siméon, J. Tivy, and P. Wadler, editors. *XQuery from the Experts: A Guide to the W3C XML Query Language*. Addison-Wesley, 2004.
11. M. Marx. XCPath, the first order complete XPath dialect. In *SIGMOD/PODS 2004*.
12. P. Wadler. Two semantics for XPath, 1999. http://www.cs.bell-labs.com/who/wadler/topics/xml.html.

XML Query Processing Using a Schema-Based Numbering Scheme

Dao Dinh Kha[1] and Masatoshi Yoshikawa[2]

[1] IMI Project of COE Program, Graduate School of Information Science
[2] Information Technology Center

Nagoya University, Japan
{dinhkha@dl, yosikawa@}.itc.nagoya-u.ac.jp

Abstract. Establishing the hierarchical order among XML elements is an essential function of XML query processing techniques. Although most XML documents have an associated DTD or XML schema, the document structure information has not been utilized efficiently in query processing techniques proposed so far. In this paper, we propose a novel technique that uses DTD or XML schema to improve the disk I/O complexity of XML query processing. We present a schema-based numbering scheme called SPIDER that incorporates both structure information and tag names extracted from the document structure descriptions. Given the tag name and the identifier of an element, SPIDER can determine the tag names and the identifiers of the ancestor elements without disk I/O. Based on SPIDER, we designed a mechanism called VirtualJoin that significantly reduces disk I/O workload for processing XML queries. Our experiments indicated that SPIDER outperforms the structural join techniques Stack-Tree and PathStack in XML query processing, especially for XML queries with heavy join workload and large data sets.

1 Introduction

Since the structure of XML [16] data can be represented by a rooted label tree, queries about XML data typically specify elements by selection predicates and their tree structural relationship. Among a number of methods proposed for verifying the structural relationship of XML elements, applying a numbering scheme is a powerful technique. Recent approaches [9], [10], [11], [12], [13] to the problem combined a numbering scheme, where each element is represented by a 3-tuple (startPos, endPos, level), with the notion of structural joins, which select the pairs of XML elements from candidate sets such that a given hierarchical order holds. The structural join approach has attracted many studies because it facilitates queries about element type, order, and predicate, which are important components of XPath expressions.

The order of elements must obey the *schematic* information described in the grammar, called the DTD or XML schema, which describes the structure of the class that the XML document belongs to. Since the document structure

Z. Bellahsène et al. (Eds.): XSym 2004, LNCS 3186, pp. 21–34, 2004.

descriptions make XML documents exchanged over the web share their grammars efficiently, most of the XML documents in use are associated with a DTD or XML schema. However, previous XML query processing techniques have not utilized the schematic information from DTD or XML schema efficiently.

A drawback of existing structural join techniques is that they require index data about all elements participating in a query to be loaded. In this paper, we propose a novel mechanism for XML query processing called `VirtualJoin` that utilizes the schematic information extracted from the DTD and XML schema to improve the disk I/O complexity of XML query processing. The core of the mechanism is a schema-based numbering scheme called `SPIDER` (for Schema-based Path IDentifiER) that incorporates both structure and tag name information about XML elements. When `SPIDER` is used, if the identifier and tag name of an element are known, the identifier and tag name of the parent element, as well as those of all of its ancestor elements, can be determined without any disk I/O. Based on this property, `VirtualJoin` reduces the number of elements, whose index data is required for processing a query.

To the best of our knowledge, `SPIDER` is the first numbering scheme that utilizes DTD and XML schema. Furthermore, `SPIDER` expresses the structure of XML documents by the identifiers of paths existing in the XML documents, rather than by the node identifiers used in previous numbering schemes.

2   Preliminaries

A DTD or an XML schema contains the description of the hierarchical relationship of XML elements. For example, a DTD may have the element type declarations shown in Figure 1(a). The element hierarchy expressed by these element type declarations is depicted in Figure 1(b).

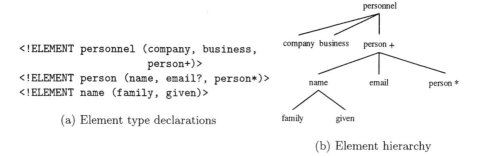

```
<!ELEMENT personnel (company, business,
                     person+)>
<!ELEMENT person (name, email?, person*)>
<!ELEMENT name (family, given)>
```

(a) Element type declarations

(b) Element hierarchy

Fig. 1. Example of DTD.

According to these declarations, any element `company` has a parent element `personnel`. The structure of an XML document is relatively simple if the tag name of the parent element of any element in the document can be determined uniquely. However, in our example, the condition is not *true* with an element `person` since its parent element may be either an element `personnel` or an element `person`. The multiple choice makes the structure of XML documents more complex. For simplicity, we use the notation of DTD in the rest of this paper.

3   SPIDER: A Schema-Based Numbering Scheme

In this section, we describe the numbering scheme SPIDER, which embeds information about both the identifiers and tag names of XML elements.

3.1   Design of SPIDER

SPIDER utilizes the structure information described by pairs of parent-child tag names in the DTD. Intuitively, each pair of tag names of parent and child nodes in the DTD is mapped to an integer called *parent-child tag indicator* PCTAGID. The mapping is designed so that the tag name of a child node and the corresponding PCTAGID can uniquely determine the tag name of the parent node. In other words, the following dependencies, called structural dependencies of the DTD, hold:

$$\texttt{parent\_tag}, \texttt{child\_tag} \longrightarrow \text{PCTAGID} \qquad (1)$$

$$\texttt{child\_tag}, \text{PCTAGID} \longrightarrow \texttt{parent\_tag} \qquad (2)$$

Note that there are many mappings (1) such that dependency (2) holds.

Representation of the DTD. The *parent-child relationship* in a DTD is represented by a table StruDTD that has three columns PARTAG, CHITAG, and PC-TAGID containing the tag names of the parent elements, the tag names of the child elements, and the corresponding parent-child tag indicator, respectively. In terms of the relational data model, dependencies (1) and (2) mean PARTAG and PCTAGID, respectively, functionally depends on the other two columns. Given a table StruDTD such that dependencies (1) and (2) hold, let mapping (1) be denoted by the function findPCTAGID and mapping (2) be denoted by the function parentTAG. The maximum value in the column PCTAGID is called the *fanout* of StruDTD. Note that the size of StruDTD is normally small enough to be kept in main memory.

The table StruDTD is constructed from the DTD or XML schema. The flexibility in design enables different variants of the table StruDTD from a given DTD or XML schema. Therefore, we can generate different variants of the SPIDER numbering scheme, depending on particular needs.

3.2   Algorithm for Constructing SPIDER

Given a table StruDTD such that dependencies (1) and (2) hold, let f denote the fanout of StruDTD. Let T denote an XML tree rooted at r. If n is a node of T then the parent node, the tag name, and the identifier of n are denoted by $parent(n)$, $n.tag$, and $n.sid$, respectively, where *sid* means "structural identifier". SPIDER

Example 1. An example of the table StruDTD corresponding to the element hierarchy in Figure 1, such that dependencies (1) and (2) hold, is shown in Table 1. Note that the pairs (personnel, person) and (person, person) have different PCTAGIDs. Figure 2 shows an example of SPIDER that uses the table StruDTD, where the identifier of a node is larger than the identifier of any of its left siblings.

Table 1. A table StruDTD.

PARTAG	CHITAG	PCTAGID
personnel	company	1
personnel	business	2
personnel	person	3
person	name	2
person	email	3
person	person	4
name	family	1
name	given	2

generates the identifiers of the nodes in an XML tree in a depth-first traversal as shown in Algorithm ConstructSPIDER.

Algorithm: ConstructSPIDER

Input: T rooted at r, StruDTD, $f = $ max (findPCTAGID())
Output: SPIDER of nodes in T
1. depth-first travel T
2.   if n is r
3. $n.sid \leftarrow 1$;
4.   else $p \leftarrow parent(n)$;
5. $pctagid \leftarrow$ findPCTAGID(p.tag, n.tag);
6. $n.sid \leftarrow f * (p.sid - 1) + 1 + pctagid$;
    endif
   endtravel

The identifier of a child node of p is the sum of a basic value computed from the identifier of p plus the parent-child tag indicator of the child node and p (steps 5 and 6). Therefore, the structure information of DTD, expressed by the table StruDTD, is incorporated into the identifiers of nodes in XML trees.

Example 2. Given a StruDTD in Table 1, suppose we have to generate the identifier of a node **name** that is the first child of a node **person**, whose identifier is equal to 4. Since ConstructSPIDER uses a depth-first traversal, the identifier of the **person** is already known. According to Table 1, findPCTAGID(person, name) is equal to 2, and max(findPCTAGID()) is equal to 4. Therefore, the identifier of the **name** is $4 \times (4 - 1) + 1 + 2$, which is equal to 15.

Coding complexity. The cost of the function findPCTAGID is equal to log_2(size(StruDTD)). Therefore, the cost of Algorithm ConstructSPIDER is equal to $O(log_2$(size(StruDTD)) $\times$ (number of nodes)).

3.3   Index Functions for SPIDER

We used the function findPCTAGID to embed the structure information into identifiers of nodes of an XML tree. For query processing, we need two index

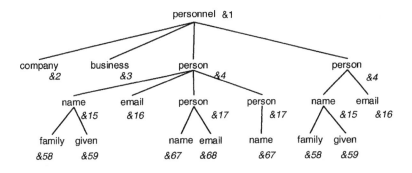

Fig. 2. Example of SPIDER

functions parentSID and nameID as a means to restore the hierarchy of XML nodes based on their identifiers. Given a node n, the index function parentSID for computing the structural identifier of the parent node of a node is defined as follows:

$$\mathsf{parentSID}(\mathbf{n}.sid) = \lfloor (\mathbf{n}.sid - 2)/f \rfloor + 1 \qquad (3)$$

This function is similar to the one introduced in [8]. However, it is worth emphasizing that we apply the function to a numbering scheme that is more comprehensive but flexible than the scheme introduced in [8].

The second index function nameID for computing PCTAGID of n in its parent node is defined as follows:

$$\mathsf{nameID}(\mathbf{n}.sid) = \mathbf{n}.sid - f \times \lfloor (\mathbf{n}.sid - 2)/f \rfloor - 1 \qquad (4)$$

Lemma 1. *Given an XML tree and a table StruDTD such that dependencies (1) and (2) hold, if the structural identifiers are generated by Algorithm Construct-SPIDER then for a given node, the structural identifier and the tag name of its parent node can be determined.*

The proof of Lemma 1 can be found in [20]. Given a node, it is possible to determine the tag names of all ancestor nodes of a node without any disk I/O by applying Lemma 1 recursively. As shown in Section 5, this property is used to avoid the intermediate structural joins and reduce the disk I/O workload for index data necessary for evaluating an XML query.

Example 3. Given an XML tree in Figure 2, let us consider the node email having the identifier equal to 68. Since $f = 4$, the function parentSID(68) is $\lfloor (68 - 2) / 4 \rfloor + 1$, which is equal to 17. The function nameID(68) is $68 - 4 \times \lfloor (68 - 2)/4 \rfloor - 1$, which is equal to 3. The function parentTAG('email', 3) returns 'person', according Table 1. Therefore, the parent node is **person** and has the identifier equal to 17.

4   Variants of SPIDER

As discussed in Section 3, since there are various ways to construct a table StruDTD such that dependencies (1) and (2) hold, we have different variants of SPIDER for a given class of XML documents. In this section, we present two coding variants for two specific purposes.

4.1   Unordered SPIDER

The unordered variant of SPIDER (or USPIDER for short) has the smallest coding size, where the *parent-child relationship is emphasized*. For example, the elements that correspond to the first b and the second b in the DTD declaration `<!ELEMENT a (b?, c*, d, b)>` are treated equally as unordered children of an element a.

We use the following observation: *for a given tag name b in a DTD, if there is only one tag a such that b appears in the element type declaration of a then dependency (2) holds whatever the value PCTAGID is.* In other words, dependency (2) is reduced to `parent tag ⟵ child tag`. For such a pair (a, b), we can assign any number, e.g. zero or one, to PCTAGID to make coding small.

Construction of the function findPCTAGID for USPIDER. Initially, the rows in the table StruDTD are generated corresponding to pairs of parent-child tags in the DTD and all the values PCTAGID are set to one. In order to make dependency (2) hold, we have to *stretch* the column PCTAGID of the table. For a given b, if $\exists$ a_1, a_2, and b such that $a_1 \neq a_2$ but findPCTAGID(a_1, b) = findPCTAGID(a_2, b) then set findPCTAGID(a_2, b) = $max_{i \neq 2}$ (findPCTAGID(a_i, b))+1. It is obvious that findPCTAGID(a_1, b) $\neq$ findPCTAGID(a_2, b). Since the cardinalities of XML DTDs are finite, the process always stops.

4.2   Sibling-Order SPIDER

This variant of SPIDER, called OSPIDER, is *sibling-order sensitive*. OSPIDER guarantees the order of sibling nodes, i.e., the identifiers of the child nodes of a node reflect the order in which these nodes appear in the parent node.

Transformation of complex DTD declarations to the basic form. In general, a DTD can be complex because of the complex specification of the type of an element. For example, an element a can be defined by a DTD declaration such as `<!ELEMENT a ((b, c, d)*, (e, c)*)>`. Theoretically, it is possible to ask the fifth element c in an element a by specifying a predicate c[5] in an XPath expression. However, such a reference is rare because although the elements c in (b, c, d)* and (e, c)* have the same tag name, they are located in different parts of the element a, so it is highly likely that these elements c have different semantics. Therefore, we decompose it using the intermediate elements to reduce the complexity. The above example declaration can be presented by an equivalent group of DTD declarations <!ELEMENT g (b, c, d)>, <!ELEMENT h (e, c)>, and <!ELEMENT a (g*, h*)>. The primary decomposition rules of DTD declarations are:

1. $(b|c)^*$ is decomposed into d^* and $d = (b|c)$
2. $(b,c)^*$ is decomposed into d^* and $d = (b, c)$
3. $b^*|c^*$ is decomposed into $d|e$ and $d = b^*$, $e = c^*$

After the transformation, all declarations can be expressed in a basic form <!ELEMENT a ($b_1\sigma_1$, $b_2\sigma_2$, ..., $b_k\sigma_k$)>, where a and b_i ($i = 1..k$) are tag names and σ_i is either empty or one of cardinalities '?', '*', and '+'.

Construction of the findPCTAGID function. Since it is desirable to reduce the size of the identifiers and make them robust on node insertion, we group the child nodes of a node in clusters and assign the same identifier to the nodes in a cluster.

Definition 1. *Among the child nodes of a given node, a c-group is the maximal group of consecutive sibling nodes having the same tag name.*

We assign an identifier to each c-group of child nodes. To determine the identifiers, we reduce the corresponding DTD declaration to its *core* form by removing the cardinalities of sub-elements from the DTD declaration. For example, <!ELEMENT a (b, c, d)> is the core form of the DTD declaration <!ELEMENT a (b, c?, d*)>. The tag names appearing in the core form of a DTD declaration are numbered by integers starting from one. The index of a c-group is the order of the corresponding tag name in the core form of the DTD declaration of the parent element.

Definition 2. *The 'core PCTAGID' of the node n in its parent node p is equal to the index of the c-group containing n in p.*

Each XML node is assigned a 'core PCTAGID' that is the index of its c-group. Note that the core PCTAGID is different from the actual index of child nodes in their parent node. To determine the *actual* PCTAGID, we stretch the core PCTAGID to make dependency (2) hold. Initially, the rows in the table StruDTD are generated corresponding to pairs of parent-child tags in the DTD and all the values PCTAGID are set to be the core PCTAGID. Since we want to maintain the order of c-groups as it is in DTD, if $\exists$ a_1, a_2, and b such that $a_1 \neq a_2$ but findPCTAGID(a_1, b) = findPCTAGID(a_2, b), then an integer value is added to the core PCTAGID of *all* of the child nodes of a_2 such that findPCTAGID(a_1, b) $\neq$ findPCTAGID(a_2, b). Since the cardinality of any DTD is finite, the stretching procedure always stops after a number of steps.

The StruDTD shown in Table 1 in Section 3.1 is of a variant of OSPIDER. Since the core PCTAGID of the pairs (personnel, person) and (person, person) are equal, i.e. three, the core PCTAGID of all pairs (person, *) were adjusted by being increased by one. After that PCTAGID of (person, person) is equal to four.

4.3   Robustness of SPIDER

SPIDER is robust on structural update since, taking into account the element descriptions from DTD or XML schema, it *anticipates* the positions of updated nodes in the associated XML documents. Let us consider two kinds of structural updates as follows:

1. **An uncertain occurrence specified by the cardinality '?' of an element** in its parent element. In the construction of SPIDER, an identifier for such an element is reserved.
2. **The insertion of a node in a group of nodes specified by the cardinalities '*' or '+'** in the declaration of a parent node. For example, according to the DTD declaration `<!ELEMENT a (b?, c*, d)>`, a node a may have a number of nodes c. Where SPIDER is used, all these nodes c have the same *sid*, so the insertion of the new node does not affect the identifiers of the others.

4.4   Coding Size

The interesting feature of SPIDER is that the fanout of findPCTAGID used to compute *sid* does not depend on the maximal degree of the nodes in the actual XML trees. In our experiments, even when the DTD was complex, the fanout of OSPIDER is relatively small. Moreover, the coding size does not depend on the actual size of tags of elements and attributes.

5   Virtual Joins with SPIDER

In this section we discuss an application of SPIDER in XML query processing. We represent each XML element by a pair [*sid*, *ord*], where *sid* is the identifier generated by SPIDER and *ord* is an actual order representation of the node in an XML instance. Among several presentations available for this purpose, we use a 3-tuple (docID, startPos, endPos) to express *ord*, where docID, startPos, and endPos have natural meanings. Using this representation, the element (docID, $startPos_1$, $endPos_1$) is an ancestor of the element (docID, $startPos_2$, $endPos_2$) iff $startPos_1 < startPos_2$ and $endPos_2 < endPos_1$.

As will be shown later, *sid* and *ord* complement each other in query processing. Although the index data of each element or attribute is a combination of both *sid* and *ord*, the actual disk I/O workload that must be loaded for processing a query is small since SPIDER provides a mechanism avoiding many intermediate structural joins in XML query processing. We call the mechanism VirtualJoin. We will describe the application of VirtualJoin to the processing of queries of the basic *path-predicate*, complex *path-predicate*, and *twig* types. First, we briefly describe several basic functions used by VirtualJoin. Detailed descriptions of the functions can be found in [20].

findParentSidAndTag determines the tag name and *sid* of the parent node of a given node. The function calls the functions parentSID and nameID to compute the *sid* of the parent node and PCTAGID of the pair of these parent-child nodes. This computed PCTAGID is used by the function parentTAG to find the tag name of the parent node.

generateNodePath establishes the full node path for a given node by recursively calling the function findParentSidAndTag.

findAncByName checks the existence of ancestors having a specific tag name of a given node specified by its *sid* and tag name. If such ancestors exist, the function returns the lowest ancestor.

5.1   Basic *Path-Predicate* Queries

A simple XML query can be represented by a path expression ending with a predicate. We call it a basic path-predicate query.

Definition 3. *An XML query is called 'a basic path-predicate' query if it is expressed in the form:* $a_1\ell_1a_2\ell_2\cdots\ell_{k-1}a_k$ *or* $a_1\ell_1a_2\ell_2\cdots\ell_{k-1}[\mathcal{P}]$, *where* $k \geq 1$, ℓ_i *(i = 1 to k-1) is either the child axis '/' or the self-or-descendant axis '//', and* $\mathcal{P}$ *is a predicate of* a_k.

The predicate $\mathcal{P}$ is optional. An example of a basic path-predicate query is "person/name/[given = 'Smith']". Using the Structural Join approach, in the basic path-predicate queries, all the nodes having the tag names a_i, $i \neq k$, and the nodes having the tag name a_k filtered by the predicate $\mathcal{P}$ participate in the structural joins. Therefore, the index data of all these nodes must be loaded into main memory.

Using SPIDER, for a given node, it is possible to establish its full node path using the function generateNodePath, and hence test if the node path *matches* the path $a_1\ell_1a_2\ell_2\cdots\ell_{k-1}a_k$. For a basic path-predicate query, VirtualJoin performs a single scan[1] over the set of nodes a_k satisfying the predicate $\mathcal{P}$. For each node of the set, it tests if the node a_k^i matches the path $a_1\ell_1a_2\ell_2\cdots\ell_{k-1}a_k$. Note that the test may terminate early for disqualified nodes and the testing process run totally in main memory. VirtualJoin requires the index data of only a_k that satisfy the predicate $\mathcal{P}$ being loaded in main memory. VirtualJoin can process the *ancestor-level* joins, where the hierarchy level is required, such as "a/b", "a/*/b", as well as the "a//b" join.

We can deduce whether the node path of a node a_k matches the path $a_1\ell_1a_2\ell_2\cdots\ell_{k-1}a_k$ from the pattern matching problem [21]. However, considering that the height of an XML tree is normally low, we proposed a simple algorithm, the details of which can be found in [20].

Note that VirtualJoin does not require the candidate nodes to be sorted and it evaluates basic path-predicate queries without disk I/O except for the index data of the output candidate set.

---

[1] For predicates with a low selectivity, there have been other approaches with a cost of an extra index.

5.2 Complex *Path-Predicate* Queries

A path query may contain a number of selection predicates.

Definition 4. *A query is called 'a complex path-predicate query' if it is expressed in the form of a finite sequence of basic path-predicate queries separated by the child axis '/' or the self-or-descendant axis '//'.*

A complex path-predicate query $B_1\ell_1B_2\ell_2\cdots\ell_{k-1}B_k$, $k \geq 1$, is evaluated by integrating the results of the basic path-predicate queries B_i, $i = 1$ to k, which are evaluated separately using `VirtualJoin`. Let $R_i = \{r_i^j\}$ denote the list of result nodes of B_i, $S_i = \{s_i^j\}$ denote the list of *sid* of the nodes in the highest hierarchical structure of B_i corresponding to $\{r_i^j\}$. From `VirtualJoin` of basic path-predicate queries, it is obvious that $\{s_i^j\}$ is generated together with $\{r_i^j\}$. The lists R_i are joined using the conventional structural join technique to produce the final result. Two elements r_i^j and r_{i+1}^l, $1 \leq i < k - 1$, are matched in the structural joins of R_i and R_{i+1} if both of the following conditions hold:

1. $r_i^j.startPos < r_{i+1}^l.startPos$ && $r_{i+1}^l.endPos < r_i^j.endPos$
2. $(\ell_i$ is '/' && $r_i^j.sid = $ parentSID$(s_{i+1}^l))||(\ell_i$ is '//' && $r_i^j.sid \leq s_{i+1}^l)$

5.3 Twig Queries

Queries about XML data typically specify elements by selection predicates and their tree structure relationship that can be represented as a node label twig pattern with or without predicates in the leaf nodes. `VirtualJoin` processes a twig query by decomposing it into subqueries (see Figure 3) that can be evaluated as complex path-predicate queries. The result elements of these queries are then joined like the joining of the intermediate results presented in 5.2.

Example 4. For being processed using `VirtualJoin`, the XQuery statement

```
FOR $b IN /site/ people/person
WHERE $b/address/[city ='Nara']
RETURN $b/name/text
```

is decomposed into three path-predicate queries "/site/people/person", "address/[city = 'Nara']", and "name/text".

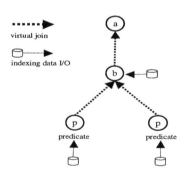

Fig. 3. Processing a twig query

In general, the disk I/O complexity of `VirtualJoin` is *optimal* since only the index data of elements that have to be verified by predicates or belong to the candidate set of the output is loaded. In Example 4, the index data of **person**, **city**, and **text** is needed to perform the joins.

6   Experiments

We implemented `VirtualJoin` to test the efficiency of this method. The main file structure for storing the index data is as follows:

<scx, element_name, add_infor>

where `scx` consists of `OSPIDER` and *ord*, `element_name` is the tag name, and `add_infor` is additional information including an element or attribute indicator and a pointer to data. The data is indexed on `scx` and `element_name` using B^+-tree sorted by the `scx.ord.startPos`.

We compared our method with the method Stack-Tree-Desc in [12] and Path-Stack in [13]. Both of the algorithms use the tuple (`docID`, `startPos`, `endPos`, `nodeLevel`) to present an XML element. Stack-Tree-Desc has the highest performance among the four methods described in [12], where stacks are used to reduce the number of match tests for the pairs of elements from the joined candidate sets in structural joins. PathStack also uses stacks to compactly present the partial and total answers to avoid large intermediate answers. For comparison, we measured the *total* time for XML query processing that includes the elapsed times for loading the index data and for performing structural joins.

6.1   Experimental Platform and Data Sets

Our experiments were coded in Java and conducted on a workstation running Windows XP Professional with a 2-GHz CPU. We used the XML data generator `xmlgen` provided by XMark [4] to generate synthetic XML documents, whose sizes ranged from 23.4 to 232.2 MB, from the DTD "auction.dtd". This DTD has a fairly complex structure to make the experiments objective. The SAX parser available from the Xerces project [18] was used to parse XML data for indexing.

6.2   Experimental Results

We use queries that featured the various complexities of structural joins. The queries contained both '/' and '//' axes and included short, medium, and long location paths.

Q_1: `//closed_auction/item`
Q_2: `//items/name`
Q_3: `//open_auction//description`
Q_4: `//open_auction//description//listitem`
Q_5: `//open_auction//description//keyword`
Q_6: `//closed_auctions/closed_auction/annotation/description/`
    `parlist/listitem/text/emph/keyword/`

The experimental results are shown in Figures 4 and 5, where our method, Stack-Tree-Desc, and PathStack are abbreviated by SCX, STD, and PS, respectively.

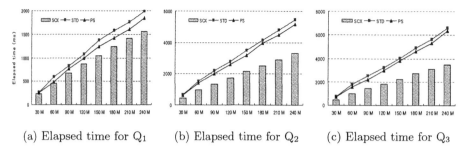

(a) Elapsed time for Q_1 (b) Elapsed time for Q_2 (c) Elapsed time for Q_3

Fig. 4. Elapsed times for processing short queries Q_1-Q_3.

Analysis. The elapsed times for processing *simple* queries with different data sets are shown in Figures 4(a)-(c). Queries Q_1 and Q_2 both involved a single parent-child join whereas the query Q_3 had an ancestor-descendant join. Although they contained only a structural join, the queries allowed us to compare the methods with the candidate sets of different cardinalities. The `VirualJoin` is slightly better than Stack-Tree-Desc in the smallest data set (Figure 4(a)) and significantly better in the bigger data sets (Figures 4(b) and (c)).

Medium complex queries Q_4 and Q_5, borrowed from [11], contained several ancestor-descendant joins. The elapsed times for processing the queries with different data sets are shown in Figures 5(d)-(e). As expected, the axis '//' could be processed efficiently using `VirualJoin`.

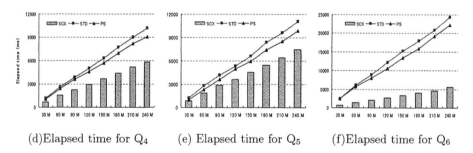

(d)Elapsed time for Q_4 (e) Elapsed time for Q_5 (f)Elapsed time for Q_6

Fig. 5. Elapsed times for processing medium and complex queries Q_4-Q_6.

A number of queries introduced in XMark [4] have *complex* structures. One example is Q_6 that means: *"Print the keywords in emphasis in annotations of closed auctions"*. The elapsed time for processing the query with different data sets is shown in Figure 5(f). For the complex query, the advantage of `VitualJoin` over STD and PS is very significant. This can be explained, for such queries, by the amount of index data saved by `VirtualJoin` from being loaded from secondary memory being larger. For the location path of Q_6, the index data of the only element `keyword` was loaded and the remaining part of the evaluation process was done in main memory.

In our query set, the join workloads increased from queries Q_1 to Q_6. In all experiments, we could see an interesting tendency that the advantage of `VirtualJoin` steadily increased in proportion to the size of the experimental data sets as well as the join workload.

7 Related Work

The structural summary has been presented as a graph for semistructured data in [7], [14], [15]. A path-based approach to query the XML data by storing all available node paths in a table of RDBMS and making queries over the pattern of the node paths has been proposed [19]. An integration of XML node numbers in query statements and an algorithm for transformation from XPath to SQL have been discussed in [5].

The presentation of XML elements by a tuple (`docID`, `startPos`, `endPos`, `nodeLevel`) and its variants for processing structural joins have been used in [3], [9], [10], [12], [13]. The indexing structures such as B^+-tree and R-tree built-in in RDBMSs have been exploited in [11] to index the presentation values.

Some current work is related to our approach [1], [2]. XML documents are embedded in a binary tree in [1], the depth of which is high in practice. XR-tree proposed in [2] manages the stab lists used to find pairs of the qualified elements in ancestor-descendant structural joins. The index implementation requires a new data structure other than the widely used B^+-tree and does not support the parent-child relationship well.

Another related work is the UID method [8] that assigns consecutive integers starting from 1 to the nodes of an XML tree in order from top to bottom and from left to right in each level, assuming that each of internal nodes has the same fan-out equal to the maximum fan-out of the nodes. The design of `SPIDER` is compact and robust on structural update, the issue that limits the application of the UID method in query processing.

Although independently developed, our approach has some similarity with a recent work [22] in using two indices to perform XML query processing.

8 Conclusion

Existing techniques for processing XML queries do not efficiently utilize the document structure described in the DTD or XML schema. In this study, we proposed `VirtualJoin`, a mechanism that enables structural joins based on `SPIDER`, a numbering scheme that incorporates both structure and tag name information extracted from DTD or XML schema. `VirtualJoin` can avoid the disk I/O for the index data of the intermediate nodes in the structure of an XML query. According to our experiments, the disk I/O improvement of `VirtualJoin` increases in proportion to the structural join workload and the sizes of data sets.

In future, we plan to investigate the application of `VirtualJoin` to querying XML data stored in an RDBMS.

References

1. Wang Wei et al., PBiTree Coding and Efficient Processing of Containment Join, ICDE, India, 2003.
2. H. Jiang, H. Lu, W. Wang, B. C. Ooi, XR-Tree: Indexing XML data for Efficient Structural Joins, ICDE, India, 2003.
3. S. Chien et al., Efficient Structural Joins on Indexed XML Documents, VLDB, Hong kong, 2002.
4. A. Schmidt, XMark: A Benchmark for XML Data Management, VLDB, Hong kong, 2002.
5. I. Tatarinov et al., Storing and Querying Ordered XML Using a Relational Database System, SIGMOD, USA, 2002.
6. S. Flesca, F. Furfaro, E. Masciari, On the minimization of XPath Queries, VLDB, Germany, 2003.
7. P. Buneman, S. Davidson, M. Fernandez, D. Suciu, Adding Structure to Unstructured Data, ICDT, Greece, 1997.
8. Y. K. Lee, S-J. Yoo, K. Yoon, P. B. Berra, Index Structures for structured documents, ICDL, USA, 1996.
9. C. Zhang, et al., On Supporting Containment Queries in Relational Database Management Systems, SIGMOD, USA, 2001.
10. Q. Li, B. Moon, Indexing and Querying XML Data for Regular Path Expressions, VLDB, Italy, 2001.
11. T. Grust, Accelerating XPath Location Steps, SIGMOD, USA, 2002.
12. S. Al-Khalifa et al., Structural Joins: A Primitive for Efficient XML Query Pattern Matching, ICDE, USA, 2003.
13. N. Bruno, N. Koudas, D. Srivastava, Holistic Twig Joins: Optimal XML Pattern Matching, SIGMOD, USA, 2002.
14. R. Goldman, J. Widom, DataGuides: enabling query formulation and optimization in semistructured databases, VLDB, 1997.
15. T. Milo, D. Suciu. Index Structures for Path Expression, ICDT, 1999.
16. W3C, Extensible Markup Language 1.0, http://www.w3.org/TR/REC-xml, 2000.
17. W3C, XML Path Language version 1.0, http://www.w3.org/TR/xpath, 2000.
18. Apache Software Foundation, Apache XML Project, http://xml.apache.org/, 2001.
19. M. Yoshikawa et al., XRel: A Path-Based Approach to Storage and Retrieval of XML Documents Using Relational Databases, ACM TOIT, 1(1), 2001.
20. Dao Dinh Kha, Masatoshi Yoshikawa and Shunsuke Uemura, Virtual Joins for XML Data, NAIST Technical Report IS-TR2003012, November 2003.
21. D. Gusfield, Algorithms on Strings, Trees, and Sequences, Cambridge University Press, New York, USA, 1997.
22. Yi Chen, Susan B. Davidson, Yifeng Zheng, BLAS: An Efficient XPath Processing System, SIGMOD, France 2004.

Implementing Memoization in a Streaming XQuery Processor

Yanlei Diao[1,2], Daniela Florescu[1], Donald Kossmann[1],
Michael J. Carey[1], and Michael J. Franklin[2]

[1] BEA Systems, U.S.A.
{danielaf, donaldk, mcarey}@bea.com
[2] University of California at Berkeley, U.S.A.
{diaoyl, franklin}@cs.berkeley.edu

Abstract. In this paper, we describe an approach to boosting the performance of an XQuery engine by identifying and exploiting opportunities to share processing both within and across XML queries. We first explain where sharing opportunities arise in the world of XML query processing. We then describe an approach to shared XQuery processing based on memoization, providing details of an implementation that we built by extending the streaming XQuery processor that BEA Systems incorporates as part of their BEA WebLogic Integration 8.1 product. To explore the potential performance gains offered by our approach, we present results from an experimental study of its performance over a collection of use-case-inspired synthetic query workloads. The performance results show that significant overall gains are indeed available.

1 Introduction

XQuery [18], while not yet a standard, is already being put to use in commercial software infrastructure products for a number of different IT purposes. For example, the XQuery language (and its sub-language XPath) has been incorporated into several products for business process management and application integration. XQuery is used in several ways there – as a transformation language for defining XML data transformations, as an expression language for making branching and looping decisions based on XML workflow variables, and as a filtering and routing language for handling message broker events. XQuery is also being used in enterprise information integration products that provide virtual XML views of disparate enterprise data sources where it is the language for defining integrated views and writing queries.

As XQuery adoption gains momentum, the performance of XQuery processing becomes increasingly important. As with any query language, XQuery is amenable to a large number of optimizations, both at compile time and at runtime. In many of the uses to which XQuery is being put, significant optimization opportunities can be obtained through the discovery and exploitation of shared processing, within or across queries. For example, in publish/subscribe, query evaluation work can be shared when matching messages against a large number of subscriptions [5]. In this

Z. Bellahsène et al. (Eds.): XSym 2004, LNCS 3186, pp. 35–50, 2004.

paper, we investigate the exploitation of such sharing opportunities to boost the performance of XQuery processing. In particular, we develop *memoization* techniques for XQuery and apply them in the context of a commercial streaming XQuery processor.

Sharing in XQuery processing. Intuitively, intermediate results of XQuery processing can be shared whenever the "same" XQuery expression(s) would otherwise be evaluated more than once with the "same" XQuery variable bindings. (We will say more about what "same" means in this context in Section 2.) This can happen in several ways:

1. The same expression can occur several times in different locations within a query.
2. The same expression can occur in different queries that are evaluated together.
3. An expression can occur within a query that is evaluated multiple times (most likely with different variable bindings).
4. An expression can occur in different queries that are executed at different times (where the query context is the same across executions).

The first case is self-explanatory. The second case arises in contexts like publish/subscribe, where an incoming XML message needs to be checked against many subscription queries. An example of the third and fourth cases is a web service call or a remote database lookup modeled as an XQuery function call, where the results of the call are known to be stable over time (at least for some specified time period).

In this work, we propose a memoization-based approach to avoiding redundant work. Memoization caches the results for an expression based on its variable bindings, and it can thus support evaluation reuse in all of the above cases.

Streaming XQuery processing. Our approach is designed to work well in the context of an XML query processor that employs stream-based processing. In the context of XML query processing, streaming is important for performance, and it can occur at a fine level of granularity. A fine-grained approach is critical given that a single XML item can be arbitrarily large, containing the equivalent of an entire table's or even database's worth of data content. To enable fine-grained streaming, the BEA XQuery engine [6], the engine on which this work is based, represents its XML operands as sequences of (potentially nested) tokens that represent smaller constituent data pieces.

The use of a token stream representation of XML provides an XQuery processor with several ways to achieve incremental query evaluation while avoiding the materialization of its inputs. The first way is *pipelining*. A given XQuery expression can consume and produce token streams incrementally, materializing only one or a few tokens at a time in order to compute and emit its output. Of course, this requires the use of a pull-based API to be truly effective. The second way is *lazy evaluation*, a technique commonly used in the implementation of functional programming languages [11]. With this technique, a result is not actually generated until requested by a consuming expression. Moreover, in XQuery, some expressions can be evaluated based on only the first few tokens of a given input – for example, nth( ), empty( ), exists( ), existential comparators, and positional predicates. These expressions enable an even lazier mode for XQuery processing, where only those (possibly few) tokens needed for the consuming expression are generated.

Contributions. In this paper, we present a memoization-based approach to sharing in XQuery processing. While both the multiple-query processing (MQP) problem [17] and the use of memoization for query processing [10] have been explored in other contexts, our contributions lie in the fact that shared XQuery query processing in a streaming environment adds significant new wrinkles to the problem. In particular, MQP in the relational setting has focused on SELECT-FROM-WHERE style constructs, whereas our work is aimed at supporting sharing for the much richer XQuery language. Memoization has been exploited for expensive functions (as in query processing) or repeatedly computed functions (as in dynamic programming), but it has not been studied for a large variety of XQuery expressions and in a stream-based processing environment. The main contributions of this work can be summarized as follows:

1. We set the scope for XQuery memoization, first in a simple but limited way, and then in an expanded range exploiting semantic data and expression equivalence.
2. We develop a number of query compilation techniques to identify interesting shareable XQuery expressions and to determine the granularity of memoization.
3. We also extend the runtime system, resolving the inherent tension between stream-based processing and memoization. Our solutions enable computation reuse while supporting pipelining and avoiding eager evaluation.
4. We summarize results from a performance study of our techniques in the context of the BEA XQuery engine. The results show significant performance gains for typical use cases of XQuery.
5. As this paper represents our initial approach towards adding memoization to XQuery processing, we identify several important open problems to be addressed.

The paper is as follows. Section 2 discusses basic issues related to XQuery memoization. Section 3 describes the BEA XQuery engine, the technical context of this work. Sections 4 and 5 describe how we have added memoization to this engine, focusing on the compile-time and runtime aspects, respectively. Section 6 reports experimental results. Section 7 covers related work. Section 8 concludes the paper.

2   Basics of XQuery Memoization

In this section we address the basic issues related to XQuery memoization. Memoization is an algorithmic technique that remembers the results returned by functions invoked with particular arguments and, if the function is called with the same arguments again, returns the result from memory rather than recalculating it [11, 13]. In the context of XQuery, the unit of computation that we adopt for memoization is the (XQuery) expression.

In its simplest form, XQuery memoization can be implemented in a straightforward way: results of an expression are shared whenever an *identical* XQuery expression is evaluated more than once with *identical* XQuery variable bindings, where the meaning of *"identical"* is based on bit-wise comparison of their binary representations.[1] The usefulness of such memoization, however, is limited by the stringent requirement of identical binary representations. To expand the scope for XQuery memoization, we would like to establish **equivalence** relationships between expressions and between variable bindings, so that ample reuse of the computed results is possible. To this end, we relax the conditions for the application of memoization along two dimensions: (1) when two XQuery *data model instances* can be determined to be equivalent; and (2) when two XQuery *expressions* can be determined to be equivalent.

XML Data Equivalence. What we seek is an equivalence relationship on XQuery data model instances that meets the following requirement for safe memoization: Given an expression E, for every pair of equivalent XQuery data model instances, the two results of evaluating E on the two instances are also equivalent. XQuery has multiple equality testing predicates (=, eq, is, deep-equal( ), ...) to compare data model instances. Unfortunately, none of these is satisfactory for establishing data equivalence for safe memoization (the analysis is omitted here in the interest of space). As a result, we define our own, more comprehensive (but still imperfect) equivalence relationship between XQuery data model instances:

Definition 1 (XML data equivalence). Two data model instances are equivalent *iff* one of the following conditions is true: (a) they both represent the empty sequence, or (b) they are both single atomic values, their primitive values are equal (based on the **eq** comparison on their respective primitive XML data types), and their type annotations are also equal (based on the **eq** comparison on their *xs:QName* data types), or (c) they are both nodes and they compare true via the **is** comparison, or (d) they are both sequences of the same length $l \geq 1$ and the corresponding items in the *ith* position ($1 <= i <= l$) are equivalent via the conditions (b) or (c).

Unfortunately, memoization based on this definition is not safe for every possible XQuery expression. For example, consider the memoization of the *string( )* function for two dateTime instances that use different time zones but have the same normalized values (i.e., the same UTC time). Based on Definition 1, the two dateTime instances are equivalent (via condition (b)), however, the results of applying *string( )* to these instances are not equivalent, due to the different time zones included in the output strings. As such, memoization in this case would cause erroneous results.

Given our goal of exploiting semantic data equivalence for memoization and the fact that doing so correctly for the full XQuery language is a very hard problem, our current solution is restricted to a subset of XQuery for which Definition 1 is guaranteed to provide safe memoization. Roughly speaking, every expression in this subset is such that each variable of the expression satisfies one of the following conditions:

---

[1] Of course, expressions that produce non-deterministic results are not suitable for memoization. Examples of such expressions include functions that read the system time (e.g., *fn:current-dateTime( )*), and user-defined functions that are declared to be variant.

(1) the type of the free variable is a node; (2) the type of the free variable is an atomic type and the computation performed by the expression is compatible with the **eq** comparison defined on this type; or (3) the type of the free variable is a sequence of items and the items in the sequence have the same type that satisfies condition (1) or (2). As our experimental results show, even this limited definition of equivalence can provide significant performance improvements for XQuery processing in use cases similar to those that we would expect to see in web services, application integration, etc.

Expression equivalence. In general, two XQuery expressions are the same if and only if they return the same result for every correct binding of their variables. This question is undecidable in general, since XQuery is Turing-complete. As a result, we identify sufficient conditions for XQuery expression equivalence based on expression normalization and detection of syntactical equivalence between normalized expressions (which will be described in detail in Section 4). As our experimental results show, these conditions permit ample reuse of computations (given typical use cases) while also being efficiently computable.

Thus, our approach represents a practical compromise between an overly restrictive definition of XQuery memoization and the difficulties that arise due to the fully-general nature of XQuery. While we believe that our approach is applicable in a large number of practical situations, expanding its range is part of our ongoing work.

3   The BEA Streaming XQuery Processor

In this section we review the aspects of the BEA XQuery engine [6] that are directly relevant to our subsequent design descriptions. The representation of XML data used internally by the BEA XQuery runtime is a sequence of tokens called the *token stream*. Despite its similarity to the SAX API, the token stream models typed XML, and is accessed via a pull-based API for producing and consuming tokens lazily. Moreover, the BEGIN tokens for documents, elements or attributes are augmented to carry the ids of the nodes in order to compare nodes for both equality and document ordering. Further details on the token stream can be found in [6].

3.1   Query Compilation

The purpose of the XQuery compiler is to parse, verify, type check, normalize and optimize a query. The result of compilation is an iterator tree that can be interpreted by the runtime system.

During compilation, a query is represented as an *expression tree*. Nodes in an expression tree represent kinds of expressions and edges represent data flow dependencies. The kinds of expressions used by the BEA XQuery processor are very close to the W3C XQuery formal semantics recommendation [20], and include *Constants*, *Variables*, *FirstOrder* expressions, *SecondOrder* expressions, *IfThenElse*, *Node Constructors*, etc. All built-in functions and operators of the XQuery standard [19] share the same representation – each is a *FirstOrder* expression. Examples include all

XPath axes (e.g., child, descendant, parent), the *data*( ) function, arithmetic functions, comparisons, and constructor functions for simple types (e.g., *float*( ), *string*( )). The *Match* expression carries out an XPath nodetest (i.e., kind of node and name of node). A *Node Constructor* creates a new XML structure. In this particular processor, node id generation is decoupled from Node Constructors and postponed until later when needed for query evaluation.[2] The family of *SecondOrder* expressions can be further classified into *Map*, *Let*, *Sort*, etc., most of which represent the high-order functions of XQuery. Map will be described more closely in the example below.

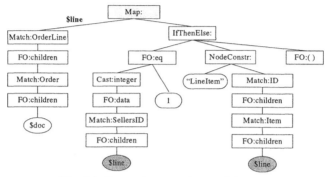

Fig. 3-1. Expression tree of query Q1.

The translation of an XQuery into an expression tree closely follows the W3C XQuery formal semantics [20]. For example, the *for* clause of a FLWOR query is translated into nested Maps, each of which defines one variable; the *where* clause into an IfThenElse expression; and so on. Consider query Q1 below, which requests line items in a purchase order document that have a particular seller.

Query Q1: *for* $line   *in* $doc/Order/OrderLine
             where xs:integer(data($line/SellersID)) *eq* 1
             return <LineItem> {$line/Item/ID} </LineItem>

Fig. 3-1 shows the expression tree for this query, where constant expressions are shown as rounded rectangles, variables as ovals, and all other expressions as rectangles. Expressions other than constants and variables are labeled with the kind of expression ("FO" for FirstOrder), followed by a colon, followed by any optional specifications of an expression, such as a particular FirstOrder function (e.g., *children*( ) or *data*( )) as well as any other parameters (e.g., the NodeTest of a Match expression). Map is the only SecondOrder expression in this example. Note that the left child of the Map expression is labeled with the name of the variable defined in the Map. Uses of the variable in the right child of the Map are denoted by shaded ovals.

A *free variable* of an expression is a variable that is not defined by any second order expressions inside this expression, essentially representing an input of the expression. For example, "$doc" is a free variable of the Map, but "$line" is not. However, "$line" is indeed a free variable of IfThenElse, the right child expression of Map, and

---

[2] This decoupling raises the potential for sharing the node construction computation.

of the expressions inside IfThenElse that contain this variable. We call a mapping between the free variables of an expression and a set of values a *binding*.

At the last step of query compilation, the compiler generates code for the query expression, resulting in an executable *iterator tree*. There is a one-to-one mapping between many of the nodes in the expression tree and iterators in the generated iterator tree; however, a few iterators implement several expressions (e.g., the *children( )* iterator implements a *child( )* expression plus a Match expression) for performance reasons. Variable expressions are implemented by a special *runtime variable* iterator that returns the value of a variable and can be *bound* to different inputs at runtime.

3.2 Runtime System

The task of the runtime system is to interpret an iterator tree to produce the query result. Like many database query engines, the BEA XQuery runtime system is based on an iterator model [9]. Its query execution model is pull-based, and data is consumed at the granularity of tokens. Using the iterator model, the runtime system naturally exploits pipelining. It also makes use of lazy evaluation; that is, an iterator only generates results on demand, with each *next( )* call. Consider the iterator that implements the *empty( )* function. This iterator consumes only a single token from its input in order to produce a Boolean result. The remaining input tokens are not consumed, and thus are not even generated. Other expressions where lazy evaluation is effective include positional predicates (e.g., $line/Item[1]) and existential quantification.

4 Query Compilation for Memoization

In this section we describe the compile-time aspects of arranging for efficient evaluation of a set of XQuery queries (referred to as the "target queries"). We restrict our attention to the cases where the target queries share the static context and most of the dynamic context (except the date and time of execution).[3] The techniques presented in this section focus on sharing among common subexpressions. Although not discussed below, sharing by caching expensive methods [10] can be easily supported by indicating such expressions to the compiler.

4.1 Expression Equivalence

Our approach to expression equivalence is based on two steps. First, all expressions are normalized by applying a set of rewriting rules. The rewriting rules include ones that "normalize" queries based on the XQuery formal semantics [20], and others that are typically applied in XQuery optimization, e.g., unnesting nested FLWOR expressions whenever possible, putting predicates in conjunctive normal form, etc. More details of these rewriting rules are provided in [6].

---

[3] XQuery memoization in the presence of different static and/or dynamic contexts poses difficulties that are beyond the scope of this paper; we leave that generalization for future work.

The second step searches for syntactical equivalence between expressions. Our approach to determining equivalence is based on the notion of *variable renaming substitutions*. We say that two expressions E1 and E2 are syntactically equivalent via a renaming substitution $S=\{x_1/y_1,....,x_n/y_n\}$, if $\{x_1,...,x_n\}$ are the free variables of E1, $\{y_1, ...,y_n\}$ are the free variables of E2, and E1 and E2 are syntactically isomorphic, up to a renaming of (free and bound) variables. For example, the expressions ($x+1)*($x-3) and ($y+1)*($y-3) are syntactically equivalent via the renaming substitution {$x/$y}.

Given this definition, we develop an algorithm that detects syntactical equivalence between two expressions E1 and E2. If E1 and E2 are syntactically equivalent via the renaming substitution $S=\{x_1/y_1, ..., x_n/y_n\}$, the algorithm returns S, otherwise it returns *null*. In the sequel, we call this algorithm "equals( )".

Given two input expressions E1 and E2, equals( ) iterates on E1 and E2 and their subexpressions from top to bottom, checking recursively at each level for syntactic isomorphism. Obviously two expressions are not (syntactically) equal if they are not of the same kind (e.g., constants, variables, Maps, etc). Moreover, it is clear that the details of the recursive algorithm depend on the kinds of the expressions E1 and E2. XQuery has more than 15 kinds of expressions. While our algorithm handles all of them, for brevity, here we describe only three:

Constant expressions. If E1 and E2 are both constant expressions, then they are equal via a renaming substitution S *iff* the given constants are equivalent via the data equivalence Definition 1 given in Section 2.

FirstOrder expressions. If E1 and E2 are both FirstOrder Expressions, then they are equal via the renaming substitution S *iff* they have the same operator and the same number of children subexpressions, and the children subexpressions are pairwise equal via the same substitution S.

Map expressions. Assume that both E1 and E2 are Map expressions of the form:

E1= *for* $var1 *in* expr1 *return* expr2

E2= *for* $var2 *in* expr3 *return* expr4

First, the algorithm will test the structural equivalence of exp1 and expr3. If this succeeds with renaming substitution S then the algorithm continues; otherwise it fails. In the positive case, the renaming {$var1/$var2} is added to the current renaming substitution S and the algorithm will continue by testing the structural equivalence of expr3 and expr4 via the new S. In case the test succeeds and an augmented substitution S is returned, the end result of the test is the substitution S *without* the renaming of the internal variables {$var1/$var2}. Otherwise the test fails.

Note that the complexity of the structural test equals( ) is linear in the size of the input expressions. Given that the potentially interesting expressions for sharing among the target queries include *all* the subexpressions of these queries, the structural test needs to be applied to all possible pairs in the Cartesian product of the subexpressions of the target queries, yielding a very expensive algorithm. Next, we describe the technique used in our implementation to avoid this exponential complexity.

4.2   Applying the Algorithm

Identifying common subexpressions is implemented as an additional step taken by the compiler after query parsing, normalization and optimization, but before code generation. In this step, the compiler iterates over the target queries and identifies common subexpressions both inside each query and between this query and earlier queries.

For each query, the compiler performs a depth first search in the query expression tree to identify the *maximal shareable subexpressions*: For each subexpression encountered that is not a constant or a variable, the compiler performs three tasks: (1) Apply *hashing* on the subexpression, ignoring all the variable names, and use the hashing result to probe the in-memory storage of all distinct subexpressions, each of which serves as a representative of an equivalence class. (2) If representatives with the same hashing result exist, for each of them call equals( ) on the representative and the subexpression in hand. (3) If any representative is equivalent to the subexpression, apply *heuristics* to filter out uninteresting cases of common subexpressions (such as inexpensive operations, e.g., a simple addition, and expressions that are not very expensive but could return large results e.g., a child path expression with wildcards). If a representative passes all these tests, the compiler determines that the representative matches the subexpression, and stops further traversal into this subexpression. Otherwise, it updates the storage of equivalence classes with the unmatched subexpression and continues the search in the children of this subexpression.

As an example, consider query Q1 from Section 3 together with Q2 given below.

Query Q2:   *for* $item   *in* $doc/Order/OrderLine
             where   xs:integer(data($item/BuyersID)) *eq* 8
             return   <LineItem> {$item/Item/ID} </LineItem>

After query Q2 is parsed, normalized, and optimized, it is represented by an expression tree similar to that in Fig. 3-1 except for the *if* expression (i.e., the leftmost branch of *IfThenElse*). Table 1 shows the results of the compilation actions applied to the expression tree of Q2 for identifying maximal shareable subexpressions after all subexpressions of Q1 have been processed. The rows contain the subexpressions considered in order of the depth first search. As Table 1 shows, Map is filtered by the first step of hashing because it contains a different path expression and a different constant in its *if* expression. Match:OrderLine and NodeConstr are the two maximal common expressions identified. Note that although FO:children and FO:( ) are equivalent via equals( ), they are filtered by our heuristics as being uninteresting sharing cases.

The implementation of code generation is also modified to take into account the identified common subexpressions. The compiler again iterates over the query set in the same order. For each query, code generation proceeds recursively in the expression tree as before, except for common subexpressions. For the instances of a common subexpression, a *CacheIterator* (which will be described in detail in the next section) is created for each instance, but all such CacheIterators point to the same memo table, which is where the results of memoization are cached at runtime.

Table 1. Identifying Common Subexpressions between Q1 and Q2

Expression	(1) hashing	(2) equals	(3) heuristics
Map	No		
Match:OrderLine	Yes	Yes	Yes
IfThenElse	No		
FO:eq	No		
Cast:integer	No		
FO:data	No		
Match:SellersID	No		
FO:children	Yes	Yes	No
NodeConstr	Yes	Yes	Yes
FO: ()	Yes	Yes	No

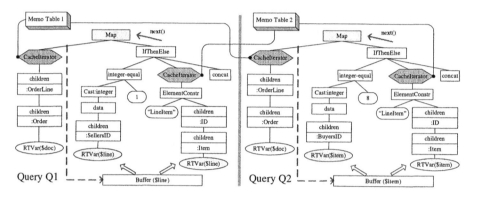

Fig. 4-1. Iterator trees of two queries containing common subexpressions

Fig. 4-1 shows the iterator trees generated for Q1 and Q2. The two queries have separate iterator trees. The structure of each iterator tree is similar to the expression tree (revisit Fig. 3-1), with abstract expressions replaced by specific iterators and some optimizations of the structure (e.g., merging *Match* and *children*). Moreover, instances of a common subexpression identified previously (as shown in Table 1) are wrapped by different *CacheIterators* that point to the same memo table.

5   Query Execution for Memoization

Having presented the compile-time aspects of our solution, we now describe the extensions required for the runtime system. These extensions are encapsulated into a new iterator called *CacheIterator*. The key data structure used by the CacheIterator is the memo table, which maps from the set of XQuery data model instances bound to the free variables of an expression to the computed/cached result of that expression. The main challenges in the memo table implementation, addressed here, stem from the inherent tension between memoization and streaming XQuery processing.

The first challenge is to obtain the "identity" of the bindings of the free variables, so that this identity can then be used as a key to probe the memo table. If the binding of a free variable is a sequence of items, the entire sequence needs to be read before the identity can be computed and any result produced, which unfortunately breaks pipelining. In addition, with lazy evaluation, the binding of a free variable which is provided by a subexpression may not yet be evaluated at the point when this key is needed. How to perform memo table lookup in the face of these conflicts is crucial for computation reuse without losing the performance benefits of stream-based processing. Our solution to this is presented in Section 5.1.

The second challenge relates to the output. Recall that a very lazy mode of execution is used for XQuery processing. That is, the result of an expression is produced token by token, upon request, rather than in its entirety. Result caching, however, works best if the whole result is pre-computed because it is unknown how many tokens of the result are to be consumed by the different consumers. We refer to the kind of caching that pre-computes the entire result as **Complete Caching**. In contrast, **Partial Caching** does not pre-compute entire results; it caches those parts of the results that have been requested by the consumers. Partial Caching is favorable from a performance perspective, but it is more difficult to integrate into a stream-based XQuery processor. These two caching schemes are described in more detail in Section 5.2.

5.1   Memo Table Lookup

The purpose of a memo table is to map the values of the free variables of a common subexpression to a (completely or partially) cached result. To this end, the memo table is implemented as a hierarchy of hash tables. Each level in this hierarchy corresponds to one free variable and is probed using the value of that free variable. Probing a memo table with a set of values bound to the free variables results in either a reference to the cached result (i.e., a memo table hit) or a *null* pointer (i.e., a memo table miss).

In order to probe the memo table and to record new entries in the memo table in the event of lookup misses, it is crucial to know the values of the free variables. As stated at the beginning of this section, a naïve implementation of memo table lookup could break lazy evaluation and pipelined processing of these values, thus adversely affecting the performance. At this point, we place an important restriction on the notion of data equivalence used for memo table lookup: we disregard condition (d) in Definition 1 (given in Section 2) for establishing equivalence between sequences of items. In other words, we only cache results of an expression if the type of each free variable of this expression is either an atomic type (e.g., integer or date) or a node (e.g., element or document). We do not cache results if the type of a free variable is a sequence of items. Our implementation of this restriction is based on type checking on free variables at compile time.

The issue with lazy evaluation still exists even with this restriction. The value of a free variable can contain an arbitrarily large number of tokens (e.g., for a document), which might be produced by another complex expression that we wish to evaluate lazily. Fortunately, this restriction does enable us to probe the memo table by only looking at the first token of the value of each free variable. If the type of the free variable is a node, the first token will contain the *id* of the node and we can use this id to probe the memo table. If the type of free variable is an atomic type, instead, we can extract the whole value from the first token and use that to probe the memo table.

5.2   Result Caching

Implementing complete result caching is easy, once the memo table lookup issue has been solved. The queries that contain a common subexpression each instantiate a CacheIterator for this common subexpression. The CacheIterators of those queries, however, share the same memo table. This memo table is used in the following way: For each binding of the free variables, the memo table is probed as described before. If the result has been cached, the CacheIterator returns it token by token (whenever its *next*( ) method is called) from the cached result. If the memo table lookup fails, the common subexpression is fully evaluated using the current binding, the entire result is cached, and the memo table is updated with the (binding, result) pair. The next time when the common subexpression needs to be evaluated with the same binding of the free variables (within the same query or for another query), the stored result is reused.

Complete Caching is simple, but it computes the entire result of a common subexpression which may never be needed. For performance reasons, we would like to compute the results of a common subexpression just as lazily as in other situations; that is, results stored in the memo table are generated only when they are needed by the consumers. This gives rise to the idea of Partial Caching that is able to cache partial results across queries and compute additional parts of the results later, if needed.

To implement Partial Caching, we need to keep the iterator tree of the common subexpression in addition to the partial results. We will use this iterator tree when additional results are needed which have not been produced yet. Furthermore, we must preserve the state of all iterators in the iterator tree, in particular, the bindings of the iterators that represent the free variables in the iterator tree. In general, preserving such states across queries can be costly and may involve further materialization.

We currently focus on a special case, for which preserving the state is relatively simple; that is, the common subexpression is *resumable*. An expression is resumable if its free variables are bound only once in one invocation of the query execution. This condition can be checked at compile time based on the static types of the expressions that compute the values of the free variables. Common examples of such expressions occur in web services where path expressions are prefixed with an external variable that will be bound to each incoming message. For a resumable expression, we simply store the iterator tree together with the partial results in the memo table and use the iterator tree whenever additional results need to be produced (with guaranteed correct state of the iterator tree). Finally, some support is also provided to prevent a query from closing its iterator tree that has been stored in a memo table at the end of its processing. Details are omitted here due to space constraints.

6   Performance Evaluation

We have implemented our techniques for shared XQuery processing in a Java-based prototype system extending the BEA XQuery processor. In this section we evaluate the effectiveness of these techniques in the context of message brokering, where queries are executed over XML message payloads (or messages, for short). The workloads are derived from use cases collected from BEA customers. These use cases demonstrate common ways of using XQuery in practice.

Starting from these use cases, we created a set of workload queries based on the Purchase Order schema from the Universal Business Language (UBL) library [15]. We also created purchase order messages using a tool based on the AlphaWorks XML generator [1]. We used a set of 1000 10KB messages in our experiments. The performance metric used is *Query Execution Time*. This is the average time for executing a set of queries on each message from the input set. It does not include the message parsing time. We compared the performance of individual execution of the queries ("no caching") and query execution with memoization ("caching"). Complete caching and partial caching perform the same, if not otherwise stated. All the experiments were performed on a Pentium III 850 Mhz processor with 768MB memory running Sun JVM 1.4.2 on Linux 2.4. The JVM maximum allocation pool was set to 500 MB. All data structures including the memo tables fit in the 500 MB allocation pool.

The first experiment was conducted in the context of subscriptions using parameterized queries, which is a common way that service instances subscribe to a message broker. The parameterized query that we used is provided below:

> *for* $price *in* $doc/Order/OrderLine/Item/BasePrice/PriceAmount
> *where*   *float*(*data*($price)) *lt* $value
> *return* $price

Thirty queries (i.e., subscriptions) were generated from this template. To obtain different degrees of query similarity, we varied the number of distinct values that the variable $value can take, called the *domain size*, from 1 to 30. For a given domain size n, the values between 1 and n were evenly distributed in the thirty queries.

The results are shown in Fig. 6-1. It is clear that memoization provides huge benefits for this workload. When all thirty queries use the same value, "caching" achieves a 10.7x performance gain. As the domain size increases, its performance benefit decreases slowly, obtaining a factor of 3.3 when every query uses a distinct value.

The next experiment focuses on the use case of message transformation for subscribers. In this case, the message broker provides a function called summarizeOrderLine (not shown here) for summarizing the line items of interest to each subscriber. An example subscription query is illustrated below.

> *for* $line *in* $doc/Order/OrderLine
> *where*   *xs:integer*(*data*($line/Item/ID)) *ge* 1 *and* *xs:integer*(*data*($line/Item/ID)) *le* 20
> *return* summarizeOrderLine ($doc, $line)

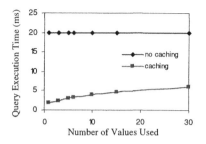
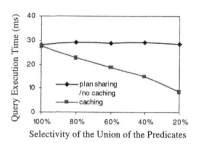

Fig. 6-1. Vary the number of distinct values used for the parameterized query

Fig. 6-2. Vary the selectivity of the union of the query predicates

In this test, we used five queries similar to the query above and fixed their selectivity to 20% each using a range predicate on the ID of line items. We varied the overlap among queries by changing the constants in the range predicates so that the selectivity of the union of the 5 predicates varied from 100% (no overlap) to 20% (full overlap).

With query overlap, the same *OrderLine* may satisfy multiple predicates, and memoization over the function summarizeOrderLine( ) can avoid redundant work among queries. This type of sharing, however, cannot be captured by the traditional plan-level sharing approach of the relational world [17]. Here, plan sharing is equivalent to individual execution of queries. The results of this experiment are shown in Fig. 6-2. It can be seen that as the overlap among queries increases, the performance of "caching" improves remarkably but that of "no caching" (or plan sharing) does not.

We also conducted experiments to evaluate the effectiveness of our approach for web services calls and message routing using path expressions, and to compare complete and partial caching for workloads where lazy evaluation is crucial. The results of these experiments show that significant overall performance gains are available.

7   Related Work

Our work is related to a number of areas in the databases and functional programming communities. We attempt to provide a rough overview of related work here.

Query execution techniques based on sorting or hashing have been used to eliminate redundant computation of expensive methods [10]. For SQL trigger execution, algorithms have been developed to extract invariant subqueries from triggers' condition and action [8]. These techniques used in the relational setting are related to ours for XQuery processing in the case of single expression, multiple bindings.

In the pioneering work on multi-query optimization [17], the problem of *MQO* is formulated as "merging" local access plans of a set of queries into a global plan with reduced execution cost. Along this line, advanced algorithms have been proposed to approximate the optimal global plan [4, 16]. Our work addresses XQuery--a much richer language--and uses different techniques for identifying common subexpressions. Moreover, as our results show, our work provides finer-grained (i.e., binding-based) sharing of intermediate results than merging relational-style access plans.

There has been a large body of work on materialized views, which *precomputes* the views used by a set of queries and stores the results to speed up query processing [7]. In contrast, our techniques consider expressions with parameters, and cache and recover expression results "on the fly" while running a set of queries. View selection [1, 3, 14] decides what subqueries to materialize based on cost models and/or reliable statistics, similar in spirit to our technique of selecting interesting shareable computations. Using partial result caching, our approach has the advantage of avoiding unnecessary materialization over the cached computations.

XQuery memoization differs from memoization in functional programming [11, 12] in two aspects. First, instead of named functions, the memoization target for XQuery is expressions, making effective detection of shareable expressions critical. Second, while memoization in functional programming is usually based on a simple "values in, value out" execution model, our approach is realized in a complex processing model that produces results lazily and pipelines them to the extent possible.

8 Conclusions

In this paper, we described a memoization-based approach to sharing in XQuery processing. We first provided an analysis of data and expression equivalence for XQuery memoization. We then addressed issues related to efficient implementation. We developed a number of query compilation techniques to identify interesting shareable expressions, and extended a pipelined runtime system with efficient memo table lookup and different caching schemes. All of these techniques have been implemented in the context of a commercial XQuery processor and their effectiveness was demonstrated using query workloads derived from the common uses of XQuery in practice.

While our results are promising, we view this as a first step towards solving the problem of efficient sharing in XQuery processing. There are many interesting and important problems to be addressed in our future work. First, as data and expression equivalence is crucial to the applicability of memoization, a thorough analysis in the context of the full XQuery language will be a main focus of our work. Second, we will consider normalization rules that rewrite queries especially to enable memoization. Such rewriting is aimed at turning variables of an expression from node-based to value-based, thus expanding the opportunities for reusing the computed results. Third, a complete solution to partial result caching that supports lazy evaluation requires further investigation. Finally, due to the diverse characteristics of shareable expressions, selective memoization is key to the performance of memoization. We plan to extend the set of compile-time heuristics and develop runtime adaptability to select those shareable expressions beneficial from the cost point of view.

Acknowledgements. We would like to thank Andrew Eisenberg for pointing out the *eq* anomaly that arises when applying the function string( ) to dateTime objects.

References

1. Agrawal, S., Chaudhuri, S., and Narasayya, V. Automated Selection of Materialized Views and Indexes in SQL Databases. In *Proc. of VLDB* 2000, 496-505.
2. AlphaWorks. XML Generator. Aug 2001.
   http://www.alphaworks.ibm.com/tech/xmlgenerator.
3. Chirkova, R., Halevy, A., and Suciu, D. A Formal Perspective on the View Selection Problem. In *Proc. of VLDB* 2001, 59-68.
4. Dalvi, N., Sanghai, S., Roy, P., et al. Pipelining in Multi-Query Optimization. In *Proc. of PODS* 2001, 59-70.
5. Diao, Y., and Franklin, M. Query Processing for High-Volume XML Message Brokering. In *Proc. of VLDB* 2003, 261-272.
6. Florescu, D., Hillery, C., Kossmann, D., et al. The BEA/XQRL Streaming XQuery Processor. In *Proc. of VLDB* 2003, 997-1008.
7. Gupta, A., and Mumick, I.S. Maintenance of Materialized Views: Problems, Techniques, and Applications. *IEEE Data Bulletin*, 18(2), 1995, 3-18.
8. Llirbat F., Fabret F., and Simon E. Eliminating Costly Redundant Computation from SQL Trigger Executions. In *Proc. of ACM SIGMD* 1997, 428-439.
9. Graefe, G. Query Evaluation Techniques for Large Databases. *ACM Computing Surveys* 25(2), 1993, 73-170.
10. Hellerstein, J., and Naughton J. Query Execution Techniques for Caching Expensive Methods. In *Proc. of ACM SIGMOD* 1997, 423-434.
11. Hudak, P. Conception, Evolution, and Application of Functional Programming Languages. *ACM Computing Surveys* 21(3), 1989, 359-411.
12. Hughes, J. Lazy Memo-functions. In *Functional Programming Languages and Computer Architecture*. Springer-Verlag LNCS 201, 1985, 129-146.
13. Michie, D. "Memo" Functions and Machine Learning. *Nature*, 218, 1968, 19-22.
14. Mistry, H., Roy, P., Sudarshan, S., et al. Materialized View Selection and Maintenance Using Multi-Query Optimization. In *Proc. of ACM SIGMOD* 2001, 307-318.
15. OASIS. Universal Business Language. Feb. 2003.
   http://www.oasis-open.org/committees/ubl/.
16. Roy, P., Seshadri, S., Sudarshan, S., et al. Efficient and Extensible Algorithms for Multi-Query Optimization. In *Proc. of SIGMOD* 2000, 249-260.
17. Sellis, T. Multiple-Query Optimization. In *ACM TODS* 13(1), 1988, 23-52.
18. XQuery 1.0: An XML Query Language. http://www.w3.org/TR/xquery/.
19. XQuery 1.0 and XPath 2.0 Functions and Operators. http://www.w3.org/TR/xpath-functions/.
20. XQuery 1.0 and XPath 2.0 Formal Semantics. http://www.w3.org/TR/xquery-semantics.

XQuery Processing with Relevance Ranking

Leonidas Fegaras

University of Texas at Arlington
416 Yates Street, P.O. Box 19015
Arlington, TX 76019-19015, USA,
fegaras@cse.uta.edu

Abstract. We are presenting a coherent framework for XQuery processing that incorporates IR-style approximate matching and allows the ordering of results by their relevance score. Our relevance ranking algorithm
is based on both stem matching and term proximity. Our XQuery processor is stream-based, consisting of iterators connected into pipelines. In
our framework, all values produced by XQuery expressions are assigned
scores, and these scores propagate and are combined when piped through
the iterators. The most important feature of our evaluation engine is the
use of structural and content-based inverse indexes that deliver data in
document order and facilitate the use of efficient merge joins to evaluate path expressions and search predicates. We present the rules for the
translation from a large part of XQuery to iterator pipeline. Our modular approach of building pipelines to evaluate XQuery scales up to any
query complexity because the pipes can be connected in the same way
complex queries are formed from simpler ones.

1 Introduction

It has been noted since its conception that the structured nature of XML allows a better representation and more precise querying of text documents. Even
though current XML query languages, such as XPath and XQuery [5], are very
powerful in expressing exact queries over XML data, they do not meet the needs
of the IR community since they do not support approximate matching based on
textual similarity with relevance ranking. There are already a number of recent
proposals on extending the XQuery language with IR-style search primitives,
such as TexQuery [3, 6], XQuery/IR [7], ELIXIR [9], XIRQL [10], XXL [17–19],
XRANK [13], and XIRCUS [15]. Furthermore, there is an ongoing effort by the
W3C community to provide usage scenarios for full-text queries [22], but there is
still no emerging standard for a full-text extension to XQuery. It is not the goal
of this paper to propose yet another document-centric language for XML documents. Instead, we present a framework for XQuery processing in which the most
important features of these emerging proposals can be seamlessly incorporated
to the XQuery semantics and can be processed efficiently.

More specifically, the objectives of this work are:

1. to use simple but powerful language extensions to XQuery based on current
   proposals to accommodate IR-style approximate matching with relevance

Z. Bellahsène et al. (Eds.): XSym 2004, LNCS 3186, pp. 51–65, 2004.

ranking; these syntactic extensions should require minimal changes to the existing XQuery semantics and should be amenable to efficient evaluation;

2. to design an indexing scheme for XML data for efficient evaluation of both search predicates and path navigation;
3. to build a highly pipelined XQuery engine, called *XQueryRank*, that evaluates XQueries against the indexes using merge joins exclusively and without materializing intermediate results;
4. this engine should consist of iterators that naturally reflect the syntactic structures of XQuery and can be composed into pipelines in the same way the corresponding XQuery structures are composed to form complex queries;
5. the XQuery translation should be concise, clean, and completely compositional, so that optimizations can be easily incorporated later;
6. even though the prototype system is not intended to be complete, since XQuery is a very complex language, it should be designed in such a way that all supported language features can be be incorporated later without strain.

The main contribution of this paper is the development of a coherent framework for XQuery processing that incorporates IR-style approximate matching and allows the ordering of results by their relevance score. Our relevance ranking algorithm is based on both stem matching and term proximity. Our XQuery processor is stream-based, consisting of *iterators* connected into pipelines [12]. This pipeline model avoids materialization of intermediate results when possible. In our framework, all values produced by XQuery expressions are assigned scores, and these scores propagate and are combined when piped through the iterators. The scoring is done implicitly by the stream iterators that evaluate the query. The most important feature of our evaluation engine is the use of structural and content-based inverse indexes that deliver data in document order and facilitate the use of efficient merge joins to evaluate path expressions and search predicates. We present the rules for the translation from a large part of XQuery (which includes the search extensions) to query plans that represent the iterator pipeline.

The closest work to ours is the TIX algebra [2]. Like the TAX algebra, TIX works on pattern trees, which captures path expressions over single documents, even though there is a proposed syntax for incorporating relevance ranking to XQuery that corresponds to the TIX operators. With XQueryRank, on the other hand, one may correlate multiple documents in the same query, may query all indexed documents at once, and may use any kind of query nesting and complexity. More importantly, we give the full details of the XQuery translation into efficient evaluation plans. Furthermore, while their term matching algorithm is limited to conjunctions of search terms, our method is as effective for disjunction and negation. Finally, in contrast to our approach, which propagates and combines relevance scores when fragments are piped through operators, TIX trees are annotated with relevance scores, called scored trees. This is a non-functional approach that does not work well with the functional semantics of XQuery, because the same tree may be assigned a different score under a different context.

2 Approximate Matching in XQuery

There are already a number of recent proposals on extending the XQuery language with IR-style search primitives. It is not the main goal of this paper to propose yet another document-centric query language; rather, we aim at developing a framework in which these query language extensions can be easily incorporated into an XQuery processor by providing a language that reflects the most important features of these proposals. We are using the following simple extensions to XQuery that have been influenced by TexQuery [3, 6]:

1. the expression document() that matches any indexed document and returns the top level elements of all these documents. The order of the documents is unspecified and may depend on the time the documents were indexed.
2. the boolean IR predicate $e \sim S$, where e is any XQuery expression, that returns true if at least one element from the sequence returned by e matches the IR *search specification*, S. The specification S has the following syntax:

$$S, S_1, S_2 ::= \text{``text''} \quad \text{phrase}$$
$$| \quad S_1 \text{ and } S_2 \quad \text{conjunction}$$
$$| \quad S_1 \text{ or } S_2 \quad \text{disjunction}$$
$$| \quad \text{not } S \quad \text{negation}$$

Note that a phrase must be present in the text of some descendant of the element e and must be in consecutive words that do not cross element boundaries.

3. the function score(e), for each element from the XQuery expression e, returns its score (the relevance assessment). A score is a real number between 0 and 1: a zero score means false, while a non-zero score means true. The closer the value score is to 1, the more the value is relevant to the query result.

For example, the following query

```
<answer>{
( for $db in document()/biblio,
      $b in $db/bib[title ~ ("XQuery processing" and "relevance")]
  where $b/abstract ~ ("SAX" and not "DOM")
  order by score($b) descending
  return <paper>{ $b/author/name, $b/title, score($b) }</paper>
) [position()<=10]
}</answer>
```

searches all indexed documents for papers that contain the phrase "XQuery processing" and the word "relevance" in the title, and whose abstract contains the word "SAX" but not the word "DOM". The resulting papers are ordered by descending order of relevance and the top ten relevant papers are returned. The result of the query consists of links to document fragments (ie, triples with the document location and the begin/end positions of an element), rather than the actual text of the fragments, because it is impossible to reconstruct the original text from the inverse indexes alone. A user may in turn dereference some of the returned links, assuming that the original XML documents are still available. Note also that, if not ordered, the resulting papers will be listed in the document order, regardless of scores, as is enforced by the XQuery semantics. Since there may be many indexed documents involved, if not ordered, the paper listings of each document would appear together and the order of documents may depend on the time they were indexed. As expected, scores are propagated and combined across path expressions and other XQuery syntactic constructs, so that results from any kind of XQuery expression can be assigned scores. Finally, words in phrases must be continuous in the XML document and term weighting is based on both stem matching and term proximity.

2.1 Semantics of the XQuery Extensions

In our framework, an XML element in an indexed XML document is assigned a triple (begin,end,level), based on its position in the document (ie, the positions of its begin/end tags) and on its depth level [21]. If an element x is a child of an element y in an XML document, then the (begin,end) region of x is contained by the corresponding region of y and the level of x is the level of y plus one. Furthermore, a preceding sibling of an element has a preceding, non-overlapping region. This numbering scheme, called *region encoding* [21], has already been used by many systems for effective XML indexing and efficient path expression evaluation.

An XML fragment (called XF) is an XML element from an indexed document that may contain text. Text is tokenized into terms (words) that reflect the linguistic tokens of a given human language. A term in an XF is assigned a pair (position,level) so that the position of the term is contained by the XF's region and the position order reflects the term order in the XF. The level of a term is equal to the level of the enclosing XF. In addition, to facilitate phrase matching and proximity calculations, our numbering scheme guarantees that consecutive terms be assigned succeeding positions.

Since the unit of XQuery processing is a sequence of XML elements, the unit of full-text searching should be a sequence of XF elements, rather than the entire document. A term in an XF can be assigned a weight $\mathcal{W}[\![term]\!]$ based on the standard IR term-frequency/inverse-document-frequency (tf-idf) relevance ranking. We are using the following weight:

$$\frac{\text{frequency-of-term-in-XF}}{\text{number-of-terms-in-XF}} \times \log\left(\frac{\text{term-level} - \text{e-level} + 1}{\text{e-level}}\right) \times \log\left(\frac{\text{XFs-containing-term}}{\text{total-number-of-XFs}}\right)$$

where e-level is the level of the element e being tested for matching. The first term is the frequency of the term in the XF, the second term depends on how close is the level of the term with that of the element under consideration, and the last term depends on how rare is the term in the database (rare terms are given higher weight). The boolean connectives in a search specification can be assigned a score based on the probabilistic interpretation of weights:

$$\mathcal{W}[\![S_1 \text{ and } S_2]\!] = \mathcal{W}[\![S_1]\!] \times \mathcal{W}[\![S_2]\!]$$

$$\mathcal{W}[\![S_1 \text{ or } S_2]\!] = \mathcal{W}[\![S_1]\!] + \mathcal{W}[\![S_2]\!] - \mathcal{W}[\![S_1]\!] \times \mathcal{W}[\![S_2]\!]$$

$$\mathcal{W}[\![\text{not } S]\!] = 1 - \mathcal{W}[\![S]\!]$$

As it can be easily proven, this interpretation preserves almost all the boolean laws, such as $\mathcal{W}[\![\text{not } (S_1 \text{ and } S_2)]\!] = \mathcal{W}[\![(\text{not } S_1) \text{ or } (\text{not } S_2)]\!]$ and $\mathcal{W}[\![\text{not } (\text{not } S)]\!]$ $= \mathcal{W}[\![S]\!]$, but does not preserve idempotent laws, such as $(S \text{ and } S) = S$. Unfortunately, this probabilistic interpretation is not very useful, since it does not take term proximity into account; the following interpretation though does.

Consider a conjunction of n terms tested against an XF

$$\text{``}T_1\text{''} \text{ and } \ldots \text{ and } \text{``}T_n\text{''}$$

where some instance of the term "T_i" is located at position p_i in the XF and has weight w_i. We abstract this conjunction with the quadruple

$$(\min(p_1, \ldots, p_n), \max(p_1, \ldots, p_n), n, w_1 \times \cdots \times w_n)$$

That is, instead of remembering all term positions, we abstract them with the smallest interval that contains these positions and assume that these n positions are distributed uniformly along this interval. In general, a conjunction of terms is represented by the quadruple (b, e, n, w) (which stand for begin-position, end-position, number-of-points, and weight). It is assigned the score $\left(1 - \frac{e-b}{n \times \text{size}}\right) \times w$, where 'size' is the XF size (the total number of terms in all descendants of the XF). The first score factor is proportional to the term proximity since $(e - b)/n$ is the average distance between terms.

To make this idea work for any type of boolean connective in a search predicate, S, we associate two sets to S: one, $\mathcal{W}[\![S]\!].T$, that contains the positive quadruples and another, $\mathcal{W}[\![S]\!].F$, that contains the negative quadruples. Since a quadruple abstracts a conjunction of terms, $\mathcal{W}[\![S]\!].T$ is the disjunction of all these conjunctions. If there are no negative terms, then the score of a search predicate S is:

$$\text{score}(S) = \oplus/\{ \tfrac{n \times \text{size}}{e-b} \times w \mid (b, e, n, w) \in \mathcal{W}[\![S]\!].T \}$$

where $\{ e \mid \ldots \}$ is a set former notation, much like the tuple relational calculus, the binary associative function $\oplus$ gives the weight of a disjunction:

$$w_1 \oplus w_2 = w_1 + w_2 - w_1 \times w_2$$

and $\oplus/\{w_1, \ldots, w_n\}$ reduces the set $\{w_1, \ldots, w_n\}$ by $\oplus$ as follows:

$$\oplus/\{w_1, w_2, \ldots, w_n\} = w_1 \oplus w_2 \oplus \cdots \oplus w_n$$

That is, each cost is proportional to both the term weight and the proximity between the constituent terms and the total score is accumulated by repeatedly applying the weighting function for disjunctions.

Before we give the general score formula for any search predicate, we describe the rules for the boolean connectives. Conjunctions are formed by merging quadruples using the following operator:

$$A \bowtie \emptyset = \emptyset \bowtie A = \{ (b, e, n, \tfrac{w}{2}) \| (b, e, n, w) \in A \}$$

$$A_1 \bowtie A_2 = \{ (\min(b_1, b_2), \max(e_1, e_2), n_1 + n_2, w_1 \times w_2) \\ \| (b_1, e_1, n_1, w_1) \in A_1 \wedge (b_2, e_2, n_2, w_2) \in A_2 \}$$

Then, the search specifications are translated as follows:

$$\mathcal{W}[\![S_1 \text{ and } S_2]\!].T = \mathcal{W}[\![S_1]\!].T \bowtie \mathcal{W}[\![S_2]\!].T \quad \mathcal{W}[\![S_1 \text{ and } S_2]\!].F = \mathcal{W}[\![S_1]\!].F \cup \mathcal{W}[\![S_2]\!].F$$

$$\mathcal{W}[\![S_1 \text{ or } S_2]\!].T = \mathcal{W}[\![S_1]\!].T \cup \mathcal{W}[\![S_2]\!].T \quad \mathcal{W}[\![S_1 \text{ or } S_2]\!].F = \mathcal{W}[\![S_1]\!].F \bowtie \mathcal{W}[\![S_2]\!].F$$

$$\mathcal{W}[\![\text{not } S]\!].T = \mathcal{W}[\![S]\!].F \qquad\qquad \mathcal{W}[\![\text{not } S]\!].F = \mathcal{W}[\![S]\!].T$$

This interpretation too preserves almost all boolean laws, as it can be seen from the following case:

$$\mathcal{W}[\![\text{not } (S_1 \text{ and } S_2)]\!].T = \mathcal{W}[\![S_1 \text{ and } S_2]\!].F = \mathcal{W}[\![S_1]\!].F \cup \mathcal{W}[\![S_2]\!].F \\ = \mathcal{W}[\![\text{not } S_1]\!].T \cup \mathcal{W}[\![\text{not } S_2]\!].T = \mathcal{W}[\![(\text{not } S_1) \text{ or } (\text{not } S_2)]\!].T$$

Furthermore, a term "T" with weight w that appears at the positions $p_1, \dots, p_n$, for $n \geq 0$, in an XF has $\mathcal{W}[\![\text{"}T\text{"}]\!].F = \emptyset$ and:

$$\mathcal{W}[\![\text{"}T\text{"}]\!].T = \{ (p_1, p_1, 1, w), \dots, (p_n, p_n, 1, w) \}$$

In addition, a phrase "$T_1 T_2 \dots T_n$" has the following $\mathcal{W}[\![\text{"}T_1 T_2 \dots T_n\text{"}]\!].T$:

$$\{ (p_1, p_n, n, w_1 \times \cdots \times w_n) \| (p_1, p_1, 1, w_1) \in \mathcal{W}[\![\text{"}T_1\text{"}]\!].T \\ \wedge \dots \wedge (p_n, p_n, 1, w_n) \in \mathcal{W}[\![\text{"}T_n\text{"}]\!].T \\ \wedge p_2 = p_1 + 1 \wedge \dots \wedge p_n = p_{n-1} + 1 \}$$

That is, terms in a phrase must have succeeding positions. Finally, the total score of any search predicate S, for a non-empty $\mathcal{W}[\![S]\!].F$, is given by:

$$\oplus / \{ \frac{|\min(e_1, e_2) - \max(b_1, b_2)|}{\text{size}} \times (1 - \frac{e_1 - b_1}{n_1 \times \text{size}}) \times w_1 \times (1 - (1 - \frac{e_2 - b_2}{n_2 \times \text{size}}) \times w_2) \\ \| (b_1, e_1, n_1, w_1) \in \mathcal{W}[\![S]\!].T \wedge (b_2, e_2, n_2, w_2) \in \mathcal{W}[\![S]\!].F \}$$

The motivation behind this formula is that negative terms should be as far as possible from positive terms. This requirement is materialized by the factor $|\min(e_1, e_2) - \max(b_1, b_2)|$, which is proportional to the distance between the positive and the negative quadruples.

In our framework, all values produced by XQuery expressions are assigned scores. This is done implicitly by the stream iterators that evaluate the query, which are described in Section 4. The unit of communication between iterators is a tuple that contains a number of elements, which typically correspond to document fragments. Each fragment is associated with a score, and these scores propagate and combined when piped through the iterators. For example, a predicate in a path expression uses the disjunction weighting function, $\oplus$, to combine the predicate scores. If the resulting score is zero, the path fragment is discarded; otherwise, its score is multiplied by the resulting predicate score. Therefore, the score of consecutive predicates in a path is the product of their constituent scores.

3   The Inverse XML Indexes

Our system uses four inverse indexes: one for XML tags, one for text terms, one for attribute names, and one for attribute values. The design of these indexes was done in a way that facilitates efficient query processing (using merge joins exclusively). Each inverse index consists of one table, called documents, which is common to all indexes, and three other tables that constitute the inverse index (the code is given in Java):

```
class InverseIndex {
    Document[]  documents;
    Key[]       keys;
    Posting[]   postings;
    Hit[]       hits;  }
```

The vector documents is a binary search vector that contains the URLs of the indexed XML documents:

```
class Document { String url; }
```

Each XML document URL appears once in the documents vector. The keys vector is a binary search vector that implements the index dictionary:

```
class Key {
    String key;
    int fragments;        // how many fragments contain this term
    int total_frequency;  // times term appears in a l l documents
    int first_posting; }  // location of the first posting
```

Each term/tag must appear once in the dictionary. That is, $\forall i, j : i < j \Rightarrow$ keys[i].key < keys[j].key. For every XML document that contains a key in keys, there is a unique entry in postings, and all these entries appear in succeeding positions ordered by document number, starting at the first_posting position of the key:

```
class Posting {
    int document;    // document location
    int frequency;   // how many times the tag appears in document
    int first_hit; } // location of the first hit
```

That is, all postings between keys[i].first_posting and keys[i + 1].first_posting are associated with the key keys[i].key and are ordered by document number. Each posting, postings[i], is associated with postings[i].frequency number of hits in the hits vector, starting from postings[i].first_hit, which are ordered by the begin/position attribute. The Hit element structure depends on the type of the index. For the tag index, it is:

```
class TagHit extends Hit {
    short begin;      // the start position of term in document
    short end;        // the end position of term in document
    short level;      // depth of term in document
    short ordinal; }  // ordinal of element within parent
```

while for the term index is:

```
class TermHit extends Hit {
    short position; // the start position of term in document
    short level; } // depth of term in document
```

The iterator used for accessing the inverse indexes delivers the Posting/Hit pairs sorted by (document_number,begin/position) order, called the *index order*. That is, the major order is the document number and the minor order is the begin position of a TagHit or the position of a TermHit. This is a very crucial property because it makes possible the implementation of both path expressions and IR search specifications using merge joins without the need of sorting the input first. Furthermore, this order is actually the document order for each document. The IndexIterator for an inverse index provides the method open(key) to open the stream for accessing key hits, and the method next() to get the next Posting/Hit from the stream:

```
class IndexIterator {
    InverseIndex index;
    int ck;          // current key
    int cp;          // current posting
    int ch;          // current hit
    int max_posting;
    boolean eos;     // is this the end of stream?
    void open ( String key ) {
        ck = binary_search (index.keys, key);
        eos = !key.equals (index.keys [ck].key);
        cp = index.keys [ck].first_posting;
        ch = index.postings [cp].first_hit;
        max_posting = cp + index.keys [ck].document_number;
    }
    void next () {
        if (ch >= index.postings [cp].first_hit
                  + index.postings [cp].frequency − 1)
            if (++cp < max_posting)
                ch = index.postings [cp].first_hit;
            else eos = true;
        else ch++;
    }
    boolean eos () { return eos; } }
```

Our system populates the indexes by parsing XML documents using SAX. The text in XF elements is tokenized, stopwords are eliminated, and each token is stemmed using Porter's algorithm [16]. The SAX events startElement and endElement, and each token in text (from the SAX event characters) are assigned succeeding positions that correspond to document order. Currently, the indexes reside entirely in memory but they can be dumped to and read from binary files. We leave the implementation of indexes using B$^+$-trees for a future work.

4   The XQuery Processor

Our XQuery processor is stream-based, consisting of iterators that read data from input streams and deliver data to the output stream. This is done in a pull-based fashion, in which iterators are connected through pipelines and an iterator (the producer) delivers a stream element to the output only when requested by the next operator in pipeline (the consumer). To deliver one stream element to the output, the producer becomes a consumer by requesting from the previous iterator as many elements as necessary to produce a single element, etc, until the end of stream. This pipeline model is very popular in database query processing [12] because it avoids materialization of intermediate results, when possible (it is not possible for blocking operations, such as sorting and grouping).

The stream unit in our framework is a fragment retrieved from the inverse indexes. Because of the complexity of XQuery, though, XML elements may be constructed on the fly and operated upon by path expressions or other XQuery operations. It is essential, therefore, to support fragments from indexed documents as well as XML elements constructed on the fly. They are all subclasses of Element:

```
abstract class Element {
    float score; }        // relevance assessment of element
```

Then, a fragment describes an element from an indexed document:

```
class Fragment extends Element {
    int document;        // document ID
    short begin;         // the start position in document
    short end;           // the end position in document
    short level; }       // depth of term in document
```

An XML element constructed on the fly is similar to a DOM element:

```
class ConstructedElement extends Element {
    String tagname;
    Element[] sequence;      // children
    Attributes attributes; } // SAX-like attributes
class PCData extends Element { String data; }
```

The support of constructed XML elements allows us to process XML documents in their native form (not indexed) using the document(url) XQuery construct.

Finally, to support queries on indexed documents effectively in the case we do not have an index key to search, such as in the query count(document()/*/*), which counts all indexed elements of level 2, we support patterns that match all indexed fragments within a given depth region:

```
class Pattern extends Element {
    int min_level;       // minimum depth in document
    int max_level; }     // maximum depth in document
```

In fact, the document() expression is translated into an iterator that produces only one element: namely, Pattern(0,0), that matches all top-level indexed elements. Later, other iterators may convert this element into a stream of Fragments, when more information is provided (such as, after a tagged projection).

Since XQuery supports FLWOR expressions with variables, all variables bindings of for-clauses are concatenated into a tuple. Recall that the values of for-clauses are always single elements, while the values of let-clauses may actually be sequences. We will see how let-variables are treated later. Thus, the unit of communication between iterators is a Tuple defined as:

```
class Tuple { Element[] components; }
```

All iterators are objects that are instances of classes that are subclasses of the class Iterator:

```
class Iterator {
    Tuple current;        // current tuple from stream
    void open ();         // open the stream iterator
    Tuple next ();        // get the next tuple from stream
    boolean eos (); }     // is this the end of stream?
```

One iterator that uses the tag index is, Child(tag,input)

```
class Child extends Iterator {
    String tag;
    Iterator input;
    IndexIterator ti;   }
```

where ti=tag_index.open(tag) is the iterator over the tag index. The body of the next() method below merges the input stream with the stream produced by the tag index. This is possible because almost all operators preserve the index order (the only exception is the order-by in FLWOR, which destroys the order and, thus, requires reordering if processed further).

```
Tuple next () {
  while (!ti.eos() && !input.eos()) {
    if (input.current[0] instanceof Fragment) {
        Fragment lf = (Fragment) input.current[0];
        Key k = ti.key();
        Posting p = ti.posting();
        TagHit h = (TagHit) ti.hit();
        if (lf.document < p.document)
           input.next();
        else if (lf.document > p.document)
           ti.next();
        else if (lf.begin < h.begin && lf.end > h.end
                && h.level == lf.level+1) {
           current = new Tuple(new Fragment(p.document,
                                 h.begin,h.end,h.level));
           ti.next();
           return current;
        } else if (lf.begin < h.begin)
           input.next();
        else ti.next();   ...
```

This method works for non-recursive schemas only. A more general algorithm that can handle recursive schemas would require a stack of ancestors (see, for example, the stack-tree algorithm [1] and the holistic twig join algorithm [8]). For example, the XQuery `document("cs.xml")/department/gradstudent/name` is translated into the following pipeline of iterators:

new Child("name", **new** Child("gradstudent", **new** Child("department",
                                        new Document("cs.xml"))))

where the Document iterator delivers a single ConstructedElement object, namely the top-level XML element of the document, after the entire document has been read and stored in memory.

For-loops in a FLWOR expression are evaluated using the Loop and Step iterators. For example, the FLWOR expression

```
for $d in document()/department, $s in $d/gradstudent
```

is translated into the pipeline:

```
Iterator  s = new Step();
new Loop(new Child("department",new Step()),
         s,
         new Child("gradstudent",new Select(0,s)));
```

The Select iterator returns a singleton tuple containing the nth element of the tuple. It basically accesses a for-variable. Our FLWOR evaluation scheme completely avoids materialization of intermediate results. Basically, the Step iterator delivers one element only and then signals the end of stream:

```
class Step extends Iterator {
    boolean first;
    Tuple tuple = new Tuple(new Pattern(0,0));
    void open () { first = true; current = tuple; }
    Tuple next () { first = false; return current; }
    void set ( Tuple t ) { tuple = t; }
    boolean eos () { return !first; } }
```

Now, the Loop iterator, which is defined as:

```
class Loop extends Iterator {
    Iterator left;
    Step right_step;
    Iterator right; }
```

processes the left stream one tuple at a time, and sets the current tuple of the Step iterator. Then it opens the right stream and processes it one tuple at a time, up to the end of stream. Then it repeats this process for the next left tuple, etc, until the end of the left stream. More specifically, the next method of Loop is:

```
Tuple next () {
    if (!left.eos()) {
        while (right.eos()) {
            left.next();
```

```
            right_step . set ( left . current );
            right . open ();  };
    current = left . current . append ( right . current );
    right . next ();
    return current;  } }
```

The same technique is used in evaluating predicates in path expressions and in
FLWOR expressions. For example, the path expression:

`document()/department/gradstudent[gpa/text()="3.5"]/name`

is translated into:

```
Iterator  s = new  Step ();
new  Child ("name" ,
    new  Predicate (new  Child ("gradstudent" ,
                    new  Child ("department" ,new  Step ())) ,
            s ,
            new  Call ("eq" ,new  Text (new  Child ("gpa" ,s)) ,
                new  Constant ("3.5" ))))
```

where the Predicate iterator operates like Loop, by reopening and processing the
condition stream for each tuple in the left stream. Two other iterators, Return
and Sort, use the same stepper to evaluate an expression (the return expression
of Return and the sorting values of Sort) for each input tuple.

   The let-bindings in FLWOR expressions are the hardest to implement because each variable may be bound to a sequence (ie, a stream of tuples), rather
than one tuple. Of course, one may materialize the bound stream into a vector, but this would be infeasible for large sequences. In our implementation, a
let-variable is bound to an Iterator that delivers the sequence of tuples, but
the Iterator stream is *cloned* as many times as the times the let-variable is accessed. The cloning is done using a queue with multiple pointers (one for each
instance of the let-variable). The size of the queue depends on the backlog between the fastest and the slowest consumer. In some extreme cases, such as
`let $v:=e return ($v,$v)`, it is the size of the entire stream (since concatenation waits for the end of the left stream before opening the right stream).

5   XQuery Translation

Figure 1 gives the rules for the translation. An XQuery e is translated into the
plan $\mathcal{T}(\llbracket e \rrbracket, \textbf{Step}())$, where the semantic brackets ($\llbracket\ \rrbracket$) enclose XQuery syntax
(ie, they represent the abstract syntax tree associated with the syntax). Basi-
cally, $\mathcal{T}(\llbracket e \rrbracket, c)$ translates the XQuery syntax e into an iterator (the consumer)
that receives stream data from the the iterator c (the producer). Function calls,
$f(a_1, \ldots, a_n)$, include binary operations, such as $+$, $*$, and, $=$, $<$, if-then-else,
etc. Element construction $< tag > \ldots < /tag >$ is equivalent to a call to
element(tag, e), where e is the concatenation of the element components (us-
ing the comma operator). Function $\mathcal{F}(\llbracket FL \rrbracket, c, s)$ translates a sequence of for/let

Translation of XQuery expressions: $e, e_1, \ldots, e_n$

$$\mathcal{T}([\![\text{``text''}]\!], c) = \mathbf{Constant}(\text{``text''}, c)$$
$$\mathcal{T}([\![\$v]\!], c) = \mathbf{Select}(v, c) \qquad \text{(a For-variable)}$$
$$\mathcal{T}([\![\$v]\!], c) = \mathbf{LetVar}(v, k) \qquad \text{(a Let-variable that uses the } k\text{th}$$
$$\text{copy of the cloned Let-binding)}$$
$$\mathcal{T}([\![path]\!], c) = \mathcal{P}([\![path]\!], c)$$
$$\mathcal{T}([\![\text{document}()]\!], c) = \mathbf{Step}()$$
$$\mathcal{T}([\![\text{document}(url)]\!], c) = \mathbf{Document}(url)$$
$$\mathcal{T}([\![\text{element}(tag, attrs, e)]\!], c) = \mathbf{Element}(tag, attrs, \mathcal{T}([\![e]\!], c))$$
$$\mathcal{T}([\![\text{score}(e)]\!], c) = \mathbf{Score}(\mathcal{T}([\![e]\!], c))$$
$$\mathcal{T}([\![e \sim S]\!], c) = \mathcal{R}([\![S]\!], \mathcal{T}([\![e]\!], c))$$
$$\mathcal{T}([\![f(e_1, \ldots, e_n)]\!], c) = \mathbf{Call}(f, \mathcal{T}([\![e_1]\!], c), \ldots, \mathcal{T}([\![e_n]\!], c))$$
$$\mathcal{T}([\![e_1, e_2]\!], c) = \mathbf{Concatenate}(\mathcal{T}([\![e_1]\!], c), \mathcal{T}([\![e_2]\!], c))$$
$$\mathcal{T}([\![\underline{\text{some}} \ \$v \ \underline{\text{in}} \ e_1 \ \underline{\text{satisfies}} \ e_2]\!], c) = \mathcal{T}([\![e_1]\!], \mathcal{T}([\![e_2]\!], c))$$
$$\mathcal{T}([\![\underline{\text{every}} \ \$v \ \underline{\text{in}} \ e_1 \ \underline{\text{satisfies}} \ e_2]\!], c) = \mathcal{T}([\![\underline{\text{not}}(\underline{\text{some}} \ \$v \ \underline{\text{in}} \ e_1 \ \underline{\text{satisfies}} \ \text{not}(e_2))]\!], c)$$
$$\mathcal{T}([\![FL \ \underline{\text{where}} \ e_1 \ \underline{\text{order by}} \ e_2 \ \underline{\text{return}} \ e_3]\!], c)$$
$$= \begin{cases} \mathbf{Assign}(w, \mathbf{Step}(), \\ \qquad \mathbf{Sort}(\mathbf{Return}(\mathbf{Predicate}(\mathcal{F}([\![FL]\!], c, \mathbf{Var}(w)), \mathbf{Var}(w), \\ \qquad\qquad\qquad\qquad \mathcal{T}([\![e_1]\!], \mathbf{Var}(w))), \\ \qquad\qquad\qquad \mathbf{Var}(w), \mathcal{T}([\![e_3]\!], \mathbf{Var}(w))) \\ \qquad\qquad \mathbf{Var}(w), \mathcal{T}([\![e_2]\!], \mathbf{Var}(w)))) \end{cases}$$

Translation of path expressions: $path$

$$\mathcal{P}([\![/A \ path]\!], c) = \mathbf{Child}(A, \mathcal{P}([\![path]\!], c))$$
$$\mathcal{P}([\![//A \ path]\!], c) = \mathbf{Descendant}(A, \mathcal{P}([\![path]\!], c))$$
$$\mathcal{P}([\![/* \ path]\!], c) = \mathbf{Any}(\mathcal{P}([\![path]\!], c))$$
$$\mathcal{P}([\![/@A \ path]\!], c) = \mathbf{Attribute}(A, \mathcal{P}([\![path]\!], c))$$
$$\mathcal{P}([\![[e] \ path]\!], c) = \mathbf{Assign}(w, \mathbf{Step}(), \mathbf{Predicate}(\mathcal{P}([\![path]\!], c), \mathbf{Var}(w), \mathcal{T}([\![e]\!], \mathbf{Var}(w))))$$
$$\mathcal{P}([\![e \ path]\!], c) = \mathcal{T}([\![e]\!], \mathcal{P}([\![path]\!], c))$$
$$\mathcal{P}([\![]\!], c) = c$$

Translation of FLWOR for/let bindings: FL

$$\mathcal{F}([\![\underline{\text{for}} \ \$v \ \underline{\text{in}} \ e \ FL]\!], c, s) = \mathcal{F}([\![FL]\!], \mathcal{T}([\![e]\!], c), s) \qquad \text{(first for-loop)}$$
$$\mathcal{F}([\![\underline{\text{for}} \ \$v \ \underline{\text{in}} \ e \ FL]\!], c, s) = \mathcal{F}([\![FL]\!], \mathbf{Assign}(w, \mathbf{Step}(), \mathbf{Loop}(c, \mathbf{Var}(w), \mathcal{T}([\![e]\!], \mathbf{Var}(w)))), s)$$
$$\mathcal{F}([\![\underline{\text{let}} \ \$v := e \ FL]\!], c, s) = \mathbf{Assign}(v, \mathbf{Clone}(\mathcal{T}([\![e]\!], s), n), \mathcal{F}([\![FL]\!], c, s)) \qquad \text{(clone } n \text{ times)}$$
$$\mathcal{F}([\![]\!], c, s) = c$$

Translation of IR search predicates: S, S_1, S_2

$$\mathcal{R}([\![\text{``phrase''}]\!], c) = \mathbf{Phrase}(c, \text{``phrase''})$$
$$\mathcal{R}([\![S_1 \ \underline{\text{and}} \ S_2]\!], c) = \mathbf{Conjunction}(\mathcal{R}([\![S_1]\!], c), \mathcal{R}([\![S_2]\!], c))$$
$$\mathcal{R}([\![\underline{\text{not}} \ S]\!], c) = \mathbf{Negation}(\mathcal{R}([\![S]\!], c))$$

Fig. 1. Translation from XQuery to Stream Iterators (w are fresh variables)

bindings *FL* in a FLWOR expression from left to right. The parameter *s* is the stepper used by the **Return** iterator of the FLWOR expression.

The Assign/Var operators do not correspond to any iterator. Instead, they are used for local assignments: Assign binds a local variable to an iterator and Var returns the value of the local variable.

As a simple example of translation, the following XQuery:

```
document("cs.xml")/department/gradstudent[gpa/text()="3.5"]/name
```

is translated into:

```
Child(name,Assign(0,Step(),
    Predicate(Child(gradstudent,Child(department,Document("cs.xml"))),
        Var(0),
        Assign(1,Var(0),Call(eq,Text(Child(gpa,Var(1))),Constant("3.5"))))))
```

6   Conclusion

Our language extensions are very simple, yet powerful enough to capture many emerging proposals for document-centric retrieval of XML data with relevance ranking. The XQueryRank evaluation engine is made out of pipelines of stream iterators that avoid materialization of intermediate results when possible and use efficient merge joins to evaluate path expressions and search predicates. Its modular approach of building pipelines to evaluate XQuery scales up to any query complexity because the pipes can be connected in the same way complex queries are formed from simpler ones.

The Java source of the prototype system is available at

http://lambda.uta.edu/XQueryRank.tar.gz

Acknowledgments: This work is supported in part by the National Science Foundation under the grant IIS-0307460.

References

1. S. Al-Khalifa, H. V. Jagadish, N. Koudas, J. M. Patel, D. Srivastava, and Y. Wu. Structural Joins. A Primitive for Efficient XML Query Pattern Matching. In ICDE 2002.
2. S. Al-Khalifa, C. Yu, and H. V. Jagadish. Querying Structured Text in an XML Database. In SIGMOD 2003, pp 4-15.
3. S. Amer-Yahia, C. Botev, and S. Shanmugasundaram. TeXQuery: A Full-Text Search Extension to XQuery. In WWW 2004.
4. S. Amer-Yahia, L. V. S. Lakshmanan, and S. Pandit. FleXPath: Flexible Structure and Full-Text Querying for XML. In SIGMOD 2004.
5. S. Boag, D. Chamberlin, M. F. Fernandez, D. Florescu, J. Robie, and J. Simeon. XQuery 1.0: An XML Query Language. W3C Working Draft. November 2003. At http://www.w3.org/TR/xquery/.

6. C. Botev, S. Amer-Yahia, and J. Shanmugasundaram. A TexQuery-Based XML Full-Text Search Engine (Demo Paper). In SIGMOD 2004.

7. J. Bremer and M. Gertz. XQuery/IR: Integrating XML Document and Data Retrieval. In WebDB 2002, pp 1-6.

8. N. Bruno, N. Koudas, and D. Srivastava. Holistic Twig Joins: Optimal XML Pattern Matching. In SIGMOD 2002, pp 310-321.

9. T. Chinenyanga and N. Kushmerick. An Expressive and Efficient Language for XML Information Retrieval. JASIST 53(6): 438-453 (2002).

10. N. Fuhr and K. Grojohann. XIRQL: A Query Language for Information Retrieval in XML Documents. In SIGIR 2001.

11. T. Grabs and H.-J. Schek. PowerDB-XML: a Platform for Data-Centric and Document-Centric XML Processing. XSym 2003.

12. G. Graefe. Query Evaluation Techniques for Large Databases. ACM Computing Surveys 25(2): 73-170 (1993).

13. L. Guo, F. Shao, C. Botev, and J. Shanmugasundaram. XRANK: Ranked Keyword Search over XML Documents. In SIGMOD 2003, pp 16-27.

14. J. Kamps, M. Marx, M. de Rijke, and B. Sigurbjornsson. Best-Match Querying from Document-Centric XML. WebDB 2004.

15. H. Meyer, I. Bruder, G. Weber, and A. Heuer. The Xircus Search Engine. 2003. At http://www.xircus.de.

16. M. Porter. An Algorithm for Suffix Stripping. Program 14(3):130-137 (1980).

17. A. Theobald and G. Weikum. Adding Relevance to XML. In WebDB 2000.

18. A. Theobald, G. Weikum. The Index-based XXL Search Engine for Querying. In EDBT 2002, pp. 477–495

19. A. Theobald, G. Weikum. The XXL Search Engine: Ranked Retrieval on XML Data using Indexes and Ontologies (Demo Paper). In SIGMOD 2002.

20. F. Weigel, H. Meuss, K. U. Schulz, and F. Bry. Content and Structure in Indexing and Ranking XML. WebDB 2004.

21. C. Zhang, J. Naughton, D. DeWitt, Q. Luo, and G. Lohman. On Supporting Containment Queries in Relational Database Management Systems. In SIGMOD 2001.

22. http://www.w3.org/TR/xmlquery-full-text-use-cases/

Information Preservation
in XML-to-Relational Mappings

Denilson Barbosa[1], Juliana Freire[2], and Alberto O. Mendelzon[1]

[1] Department of Computer Science – University of Toronto
{dmb,mendel}@cs.toronto.edu
[2] OGI School of Science and Engineering – Oregon Health and Sciences University
juliana@cse.ogi.edu

Abstract. We study the problem of storing XML documents using relational mappings. We propose a formalization of classes of mapping schemes based on the languages used for defining functions that assign relational databases to XML documents and vice-versa. We also discuss notions of information preservation for mapping schemes; we define *lossless* mapping schemes as those that preserve the structure and content of the documents, and *validating* mapping schemes as those in which valid documents can be mapped into legal databases, and all legal databases are (equivalent to) mappings of valid documents. We define one natural class of mapping schemes that captures all mappings in the literature, and show negative results for testing whether such mappings are lossless or validating. Finally, we propose a lossless and validating mapping scheme, and show that it performs well in the presence of updates.

1 Introduction

The problem of storing XML documents using relational engines has attracted significant interest with a view to leveraging the powerful and reliable data management services provided by these engines. In a mapping-based XML storage system, the XML document is represented as a relational database and queries (including updates) over the document are translated into queries over the database. Thus, it is important that the translation of XML queries and updates into SQL transactions be correct. In particular, only updates resulting in *valid* documents should be allowed. To date, the focus of the work in designing mapping schemes for XML documents has been on ensuring that XML queries over the documents can be answered using their relational representations. In this paper, we study the problem of designing mapping schemes that ensure only valid update operations can be executed.

An important requirement in mapping systems is that any query over the document must be computable from the database that represents the document. In particular, the mapping must be *lossless*, that is, the document itself must be recoverable from its relational image. When updates are considered, one must be able to test whether an operation results in the representation of a valid document *before* applying the operation to the database. This amounts

Z. Bellahsène et al. (Eds.): XSym 2004, LNCS 3186, pp. 66–81, 2004.

to checking whether the resulting database represents a well-formed document (i.e., a tree) and that this document conforms to a document schema. Several works [4,22] exploit information about a document schema for designing better mapping schemes; the metric in most of these is query performance, for example, the number of joins required for answering certain queries. However, to the best of our knowledge, there has been no work on ensuring that only valid updates can be processed over relational representations of documents.

1.1   Related Work

There is extensive literature on defining *information preserving* mappings for relational databases [17]; our notion of *lossless* mapping schemes is inspired by that of lossless decompositions of relations. The incremental checking of relational view/integrity constraints has also been widely studied [15,12]. Some of the view maintenance techniques have been extended to semi-structured models that were precursors of XML [23]. Another related problem, the incremental validation of XML documents w.r.t. XML schema formalisms, has been studied in [3,5,19]; we use the incremental algorithms proposed in [3] in this work.

The literature on mapping XML documents to relational databases is also vast [16]. One of the first proposals was the Edge [14] scheme, a generic approach that explicitly stores all the edges in a document tree. Departing from generic mappings, several specialized strategies have been proposed which make use of schema information about the documents to generate more efficient mappings. Shanmugasundaram *et al.* [22] describe three specialized strategies which aim to minimize data fragmentation by *inlining*, whenever possible, the content of certain elements as columns in the relation that represents their parents. LegoDB [4] is a cost-based tool that generates relational mappings using inlining as well as other operations [21]; the goal there is to find a relational configuration with lowest cost for processing a given query workload on a given XML document. STORED [11] is a hybrid method for mapping semistructured data in which relational tables are used for storing the most regular and frequent structures, while *overflow* graphs store the remaining portions of the semistructured database. None of these works deals with checking the validity of updates.

Orthogonal to designing mapping approaches is the translation of constraints in the document schema to the relational schema for the mappings. For instance, the propagation of keys [9] and functional dependencies [8] have been studied. Besides capturing the semantics of the original document schema, these techniques have been shown to improve the mappings by, e.g., reducing the storage of redundant information [8]. However, these works do not consider the translation of the constraints defined by the content models (i.e., regular expressions) in the document schema, which is the focus of this work. We note that these techniques can be applied directly in our method.

Designing relational mappings for XML documents can be viewed as the reincarnation of the well-known problem of "simulating" semantic models in relational schemas [1], and there are mapping schemes that follow this "classical" approach. However, the semantic mismatch between the XML and relational models is much more pronounced than in previously considered models. For example, XML data is inherently ordered; moreover, preserving this ordering is crucial for deciding the *validity* of the elements in the document. Mani and Lee [18] define an extended (yet unordered) ER model for describing XML data, and provide algorithms for translating these models into relational schemas.

For this study, we had to fix an update language; we settled for a simple language, as the goal was to verify the feasibility of our approach rather than proposing a new language. For a discussion on updating XML, see [24].

Contributions and Outline. In Section 3, we provide a formalization of mapping schemes as pairs of functions, the mapping and publishing functions, that assign relational databases to XML documents and vice-versa. We introduce in Section 3.1 the notion of parameterized classes of mapping schemes, which are defined by the languages used for specifying the mapping function, the publishing function, and the relational constraints in the target schema. In Section 3.2 we introduce $\mathcal{XDS}$: a natural class of mapping schemes powerful enough to express all, to the best of our knowledge, mapping schemes in the literature. In Section 4, we characterize mapping schemes with respect to information preservation. In particular, we define *lossless* mapping schemes as those that ensure all XML queries over a document can be executed over its corresponding database; and *validating* mapping schemes, which ensure only valid updates can be effected. We also show that testing both properties for $\mathcal{XDS}$ mapping schemes is undecidable. In Section 5 we propose an $\mathcal{XDS}$ mapping scheme that is both lossless and validating, and discuss the incremental maintenance of the constraints in such mappings in the presence of updates in Section 6.

2   Preliminaries

We model XML documents as ordered labeled trees with element and text nodes. The root of the tree represents the whole document and has one child, which represents the outermost element. Following the XML standard [27], the *content* of an element node e is the (possibly empty) list of element or text nodes that are children of e. For simplicity, in an element with *mixed* content (i.e., element and text nodes as its children), we replace each text node by an element node whose label is #PCDATA and whose only child is the given text node. Thus, each element in the tree has either text or element nodes as its content; also, all text nodes are leaf nodes in the tree.

More precisely, we define the following. Let $\mathcal{I}$, $\mathcal{D}$ be two disjoint, countably infinite sets of node ids and values.

Definition 1 (XML Document) *An XML document is a tuple $\langle T, \lambda, \tau, \nu \rangle$, such that T is an ordered tree whose nodes are elements of $\mathcal{I}$, $\lambda : \mathcal{I} \to \mathcal{D}$ is an assignment of labels to nodes in T, $\tau : \mathcal{I} \to \{element, text\}$ is an assignment of node types to the nodes in T, and $\nu : \mathcal{I} \to \mathcal{D}$ is an assignment of values to text nodes in T (i.e., ν is undefined for a node e if $\tau(e) \neq text$).*

We model document schemas as sets of rules which constrain the structure and the labels of the elements in the document. Such *element declaration rules* assign *content models* to *element types*. An element type is defined by a path expression of the form $[c_i]/l_i$ where l_i is an element label and c_i is an optional path expression specifying the *context* in which l_i occurs. We restrict contexts to be path expressions matching $E := a \mid E/E \mid E//E$, where a is either an element label or the wildcard $*$ for matching elements of any label. We say an element is of type t_i if it is in the result set of evaluating $[c_i]/l_i$ over the document. Following the XML standard, a content model is specified by a 1-unambiguous regular expression [6] of the form $E := \varepsilon \mid a \mid \#\text{PCDATA} \mid (E) \mid E|E \mid E, E \mid E* \mid E+ \mid E?$, where ε represents the empty string, a is an element label, and #PCDATA represents textual content. Note that this captures all four content models for XML elements [27].

Definition 2 (Document Schema) *A document schema X is a set of element declaration rules of the form $t_i \leftarrow r_i$ where t_i is an element type and r_i is a content model, such that for any document D that is valid with respect to X (as defined below), for each element e in D, there is exactly one element type t_i such that e is of type t_i.*

Let e be an element of type t_i, and $c_1, \ldots, c_n$ be its (ordered) children; we say e is *valid* with respect to rule $t_i \leftarrow r_i$ if the string $\lambda(c_1) \cdots \lambda(c_n)$ matches r_i. We say a document D is valid with respect to a document schema X, denoted $D \in L(X)$ if all elements in D are valid with respect to the rules in X corresponding to their respective types.

Let $\mathfrak{I}$, $\mathcal{D}$ be two disjoint countably infinite sets of surrogates and constants. We define relational database as follows:

Definition 3 (Relational Database) *Each relation scheme R has a set (possibly empty) of attributes of domain $\mathfrak{I}$, called the surrogate attributes of R, and a set (possibly empty) of attributes with domain $\mathcal{D}$. Everything else is defined as customary for the relational model.*

Intuitively, renaming node ids in a document does not yield a new document. Similarly, renaming surrogates in a database does not create a new mapping. In order to capture these properties, we define:

Definition 4 (Document Equivalence) *XML documents $D_1 = \langle T_1, \lambda_1, \tau_1, \nu_1 \rangle$, and $D_2 = \langle T_2, \lambda_2, \tau_2, \nu_2 \rangle$, are equivalent, denoted by $D_1 \equiv D_2$, if there exists an isomorphism ϕ between T_1 and T_2 s.t. $\lambda_1(v) = \lambda_2(\phi(v))$, $\tau_1(v) = \tau_2(\phi(v))$, and $\nu_1(v) = \nu_2(\phi(v))$, for all $v \in T_1$.*

Definition 5 (Database Equivalence) *Two database instances I_1, I_2 are equivalent, written $I_1 \equiv I_2$ if there exists a bijection on $\mathfrak{I} \cup \mathcal{D}$ that maps $\mathfrak{I}$ to $\mathfrak{I}$, is the identity on $\mathcal{D}$, and transforms I_1 into I_2.*

(The notion of database equivalence discussed above has been called *OID equivalence* in the context of object databases [1].)

3   XML-to-Relational Mappings

We define an XML-to-relational *mapping scheme* as a triple $\mu = (\sigma, \pi, S)$, where S is a relational schema; σ is a *mapping function* that assigns databases to XML documents; and π is a *publishing function* that assigns XML documents to databases. More precisely, let $\mathcal{X}$ be the set of all XML documents; we define:

Definition 6 (Mapping Scheme) *A mapping scheme is a triple* $\mu = (\sigma, \pi, S)$, *where* $\sigma : \mathcal{X} \to \mathcal{R}(S)$ *is a partial function, and* $\pi : \mathcal{R}(S) \to \mathcal{X}$ *is a total function. Moreover:*

1. for all D_1, D_2 $D_1 \equiv D_2$ *implies* $\sigma(D_1) \equiv \sigma(D_2)$,
2. for all I_1, I_2 $I_1 \equiv I_2$ *implies* $\pi(I_1) \equiv \pi(I_2)$.

Defining σ to be a partial function allows mapping schemes where the relational schemas are customized for documents conforming to a given document schema X [4,22]; in other words, mapping schemes where $\mathrm{Dom}(\sigma) = L(X)$. On the other hand, requiring π to be total ensures that any legal database (as defined below) can be mapped into a document. Conditions 1 and 2 in Definition 6 ensure that both σ and π are *generic* (in the sense of database theory [1]): they map equivalent documents to equivalent databases and vice-versa.

3.1   Parameterized Classes of Mapping Schemes

We define classes of mapping schemes based on the languages used for specifying σ, S, and π. The power of these languages determines what kinds of mappings can be specified. For example, some sort of counting mechanism in the mapping language is required for specifying mapping functions that encode "interval-based" element ordering [10].

3.2   The $\mathcal{XDS}$ Class of Mappings

We now describe one particular class of mapping schemes that captures all mappings proposed in the literature. In summary, we use an XQuery-like language for defining σ, we allow boolean datalog queries with inequality and stratified negation to be specified in the relational schema, and we use XQuery coupled with a standard publishing framework such as SilkRoute [13]. We will call this class of mappings $\mathcal{XDS}$, (for XQuery, Datalog, and SilkRoute).

The Mapping Language. The language consists of XQuery augmented with a clause `sql ... end` for specifying SQL insert statements, and to be used instead of the `return` clause in a FLOWR expression. The semantics of the mapping expressions is defined similarly to the usual semantics of FLOWR expressions: the `for`, `let`, `where`, `order by` clauses define a list of tuples which are passed, one at a time, to the `sql ... end` clause, and one SQL transaction is issued per such tuple. Unlike a query, a mapping expression does not return any values, and is declared within a `procedure`, instead of an XQuery function.

The Relational Constraints. In $\mathcal{XDS}$ mapping schemes, each constraint in the relational schema is a boolean query that must evaluate to false unless the constraint is violated. We say that a relational instance is *legal* if it does not violate any of the constraints. Each of these queries is expressed as a set of datalog rules, augmented with stratified negation and not-equals. This language allows easy expression of standard relational constraints such as functional dependencies and referential integrity, while the recursion in datalog can be used to express, for example, that the children of an element conform to the element's content model, as shown in the Edge^{++} mapping of Section 5.

The Publishing Language. Publishing functions are arbitrary XQuery expressions over a "canonical" XML view of a relational database. That is, each relation is mapped into an element whose children represent the tuples in that relation in the standard way (i.e., one element per column). This is the approach taken by SilkRoute [13] and XPERANTO [7]. Of course, there are several different "canonical" views (i.e., documents) that represent the same database, as no implicit ordering exist among tuples or relations in the database.

It is easy to see that fairly complex mapping schemes are possible in the $\mathcal{XDS}$ class. In fact, all mapping schemes that we are aware of in the literature are in $\mathcal{XDS}$. Below, we give an example of such a mapping scheme.

Example 1. The Edge mapping scheme [14] belongs to $\mathcal{XDS}$ and can be described as follows. The relational schema S contains the relations (primary keys are underlined):

$$\text{Edge}(parent : \mathfrak{I}, \underline{child} : \mathfrak{I}, ordinal : \mathcal{D}, label : \mathcal{D}), \quad \text{Value}(\underline{element} : \mathfrak{I}, value : \mathcal{D})$$

The Edge relation contains a tuple for each element-to-element edge in the document tree, consisting of the ids of the parent and child, the child's ordinal, and the child's label. The Value relation contains a tuple for each leaf in the tree. The relational schema also contains constraints for ensuring that: there is only one root element; every child has a parent; every element id in Value appears also in Edge; and that the ordinals of nodes in the tree are consistent. Note these constraints are easily expressed as boolean datalog programs.

The mapping function σ is defined by a recursive procedure that visits the children of a given node, storing the element nodes in the Edge relation and the text nodes in Value relation:

```
define procedure map_node($e as node){
  for $n at $i in $e/*
  if ($n instance of element()) then
    sql INSERT INTO Edge VALUES (id($e),id($n),$i,name($n)) end;
    map_node($n);
  if ($n instance of text()) then
    sql INSERT INTO Value VALUES (id($e),$n) end; }

(: to map the document :)
map_node(doc("doc.xml"));
```

```
<a>
  <b>foo</b>
    mixed
  <b>bar</b>
</a>

(a) Document
```

Edge:

parent	child	ordinal	label
0	1	0	a
1	2	0	b
1	3	1	#PCDATA
1	4	2	b

Value:

element	value
2	foo
3	mixed
4	bar

(b) Edge mapping

Fig. 1. Edge mapping of a document.

The id() function used in the procedure above can be any function that assigns a unique value to each node in the tree; for concreteness, we assume the function returns the node's discovery time in a DFS traversal of the tree, and that the discovery time of the document node (i.e., the node that is the parent of the root element in the document) is 0. Figure 1 shows a document and its image under the Edge mapping.

Finally, the publishing function π is defined as follows. The publishing of an element e is done by finding all its children in the Edge and Value elements in the "canonical" published views, and returning them in the same order as their ordinal values. We use the order by clause in the FLOWR expression to reconstruct the sequence of element and text nodes in the same order as in the original document.

4   Preserving Document Information

As discussed in Section 1, a mapping-based storage system for an XML document should correctly translate any query over the document, including updates, into queries over the mapped data. In this section, we discuss two properties that ensure that queries and valid updates can always be processed over databases that represent documents.

The generally assumed notion of information preservation for a mapping scheme is that it must be *lossless*; that is, one must be able to reconstruct any (fragment of a) document from its relational image [11]. More precisely, we define:

Definition 7 (Lossless Mapping Scheme) *A mapping scheme $\mu = (\sigma, \pi, S)$ is* lossless *if for all $D \in \text{Dom}(\sigma)$, $\pi(\sigma(D)) \equiv D$.*

Informally, losslessness ensures that all queries over the documents can be answered using their mapped images: besides the naive approach of materializing $\pi(\sigma(D))$ and processing the query, there are several techniques for translating the XML queries into SQL for specific mappings and XML query languages [16]. The following is easy to verify:

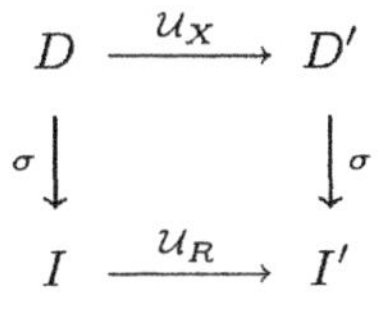

$$D \xrightarrow{\ u_X\ } D'$$

$$\sigma \downarrow \qquad\qquad \downarrow \sigma$$

$$I \xrightarrow{\ u_R\ } I'$$

Fig. 2. Updating documents and their mapping images.

Proposition 1 *The Edge mapping scheme is lossless.*

While losslessness is necessary for document reconstruction, it does not en-sure that databases represent valid documents, nor that updates to representa-tions of valid documents result in databases that also represent a valid docu-ments. As an example, consider a mapping scheme for documents conforming to the schema $X : a \leftarrow (b|\#\mathrm{PCDATA})*$; $b \leftarrow \#\mathrm{PCDATA}$, and recall the (loss-less) Edge mapping scheme discussed in Example 1. Figure 1(a) shows a valid document with respect to X, and its relational representation is shown in Fig-ure 1(b). It is easy to see that any *permissible* update (i.e., an update resulting in a valid document) to the document can be translated into an equivalent SQL transaction over the document's representation. However, it is also possible to update the representation in a way that results in a legal database that does not represent a valid document with respect to X. For instance, the SQL trans-action that inserts the tuple (3,4,0,c) into Edge and (4,0,foo) into Value, which results in a legal database, has no equivalent permissible XML update because it corresponds to inserting an element labeled c as a child of the second b element, which violates the document schema.

We define a property of mapping schemes that ensures that all and only valid documents can be represented:

Definition 8 (Validating Mapping Scheme) $\mu = (\sigma, \pi, S)$ *is* validating with respect to document schema X *if* σ *is total on* $L(X)$*, and for all* $I \in \mathcal{R}(S)$*, there exists* $D \in L(X)$ *such that* $I \equiv \sigma(D)$.

For simplicity, we drop the reference to the document schema X when dis-cussing a validating mapping scheme, and just say that a document is valid if it is valid with respect to X. Intuitively, a mapping scheme is *validating* with respect to X if it maps all valid documents to some legal database and if every legal database is (equivalent to) the image of some valid document under the mapping. This implies that all permissible updates to documents can be trans-lated into equivalent updates over their mappings, and vice-versa, as depicted in the diagram in Figure 2.

We conclude this section by showing that there are theoretical impediments to the goal of automatically designing lossless and/or validating $\mathcal{XDS}$ mappings. The following results are direct consequences of the interactions of context-free languages and chain datalog programs[1] [25,26]. The proofs are omitted in the interest of space and are given in the full version of the paper [2].

Theorem 1 *Testing losslessness of $\mathcal{XDS}$ mapping schemes is undecidable.*

Theorem 2 *Testing validation of $\mathcal{XDS}$ mapping schemes is undecidable.*

5   A Lossless and Validating $\mathcal{XDS}$ Mapping Scheme

In this section we introduce Edge^{++}: a lossless and validating mapping scheme in $\mathcal{XDS}$. The Edge^{++} mapping scheme is an extension of the Edge mapping scheme that includes constraints for ensuring the validation property. In this section we fully describe the procedure for creating a mapping scheme $\mu = (\sigma, \pi, S)$ given a document schema X, and show that μ is both lossless and validating with respect to X.

5.1   The Relational Schema

Recall the definition of relational databases in Section 2. Let $\mathfrak{I}' = \mathfrak{I} \cup \{\#\}$, $\# \notin \mathfrak{I}$ (the symbol $\#$ will be used for marking elements that have no children); also, let $\mathfrak{Q} \subseteq \mathcal{D}$ be a set of states, $\mathfrak{T} \subseteq \mathcal{D}$ be a set of type identifiers, and $\mathcal{B} \subseteq \mathcal{D}$ denote the set of boolean constants. The relational schema of Edge^{++} is as follows:

$$\text{Edge}(parent : \mathfrak{I}, \underline{child} : \mathfrak{I}, label : \mathcal{D}), \quad \text{FLC}(\underline{parent} : \mathfrak{I}, first : \mathfrak{I}', last : \mathfrak{I}'),$$

$$\text{ILS}(left : \mathfrak{I}, \underline{right} : \mathfrak{I}), \quad \text{Value}(\underline{element} : \mathfrak{I}, value : \mathcal{D}), \quad \text{Type}(\underline{element} : \mathfrak{I}, type : \mathfrak{T}),$$

$$\text{Transition}(\underline{type} : \mathfrak{T}, \underline{from} : \mathfrak{Q}, symbol : \mathcal{D}, to : \mathfrak{Q}, isAccepting : \mathcal{B})$$

The Edge and Value relations are used essentially as in the Edge mapping scheme, except that the ordering of the element nodes is not explicitly stored. Instead, we use the FLC and ILS relations to represent the successor relation among element nodes that are children of the same parent element (ILS stands for "immediate-left-sibling" and FLC stands for "first-last-children"). The choice of keeping the ordering of the elements using the FLC and ILS relations is motivated by the fact that they allow faster updates to the databases, as we do not need to increase (resp. decrease) the ordinals of potentially all children of an element after an insertion (resp. deletion). The constraints that we discuss here require only that we can access the next sibling of any element, and, of course, can be adapted to other ordering schemes (e.g., interval-based).

More precisely, the FLC relation contains a tuple for each element e in the document whose content model is not #PCDATA, consisting of the id of e and the ids of its first and last children; if e has no content (i.e., no children), a tuple $(s_e, \#, \#)$ is stored in FLC, where s_e is the surrogate to e's id. The ILS relation contains a tuple consisting of the ids of consecutive element nodes that

---

[1] Chain datalog programs seek pairs of nodes x and y in a graph such that there exists a path $x \rightsquigarrow y$ whose labels spell a word in an associated language.

are children of the same parent. Thus, if $c_1, \ldots, c_n$ are the ordered children of an element e; we have $(s_e, s_{c_1}, s_{c_n}) \in \mathsf{FLC}$, and $\{(s_{c_1}, s_{c_2}), \ldots, (s_{c_{n-1}}, s_{c_n})\} \subseteq \mathsf{ILS}$. The Type relation contains the types of each element in the document. Finally, the Transition relation stores the transition functions of the automata that correspond to the content models in the document schema.

Next, we discuss the two kinds of constraints defined in the relational schema.

Structural Constraints. Similarly to the Edge mapping scheme, the structural constraints ensure that any legal database encodes a well-formed XML document (i.e., an ordered labeled tree). We also need to ensure that the ordering of the element nodes is consistent, and that each element has a type. We note that these constraints are easily encoded as boolean datalog programs. For instance, the following constraint ensures that no element that is marked as having no children is the parent of any other element:

$$\mathsf{invalid} :- \mathsf{FLC}(p, \#, \#), \mathsf{Edge}(p, \_, \_)$$

Validation Constraints. The validation constraints encode the rules in the document schema into equivalent constraints over the relations in S, to ensure that the document represented by the mapping is indeed valid. For each rule $t_i \leftarrow r_i$ in the document schema, we define the following datalog program:

$$\mathsf{reach}_{t_i}(p, \#, s) :- \mathsf{FLC}(p, \#, \#), \mathsf{Type}(p, t_i), \mathsf{Transition}(t_i, q_0, \varepsilon, s, \_) \tag{1}$$

$$\mathsf{reach}_{t_i}(p, c, s) :- \mathsf{Edge}(p, c, x), \mathsf{FLC}(p, c, \_), \mathsf{Type}(p, t_i), \mathsf{Transition}(t_i, q_0, x, s, \_) \tag{2}$$

$$\mathsf{reach}_{t_i}(p, c, s) :- \mathsf{reach}_{t_i}(p, x, y), \mathsf{ILS}(x, c), \mathsf{Type}(p, t_i), \mathsf{Edge}(p, c, w), \tag{3}$$
$$\mathsf{Transition}(t_i, y, w, s, \_)$$

$$\mathsf{accept}_{t_i}(p) :- \mathsf{reach}_{t_i}(p, c, s), \mathsf{FLC}(p, \_, c), \mathsf{Type}(p, t_i), \mathsf{Transition}(t_i, \_, \_, s, true)$$

$$\mathsf{invalid}_{t_i} :- \mathsf{FLC}(p, \_, \_), \neg\mathsf{accept}_{t_i}(p)$$

The boolean view $\mathsf{invalid}_{t_i}$ evaluates to true iff there is some element p of type t_i whose contents are invalid with respect to r_i. The recursive view reach_{t_i} simulates the automaton using the labels of the children of each element p as follows. The simulation starts with rules (1) or (2); rule (1) applies only if the element has no content (the constant q_0 denote the starting state of the automaton for r_i). Rule (3) carries out the recursion over the children of p. Finally, the accept_{t_i} rule checks that the computation is accepting if the state s reached after inspecting the last child c (note that c could be $\#$ if the element has no content) is accepting.

5.2   The Mapping Function

As in Edge, we define a recursive function that maps all nodes in the document tree. Besides that, the mapping procedure in Edge^{++} also assigns types to the elements in the document. Of course, the types assigned to elements must match those stored in the Transition relation; for concreteness, we assume that type t_i is represented by the integer i. The mapping of the document is then defined by the following function shown in Figure 3.

```
define procedure map_node($e as node){
  let $cc := $e/*
  for $n in $cc
  if ($n instance of text()) then
    sql INSERT INTO Value VALUES (id($e), data($e)) end;
  else
  if ($n instance of element()) then
    if count($cc)=0 then (:the element has no children:)
      sql INSERT INTO FLC VALUES (id($e),'#','#') end;
    else
      let $first := $cc[1], $last := $cc[count($cc)]
      for $c at $i in $cc
      sql INSERT INTO Edge VALUES (id($e),id($c), name($c));
          INSERT INTO FLC VALUES (id($e), id($first), id($last));
      end;
      if ($i > 1) then
        let $j := $cc[$i-1];
        sql INSERT INTO ILS VALUES (id($c),id($j)) end;
      else ()
    map_node($n);
}
map_node(doc("doc.xml"));

(: the following assign the types to elements :)
for $e in $d/t_1 sql INSERT INTO Type VALUES (id($e),1) end;
...
for $e in $d/t_n sql INSERT INTO Type VALUES (id($e),n) end;
```

Fig. 3. Mapping function for Edge^{++}.

5.3   The Publishing Function

The publishing function π in Edge^{++} is straightforward. Note that publishing a single element e of type x is done by visiting all elements in the published view that have e as parent. In order to retrieve the elements in their original order, we use a recursive function that returns the next sibling according to the successor relation stored in ILS. In order to publish a subtree one can recursively apply the simple method above.

The following is easy to verify:

Proposition 2 *Let X be a document schema, then the Edge^{++} mapping scheme $\mu = (\sigma, \pi, S)$ is lossless and validating with respect to X.*

6   Updates and Incremental Validation

Any update (i.e., SQL transaction) over an Edge^{++} mapping succeeds only if the resulting database satisfies the constraints in the schema (i.e., represents a valid document). Evidently, testing all constraints after each update is inefficient and, in most cases, unnecessary [15]. In this section, we discuss efficient ways of checking the validity of the Edge^{++} constraints in the presence of updates. We start by briefly discussing a simple update language for XML documents which can be effectively translated into SQL transactions over Edge^{++} mappings.

6.1   The Update Language

The update language provided to the user has a significant impact on the performance of a mapping-based storage system. In particular, there may be constraints in the relational schema that can be dropped if the user is not allowed to issue arbitrary SQL updates over the mapped data.

Consider the constraint in the Edge mapping scheme discussed in Example 1 that specifies that "every element that appears in the Value relation must also appear in the Edge relation". This constraint ensures that every #PCDATA value stored in the database is the content of some element in the document. Note that this constraint is necessary only if the user can write arbitrary SQL update statements that modify the Value relation, but can be dropped if inserting elements with textual content is always done by a transaction that inserts tuples in Edge and Value relations at the same time.

We note that it is reasonable to assume the user updates are issued in some XML update language, and these are translated into SQL transactions in a way that the "structural" constraints are preserved, so they need not be checked after each transaction.

Update Operations. To date, there is no standard update language for XML, and proposing a proper update language is outside the goals of this work; instead, we use a minimal set of atomic operations, consisting basically of insertions and deletions of subtrees.

- **Append**(p,y), where both p and y are elements, results in inserting y as the last child of p;
- **InsertBefore**(x,y), where both x and y are elements, results in inserting y as the immediate left sibling of x; this operation is not defined if x is the root of the document being updated;
- **Delete**(x), where x is an element, results in deleting x from the document.

For the Edge^{++} mapping scheme, it is straightforward to translate the primitive operations above into SQL transactions in a way that preserves structural validity.

6.2   Incremental Checking of Validating Constraints

The validating constraints in Edge^{++} mappings are recursive datalog programs that test membership in regular languages, which is a problem that has been shown to have low complexity. Patnaik and Immerman [20] show that membership in regular languages can be incrementally tested for insertion, deletion or single-symbol renaming in logarithmic time. By viewing the sequence of children of an element as a string generated by the regular expression for that element, Barbosa et al. [3] give a constant time incremental algorithm for matching strings to certain 1-unambiguous regular expressions. The classes of regular expressions considered in that work capture those most commonly used in real-life document schemas.

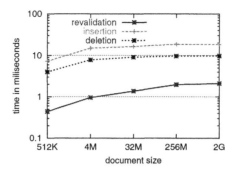

Fig. 4. Updates and incremental validation times.

Essentially, the idea behind the algorithms in [20,3] is to store the *paths* through the automata (i.e., sequence of states) together with the strings. Testing whether an update to the string is valid amounts to testing whether the corresponding path can be updated accordingly, while yielding another accepting path. As shown in [3], this test can be easily implemented as an efficient datalog program.

7 Experimental Evaluation

We show preliminary experimental results for the incremental maintenance of the validation constraints as defined in Section 5.1. Our experiments were run on a Pentium-4 2.5 GHz machine running DB2 V8.1 on Linux. We used several XMark documents of varying sizes (512KB, 4MB, 32MB, 256MB and 2GB); we note that the regular expressions used in the XMark DTD follow the syntactic restrictions discussed in the previous section, and, thus, are amenable to the simple algorithm discussed.

The implementation used in our experiments uses a more efficient relational schema than the one discussed in Section 5, which consists of horizontally partitioning the Edge relation based on the type of the parent element in each edge. That is, for each element type t_i, we define $\mathsf{Edge}_{t_i}(p, c, l)\text{:-}\mathsf{Edge}(p, c, l), \mathsf{Type}(p, t_i)$; the Transition table is partitioned in a similar fashion. Note that this results in eliminating some of the joins in the validating constraint. The workload in our experiments consists of 100 insertions and deletions of items for auctions in the North America region, each performed as a separate transaction. Each element inserted is valid and consists of an entire subtree of size comparable to those already in the document, and each delete operation removes one of the items inserted.

Figure 7 shows the times for executing the insertions, deletions and for incrementally recomputing (and updating) the validation constraints. The graph shows that, in practice, Edge^{++} can achieve good performance: per-update costs are dominated by SQL insert and delete operations; and the costs scale well with document size, which is consistent with the results in [3]. It is worthy of note that, in this experiment, all transactions were executed at the "user level", thus incurring overheads (e.g., compiling and optimizing the queries for incremental maintenance of the validating constraints) that can be avoided in a native (inside the database engine) implementation. Even with these overheads, the cost for maintaining the validating constraints is roughly 10 times smaller than the cost of performing the actual update operations.

8   Conclusion

In this paper we have proposed a simple formal model for XML-to-relational mapping schemes. Our framework is based on classes of mapping schemes defined by the languages used for mapping the documents, specifying relational constraints, and publishing the databases back as XML documents. We introduced a class of mappings called $\mathcal{XDS}$, which captures all mapping schemes in the literature. We proposed two natural notions of information preservation for mapping schemes, which ensure that queries and valid updates over the documents can be executed using these mappings. We showed that testing either property for $\mathcal{XDS}$ mappings is undecidable. Finally, we have proposed a lossless and validating $\mathcal{XDS}$ mapping scheme, and shown, through preliminary experimental evaluation that it performs well in practice.

We are currently working on designing *information preserving* transformations to derive lossless and validating mapping schemes from other such mappings. We have observed that virtually all mapping transformations proposed in the literature (e.g., inlining) can be modified to preserve the losslessness and validation properties in a simple way. We also hope that our simple formalization can be used by other researchers for studying other classes of mapping schemes, using other languages and possibly other notions of document (or database) equivalence.

Acknowledgments. This work was supported in part by grants from the Natural Science and Engineering Research Council of Canada. D. Barbosa was supported in part by an IBM PhD. Fellowship. J. Freire was supported in part by The National Science Foundation under grant EIA-0323604.

References

1. S. Abiteboul, R. Hull, and V. Vianu. *Foundations of Databases*. Addison Wesley, 1995.
2. D. Barbosa, J. Freire, and A. O. Mendelzon. Information Preservation in XML-to-Relational Mappings. Technical report, University of Toronto, 2004.
3. D. Barbosa, A. O. Mendelzon, L. Libkin, L. Mignet, and M. Arenas. Efficient Incremental Validation of XML Documents. In *International Conference on Data Engineering*, pages 671–682, Boston, MA, USA, 2004.

4. P. Bohannon, J. Freire, P. Roy, and J. Siméon. From XML Schema to Relations: A Cost-based Approach to XML Storage. In *Proceedings of the 18th International Conference on Data Engineering*, pages 64–75, February 26-March 1 2002.
5. B. Bouchou and M. Halfeld-Ferrari-Alvez. Updates and Incremental Validation of XML Documents. In *9th International Workshop on Database Programming Languages*, pages 216–232, Potsdam, Germany, September 6-8 2003.
6. A. Brüggemann-Klein and D. Wood. One-Unambiguous Regular Languages. *Information and Computation*, 142:182–206, 1998.
7. M. J. Carey, J. Kiernan, J. Shanmugasundaram, E. J. Shekita, and S. N. Subramanian. XPERANTO: Middleware for Publishing Object-Relational Data as XML Documents. In *Proceedings of the 26th International Conference on Very Large Data Bases*, pages 646–648, Cairo, Egypt, September 10-14 2000.
8. Y. Chen, S. Davidson, C. S. Hara, and Y. Zheng. RRXF: Redundancy reducing XML storage in relations. In *Proceedings of 29th International Conference on Very Large Data Bases*, pages 189–200, Berlin, Germany, September 9-12 2003.
9. S. Davidson, W. Fan, C. Hara, and J. Qin. Propagating XML Constraints to Relations. In *Proceedings of the 19th International Conference on Data Engineering*, Bangalore, India, March 5 - 8 2003.
10. D. DeHaan, D. Toman, M. P. Consens, and M. T. Özsu. A Comprehensive XQuery to SQL Translation using Dynamic Interval Encoding. In *Proceedings of the 2003 ACM SIGMOD International Conference on on Management of Data*, pages 623–634, San Diego, California, June 9-12 2003.
11. A. Deutsch, M. Fernández, and D. Suciu. Storing Semistructured Data with STORED. In *Proceedings of the 1999 ACM SIGMOD International Conference on Management of Data*, pages 431–442, Philadelphia, Pennsylvania, USA, May 31-June 03 1999.
12. G. Dong and J. Su. Incremental Maintenance of Recursive Views Using Relational Calculus/SQL. *SIGMOD Record*, 29(1):44–51, 2000.
13. M. Fernández, Y. Kadiyska, D. Suciu, A. Morishima, and W.-C. Tan. SilkRoute: A Framework for Publishing Relational Data in XML. *ACM Transactions on Database Systems*, 27(4):438–493, 2002.
14. D. Florescu and D. Kossmann. Storing and Querying XML Data Using an RDBMS. *IEEE Data Engineering Bulletin*, 22(3), September 1999.
15. A. Gupta and I. S. Mumick, editors. *Materialized Views - Techniques, Implementations and Applications*. MIT Press, 1998.
16. R. Krishnamurthy, R. Kaushik, and J. F. Naughton. XML-SQL Query Translation Literature: the State of the Art and Open Problems. In *Proceedings of the First International XML Database Symposium*, pages 1–18, Berlin, Germany, September 8 2003.
17. D. Maier. *The Theory of Relational Databases*. Computer Science Press, 1983.
18. M. Mani and D. Lee. XML to Relational Conversion Using Theory of Regular Tree Grammars. In *Efficiency and Effectiveness of XML Tools and Techniques and Data Integration over the Web. VLDB 2002 Workshop EEXTT and CAiSE 2002 Workshop DTWeb. Revised Papers*, pages 81–103. Springer, 2002.
19. Y. Papakonstantinou and V. Vianu. Incremental Validation of XML Documents. In *Proceeedings of The 9th International Conference on Database Theory*, pages 47–63, Siena, Italy, January 8-10 2003.
20. S. Patnaik and N. Immerman. Dyn-FO: A Parallel, Dynamic Complexity Class. In *Proceedings of the 13th ACM SIGACT-SIGMOD-SIGART Symposium on Principles of Database Systems*, pages 210–221, Minneapolis, Minnesota, May 24-26 1994.

21. M. Ramanath, J. Freire, J. R. Haritsa, and P. Roy. Searching for Efficient XML-to-Relational Mappings. In *Proceedings of the First International XML Database Symposium*, pages 19–36, Berlin, Germany, September 8 2003.
22. J. Shanmugasundaram, K. Tufte, C. Zhang, G. He, D. J. DeWitt, and J. F. Naughton. Relational Databases for Querying XML Documents: Limitations and Opportunities. In *Proceedings of 25th International Conference on Very Large Data Bases*, pages 302–314, Edinburgh, Scotland, UK, September 7-10 1999.
23. D. Suciu. Query Decomposition and View Maintenance for Query Languages for Unstructured Data. In *Proceedings of 22th International Conference on Very Large Data Bases*, pages 227–238, Mumbai (Bombay), India, September 3-6 1996.
24. I. Tatarinov, Z. G. Ives, A. Y. Halevy, and D. S. Weld. Updating XML. In *Proceedings of the 2001 ACM SIGMOD International Conference on Management of Data*, pages 413 – 424, Santa Barbara, California, United States, 2001.
25. J. D. Ullman. The Interface Between Language Theory and Database Theory. In *Theoretical Studies in Computer Science*, pages 133–151. Academic Press, 1992.
26. J. D. Ullman and A. V. Gelder. Parallel Complexity of Logical Query Programs. *Algorithmica*, 3:5–42, 1988.
27. Extensible Markup Language (XML) 1.0 - Second Edition. W3C Recommendation, October 6 2000. Available at: `http://www.w3.org/TR/2000/REC-xml-20001006`.

A Signature-Based Approach for Efficient Relationship Search on XML Data Collections[*]

Giuseppe Amato[1], Franca Debole[1], Fausto Rabitti[1], Pasquale Savino[1], and
Pavel Zezula[2]

[1] ISTI-CNR, Pisa, Italy
firstname.lastname@isti.cnr.it
[2] Masaryk University, Brno, Czech Republic
zezula@fi.muni.cz

Abstract. We study the problem of finding relevant relationships among user defined nodes of XML documents. We define a language that determines the nodes
as results of XPath expressions. The expressions are structured in a conjunctive
normal form and the relationships among nodes qualifying in different conjuncts
are determined as tree twigs of the searched XML documents. The query execution is supported by an auxiliary index structure called the tree signature. We
have implemented a prototype system that supports this kind of searching and we
have conducted numerous experiments on XML data collections. We have found
the query execution very efficient, thus suitable for on-line processing. We also
demonstrate the superiority of our system with respect to a previous, rather restricted, approach of finding the lowest common ancestor of pairs of XML nodes.

1 Introduction

A typical characteristic of XML objects is that they combine in a single unit data values
and their structure. Such encapsulation of data and structure is very convenient for
exchanging data, because the separation of schema and data instances in traditional
databases might cause problems in keeping proper relationships between these two
parts.

XML is becoming the preferable format for the representation of heterogeneous
information in many and diverse application sectors, such as electronic data interchange,
multimedia information systems, publishing and broadcasting, public administration,
health care and medical applications, and information outside the corporate database.
This widespread use of XML has posed a significant number of technical requirements
for storage and content-based retrieval of XML data – many of them are still waiting for
effective solutions. In particular, retrieval of XML data, based on content and structure,
has been widely studied and the problem has been formalized by the definition of query
languages such as the XPath and XQuery. Consequently, most of the implementation

* This work was partially supported by the ECD project (Extended Content Delivery), funded by
the Italian government, by the VICE project (Virtual Communities for Education), also funded
by the Italian government, and by DELOS NoE, funded by the European Commission under
FP6 (Sixth Framework Programme).

effort have concentrated on the development of systems able to execute queries expressed in these languages. To tackle the problem of structural relationships, the main stream of research on XML query processing has concentrated on developing indexing algorithms that respect the structure. Though other alternatives exist, the *structural or containment join* algorithms, such as [ZND+01], [LM01], [SAJ+02], [CVZ+02], and [BKS02], are most popular. They all take advantage of the *interval based* tree numbering scheme.

However, many other research issues are still open. A new significant problem is that of searching for relationships among XML components, that is either nodes and/or values. Indeed, there are many cases where the user may have a vague idea of the XML structure, either because it is unknown, or because it is too complex, or because many different, semantically close or equivalent, structure forms are used for XML coding. In these cases, what the user may need to search for are the relationships that exist among the specified components. For instance, in an XML encoded bibliography dataset, one may want to search for relationships between two specific persons to discover whether they were co-authors, editors, editor and co-author, cited in the bibliography, etc. In all these cases, the user may obviously have problems with languages that require to specify (as precisely as possible) the search paths. Any vagueness may result in a significant imprecision of search results and certainly in an undesirable increase of the computational costs. For example, provided that the schema is known, a very complex XQuery – taking into account all possible combinations of person roles – or several queries should be expressed in order to obtain the same result, with an obvious performance drawback. In Section 4.3 we give a real example on a car insurance policy application. This will show the suitability of our approach both in terms of the expressiveness of the query language and the performance efficiency.

In fact, there have been attempts to base search strategies on explicitly unknown structure of data collections. Algorithms for the proximity search in graph structured data are presented in [GS98]. The objective is to *rank* retrieved objects in one set, called the *Find* set, according to their proximity to objects in another given set, called the *Near* set. Specifically, applications generate the *Find* and *Near* queries on the underlying database. The database (or information retrieval) engine evaluates the queries and passes the *Find* and *Near* object result sets to the *proximity engine*. The proximity engine then ranks the *Find* set using available distance function represented as the length of the shortest path between a pair of objects from the *Find* and *Near* sets. In [GS98], the formal framework is presented and several implementation strategies are experimentally evaluated. However, the performance remains the main problem.

The Nearest Concept Queries from [SKW01] are defined for the XML data collections, and the queries use advantage of the *meet operator*. For two nodes o_1 and o_2 in given XML tree, the meet operator, $meet(o_1, o_2)$, simply returns the *lowest common ancestor*, l.c.a., of nodes o_1 and o_2. Such node is called the *nearest concept* of nodes o_1 and o_2 to indicate that the type, i.e. the node's tag, of the result is not specified by the user. Though extensions of this operator to work on a set of nodes are also specified, reported experiments only consider pairs of nodes. Further more, the response time dramatically depends on the actual distance between the nodes.

Very recently, a semantic search engine XSEarch has been proposed in [CMK+03]. It is based on a simple query language that is suitable for a naive user, and it returns

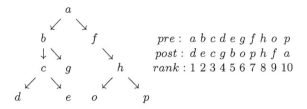

Fig. 1. Preorder and postorder sequences of a tree

semantically related document fragments that satisfy the user's query. By application of the Information Retrieval techniques, the retrieved results are ranked by estimated query relevance.

Our approach can be seen as an extension or a generalization of [SKW01] and [GS98], assuming the XML structured object collections. In principle, the result of a relationship (or structure) search query can be represented as a set of twigs of the searched data. In this way, all structural relationships, not only the l.c.a., are encapsulated and made available to the user for additional elaboration or ranking. To achieve high performance, we use the *tree signature* concept [ZAR03], which is a compressed XML tree representation supporting efficient search and navigation operations. The signatures have already been applied to the traditional XML searching with good success – see [ZAD03] for the *ordered* and [ZMM04] for the *unordered* inclusion of query trees in the data trees.

In the following, we summarize the concept of tree signatures in Section 2 and define their analytic properties. In Section 3, we specify the structure search queries and elaborate on procedures for their efficient evaluation. We describe our prototype implementation in Section 4 where we also report results from experimentation. Final discussion and our future research plans are in Section 5.

2   Tree Signatures

The idea of the tree signature [ZAD03,ZAR03,ZMM04] is to maintain a space effective representation of the XML tree structures. Formally, the XML data tree T is seen as an ordered, rooted, labelled tree. To linearize the trees, the *preorder* and *postorder ranks* from [Die82] are applied as the coding scheme. For illustration, see the preorder and postorder sequences of a sample tree in Figure 1 – the node's position in the sequence is its preorder/postorder rank, respectively.

The basic (short) signature of tree T with $m = |T|$ nodes has the following format

$$sig(T) = \langle t_1, post(t_1); t_2, post(t_2); \dots ; t_m, post(t_m)\rangle,$$

where t_i represents the name of node with preorder i and postorder $post(t_i)$. A more rich version of the tree signature, called the *extended signature*, is a sequence

$$sig(T) = \langle t_1, post(t_1), ff(t_1), fa(t_1); \dots ; t_m, post(t_m), ff(t_m), fa(t_m)\rangle,$$

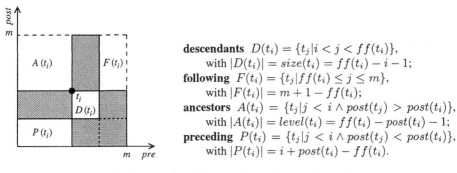

$$\textbf{descendants } D(t_i) = \{t_j | i < j < ff(t_i)\},$$
$$\text{with } |D(t_i)| = size(t_i) = ff(t_i) - i - 1;$$
$$\textbf{following } F(t_i) = \{t_j | ff(t_i) \le j \le m\},$$
$$\text{with } |F(t_i)| = m + 1 - ff(t_i);$$
$$\textbf{ancestors } A(t_i) = \{t_j | j < i \wedge post(t_j) > post(t_i)\},$$
$$\text{with } |A(t_i)| = level(t_i) = ff(t_i) - post(t_i) - 1;$$
$$\textbf{preceding } P(t_i) = \{t_j | j < i \wedge post(t_j) < post(t_i)\},$$
$$\text{with } |P(t_i)| = i + post(t_i) - ff(t_i).$$

Fig. 2. Properties of the preorder and postorder ranks.

where $ff(t_i)$ is the pointer to (preorder value of) the *first following* node, and $fa(t_i)$ refers to the *first ancestor*, that is the parent node of t_i. If there are no following nodes, $ff(t_i) = m + 1$. Since the root t_1 has no ancestors, $fa(t_1) = 0$. For illustration, the extended signature of the tree from Figure 1 is

$$\langle a, 10, 11, 0; b, 5, 7, 1; c, 3, 6, 2; d, 1, 5, 3; e, 2, 6, 3; \ldots ; h, 8, 11, 7; o, 6, 10, 8; p, 7, 11, 8\rangle$$

Given a node t_i with $pre(t_i) = i$, all the other nodes can be divided into four disjoined subsets of computable cardinalities, as illustrated in Figure 2. By definition of the nodes' ranks, the *descendant D* nodes (if they exist) form a continuous preorder as well as a postorder sequences. Further more, the *following F* nodes end the preorder sequence and the *preceding P* nodes start the postorder sequences. So there is actually some empty space in the *pre/post* plain as highlighted by the dark area in Figure 2 (left). In the preorder sequence, the *ancestor A* nodes interleave with the preceding nodes, in the postorder sequence, the ancestor nodes interleave with the following nodes.

As demonstrated in [ZAD03], the signatures also efficiently support execution of tree operations such as the leaf detection, path slicing, (sub-)tree inclusion tests, and many others. The *lowest common ancestor*, l.c.a., of nodes t_i and t_j is the node with highest preorder of $\{A(t_i) \cap A(t_j)\}$. Assuming $i < j$, an efficient algorithm to find l.c.a. recursively follows the fa pointer to find the first node t_k, such that $ff(t_k) > j$. Without any increase of complexity, this strategy can easily be generalized to finding the l.c.a. of n nodes.

A *sub-signature*, $sub\_sig_S(T)$, is a specialized (restricted) view of T through signatures, which retains the original hierarchical relationships of nodes in T, but it is not necessarily forming a tree. Considering $sig(T)$ as a sequence of individual entries representing nodes of T,

$$sub\_sig_S(T) = \langle t_{s_1}, post(t_{s_1}); t_{s_2}, post(t_{s_2}); \ldots ; t_{s_k}, post(t_{s_k})\rangle$$

is a sub-sequence of $sig(T)$, defined by the ordered set $S = \{s_1, s_2, \ldots s_k\}$ of indexes (preorder values) in $sig(T)$ with $1 \le s_i \le m$ for all i.

3 Structure Search Queries

The key construct of most XML query models and languages is the *tree pattern*, TP. Accordingly, research on evaluation techniques for XML queries has concentrated on tree pattern matching defined by the pair $Query = (Q, C)$, where $Q = (B, E)$ is the *query tree* in which each node from B has a name (label), not necessarily different, each edge from E represents the *parent-child* or the *ancestor-descendant* relationship between pairs of nodes from B. The *constraint* C is a formula specifying restrictions on the nodes and their properties, including in general their tags, attributes, and contents. In order to improve query efficiency, this concept was recently extended in [CJL+03] into the *generalized tree pattern* query, GTP, where edges of the query tree Q can be *optional* or *mandatory* and each node carries a real number valued *score*. The tree signature concept has already proved to be highly competitive with respect to numerous other alternatives to accelerate execution of TP queries both considering the query trees as ordered [ZAD03,ZAR03] and also unordered [ZMM04].

In this paper, we consider a different concept of query. It does not explicitly declare relationships among qualifying data tree nodes. Discovering relationships is actually the objective of querying to find hierarchically dependent subsets forming a tree. In the following, we first define the query model, then define its evaluation principles, and finally specify an efficient algorithm for the query execution.

3.1 Structure Search Query Model

We define the structure search query SS_Q as a conjunctive normal form of node specification expressions E_i^j as

$$SS\_Q = (E_1^1 \vee \ldots \vee E_{n_1}^1) \wedge \ldots \wedge (E_1^k \vee \ldots \vee E_{n_k}^k),$$

where each E_i^j is an XPath expression determining candidate nodes to be used as a starting point for relationships discovery. The result of such a query is the set of twigs, of the searched data tree, where structural relationships existing among nodes qualifying E_i^j of different conjuncts are made explicit. Individual nodes can be constrained by full or partial name-path specifications as well as by content predicates. Observe that an E_i^j expression might also search for all elements having a specific content, no matter what is the name of the element, or it might search for all elements of a certain name, independently of their content and structural relationships in the data tree.

Provided the XML schema is known, traditional XML processing tools, e.g. XQuery, can also determine instances of all such structural relationships. However, this would require execution of multiple TP queries, each of which considering a specific node relationships constraint. Our approach has a higher expressive power, because it does not require a priori knowledge of the structure of the XML documents and, as we will see later, offers higher processing performance.

More formally, the answer to a structure search query SS_Q is a set of sub-trees (or *twigs*) of the data tree, obtained as follows. Let T be the data tree and SS_Q a structure search query consisting of k conjuncts. Let R^Q be a *pattern of k nodes* of T such that:

- each node qualifies in a different conjunct, and

– all the nodes share a common ancestor.

Then, a qualifying twig T^Q is the sub-tree of T induced by R^Q. T^Q consists of all nodes of R^Q, but can also include additional, *induced*, nodes, which are the ancestors of nodes from R^Q up to their l.c.a., that is the root of the twig. Since T^Q is a sub-tree of T, the relationships of nodes in T^Q are the same as in T. In the following, we denote the pattern of induced nodes as I^Q. For formal manipulations, we see the patterns R^Q and I^Q as well as the twig T^Q as sub-signatures of $sig(T)$, designated, respectively, as $sub\_sig_{SR}(T)$ and $sub\_sig_{SI}(T)$. For brevity, we use $sub\_sig_S(T)$ whenever explicit distinctions between the patterns and twigs are not necessary.

For illustration, consider the following query.

```
(//person[name=John] ∨ //person[name=Jack])
∧ (//person[name=Ted]).
```

The qualifying patterns are pairs, because the query consists of two conjuncts. Furthermore, one node of the pair is always a person with name Ted and the other is a person with name John or Jack. However, the resulting twigs can be quite different even for a specific pair of nodes. For example, Jack and Ted can appear below the element `<author>`, which implies that they are coauthors of the same article. But they can have the `<journal>` element as their l.c.a. where several alternatives for twigs can occur. Two persons can be authors of different journal papers, but they can also be editors of this journal, or one of them can be the editor and the other the author.

Level constrained structure search. In some cases, it might be desirable to find twigs with the root at level of at least certain value – we assume the document's root to be at level 0. For example, consider the DBLP XML data set [DBLP]. It consists of just one large XML document (file), having the `<dblp>` element as its root. In this case, structure search queries would typically produce a large set of results, because all possible query patterns have at least the `<dblp>` element as the root. Further more, the fact that two names with the l.c.a. `<dblp>` appear in the DBLP bibliography is probably of low significance. It would be more useful to search for structural relationships excluding the `<dblp>` root element, that is searching for twigs with the root element on levels greater than 0. We denote such *level constrained* structure search queries as $SS\_Q^{lev_{min}}$, indicating that the level of the roots of the qualifying twigs should be greater than or equal to lev_{min}.

3.2   Query Evaluation Principles

Assume a collection of XML documents and an $SS\_Q^{lev_{min}}$ query. Suppose each conjunct produces a non-redundant list L_i, $i = 1, 2, \ldots, k$ of preorder values of qualifying nodes in T. The central problem of the query evaluation is to determine the query patterns R^Q as the sub-signature $sub\_sig_{SR}(T) \mid S^R = \{s_1, s_2, \ldots, s_k\}$, which satisfies the following properties:

1. each s_j is from exactly one list L_i and no two instances are from the same list;
2. the constraint $s_1 < s_2 < \ldots < s_k$ is satisfied;
3. the l.c.a. of $\{s_1, s_2, \ldots, s_k\}$ exists on level $\geq lev_{min}$.

For example, if the query is $(//\mathrm{g}) \wedge (//\mathrm{f}) \wedge (//\mathrm{c})$, then the qualifying pattern in tree T from Figure 1 is $sub\_sig_{SR}(T) = \langle c, 3; g, 4; f, 9 \rangle$, because $S^R = \{3, 6, 7\}$. The l.c.a. of nodes c, g, and f is a, that is a node at level 0.

3.3   Structure Search Query Evaluation Strategies

The query evaluation proceeds in the following four phases: 1) evaluation of the expressions E_i^j; 2) evaluation of the conjuncts; 3) generation of the node patterns R^Q 4) generation of resulting twigs T^Q. This sub-section discusses efficient execution of phases 1), 2), and 3). Section 3.5 concerns the evaluation of the phase 4).

The evaluation of each expression E_i^j returns a list LE_i^j of nodes qualifying for the corresponding XPath expression. We suppose that these lists are ordered according to the preorder ranks. The efficient evaluation of expressions E_i^j and ordering of the lists LE_i^j can be obtained by using XML path indexes and/or the XML tree signatures, as discussed in [ADR+03,ZAD03].

The result of the j-th conjunct is the union of the lists LE_i^j for all i and a specific j. Since the lists LE_i^j are ordered with respect to the preorder ranks, multiple merge of corresponding lists ensures efficiency of this procedure. This will produce k lists L_i of nodes, one for each conjunct, still ordered by the preorder ranks.

A naive way to obtain patterns R^Q is to first produce the Cartesian product of the k lists L_i, and then eliminate those k-tuples that do not satisfy the conditions defined in Section 3.2. However, the cost of such process can be very high, because the Cartesian product can produce many tuples among which only a few are finally qualifying. Such approach also assumes complete k lists to be available. In the following, we propose a new algorithm, called the *structure join*, which performs this step of query execution efficiently. The algorithm produces all patterns R^Q.

Table 1. Structure Join Algorithm

1: **procedure** STRUCTUREJOIN($L_1, \ldots, L_k, lev_{min}$)
        ▷ $L_1, \ldots, L_k$ are the lists with elements sorted with respect to preorder numbering;
        ▷ lev_{min} is the minimum level accepted for roots of qualifying twigs;
        ▷ $L_i(j)$ is the j-th element in list L_i;

2:     $result := \varnothing$;
3:     **if** $(\exists i : L_i = \varnothing)$ **then return** $result$;
4:     **else**
5:        $c_i := 1[\forall i, i = 1, \ldots, k]$;   ▷ Cursors pointing to current tops of the lists
6:        $P := max\{ pre(L_i(c_i))| \ i = 1, \ldots, k\}$;
7:        $M \in \{ j| \ pre(L_j(c_j)) = P \wedge \ 1 \leq j \leq k\}$;
8:        $a_M \in \{a| \ a \in ancestors(L_M(c_M)) \wedge level(a) = lev_{min}\}$;
9:        **if**$(a_M = null)$ **then** $c_M := c_M + 1$; **goto step** 6; **end if**
10:       **if** $(\exists i : \ pre(L_i(c_i)) \leq pre(a_M))$ **then**
11:          $c_i := min\{c| \ pre(L_i(c)) > pre(a_M)\}[\forall i : i = 1, \ldots, k]$;
12:          **if**$(\exists i : \ c_i > length(L_i))$ **then return** $result$; **else goto step** 6;
13:       **else**
14:          $pl_M := ff(a_M) - 1$;   ▷ pl_M is the preorder of the last node of the sub-tree rooted at a_M
15:          $SL_i := \{L_i(c)|c_i \leq c \wedge pre(L_i(c)) \leq pl_M\}[\forall i : i = 1, \ldots, k]$;
16:          <Generate sub-signatures of length k with each element from a different SL_i; put them in $result$ >
17:          $c_i := min\{c|pre(L_i(c)) > pl_M\}[\forall i : i = 1, \ldots, k]$;
18:          **if**$(\exists i : \ c_i > length(L_i))$ **then return** $result$; **else goto step** 6;
19:       **end if**
20:     **end if**
21: **end procedure**

The **StructureJoin** algorithm specified in Table 1 takes as input k lists of qualifying nodes, with elements sorted with respect to preorder numbering, and the level constraint lev_{min}. The algorithm avoids the unnecessary generation of not valid sub-signatures by restricting the computation of the Cartesian product to portions of the lists L_i that contain elements which belong to the same potentially qualifying sub-tree. Step 3 checks for an empty list, which terminates the algorithm. Then cursors c_i are set to refer the first element of the lists in Step 5. Steps 6 and 7 choose M as the index of the list that has the element $L_M(c_M)$ with the maximum preorder. Provided a pattern of nodes with structural relationships with $L_M(c_M)$ exists, the corresponding sub-signatures will have $L_M(c_M)$ as the last node. Step 8 determines the ancestor a_M of $L_M(c_M)$ which has level lev_{min}. The ancestor can be efficiently obtained by using the tree signature. This ancestor is the root of the sub-tree containing all possible nodes that can be joined with $L_M(c_M)$ (i.e. having valid structural relationships with $L_M(c_M)$). If a valid ancestor cannot be found, i.e. $level(L_M(c_M)) < lev_{min}$, the element is discarded by moving the cursor forward (Step 9). Step 10 checks that the top element of all lists belongs to the sub-tree rooted at a_M, that is, checks that the preorder of the top elements is greater than or equal to $pre(a_M)$. If the top element of at least one list is smaller than $pre(a_M)$, then the cursor of that list should be moved to the first element with preorder greater than $pre(a_M)$ (Step 11) and if the end of the list is reached, the algorithm ends (Step 12). If the top element of all lists is greater than $pre(a_M)$ then Step 14 uses the first following pointer, contained in the signatures, to compute pl_M, the preorder of the last node in the sub-tree rooted at a_M. Note that at this point no list can have a top element with preorder greater than pl_M, because that list should have been selected at Steps 6 and 7. All nodes in the lists that have preorder included between $pre(a_M)$ and pl_M are used to generate qualifying sub-signatures, that is, the Cartesian product will be computed only using the consecutive portions of the lists corresponding to elements having preorder between $pre(a_M)$ and pl_M. In fact, Step 15 determines the set of elements in each list that should be used for the Cartesian product – sub-lists SL_i always form a continues sequence in corresponding lists L_i. Step 16 computes the Cartesian product by generating all possible combination of nodes belonging to the sub-tree rooted at a_M present in the lists, and arranges the obtained tuples to form valid sub-signatures. Step 17 moves the cursor to point to the new top element corresponding to the next sub-tree in each list. If the end of at least one list is reached, the algorithm ends (Step 18).

Example: We illustrate the behavior of the algorithm with an example. Figure 3 shows a data tree template (on the left) and the manipulation process of the joined lists (on the right). Suppose a structure search query with three conjuncts, where the phases 1) and 2) have produced the ordered lists L_1, L_2, and L_3. Sub-trees involved in the algorithm execution are labelled from 1 to 4. The nodes of these sub-trees contained in the lists are highlighted with rectangles also labelled as the corresponding sub-trees. Finally, suppose to be at the beginning of a generic iteration of the algorithm with cursors pointing to positions c_1^1, c_2^1, and c_3^1. Steps 6 and 7 choose M^1 such that the preorder of $L_{M^1}(c_{M^1}^1)$ is the maximum (i.e. the rightmost) among the elements pointed by the list cursors. Step 8 determines a_{M^1} as the highest possible ancestor of such a node. Elements with admissible structural relationships with $L_{M^1}(c_{M^1}^1)$ should be in the sub-tree rooted at a_{M^1}. Step 10 detects that there are lists where the first element is not in the currently considered sub-tree. In fact, the first element of list L_1 is from sub-tree 1. Note that in order to have valid structure relationships involving elements of sub-tree 1, all other lists must have elements of that sub-tree. However, the fact that cursors of the other lists refer elements of sub-list 3 means that no elements from sub-tree 1 were found in previous iterations. Step 11 moves cursors of the lists to point the first element with preorder greater than $pre(a_{M^1})$. Note that also elements of sub-tree 2 in list L_1 are skipped at this step. Now, Step 6 and 7 chose the new rightmost element $L_{M^2}(c^2_{M^2})$, which now belongs to sub-tree 4. Step 8 determines a_{M^2}, which now is the root of sub-tree 4. Step 10 determines that there are lists whose first element does not belong to sub-tree 4 (both lists L_2 and L_3 have the first element from sub-tree 3). As before, Step 11 moves the cursors forward to refer elements after a_{M^2}. Current situation is that now all lists have elements from sub-tree 4. Therefore the algorithm arrives at Step 14 were the preorder pl_{M^3} of the last element of sub-tree 4 is determined and the Cartesian product of sub-lists with elements of sub-tree 4 is performed at Step 16. Step 17 moves the cursor to the next sub-tree in the lists and goes for a new iteration.

3.4 Algorithmic Complexity Considerations

It is important to point out that this algorithm computes the Cartesian products of small (continues) portions of the lists, provided the width of the sub-trees is small. In fact, just elements belonging to the same sub-tree are joined.

From this observation we can show that the complexity of our algorithm, in the average case, can be considered linear with respect to the dimension of the input. In fact, the complexity of a single Cartesian product is equal to the product of the sizes of the sub-lists SL_i. This can be realistically bounded by the average size of the sub-trees. Let's call s_{avg} that size. Then, the complexity of the Cartesian product is $O((s_{avg})^k)$. The number of Cartesian products computed is bounded by the number of sub-trees, because the algorithm computes at most one Cartesian product for every sub-tree. The number of sub-trees can be estimated as n/s_{avg}, where n is the total number of elements in the dataset. Therefore, the complexity of the algorithm is

$$O((s_{avg})^k \times (n/s_{avg})) = O((s_{avg})^{k-1} \times n).$$

In case that the average size of the sub-trees is much smaller than the size of the dataset ($s_{avg} \ll n$), which is true for large databases, the complexity is linear with the size n of the input. Of course, in the worst case, i.e. when the lev_{min} is set to 0 and the data set is composed of one large XML file, the result is that $s_{avg} = n$ and the complexity is $O(n^k)$. However, such kind of searching has very little semantic meaning, as we have already explained.

3.5 Data Twig Derivation

In order to derive a qualifying twig T^Q for query SS_Q in tree T, we start with the sub-signature $sub\_sig_{SR}(T)$ representing the query's qualifying pattern. Then for each ancestor set $A(t_{s_i})$, $i = 1, 2, \ldots, k$, we determine a sub-signature $sub\_sig_{S_i}(T)$ of the

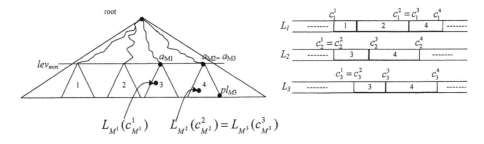

Fig. 3. Structure Join execution example

path from the node t_{s_i} to the l.c.a. of all nodes in S^R. In this way, we obtain sets S_i, and the qualifying twig is obtained as a tree induced from the pattern as

$$sig(T^Q) = sub\_sig_{S^T}(T)|S^T = \cup_{i=1}^n S_i \cup S^R,$$

considering the sets S_i as ordered – the set S^R is also ordered.

Provided $S^T = \{s_1, s_2, \ldots s_h\}$, the sub-signature $sub\_sig_{S^T}(T)$ defines a tree twig T^Q with root t_{s_1} of preorder value s_1 in T. Since the preorder/postorder values in sub-signatures are those of the original tree, leaves in sub-signatures are not necessarily leaves of T, so they can only be recognized by checking consecutive entries of the sub-signature. Specifically, if $post(t_{s_i}) < post(t_{s_{i+1}})$ then the i-th entry in the sub-signature is a leaf of the twig T^Q. Naturally, the last element, t_{s_h} in our case, is always a leaf. The element t_{s_1} needs not be checked, because it is the root of T^Q.

If we continue with our previous example of the structure search query $(//\text{g}) \wedge (//\text{f})$ $\wedge (//\text{c})$, resulting in the query pattern sub-signature $sub\_sig_{S^R}(T) = \langle c, 3; g, 4; f, 9 \rangle$ $|S^R = \{3, 6, 7\}$, the sub-signatures of the ancestors define the sets $S_1 = \{1, 2\}$ (for the node c), $S_2 = \{1, 2\}$ (for the node g), and $S_3 = \{1\}$ (for the node f). The union of the ordered sets of $S^R, S_1, S_2,$ and S_3 is $S^T = \{1, 2, 3, 6, 7\}$, which is a sub-tree of nodes a, b, c, g, f from T, rooted at node a. If we change our query to $(//\text{g}) \wedge (//\text{c})$, we get $sub\_sig_{S^R}(T) = \langle c, 3; g, 4; \rangle |S^R = \{3, 6\}$, so $S_1 = \{2\}$ and $S_2 = \{2\}$, because the lowest common ancestor of c and g is b. When we make the ordered union of all these sets, we get $S^T = \{2, 3, 6\}$, which defines a sub-tree rooted at node b.

4 Experimental Evaluation

In this section we validate the **Structure Join** algorithm from the performance point of view. Our algorithm, as demonstrated in Table 1, offers very high performance and scales very well with the increasing size of the joined lists. The structure join algorithm was implemented in Java, JDK 1.4.0 and the experiments run on a PC with a 1800 GHz Intel pentium 4, 512 Mb main memory, EIDE disk, running Windows 2000 Professional edition with NT file system (NTFS).

We have conducted most of our experiments on the XML DBLP dataset, consisting of about 200 MB [DBLP] of data. The size of the signature file is about 30% of the data size. We have verified the performance of the structure join algorithm in three tests. First, we have measured its performance using different queries, which have different number of conjuncts and different sizes of the input sets (see Section 4.1). Second, we have compared the efficiency of our structural join with the *meet* operator proposed in [SKW01] (see Section 4.2) . Finally, we have run experiments in a real application scenario of insurance records (see Section 4.3).

4.1 Performance Measurements

The queries that we have used to run the first group of experiments are listed in the first column of Table 2. Each query is coded as "QD_n", where D indicate the size of the input set (which can be Small S, Medium M, or Large L) and n can be 2 or 3 to indicate the number of conjuncts. For all our queries, the level constraint lev_{min} was set to 1 (just below the root element that is on level 0). For each query, Table 2 reports the size of the corresponding input set, the size of the output set, the number of Cartesian products computed (that is the number of qualifying sub-trees containing elements in the input set), the average number of iterations executed in each Cartesian product, and the elapsed time to complete the structure join in milliseconds.

Table 2. Performance of Structure Join algorithm. In the last but one column **#CP** indicate the number of Cartesian products and **#ICP** the average number of iterations for each Cartesian product.

Queries		#input set	#output set	#CP (#ICP)	Time (ms)
QS_2	//phdthesis/title ∧ //phdthesis/author	72 72	72	72 (1)	<1
QM_2	//incollection/title ∧ //incollection/author	1410 2931	2931	1400 (2)	30
QL_2	//inproceedings/title ∧ //inproceedings/author	22004 53243	53243	21977 (2)	392
QS_3	QS_2 ∧ //phdthesis/year	72-72 72	72	72 (1)	<1
QM_3	QM_2 ∧ //incollection/year	1410-2931 1410	2931	1400 (2)	37
QL_3	QL_2 ∧ //inproceedings/year	22004-53243 22004	53243	21977 (2)	512

The reported processing time is obtained as the average over one hundred independent executions of the algorithm. It only includes the processing time required for the structure join algorithm and it does not include the time needed to obtain the input sets. The experiments demonstrate the linear trend with respect to the cardinality of largest input set, confirming our expectation of linear complexity.

As explained previously, a trivial technique to execute the structure search is to compute a Cartesian product of the input sets and to eliminate the non qualifying tuples.

The complexity of such a strategy would have been polynomial. In particular the number of iterations required would have been equal to the product of the cardinalities of the input sets. Our algorithm, on the other hand, computes several Cartesian products and the number of iterations in each product is small. Therefore, the overall cost of our algorithm is linear.

Note that the number of computed Cartesian products increases linearly with sizes of the input sets (given that the number of qualifying sub-trees increases linearly with the sizes of the input sets). On the other hand, the number of iterations computed in each Cartesian product is independent of the sizes of the input sets, it is very small in practical cases (and it can be considered constant). This is explicated considering the actual number of Cartesian products computed, the average number of iterations in each product, and the elapsed time reported in Table 2.

For example, the trivial Cartesian product technique would have required 72*72*72 iterations to process query QS_3, while our technique needs only 72*1 iterations. The trivial Cartesian product technique would have required 22004*53243*22004 iterations to process query QL_3, while our technique requires just 21977*2 iterations. Note that the number of computed Cartesian products (21977) is smaller than the size of the smaller input set (22004). This is due to the fact that sometimes elements were discarded, because no elements from the same sub-trees were found in the other input sets (inproceedings with title and without authors or years).

4.2   Comparison with Other Techniques

To compare our algorithm with the meet operator, we have repeated the experiments from [SKW01]. Specifically, we have searched DBLP for the string "ICDE" and for the year records, incrementally including years from 1999 to 1984. We have performed the structure join on this two sets and we have computed the elapsed time of our algorithm. Figure 4 compares the elapsed time of the original meet operator and our algorithm varying the size of the input set (obtained in correspondence of the number of years included in one input set). The graph on the left side shows the performance of our algorithm, while the graph on the right shows the performance of the meet operator. Our technique is about two orders of magnitude faster than the meet operator – the time scale of the graph on the left is 100 times smaller than that of the graph on the right. For instance, with the maximum input set sizes, our technique is 96 times more efficient than the meet operator technique. Specifically, our algorithm processes the query in about 30 ms, while the meet operator needs about 3 seconds.

4.3   On-the-Field Experiment

In addition to the previous performance tests, we have also conducted experiments with a dataset related to a more realistic and complex scenario. Figure 5 sketches the XML structure of information used by a car insurance company to keep track of the customers and their record of accidents, that is an information about the type of accident, its status, those involved in the accident as witnesses, those injured, etc. In order to detect possible frauds, the insurance company may be interested in discovering all relationships between two (or more) of their customers. Examples of requests are as follows: have they been

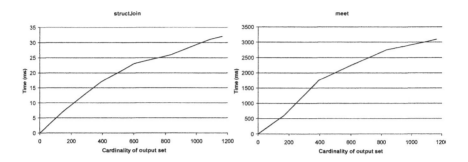

Fig. 4. Comparison between our structJoin algorithm and the meet operator

involved in many accidents, possibly with different roles (i.e. causing the accident, witness, injured person, etc.)? Who were those involved as witness or as injured persons or as the insurance owners?

The size of this dataset is 45 Mb and it contains 10000 insurance policies. In the experiment, we have searched for co-occurrences of four specific persons, identified by their names, using as the level thresholds (lev_{min}) 0, 1 and 2, corresponding, respectively, to elements <Insurance Policy>, <Risk>, and <Accident>. In the first case, we implicitly searched for co-occurrences of the four persons either as an owner, witness, or subject involved in accidents of the same insurance policy. In the second case, we implicitly searched for co-occurrences as a witness or subject involved in accidents of the same policy. In the last case, we searched for co-occurrences in the same accident. The number of twigs that we have found, i.e. those which satisfy the search criteria, are 6 for the level 0, 2 for the level 1, and 1 for the level 2. An interesting observation was that the specified persons were somehow involved together in 6 different insurance policies and the related accidents with different roles. This could suggest that further investigation should be performed by the insurance company on these subjects. The time required for processing such queries was, respectively, 7, 5, and 4 milliseconds, confirming the high performance of the technique in real application scenarios.

5   Conclusions

Contemporary XML search engines reason about the meaning of documents by considering the structure of documents and content-based predicates, such as the set of key-words or similarity conditions. However, the structure of the documents is not always known, so it can become the subject of searching.

In this paper, we have introduced a new type of queries, called the structure search, that allows users to query XML databases with value predicates and node names, but without specification of their actual relationships. The retrieved entities are sub-trees of the searched trees (twigs), which obviate the structural relationships among determined tree nodes, if they exist. The twigs can also contain additional tree nodes, not explicitly required by the query, so the transitive relationships are also discovered. Our prototype implementation demonstrates that the proposed algorithms yield useful results on real

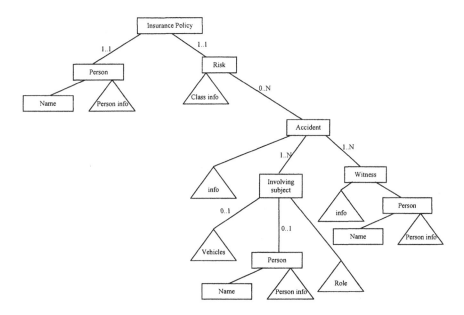

Fig. 5. Schema of the insurance records dataset

world data and scale well, enabling interactive querying. In this way, our approach can be seen as a considerable extensions of previous approaches to proximity searching in structured data. With the help of tree signatures, it also has a very efficient implementation as needed for processing of large XML data collections available on the web. Results are confirmed by systematic experiments on the DBLP dataset. A possible application is outlined by the structure search on insurance records including performance evaluation.

Our future plans concern introducing even more flexibility or vagueness to the specification of expressions determining nodes. For example by considering alternative names, such as Author or Writer, which can be automatically chosen from proper dictionaries or lexicons. We are also working on developing of *ranking* mechanisms that would order or group the retrieved twigs according to their relevance with respect to the query. In this place, the analytic properties of tree signatures will play an indispensable role.

References

[ADR+03] G. Amato, F. Debole, F. Rabitti, and P. Zezula. YAPI: Yet another path index for XML searching. In *ECDL 2003, 7th European Conference on Research and Advanced Technology for Digital Libraries, Trondheim, Norway, August 17-22, 2003*, 2003.

[BKS02] N. Bruno, N. Koudas, and D. Srivastava. Holistic Twig Joins: Optimal XML Pattern Matching. In *Proceedings of the 2002 ACM SIGMOD International Conference on Management of Data*, pp. 310-321, Madison, Wisconsin, USA, June 2002.

[CVZ+02] S. Chien, Z. Vagena, D. Zhang, V. J. Tsotras, and C. Zaniolo, Efficient Structural Joins on Indexed XML Documents. In *Proceedings of the 28th VLDB Conference*, Hong Kong, China, September, 2002, Morgan Kaufmann, 2002, pp. 263-274.

[CMK+03] S. Cohen, J. Mamou, Y. Kanza, and Y. Sagiv, XSEarch: A Semantic Search Engine for XML. In *Proceedings of the 29th VLDB Conference*, Berlin, Germany, September, 2003, Morgan Kaufmann, 2003, pp. 45-56.

[CJL+03] Z. Chen, H.V. Jagadish, V.S. Lakshmanan, and S. Paparizos. From Tree patterns to Generalized Tree Patterns: On Efficient Evaluation of XWQuery. In *Proceedings of the 29th VLDB Conference*, September 2003, Berlin, Germany, pp. 237-248.

[Die82] P.F. Dietz. Maintaining Order in a Linked List, In *Proceedings of STOC, 14th Annual ACM Symposium on Theory of Computing*, May 1982, San Francisco, CA, 1982, pp. 122-127.

[DBLP] M.Ley. DBLP Bibliography http://dblp.uni-trier.de/xml/.

[GS98] R. Goldman and N. Shivakumar. Proximity Search in Databases. In *Proceedings 1998 VLDB Conference*, pp. 26-37, New York, USA.

[Gr02] T. Grust. Accelerating XPath location steps. In *Proceedings of the 2002 ACM SIG-MOD International Conference on Management of Data*, Madison, Wisconsin, 2002, pp. 109-120.

[LM01] Q. Li and B. Moon, Indexing and Querying XML Data for Regular Path Expressions. In *Proceedings of 27th International Conference on Very Large Data Bases, VLDB01* September 11-14, 2001, Roma, Italy, Morgan Kaufmann, 2001, pp. 361-370.

[SKW01] A. Schmidt, M. Kersten, and M. Windhouwer Querying XML Documents Made Easy: Nearest Concept Queries. Proceedings of the *17th International Conference on Data Engineering*, April 02 - 06, 2001 Heidelberg, Germany, IEEE, pp. 321-329.

[SAJ+02] D. Srivastava, S. Al-Khalifa, H. V. Jagadish, N. Koudas, J. M. Patel, and Y. Wu, Structural Joins: A Primitive for Efficient XML Query Pattern Matching. In *Proceedings of the 18th International Conference on Data Engeneering, ICDE 2002*, March 2002, San Jose, California, 2002, pp. 161-171.

[ZAD03] P. Zezula, G. Amato, F. Debole, and F. Rabitti. Tree Signatures for XML Querying and Navigation. In *Proceedings of the XML Database Symposium, XSym 2003*, Berlin, September 2003, LNCS 2824, Springer, pp. 149-163.

[ZAR03] P. Zezula, G. Amato, and F. Rabitti. Processing XML Queries with Tree Signatures. In *Intelligent Search on XML Data, Applications, Languages, Models, Implementations, and Benchmarks.*, 2003, LNCS 2818, Springer, pp. 247-258.

[ZMM04] P. Zezula, F. Mandreoli, R. Martoglia. Tree Signatures and Unordered XML Pattern Matching. In *Proceedings of the 30th SOFSEM Conference on Current Trends in Theory and Practice of Informatics.*, Czech Republic, January 2003, LNCS 2932, Springer, pp. 122-139.

[ZND+01] C. Zhang, J. Naughton, D. DeWitt, Q. Luo, and G. M. Lohman, On Supporting Containment Queries in Relational Database Management Systems. In *ACM SIGMOD Conference 2001*: Santa Barbara, CA, USA, ACM-Press, 2001.

Correctors for XML Data*

Utsav Boobna[1] and Michel de Rougemont[2]

[1] I.I.T Kanpur, India utsav@iitk.ac.in
[2] University Paris II & LRI, France mdr@lri.fr

Abstract. A corrector takes an invalid XML file F as input and produces a valid file F' which is not far from F when F is $\epsilon-$close to its DTD, using the classical Tree Edit distance between a tree T and a language L defined by a DTD or a tree-automaton. We show how testers and correctors for regular trees can be used to estimate distances between a document and a set of DTDs, a useful operation to rank XML documents.
We describe the implementation of a linear time corrector using the Xerces parser and present test data for various DTDs comparing the parsing and correction time. We propose a generalization to homomorphic DTDs.

1 Introduction

For classification, search and querying semistructured data, it is important to detect approximate validity, i.e. if a file F approximately follows a structure M. In the case of XML data, the structure is a DTD or a schema and we want to decide if a file F approximately follows a DTD M. A search engine for structured data would specify a finite set $M_1, ..., M_k$ of structures and would like to efficiently rank all documents by estimating their distances to these DTDs. The documents were valid for their own DTD when they were created, but are most likely invalid for $M_1, ..., M_k$ because of linguistic differences in tags, small changes in the internal structure of DTDs and potential errors in the file. It is therefore important to efficiently estimate how close they are to a fixed set of DTDs.

A given file is well-formed if the tags follow a tree-like structure and is valid if the tree is accepted by the automaton associated with the DTD. The tool Tidy [13] takes an XML file as input and corrects it if it is not well-formed: it adds the missing tags and removes the incorrect ones to obtain a well-formed file close to the original one. We first describe the implementation of a similar tool for validity. It takes a well-formed XML file and a DTD as input and corrects it if it is invalid: it adds the missing leaves and subtrees, removes or modifies the incorrect ones to obtain a valid file close to the original one. Moreover it estimates in linear time the distance between a file and several DTDs which can be used to *rank documents* relative to these DTDs.

* Work supported by *ACI Sécurité Informatique: VERA* of the French Ministry of Research.

Z. Bellahsène et al. (Eds.): XSym 2004, LNCS 3186, pp. 97–111, 2004.
© Springer-Verlag Berlin Heidelberg 2004

The distance between two XML files is the classical Tree Edit Distance [14,12, 2] applied to the DOM trees associated with the files. It measures the number of insertions and deletions of nodes and edges, and the number of label changes to a given node. It generalizes the classical Edit Distance on strings which measures the number of insertions, deletions and modifications of characters necessary to apply to a string s to obtain a string s'. These Edit Distances have many extensions when additional operators are used, such as Moves of substrings, Permutations and Cut/Paste operations. In this paper two distances are used on unranked ordered trees: the Tree Edit distance and the Tree-Edit distance with moves where we also allow to move an *entire subtree* in one step.

Correctors are related to the self-testers of [3,4] in the theory of program verification. The related notion of *property testing* was proposed in [11], its applications to graphs were studied in [8] and its applications to regular words in [1]. These last authors prove that regular properties of words have testers, i.e. we can decide by sampling a word in constant time, if it belongs to a regular language or if it is far from the language, i.e. at distance more than $\epsilon \cdot n$ if n is the length of the string. An XML tester for a DTD and some ϵ takes an XML file F and decides with high probability in constant time if F is valid or if F is ϵ−far from the DTD. In [9], we prove the existence of such a tester for regular trees and the Tree Edit Distance with moves.

A corrector for regular words transforms a word s close to a regular language, i.e. at a distance less than $\epsilon \cdot n$ into a word s' in the language such that s' is close to s. For regular tree properties, i.e. properties defined by tree automata, or by DTDs, such correctors have been introduced in [9] for the Tree-Edit distance with moves. A basic corrector was introduced in [7] for the classical Tree-Edit distance. It is a linear algorithm which takes a general invalid file F and a DTD M as input and produces a valid file F' close to F as output, when the distance between F and the DTD is constant, i.e. if there are not too many errors. It used the notion of a *global correction* which implied a time linear in n but exponential in the number of errors.

In this paper, we first emphasize a fundamental difference between the two Tree Edit distances. If we allow moves, we prove that the distance problem is NP-complete and non-approximable. Yet we can approximate it very efficiently in the sense introduced by testers and correctors: we can quickly decide if it close or far and we can approximate it when it is close. Ordered trees with moves behave as unordered trees and this fundamental difference becomes very important for XML schemas where operators such as *interleave* are restricted in order to allow for an efficient implementation.

We give a global presentation of correctors and describe the implementation of a *local corrector* for the classical Tree Edit distance (without moves), i.e. an algorithm which is both linear in n and the number of errors but may not yield the best correction. We describe its implementation using the Xerces parser and give test data for invalid files which follow three DTDs: the first represents deep trees, the second wide trees, and the third a combination of deep and wide trees.

The main result of the paper is to show that the correction time is always less than the parsing time and therefore scales up.

We discuss the generalization of a corrector to close DTDs. We consider a file (F, M_1) where M_1 is the DTD of F, and an external DTD M_2 close to M_1, having defined the distance between two DTDs. We estimate the distance between (F, M_1) and M_2, when F is close to M_1, M_2 close to M_1 and therefore F is close to M_2.

In section 2, we present the notations, the Tree Edit distances, property testing on trees, its connection with the correctors and prove that the distance problem for ordered trees with the Tree Edit distance with moves is NP-complete. In section 3, we describe the structure of correctors, the implementation of a local corrector and give an example. In section 4, we provide general figures on the relative parsing and correction time for three DTDs. In section 5, we introduce a distance on DTDs and generalize the approach to homomorphic DTDs.

2   Preliminaries

A well-formed XML file is composed of two parts: a *ranked ordered labelled tree* and a Document Type Definition DTD or Schema. We define these two objects, the Tree Edit Distance which gives a measure between ordered labelled trees and between a tree and a DTD, and the basic notions of testers and correctors.

2.1   Ranked Ordered Labelled Trees

A *ranked labelled ordered tree* is a ranked ordered tree with labels, i.e. a structure $\mathcal{T}_{rl} = (D_n, Child_i, Label_j, root)_{i \leq m, j \leq p}$ where the domain $D_n = \{1, ..., n\}$ is the set of nodes, the binary relation $Child_i(u, v)$ is satisfied if u is the i-th child of v for $i \leq m$ and a fixed m and $root$ is a distinguished element of D_n with no predecessors. The graph of the $Child_i(u, v)$ is a tree, $Label_j$ is a unary relation on D_n and the set $\{Label_j\}_{1j \leq p}$ is a partition of D_n.

Let $\mathcal{L} = \{l_1, l_2...l_j...l_p\}$ be the set of labels also called *tags*. A DTD defines one label as a *root* and declares a set of rules $l : (m)$ where l is a tag and m a regular expression on $\mathcal{L}$, also called the *content model m*. The content model (#PCDATA) indicates a leaf. Each rule $l : (m)$ specifies a transition of a special unranked tree-automaton. In this paper we consider bottom-up tree automata on labelled trees but we may have taken equivalent models.

Our implementation uses the standard parsing tools, Sax and Xerces. After reading the file, we obtain a DOM tree, which is parsed bottom-up. We describe how to handle parsing errors, in order to modify a DOM tree and obtain a valid one. We interleave parsing steps with correction steps and obtain two outputs: a corrected file and an estimation of the Tree Edit Distance. It is possible that a Sax-based corrector would directly give an estimated distance without building a corrected file and hence avoid the DOM construction.

2.2   The Tree Edit Distance

The Edit Distance on strings has been introduced in [14] for comparing strings and generalized in [12] for trees. The survey [2] describes hardness results for unordered trees and classical polynomial algorithms for ordered trees. Basic operations on ordered labelled trees include: *change* a label, *insertion* of a node on a given edge (transformed in two edges), *insertion* of an edge or *deletion* of an edge.

Definition 1 *The distance between T and T' is the minimum number of Tree Edit operations necessary to reach T' from T, noted $Dist(T, T')$. The distance between T and a language L, noted $Dist(T, L)$ is the minimum distance between $Dist(T, T')$ for $T' \in L$*

We say that two trees T and T' are k-close if their distance is less than k, and that T is ϵ-close to a DTD if the distance between T and the language L associated with the DTD is less than $\epsilon \cdot n$, if T has n nodes. T is ϵ-far from a DTD if it is not ϵ-close. It is a classical observation that the distance is P-computable for ordered trees and NP-complete on unordered trees. In the context of XML, several papers [10,5] estimate similarities between files using variations of the P-algorithm based on dynamic programming, an $O(n^2)$ algorithm. The methods we introduce can decide if the distance to a DTD is small or large in constant time (depending on ϵ) but independent of n when we use a tester. A corrector produces a corrected file in linear time.

Distances with moves. On strings, a *move* is simply the possibility to isolate an arbitrary substring t and a position i in a string s of size n and to *move* t in position i, shifting the word to the right in one step. The new Edit distance, called *Edit distance with moves* introduced in [6] for strings has many applications in the database streaming model. In the case of trees, a *move* is the possibility to isolate a subtree t and a leaf i in a tree T of size n. We move t to position i in one step, as shown in the figure below.

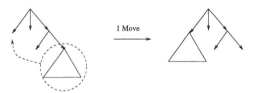

Fig. 1. Tree Edit Distance with moves.

This construction is indeed feasible in the DOM tree model by modifying two edges. The distance problem changes completely as the next result shows because ordered trees with moves behave as unordered trees.

Proposition 1 *The distance problem on ordered trees with the Edit distance with moves is NP-complete.*

Proof. We reduce an NP-complete problem 3SM (3-Set Matching or Exact Cover by 3-Sets) to the distance problem on unranked trees. We use unranked trees similar to the ones mentioned in [2] where it is shown that the distance problem on unordered trees is NP-complete. Consider a set $U = \{u_1, u_2, \ldots\ldots u_{3k}\}$ and n sets of 3 elements of U, *i.e.* $S_1 = \{u_{1_1}, u_{1_2}, u_{1_3}\}, \ldots, S_i = \{u_{i_1}, u_{i_2}, u_{i_3}\}, \ldots, S_n = \{u_{n_1}, u_{n_2}, u_{n_3}\}$. We have to decide if there are k subsets $S_{i_1}, \ldots, S_{i_k}$ which partition U, i.e. whose intersection is empty and their union is U.

Consider the two unranked trees below, T_1 and T_2 on an alphabet $\Sigma = \{u_1, u_2, \ldots, u_{3k}, S_1, \ldots, S_n, a, t\}$. The tree T_1 is built from the n sets $S_1 = \{u_{1_1}, u_{1_2}, u_{1_3}\}, \ldots, S_i = \{u_{i_1}, u_{i_2}, u_{i_3}\}, \ldots, S_n = \{u_{n_1}, u_{n_2}, u_{n_3}\}$ as in Figure 2 and the distance between the node S_i and the three leaves is $n + 5k$. The tree T_2 has $u_1, \ldots, u_{3k}$ as successors and a node labelled t with $3(n - k)$ leaves at distance $n + 5k$ labelled t.

If we can partition U with k such sets, we can use k delete of edges (a, S_i) followed by k moves to place the $u_{i_1}, u_{i_2}, u_{i_3}$ to the left. We reorder all the u_{i_j} and use up to $3k$ moves to obtain the left part of T_2. We then use $n - k$ merges on the other sets to obtain the right part of T_2 and $3(n - k) + 1$ modifications of labels after we change all the labels to t. In the worst-case we make $2k + 3k + (n - k) + 3(n - k) + 1 = 4n + 2k + 1 = p$ operations.

If the instance of 3SM is positive, the distance between T_1 and T_2 is less than p. If the instance of 3SM is negative, let us show that the distance is greater than p. The transformation of the second part of the tree requires $3(n - k) + 1$ operations. If we select any subset of size k, there will be at least one duplicate u_i which requires $n + 5k$ operations to remove and in the best case, we apply $k + n + 5k$ delete. The distance is at least $4n + 3k + 1$. This proves that the distance problem on unranked trees with an infinite alphabet is NP-complete.

To reduce the problem to a finite alphabet by replacing nodes labelled by a letter of $\Sigma = \{u_1, u_2, \ldots, u_{3k}\}$ by a binary tree of size $\log(3k)$ and suppressing the labels $S_1, \ldots, S_n$. Construct larger trees T_1' and T_2' from T_1 and T_2 by replacing the nodes labelled $u_{i_1}, u_{i_2}, u_{i_3}$ by such finite trees. We keep the same construction but instead of $3(n - k) + 1$ modifications of labels, we first need to apply $3(n - k) \log(3k)$ deletions of edges to remove the finite binary trees, and then apply the $3.(n - k) + 1$ modifications of labels. We just take $p' = 2k + 3k + (n - k) + (3(n - k) + 1) \log(3k) = (3(n - k) + 1) \log(3k) + n + 4k$. This concludes that the distance problem on unranked trees is NP-complete. If we code the trees T_1' and T_2' by binary trees T_1'' and T_2'' using a standard encoding, we notice that if $(T_1', T_2') = k$ then $(T_1'', T_2'') = 2k$: we reduce the distance problem on unranked trees to the distance problem on ranked trees.   □

The argument can be also used to show that the distance problem is not approximable as we can maintain an arbitrarily large gap between positive and negative instances. Although this distance is hard to compute, it becomes easy to approximate in the sense introduced by testers.

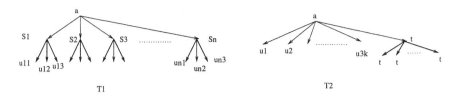

Fig. 2. Trees T_1 and T_2.

2.3   Testers and Correctors

In the late eighties, the theory of *program checking* and *self-testing/correcting* was initiated in [3,4]. Correctors in this context take a program, incorrect on a few instances, as an oracle and produce a correct program with high probability. Many interesting correctors for numerical computations and linear algebra are presented in [3].

The related notion of *property testing* was first proposed in [11]: it is an approximate randomized test which separates with high probability inputs which satisfy a property from those which are far from the property, using the Hamming distance to compare structures. For graphs, [8] investigated property testing for several properties such as *c*-colorability which can be approximately tested in constant time. In [1], the authors prove that any regular property of strings can be tested and this result is generalized for the Edit Distance in [9]. For trees with the Tree Edit distance with moves, [9] provides a randomized algorithm A which given a tree T of size n and a regular tree language L defined by a DTD is such that: A accepts if $T \in L$ and A rejects with high probability if T is ϵ-far from L, i.e. the distance between T and L is greater than $\epsilon \cdot n$. The time of the algorithm is independent of n and depends on ϵ only. Such an algorithm samples the DOM tree by selecting a random node and a finite local subtree of size $1/\epsilon$, and finally checks a local property.

There is a corrector which takes a tree T ϵ-close to L, i.e. at distance less than $\epsilon \cdot n$ as input and produces a tree $T' \in L$, which is ϵ'-close to T, as output.

Notice that the Tree Edit distance with moves is hard to compute but we can estimate it if it small. First use the tester to detect if it is large. If it is small, use a corrector for an estimate.

3   Correctors for XML

A Corrector takes an XML file (which may not be valid) and the corresponding DTD as input and produces a valid XML file close to the original one and the approximate Edit distance, as output. For the Tree Edit distance without moves, we don't know correctors which would correct up to distances $\epsilon \cdot n$ but we know correctors which correct up to a constant distance. We now present two classes of correctors and an implementation for this distance.

3.1   Corrector for the Tree Edit Distance

There are two distinct steps proposed in [7], after having read a file.

    1. **Inductive *-Marking of the DOM tree.** *Follow a bottom-up run on the DOM tree and mark with a * the nodes where a parsing error occurs. The root of a subtree which contains *-nodes is a *-node if all substitutions of * with feasible tags in the suntree lead to a parsing error.*

    2. **Recursive correction of the *-subtrees.** *Proceed top-down and propose local modifications in the neighborhood of the * node of maximum height. Compute the global distance obtained when the leaves are reached and choose the modification of minimum distance.*

This algorithm guarantees that the obtained DOM tree is valid and at a predictable distance of the original tree if the original file was at distance k to the DTD. Notice that the number of * nodes is a first estimate of the distance. It is $O(n)$ if n is the size of the tree, but exponential in the distance k. We therefore consider Local Correctors where a local correction is made at each * node, in order to remove this exponential constant factor.

3.2   Local Correctors

An l-local Corrector makes corrections at each * node, looking at a finite neighborhood at distance l, below the node. Clearly local corrections may not be as good as a global correction, but they are more efficient as they remove the exponential constant factor 2^k. We propose a 1-local Corrector, or Local Corrector, i.e. look at the direct successors of a * node or neighborhood of size 1 below the node.

A local correction at a * node proceeds as follows. We propose a new label t for a * node which guarantees that the tree T will be valid. We consider the string s of labels of the successors of the * node, select a rule of the DTD which minimizes the Tree Edit Distance and apply a local correction.

    Local Corrector
Input: *a file F and a DTD.*
Output: *a valid file F' close to F.*

    1. **Inductive *-Marking of a tree.** *Follow a bottom-up run on the DOM tree and mark with a * the nodes where a parsing error occurs.*

    2. Iterate Top-down at each * node. Propose a valid tag, i.e. a tag which leads to a valid tree, to a * node, apply a local correction at each node.

    Local Correction
Input: *a * node and its new label t, the string s of labels of successor nodes and a DTD.*
Output: *the closest string s' of the DTD, the Edit distance and a sequence of local corrections at the * node.*

    1. Consider all rules of type $t : m$ where m is a content model, i.e. a regular expression in the language of $\mathcal{L}$.

    2. Compute the Edit-distance between m and s. Select the rule with the minimum distance and closest string s'. Make the local correction, i.e. the sequence of Deletion, Insertion and Modification to s to obtain s'.

The key function is to compute the distance between a string and a regular expression and there are efficient algorithms for this problem as in [15]. We then obtain a distance and a corrected string s' where nodes are added, removed or modified. In order to solve very efficiently the distance to a regular expression problem, we assume the DTD uses only the $*, +$ operators to a *single tag* and we say that such a DTD is in *Unary Normal Form*. If we compute the distance between s and a regular expression for the Edit distance with Moves, we would generalize the local corrector to the Tree Edit distance with Moves.

3.3   Java Implementation Details

An implementation of the corrector using the notion of local correction at every error node is available on the site *http://www.lri.fr/~mdr/xml*. It uses the Sax and Xerces parsers and its key features are:

Phase 1: Parsing. As we read the file, we read the DTD with the Sax Parser, stores the declaration of each element in a class and obtain the DOM structure of the document by parsing it with the Xerces-j parser. We travel the DOM structure Bottom-up, and assign *Height* and *SubtreeSize* to each node as attribute. *Height* will be used to set the preference for correction whereas *SubtreeSize* will be used to calculate the approximate edit distance. We isolate the error nodes (* nodes) along with the error statement as we consider several parsing possibilities. We store these nodes in an array. If there is any fatal error (i.e., the given XML document is not well formed) then exit, else go to the Correction phase.

Phase 2: Correction. For each * node, we derive possible tags for that node such that the root of the tree accepts. For each possible tag t, we access the DNF of its Content Model, the minimum height of its subtrees (to compute the Edit distance while inserting or removing nodes) and the string s of tags of the successors. For each content model m, compute the Edit distance between s and m. Choose the model m with the minimum Edit distance. We obtain the string s' closest to s and a sequence of basic operations among M (Match), D (Delete), I (Insert), C (Change) which have to be realized for each letter of s. Modify the tree following these modifications. Check the attributes of each child node. If some attribute is missing then add it, if there is an undeclared attribute then remove it and if the attribute is not correctly defined then modify it.

Compute the total Edit distance, for all the corrections done. Remove the attributes added as part of this program. Serialize this DOM structure to an XML Document.

3.4   Example of a Corrected File

Consider the following DTD which defines a class of right-branch trees.

```
<?xml version="1.0"?>
<!DOCTYPE a [<!ELEMENT a (l,r)><!ELEMENT r ((l,r)|q ) >
<!ELEMENT l (#PCDATA) ><!ELEMENT q (#PCDATA) >]>
```

Consider a file F whose DOM tree is represented in (a) of the following figure. At parsing time we generate two * nodes. Correcting top-down, the first * node is labelled r and the string s below at distance 1 is r. There are two possibilities for s': $s'_1 = l, r$ or $s'_2 = q$ from the DTD. In the first case, we correct by introducing a left branch l and the Tree Edit Distance is 1. In the second case we drop the subtree labelled r and replace it by a branch labelled with q. The Tree Edit Distance is the size of the subtree, i.e. 11 and this choice is not taken. We proceed until the next * node labelled r and $s = l, r, q$. In this case $s' = l, r$ and we drop the q branch. The total Edit Distance is 2.

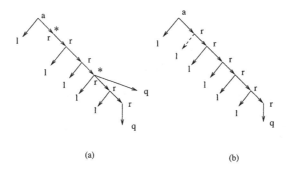

(a)   (b)

Fig. 3. Correction of a DOM tree.

4   Comparative Study

We consider three different DTDs and analyze the parsing and the correction time of files up to 800 nodes. The first DTD defines deep binary trees, the second DTD defines wide trees and the third DTD defines a mixture od deep and wide trees.

4.1   Deep Tree Example

The first DTD defines the class of right-branch trees with the tags a, l, r, q, as in the example of section 3.5. Given a valid binary tree, we randomly add extra branches to a node r, remove some left branches and change some of the r tags. Assume a distance of 10, i.e. we add 10 errors to various files from 50 nodes to 800 nodes.

The Figure 5 shows the approximate time in milliseconds taken for the parsing as well as the correction time of the XML document. It clearly indicates a correction time negligible compared to the parsing time. In this case, the possible expanded words w at each stage are very short and the Edit distance computations are very efficient.

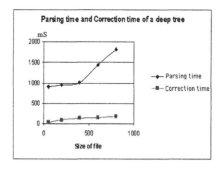

Fig. 4. Analysis of Deep trees.

4.2 Wide Tree Example

The second DTD is closer to classical examples in databases where the branching degree is large. We represent a document with a title and many lines, each one composed of many chars. We introduce 10 random errors in wide valid trees of size 50 up to 800 nodes.

```
<?xml version="1.0" encoding="UTF-8"?><!DOCTYPE d [
<!ELEMENT d (title,line*)><!ELEMENT line (b,char*,c)>
<!ELEMENT title (#PCDATA)><!ELEMENT char (#PCDATA)>
<!ELEMENT b (#PCDATA)><!ELEMENT c (#PCDATA)>]>
```

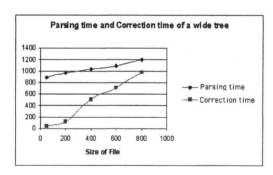

Fig. 5. Analysis of Wide trees.

In this case, the discrepancy in the parsing and correction time is due to the large number of expansions of the regular expressions to be considered. This number increases drastically and we need to compute the edit distance for many probable corrections and then sort out the smallest one. Notice that the correction time is still less than the parsing time.

4.3   Deep Tree Having Some Wide Branches

We now define a mixture of the previous DTDs. We have many *b*s nodes below which we attach a right-branch tree, as defined by the first DTD. Starting from valid trees, we generate invalid trees with 10 random errors of size 50 up to 800 nodes.

```
<?xml version="1.0"?><!DOCTYPE b [<!ELEMENT b ((a|b),r)>
<!ELEMENT a (l,r)><!ELEMENT r ((l,r)|q ) >
<!ELEMENT l (#PCDATA) ><!ELEMENT q (#PCDATA) >]>
```

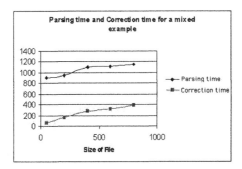

Fig. 6. Wide branches of deep trees.

In this last case, the correction time is the average of the two previous example and significantly less than the parsing time.

If we had considered the global correction, the situation would have been quite different. We would need to check all the permutations of all possible corrections at each error node and then select the best correction. For deep trees, it would be very inefficient whereas for wide trees, it would be acceptable. The global method may have produced a better correction, but very inefficient for deep trees.

4.4   The Book Example

Consider the following standard realistic DTD describing a *book* document. On the site *http://www.lri.fr/~mdr/xml*, there are several examples of invalid files with few errors and the corrected valid file is obtained on-line. In general, the user can upload his own file, provided the DTD is included and in Unary Normal Form. If the distance is not too large, he will obtain a corrected valid file on-line.

```
<?xml version='1.0' ?>
<!ELEMENT book (chapter*,title,author)>
<!ELEMENT chapter (title,para*)><!ELEMENT title (#PCDATA)>
<!ELEMENT para (#PCDATA)><!ELEMENT author (#PCDATA)>
```

A more general problem concerns the correction of a file F, using a DTD M_1 with respect to a close DTD M_2. It is essential to rank Web documents relative to a given DTD. We have to consider not only the given DTD but also close ones, in particular to adjust with the different languages used on the Web. The following DTD is a close french version of the previous one. If we wish to rank documents of type *Book* with their Edit-distance, we need to also consider french books, chinese books and so on.

```
<?xml version='1.0' ?>
<!ELEMENT livre (chapitre*,editeur,auteur,titre)>
<!ELEMENT chapitre (titre,para*)>
<!ELEMENT titre (#PCDATA)><!ELEMENT para (#PCDATA)>
<!ELEMENT auteur (#PCDATA)><!ELEMENT editeur (#PCDATA)>
```

We show that we can generalize the corrector to handle DTDs which are close to a given DTD.

5   A Corrector for Homomorphic Data Type Definitions

The correction algorithm can be generalized to DTDs which may not be the original DTD of the file, provided they are close. If a document F is a french book with a DTD close to the english one, we wish to find a mapping between french and english tags and an approximate distance between the french document and the english DTD. We generalize the distance between a tree and a DTD to a distance between two DTDs by defining a function of n, as the maximum of the distances between pairs of trees in M_1, M_2 of size n, making the definition symmetric. When they are close, i.e. the distance is $O(1)$, we propose to adapt the previous corrector.

5.1   Distance on *DTDs*

Consider two regular expressions or two DTDs. We first consider the case when they use the same language of tags $\mathcal{L}_1$ and then different languages $\mathcal{L}_1$ and $\mathcal{L}_2$.

Definition 2 *The distance between two regular expressions r and t on the same language $\mathcal{L}_1$ is the function $Dist(n, r, t) = Max\{ Dist1(n, r, t), Dist1(n, t, r) \}$ where*

$$Dist1(n, r, t) = Max_{w \in r, |w|=n}\{ dist(w, t) \}$$

Similarly, the distance between two DTDs M_1 and M_2 on the same language $\mathcal{L}_1$ is the function $Dist(n, M_1, M_2) = Max\{ Dist1(n, M_1, M_2), Dist1(n, M_2, M_1) \}$ where

$$Dist1(n, M_1, M_2) = Max_{F \in M_1, |F|=n}\{ dist(F, M_2) \}$$

We say that two DTDs are at distance $O(1)$ or at constant distance if $Dist(n, r, t) = O(1)$. We are interested in short distances, say up to $\log n$, as we wish to capture close DTDs. In the sequel we only consider DTDs at constant distances.

Example 1. Let $\mathcal{L}_1 = \{a, b, c, d, u, v\}$. If $r = au * bv * cd$ and $t_1 = au * abv * c$ then $Dist(n, r, t_1) = O(1)$. If $t_2 = ab * v * c$ then $Dist(n, r, t_2) = O(n)$.

If regular expressions or DTDs use different languages $\mathcal{L}_1$ and $\mathcal{L}_2$, we wish to generalize this definition. We consider mappings π from $\mathcal{L}_1 \cup \{\bot\}$ to $\mathcal{L}_2 \cup \{\bot\}$ such that $\pi(\bot) = \bot$. We then extend the previous definition to two regular expressions r and t by taking the Minimum over all π of the distance between $\pi(r)$ and t. We interpret $\bot$ as the empty symbol, i.e. $a.\bot = \bot.a = a$

Definition 3 *Two regular expressions r and t are isomorphic if there exists a mapping π between the symbols (tags) of r in $\mathcal{L}_1$ and the symbols (tags) of t in $\mathcal{L}_2$ such that $\pi(r) = t$. Two regular expressions r and t in Unary Normal Form such that $|r| \geq |t|$ are homomorphic if there exists a mapping π between $\mathcal{L}_1 \cup \{\bot\}$ and $\mathcal{L}_2 \cup \{\bot\}$ such that the distance between $\pi(r)$ and t is $O(1)$.*

In case $|r| \leq |t|$, consider mappings from $\mathcal{L}_2$ into $\mathcal{L}_1$ and check $\pi(t)$ with r.

Example 2. Let $\mathcal{L}_1 = \{a, b, c, d, u, v\}$ and $\mathcal{L}_2 = \{a, b, c, d, u, v\}$ If $r = au * bv * cd$ and $t_1 = cx * y * e$ then $Dist(n, r, t_1) = O(1)$ with π such that $\pi(a) = c$, $\pi(u) = x, \pi(b) = \bot, \pi(v) = y, \pi(c) = e$ and $\pi(a) = c$. Hence $au * bv * cd$ and $cx * y * e$ are homomorphic.

If $t_2 = cx * y * e*$ then $Dist(n, r, t_2) = O(n)$ for any mapping π and these regular expressions are not homomorphic.

We generalize now the previous definition to two DTDs on different languages, assuming they are reduced, i.e. each rule influences the tree language associated with the DTD. Consider that the DTD provides the DNF form for each tag. For a tag a, let $DNF(a)$ be the regular expression which defines a. Suppose without loss of generality that $|\mathcal{L}_1| \geq |\mathcal{L}_2|$. Call a tag a *recursive* if either $a*$ occurs in some content model or if a occurs in the DNF form of a or if a is on a loop in the dependency graph whose nodes are tags and edges link a tag b with all the tags in its DNF.

Definition 4 *Two DTDs M_1 and M_2 with roots r_1 and r_2 are homomorphic if there exists a mapping π between $\mathcal{L}_1 \cup \{\bot\}$ and $\mathcal{L}_2 \cup \{\bot\}$ such that:*

- *if a is recursive in M_1 then $\pi(a)$ is recursive in M_2 and $\pi(DNF(a))$ is isomorphic to $DNF(\pi(a))$*
- *if b is non recursive in M_1 then $\pi(DNF(b))$ is homomorphic to $DNF(\pi(b))$.*
- *$\pi(r_1) = \pi(r_2)$.*

If $|\mathcal{L}_1| \leq |\mathcal{L}_2|$, we require π to map $\mathcal{L}_2 \cup \{\bot\}$ into $\mathcal{L}_1 \cup \{\bot\}$ as before.

Example 3. Let $\mathcal{L}_1 = \{book, chapter, title, author, para\}$ for the french DTD and $\mathcal{L}_2 = \{livre, chapitre, titre, auteur, para, editeur\}$ for the english DTD. In this case *chapitre, para, titre* are recursive in the french DTD M_2.

Let π such that $\pi(livre) = book$, $\pi(chapitre) = chapter, \pi(titre) = title, \pi(auteur) = author, \pi(para) = para, \pi(editeur) = \bot$.

In this case the recursive tags are mapped to isomorphic DNFs and the non recursive tag *livre* is mapped to a homomorphic DNF as $\pi(chapitre*, editeur, auteur, titre) = (chapter*, title, author)$ is at a constant distance from $(chapter*, author, title)$.

Proposition 2 *Two homomorphic regular expressions r, t are at distance $O(1)$. Two homomorphic DTDs are at distance $O(1)$.*

Given a file F with a DTD M_1, and another external DTD M_2, we wish to estimate the distance between F and M_2. We can look for all possible π which are homomorphisms between M_1 and M_2, and look at the distance between $\pi(F)$ and M_2 with the previous corrector. This procedure would be exponential in the number of tags and inefficient in practice. We can however generalize the approach of a corrector: we build bottom-up a possible π and correct top-down as before.

5.2   Generalized Local Corrector

A (d, l)-local Generalized Corrector looks bottom-up at finite neighborhoods at distance d above a node and constructs the π which minimizes the edit distance. As we proceed, bottom-up, we only extend a given π and quit if the distance is too large. We apply the corrector top-down as before to estimate the distance between F and an external DTD M_2.

The local construction of a π is not as good as the exhaustive search for the best π but is very efficient. We propose a $(2, 1)$-local Generalized Corrector: we look at depth 2 above as we proceed bottom-up and at depth 1 top-down as before. It has the advantage of catching quickly the expressions $a*$ which have to be matched to a $b*$ in the other DTD. We call GLC for Generalized Local Corrector such a $(2, 1)$-local Generalized Corrector.

> GLC
> **Input:** a file (F, M_1), an external DTD M_2 and parameter k.
> **Output:** the approximate distance between F and M_2, when it is less than k and a corrected file F'.
>
> 1. Follow a bottom-up run on the DOM tree and inductively construct the best π. Mark with a * the nodes where a parsing error for M_2 occurs.
>
> 2. Proceed Top-down as in the classical Corrector. Propose a valid tag, i.e. a tag which leads to a valid tree, to a * node, apply a local correction at each node.

We build a potential mapping π, bottom-up and estimate the Edit Distance. If it is greater than k, we stop and consider another mapping. If we reach the root with a potential mapping π, we correct $\pi(F)$. The advantage of this construction is that very few possible π are considered, especially when started with a random subtree of depth 2 from the leaves. We construct an approximate π bottom-up and obtain with the Corrector an approximate distance Top-down.

6   Conclusion

A corrector for XML documents can estimate in linear time the distance between a document and a DTD when this distance is small. It is a useful operation to rank documents relative to several DTDs. The proposed implementation of a local corrector uses the Xerces parser and shows that in general the correction time is less than the parsing time and therefore scales up. It only corrects documents for a fixed constant distance but we intend to generalize the corrector for the Tree Edit distance with moves. In this case we would correct for a distance up to $\epsilon \cdot n$, as predicted by the theory.

We proposed the generalization of a corrector to external DTDs, i.e. to handle a file (F, M_1) whose DTD is M_1 with an external DTD M_2, provided the distance between M_1 and M_2 is constant. At the heart of the problem lies the approximate equivalence of regular expressions.

References

1. N. Alon, M. Krivelevich, I. Newman, and M. Szegedy. Regular languages are testable with a constant number of queries. *IEEE Symposium on Foundations of Computer Science*, 1999.
2. A. Apostolico and Z. Galil. Pattern matching algorithms, chapter 14: Approximate tree Pattern matching. *Oxford University Press*, 1997.
3. M. Blum and S. Kannan. Designing programs that test their work. *ACM Symposium on Theory of Computing*, pages 86-97, 1989.
4. M. Blum, M. Luby, and R. Rubinfeld. Self-testing/correcting with applications to numerical problems. *ACM Symposium on Theory of Computing*, pages 73-83, 1990.
5. S. Chawathe, A. Rajaraman, H. Garcia-Molina, and J . Widom. Change detection in hierarchically structured information. In *Proceedings of the A CM SIGMOD*, pages 493-504, 1996.
6. G. Cormode. Sequence distance embeddings. *Ph.D. thesis, University of Warwick*, 2003.
7. M. de Rougemont. A corrector for XML. ISIP: Franco-Japanese Workshop on Information Search, *Integration and Personalization, Hokkaido University, http://ca.meme.hokudai.ac.jp/project/fj2003/*, 2003.
8. O. Goldreich, S. Goldwasser, and D. Ron. Property testing and its connection to learning and approximation. In *IEEE Symposium on Foundations of Computer Science*, pages 339-348, 1996.
9. F. Magniez and M. Rougemont. Property testing of regular tree languages. *ICALP*, 2004.
10. A. Nierman and H. V. Jagadish. Evaluating structural similarity in XML documents. In *Proceedings of the fifth International Workshop on the Web and Databases*, pages 61-66, 2002.
11. R. Rubinfeld and M. Sudan. Robust characterizations of polynomials with applications to program testing. *SIAM Journal on Computing*, 25:23-32, 1996.
12. K. C. Tai. The tree-to-tree correction Problem. *Journal of the Association for Computing Machinery*, 26: 422-433, 1979.
13. Tidy. *HTML Tidy Library Project, http://tidy.sourceforge.net.* 2000.
14. R. Wagner and M. Fisher. The string-to-string correction Problem. *Journal of the Association for Computing Machinery*, 21:168-173, 1974.
15. S. Wu, U. Manber, and E. Myers. A subquadratic algorithm for approximate regular expression matching. *Journal of algorithms*, 19:346-360, 1995.

Incremental Constraint Checking for XML Documents

Maria Adriana Abrão[1]*, Béatrice Bouchou[1], Mírian Halfeld Ferrari[1],
Dominique Laurent[2], and Martin A. Musicante[3] **

[1] Université François Rabelais - LI/Antenne de Blois, France
adriana.abrao@etu.univ-tours.fr, {bouchou, mirian}@univ-tours.fr
[2] Université de Cergy-Pontoise - LIPC, France
dominique.laurent@dept-info.u-cergy.fr
[3] Universidade Federal do Paraná - Departamento de Informática, Brazil
mam@inf.ufpr.br

Abstract. We introduce a method for building an XML constraint validator from a given set of schema, key and foreign key constraints. The XML constraint validator obtained by our method is a bottom-up tree transducer that is used not only for checking, in only one pass, the correctness of an XML document but also for incrementally validating updates over this document. In this way, both the verification from scratch and the update verification are based on regular (finite and tree) automata, making the whole process efficient.

1 Introduction

We address the problem of incremental validation of updates performed on an XML document that respects a set of schema and integrity constraints (*i.e.*, on a valid XML document). Given a set of schema and integrity constraints $\mathcal{D}$, we present a method that translates $\mathcal{D}$ into a bottom-up tree transducer $\mathcal{U}$ capable of verifying the validity of the document. We only address meaningful specifications [11], *i.e.*, ones in which integrity constraints are consistent with respect to the schema. The aim of this work is the construction of a transducer $\mathcal{U}$ that allows incremental validation of updates. In this paper, we deal mostly with the verification of key and foreign key constraints. The validation of updates taking into account schema constraints (DTD) is performed by $\mathcal{U}$ exactly as proposed in [5]. Our framework takes into account attributes as well as elements: details concerning the treatment of attributes are presented in [5,6]. Here, for the sake of simplicity, we disregard specificity of attributes. The main contributions of the paper are:

- A method for generating a validator from a given specification containing schema, key and foreign key constraints.
- An unranked bottom-up tree transducer, which represents the validator, where syntactic and semantic aspects are well separated.
- An incremental schema, key and foreign key validation method.

* Supported by CAPES (Brazil) BEX0706/02-7
** This work was done while the author was on leave at Université François Rabelais. Supported by CAPES (Brazil) BEX1851/02-0.

Z. Bellahsène et al. (Eds.): XSym 2004, LNCS 3186, pp. 112–127, 2004.

- An index tree that allows incremental updates on XML document. This key index can also be used for efficiently evaluate queries.

This paper is organized as follows: section 2 gives an overview of the incremental constraint checking framework. Section 3 presents our method to build a tree transducer from a given specification containing a DTD and a set of keys and foreign keys. We also show how the transducer is used to efficiently verify all the imposed constraints. Section 4 shows how incremental validation is performed on updates. Section 5 concludes and describes our future research directions.

2   General Overview

An XML document is a structure $\mathcal{T}$ composed by an unranked labeled tree t and functions *type* and *value*. Tree t is a mapping $t : dom(t) \rightarrow \Sigma$ where $dom(t)$, called the set of t's positions, is a set of finite strings of positive integers closed under prefixes (see Fig. 1). We write $t(p) = a$ for $p \in dom(t)$ to indicate that the symbol a is the label in Σ associated with the node at position p. The function $type(t, p)$ indicates the type (*element*, *attribute* or *data*) of the node at position p. The function $value(t, p)$ gives the value associated with a data node.

Fig. 1 shows part of the labeled tree representing the document used in our examples. It describes menus and combinations in some French restaurants. Differently from the *à la carte* style, a combination is a grouping of dishes and drinks, reducing both the choice and the price for clients. Each node in the tree has a position and a label. Elements and attributes associated with arbitrary text have a child labeled *data*. In Fig. 1 attribute labels are depicted with a preceding @.

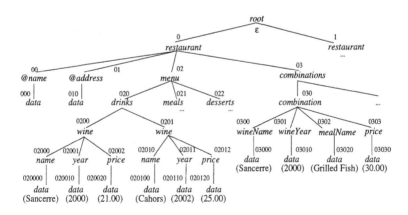

Fig. 1. Labeled tree t of an XML document

Definition 1. Key and foreign key syntax [8]: A key is represented by $(P, (P', \{P^1, \ldots, P^m\}))$. A foreign key is represented by $(P_0, (P'_0, \{P_0^1, \ldots, P_0^m\})) \subseteq K$ where $K = (P, (P', \{P^1, \ldots, P^m\}))$ is a key such that $P = P_0$. In a key, path P is called the *context path*; P' the *target path* and $P^1, \ldots, P^m$ the *key paths*. The same applies for a foreign key, except for $P_0^1, \ldots, P_0^m$ that are called *foreign key paths*.   □

All the paths in the definition above use only the child axes. Context and target paths should reach element nodes. Key (or foreign key) paths are required to end at a node associated to a value, *i.e.*, attribute nodes or elements having just one child of type *data*. The next example gives the intuition of the semantics of key and foreign key constraints over the document of Fig. 1.

Example 1. Let $K_1 = (/restaurant,(./menu/drinks/wine, \{./name, ./year\}))$ be a key constraint indicating that, in the context of a restaurant, a wine (the target node) can be uniquely identified by its name and its year. Let $FK_2 = (/restaurant, (./combina-tions/combination, \{./wineName, ./wineYear\})) \subseteq K_1$ be a foreign key constraint indicating that, for each restaurant, a combination is composed by a wine that should appear in the menu of the restaurant.   □

Definition 2. Key and foreign key semantics: An XML tree $\mathcal{T}$ satisfies a key $(P, (P', \{P^1, \ldots, P^m\}))$ if for each context position p defined by P the following two conditions hold: (i) For each target position p' reachable from p via P' there exists a unique position p_h from p', for each $P^h(1 \leq h \leq m)$. (ii) For any target positions p' and p'', reachable from p via P', whenever the values reached from p' and p'' via $P^h(1 \leq h \leq m)$ are equal, then p' and p'' must be the same position. Similarly, an XML tree $\mathcal{T}$ satisfies a foreign key $(P_0, (P_0', \{P_0^1, \ldots, P_0^m\})) \subseteq K$ if: (i) it satisfies its associated key K and (ii) each tuple τ of values, built following paths $P_0/P_0'/P_0^1, \ldots, P_0/ P_0'/P_0^m$ (in this order), can also be obtained by following the paths $P/P'/P^1, \ldots, P/P'/P^m$ (in this order).   □

In the following, we assume an XML tree $\mathcal{T}$ and a set of schema and integrity constraints $\mathcal{D}$ and we survey (i) the validation of $\mathcal{T}$ from scratch which is performed in only one pass on the XML tree and (ii) the incremental validation of updates over $\mathcal{T}$.

2.1 Validation from Scratch

Our method consists in building a tree transducer capable of expressing all the constraints of a given specification $\mathcal{D}$. The tree transducer is composed by a bottom-up tree automata (to verify the syntactic restrictions) and a set of actions defined for each key and foreign key. These actions manipulate values and are used to verify the semantic aspects of constraints. The execution of the tree transducer consists in visiting the tree in a bottom-up manner[1], performing, at each node:

A) *The verification of schema constraints.* Schema constraints are satisfied if all positions of a tree t can be associated to a state and if the root is bound to a final state (defined by the specification). A state q is assigned to a position p if the children of p in t verify the element and attribute constraints established by the specification. Roughly, a schema constraint establishes, for a position labeled a, the type, the number and (for the sub-elements) the order of p's children. We assume that the XML document in Fig. 1 is valid wrt schema constraints (see [5] for details).

---

[1] Notice that it is very easy to perform a bottom-up visit even using SAX [14](with a stack).

B) *The verification of key and foreign key constraints.* In order to validate key and foreign key constraints we need to manipulate data values. To this end, we define the values to be carried up from children to parents in an XML tree. The following example illustrates how the transducer treats values being carried up for each node. This treatment depends on the role of the node's label in the key or foreign key.

Example 2. We assume a tree transducer obtained from specification $\mathcal{D}$ (containing a given DTD together with K_1, FK_2 of Example 1) and we analyze its execution over $\mathcal{T}$ (Fig. 1):

1. The tree transducer computes the values associated to all nodes labeled *data*. We consider $value(020000) = value(03000) = Sancerre$ and $value(020010) = value(03001) = 2000$ as some of the values computed in this step.
2. The tree transducer analyzes the parents of the *data* nodes. If they are key or foreign key nodes, they receive the values computed in step 1. Otherwise, no value is carried up. In our case, the value *Sancerre* is passed to key node 02000 and to foreign key node 0300. The value 2000 is passed to key node 02001 and to foreign key node 0301.
3. The tree transducer passes the values from children to parent until it finds a target node. At this level the values for each key or foreign key are grouped in a list. Node 0200 is target for K_1, and as the key is composed by two items, the list contains the tuple value ⟨*Sancerre*, 2000⟩. Similarly, node 030 (target node for FK_2) is associated to ⟨*Sancerre*, 2000⟩.
4. The transducer carries up the lists of values obtained in step 3 until finding a context node. At a context node of a key, the transducer tests if all the lists are distinct, returning a boolean value. Similarly, at a context of a foreign key, the transducer tests if all the tuples exist as values of the referenced key. In our case, *restaurant* is the context node for both K_1 and FK_2. As context node for K_1, it receives several lists, each containing a tuple with the wine name and year. The test verifies the uniqueness of those tuples. As context node for FK_2, it receives several lists, each containing a tuple with the name and year of a wine of a combination. The test verifies if each tuple is also a tuple for key K_1. For instance, ⟨*Sancerre*, 2000⟩ that represents a wine in a combination, appears as a wine in the menu of the restaurant.
5. The boolean values computed in step 4 are carried up to the root. K_1 and FK_2 are satisfied if the conjunction of the boolean values results in *true*.   □

Notice that, at each context node, key and foreign key constraints are verified by respecting a specific order: only after testing all key constraints, the transducer verifies foreign key constraints (wrt key values already tested). We recall that the context path of a foreign key must be the same as the context path of its corresponding key.

2.2 Incremental Validation of Updates

Let us now consider updates over valid XML trees. To this end, we suppose that:

– Updates are seen as changes to be performed on the XML tree $\mathcal{T}$.

– Only updates that preserve the validity of the document (with respect to schema, key and foreign key constraints) are accepted. If the update violates a constraint, then it is rejected and the XML document remains unchanged.
– The acceptance of an update relies on *incremental validation* tests, *i.e.*, only the validity of the part of the original document directly affected by the update is checked.

We focus on two kinds of update operations. The insertion of a subtree $\mathcal{T}'$ at position p of $\mathcal{T}$ and the deletion of the subtree rooted at p in $\mathcal{T}$. To verify if an update should be accepted, we perform incremental tests, summarized as follows:

1. *Schema constraints:* We consider the run of the tree transducer on the subtree of $\mathcal{T}$ composed just by the updated position p, its siblings and their father. If the state assigned to p's father does not change due to the update, *i.e.*, the tree transducer maintains the state assignment to p's father as it was before the update, then schema constraints are not violated (see [5] for details).

2. *Key and foreign key constraints:* To facilitate the validation of keys and foreign keys for an update operation, we keep an index tree of those tuples in $\mathcal{T}$ defined by each key. For each key tuple a reference counter is used in order to know how many times the tuple is used as a foreign key.

   The verification of key and foreign key constraints changes according to the update operation being performed. Firstly we have to find (for each key and foreign key) the corresponding context node p', concerned by the insertion or the deletion. Then, in order to insert a subtree $\mathcal{T}'$ at position p of $\mathcal{T}$ we should perform the following tests: (i) verify whether $\mathcal{T}'$ does not contain duplicate key values for context p', (ii) verify whether $\mathcal{T}'$ does not contain key values already appearing in $\mathcal{T}$ for context p', (iii) verify whether $\mathcal{T}'$ does not contain foreign key values not appearing nor in $\mathcal{T}'$ neither in $\mathcal{T}$ for context p' and (iv) for each key tuple in context p' being referenced by a foreign key in $\mathcal{T}'$, increase its reference counter.

   Similarly, to delete a subtree $\mathcal{T}'$, rooted at position p, from an XML tree $\mathcal{T}$ we should perform the following tests, for each context p': (i) verify if $\mathcal{T}'$ contains only key values that are not referenced by foreign keys (not being deleted) and (ii) for each key tuple in context p' being referenced by a foreign key in $\mathcal{T}'$, decrease its reference counter.

The acceptance of an update over an XML tree $\mathcal{T}$ wrt keys and foreign keys requires information about key values in $\mathcal{T}$. Given an XML tree $\mathcal{T}$, the tree transducer is used once to verify its validity (from scratch). During this first execution of the tree transducer an index tree, called *keyTree*, is built for each key constraint K that should be respected by $\mathcal{T}$. Each *keyTree*$_K$ is a tree structure that stores the position of each context and target node together with the values associated to each key node in $\mathcal{T}$. Fig. 2 describes this index structure using the notation of DTDs and Fig. 3 shows a *keyTree* for key K_1 of Example 1. The next example illustrates the validation of updates.

Example 3. Given the XML tree of Fig. 1, we show its incremental verification due to the insertion of a new wine in the menu of a restaurant (*i.e.*, the insertion of a labeled tree t' at position $p = 0200$ of t). Moreover, we consider a specification stating that a position p labeled *drinks* should respect the following schema constraint: the concatenation of

```
<!DOCTYPE keyTree[
<!ELEMENT keyTree (context*)>
<!ATTLIST keyTree nameKey CDATA #REQUIRED>
<!ELEMENT context (target+)>
<!ATTLIST context pos CDATA #REQUIRED>
<!ELEMENT target (key+)>
<!ATTLIST target pos CDATA #REQUIRED refCount CDATA #REQUIRED>
<!ELEMENT key #PCDATA>]
```

Fig. 2. DTD specifying structure *keyTree*

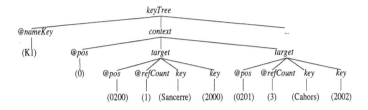

Fig. 3. *KeyTree*$_{K_1}$ built over the document of Fig. 1

the labels associated with p's children composes a word that corresponds to the regular expression $q_{wine}{}^*$.

The verification of the update with respect to schema constraints consists in: (i) considering that the update is performed (without performing it yet) and (ii) verifying if the state q_{drinks} can still be associated with position 020 (0200's father) by analyzing the schema constraint imposed over nodes labeled *drinks*. To this end, we build the sequence of states associated with 020's children. The insertion consists of shifting to the right the right siblings of p. Thus, we consider state q_{wine} associated to positions 0201 and 0202 and we only calculate the state associated with the update position 0200. As the root of t' (at position 0200) is associated to the state q_{wine}, we obtain the word $q_{wine}\, q_{wine}\, q_{wine}$. This word matches the regular expression $q_{wine}{}^*$. Thus, the update respects the schema constraints [5].

Now we verify whether K_1 and FK_2 (Example 1) are preserved by the insertion. As the inserted subtree contains only one key value, it contains no key violation by itself (no duplicate of key values). Then we assume that the update is performed (without performing it yet) and we verify whether the key value being inserted is not in contradiction with those already existing in the original document. In our case, we suppose that the wine being inserted is identified by the key tuple ⟨*Bordeaux*, 1990⟩. Comparing this value to those stored in the *keyTree*$_{K_1}$ (Fig. 3), we notice that no violation exists. The inserted subtree does not contain foreign key values and, thus, we can conclude that the update is possible with respect to key and foreign key constraints.

As the above tests succeed, the insertion can be performed. The performance of an update implies changes not only on the XML tree but also on index trees *keyTrees*.   □

3   Tree Transducers for XML

We first present the definition of our tree transducer. This transducer combines a tree automaton (expressing schema constraints) with a set of output functions (defining key and foreign key constraints). In this paper we disregard the specificity or attributes.

Definition 3. Output function: Let $\mathbf{D}$ be an infinite (recursively enumerable) domain and let $\mathbf{D}^*$ denote the set of all lists of items in $\mathbf{D}$. Let $\mathcal{T} = (t, type, value)$ be an XML tree. An *output function* f takes as arguments: (i) a tree position $p \in dom(t)$ and (ii) a list l of items in $\mathbf{D}$. The result of applying $f(p, l)$ is a list of items in $\mathbf{D}$. In other words, $f : dom(t) \times \mathbf{D}^* \to \mathbf{D}^*$. □

We recall the process described in Example 2: at each node, data values are collected from children nodes and can be used to perform tests. Output functions are defined to perform these actions: for the node at position p, each output function takes as parameters the list l of values coming from p's children. One output function is defined for each key and foreign key.

Definition 4. Unranked bottom-up tree transducer (UTT): A UTT over Σ and $\mathbf{D}$ is a tuple $\mathcal{U} = (Q, \Sigma, \mathbf{D}, Q_f, \Delta, \Gamma)$ where Q is a set of states, $Q_f \subseteq Q$ is a set of final states, Δ is a set of transition rules and $\Gamma = \{f_1, ..., f_n\}$ is a set of output functions.

Each transition rule in Δ has the form $a, E \to q$ where (i) $a \in \Sigma$; (ii) E is a regular expression over Q and (iii) $q \in Q$. Each output function in Γ has the form $f_j(p, l) = l'$ as in Definition 3. □

Key and foreign key constraints are expressed by output functions in Γ. As the tree is to be processed bottom-up, the basic task of output functions is to define the values that have to be passed to the parent position, during the run.

3.1   Generating Constraint Validators

Given a specification $\mathcal{D} = (D, \mathbf{K})$ where D is a set of schema constraints and $\mathbf{K}$ is composed by a set of keys and foreign keys, we propose a method to translate $\mathcal{D}$ into a UTT. In this sense, we present an algorithm to generate a validator from a given specification. This validator is executed to check the constraints in $\mathcal{D}$ for any XML tree.

Let $\mathcal{U} = (Q, \Sigma, \mathbf{D}, Q_f, \Delta, \Gamma)$ be a UTT whose transition rules in Δ are obtained from the translation of a DTD D (part of $\mathcal{D}$). Each output function in Γ is related to a finite state automaton that indicates which nodes play a role in keys and foreign keys. Notice that context, target and key nodes in each key K_j or foreign key FK_j are defined in a top-down fashion. In order to identify these nodes using a bottom-up tree automaton, we must traverse the paths stated by each key K_j or foreign key FK_j in reverse. If we see paths as regular expressions, then we can associate finite state automata with them. Paths in reverse are recognized by reversing all the transitions of these automata [13].

Given a key constraint K_j $(1 \leq j \leq k)$ or a foreign key constraint FK_j $(k + 1 \leq j \leq n)$, we use the following notations: for context path P_j, we have $M_j = \langle \Theta_j, \Sigma, \delta_j, e_j, F_j \rangle$; for target path P'_j, $M'_j = \langle \Theta'_j, \Sigma, \delta'_j, e'_j, F'_j \rangle$; for key or foreign key paths $P_j^1 \mid ... \mid P_j^{m_j}$, $M''_j = \langle \Theta''_j, \Sigma, \delta''_j, e''_j, F''_j \rangle$. For the sake of homogeneity, we define $M_F = \langle \{e_0, e_f\}, \{root\}, \{\delta(e_0, root, e_f)\}, e_0, \{e_f\} \rangle$ as the finite state automaton recognizing the path formed just by the symbol *root*. Fig. 4 illustrates the finite state automata that recognize the paths in K_1 and FK_2 of Example 1 in reverse.

Remark: We denote by $M.e$ the current state e of the finite state automaton M, and we call it a *configuration*.

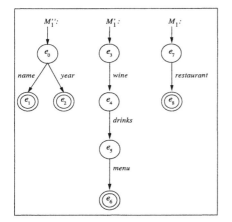 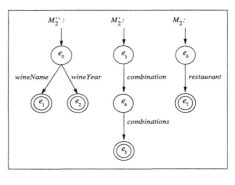

Fig. 4. Automata corresponding to the paths of K_1 and FK_2 in reverse

Algorithm 1 - Key constraints as output functions:

Input: A set of k keys $\{K_j = (P_j, (P_j', \{P_j^1, ..., P_j^{m_j}\})) \mid 1 \leq j \leq k\}$, a set of $(n-k)$ foreign keys $\{FK_j = (P_j, (P_j', \{P_j^1, ..., P_j^{m_j}\})) \subseteq K \mid (k+1) \leq j \leq n; K \text{ is a key }\}$

Output: A set of output functions $\Gamma = \{f_1, ..., f_n\}$.

begin
    $\Gamma = \emptyset$
    for each K_j and FK_j do
        Build the finite automata M_j, M_j' and M_j''
        Use M_j, M_j' and M_j'' to specify the function f_j
        $\Gamma = \Gamma \cup \{f_j\}$
    return Γ
end

Each output function $f_j \in \Gamma$ is specified by the algorithm below:

Algorithm 1.1 - Specification of output functions

Input: Automata concerning a key K or a foreign key FK.

A position p and a list l of pairs in **D**. For each pair, the first element is an automaton configuration and the second element is a list of values.

Output: A list of pairs in **D**.

begin
  Let $a := t(p)$ //a is the label of position p
  (1) If $a = data$ then return $[(M''.e'', [value(t,p)])]$
  (2) If a is a target label for K or FK
      then return $[(M'.\delta'(e',a), checkArity(concat(filter_{key}(l))))]$

Function $filter_{key}$ leaves in the key lists only the values associated to key positions of K (or FK). For that purpose, it selects the singletons whose configuration corresponds to a final state of M'. Function $concat$ returns the concatenation of all its argument lists into one list. If the length of the resulting list does not correspond to the length m of K, then function $checkArity$ replaces it by an empty list. For foreign keys the length is not tested.

(3) If a is a context label for a key K

then return $[(M.\delta(e, a), checkKey(filter_{target}(l)))]$

where $checkKey([v_1 \ldots v_m]) = \begin{cases} [true] & \text{if } v_1 \ldots v_m \text{ are all nonempty distinct lists.} \\ [false] & \text{otherwise.} \end{cases}$

(4) If a is a context label for a foreign key FK

then return $[(M.\delta(e, a), checkForeign(filter_{target}(l)))]$

where $checkForeign([v_1 \ldots v_m]) = \begin{cases} [true] & \text{if } v_1 \ldots v_m \text{ are lists whose values appear} \\ & \text{in the key taking part in the} \\ & \text{definition of } FK. \\ [false] & \text{otherwise.} \end{cases}$

Remark: In cases (3) and (4) above, function $filter_{target}$ rejects all the values not belonging to target lists of key K (or foreign key FK), *i.e.*, those whose configuration does not correspond to the final state of M'.

(5) If a is the root label then return $[(M_F.e_f, concat(filter_{context}(l)))]$

Function $filter_{context}$ rejects all the values not belonging to context lists (configuration different from the final state of M).

(6) In all other cases

(*i.e.*, when $a \neq data$ and a is not a target label, nor a context label, nor the root)

return $carryUp(l)$

where function $carryUp$ is defined as follows:

```
function carryUp (L : list of pairs)
var result : list of pairs
begin
result ← [ ]
for each c = (M.e, v) in L //* M stands for M, M' or M''
    if δ(e, a) = e' is a transition in M then result ← concat(result, [(M.e', v)])
return result
end
```

end   □

In cases (1) to (5) the resulting list contains only one pair. A pair is always composed by:

(A) A configuration $M.e$ where M is one of the finite automata representing paths in keys, and e is a state of M. For example, in case (2), M is M', the target automaton for K or FK. This configuration is obtained by performing the first transition at automaton M', using the symbol a as input. Notice that $\delta'(e', a)$ is a state of M'. Other cases are similar.

(B) A list of values. From data nodes to target nodes the list contains only one value. From target nodes to context nodes the list contains the values composing a key (or foreign key). From context nodes to the root the list contains one boolean value indicating that within a given context, K or FK holds or not.

Notice that for foreign key context level (case (4)), FK and its associated key have the same context and the tuples representing the key are computed before those that represent foreign key FK (since $K_j (1 \le j \le k)$ and $FK_j (k + 1 \le j \le n)$). Once computed, key tuples are stored in *keyTrees*, then foreign key tuples can be checked (as shown in the next section). At root level (case (5)), we have the boolean values that were obtained for each subtree rooted at the context level. In case 6, values are carried up by function *carryUp*. This function selects pairs from children nodes belonging to key and foreign key paths, by checking configurations in these pairs. The resulting list can contain more than one pair. If nodes are not concerned by any key or foreign key, the function *carryUp* does not transmit any value.

3.2 Validating XML Documents

The verification of keys and foreign keys are performed simultaneously, in one pass, together with schema validation, during the execution of the UTT over an XML tree. Example 4 illustrates such an execution while Definitions 5 and 6 formalize it. The index *keyTree*, necessary to perform incremental updates on XML documents, is dynamically built. Similarly to the one proposed in [9], it is a tree structure containing levels for the key name, context, target, key and data nodes as defined in Fig. 2.

Example 4. We consider a specification $\mathcal{D}$ containing K_1 and FK_2 (Example 1). The finite state automata associated to K_1 and FK_2 are the ones given in Fig. 4. To verify if the XML tree $\mathcal{T}$ of Fig. 1 satisfies K_1 and FK_2 we run the transducer $\mathcal{U}$ (from $\mathcal{D}$) over $\mathcal{T}$ (recall that $\mathcal{U}$ contains two output functions f_1 and f_2 defined from K_1 and FK_2 (respectively), following Algorithm 1):

1. For the data nodes, each output function returns a singleton list that contains a pair: the initial configuration of the key (or foreign key) automaton M'', and the value of the node. Positions 020000 and 03000 are data nodes, then we have:
   $$f_1(020000, [\,]) = [(M_1''.e_0, [Sancerre])]; \quad f_2(03000, [\,]) = [(M_2''.e_0, [Sancerre])].$$

2. The fathers of data nodes which are key (or foreign key) nodes should carry up the values received from their children. Thus, each of them executes a first transition in M'' using each key (or foreign key) label as input. For each father of a data node which is not a key (or a foreign key) node, the output function returns an empty list. For instance, position 02000 is a key node for K_1 and position 0300 is a foreign key node for FK_2. Then, reading the label *name* from state e_0 of M_1'', we reach state e_1, and we carry up the value *Sancerre*. We obtain a similar result for FK_2 when reading label *wineName*: $f_1(02000, [(M_1''.e_0, [Sancerre])]) = [(M_1''.e_1, [Sancerre])];$
   $f_2(0300, [(M_2''.e_0, [Sancerre])]) = [(M_2''.e_1, [Sancerre])].$
   At this stage the construction of *keyTree*$_{K_1}$ starts by taking into account the information associated to each key node (e.g., *keyTree*$_{K_1}[t, 02000]$ is the subtree rooted at *key* and associated with the value *Sancerre* in Fig. 3).
3. For node 0200, *wine* is a target label of K_1 and for node 030, *combination* is a target label of FK_2. In order to transmit only key (or foreign key) values, the output function of a target label (i) selects those that are preceded by a final state of the key automaton M'', (ii) joins them in a new list, and (iii) executes the first transition

of the target automaton M'. In this way, at a target position the tuple value of a key (or foreign key) is built:

$$f_1(0200, [(M_1''.e_1, [Sancerre]), (M_1''.e_2, [2000])]) = [(M_1'.e_4, [Sancerre, 2000])];$$
$$f_2(030, [(M_2''.e_1, [Sancerre]), (M_2''.e_2, [2000])]) = [(M_2'.e_4, [Sancerre, 2000])].$$

The construction of $keyTree_{K_1}$ continues and $keyTree_{K_1}[t, 0200]$ is obtained taking into account the information available at position 0200. (See subtree rooted at *target* in Fig. 3).

4. The computation continues up to the context, verifying whether the labels visited are recognized by the target automaton or not and carrying up the key (or foreign key) values. For instance, we reach state e_5 in M_1' by reading the label "*drinks*" (Fig. 4):

$$f_1(020, [(M_1'.e_4, [Sancerre, 2000])]) = [(M_1'.e_5, [Sancerre, 2000])];$$

5. For the node 0, the label *restaurant* is a context label of both K_1 and FK_2. For K_1 (respectively FK_2) the output function selects the sublists associated to a final state of the target automaton M_1' (respectively M_2'). The output function of K_1 checks if all the selected sublists are distinct. The output function of FK_2 verifies if the selected sublists correspond to lists of values obtained for K_1. In both cases, the output functions return a boolean value that will be carried up to the root:

$$f_1(0, [(M_1'.e_6, [Sancerre, 2000]), (M_1'.e_6, [Cahors, 2002])]) = [(M_1.e_8, [true])];$$
$$f_2(0, [(M_2'.e_5, [Sancerre, 2000])]) = [(M_2.e_7, [true])].$$

At this point, we have $keyTree_{K_1}[t, 0]$ represented by the subtree rooted at *context* in Fig. 3. Notice that the attribute refCount for tuple $\langle Sancerre, 2000 \rangle$ has value 1 because at this context node, the tuple $\langle Sancerre, 2000 \rangle$ exists for foreign key FK_2. Indeed, at the context level we increment the refCount of each key tuple that corresponds to a foreign key tuple obtained at this level. Supposing that the tuple $\langle Cahors, 2002 \rangle$ appears in three different combinations (not presented in Fig. 1), we would have refCount= 3 for it.

6. At the root position the last output function selects the sublists that are preceded by a final state of the context automaton M and returns all boolean values in these sublists. The construction of $keyTree_{K_1}$ finishes by a label indicating the name of the key (Fig. 3).   □

Definition 5. A run of $\mathcal{U}$ on a finite tree t: Let t be a Σ-valued tree and $\mathcal{U} = (Q, \Sigma, \mathbf{D}, Q_f, \Delta, \Gamma)$ be a UTT. Given the keys $K_1, \ldots, K_k$ and foreign keys FK_{k+1}, $\ldots, FK_n$ a **run** of $\mathcal{U}$ on t is: *(i)* a tree $r : dom(r) \to Q$ such that $dom(r) = dom(t)$; *(ii)* a function $\$: dom(r) \to (\mathbf{D}^*)^n$ and *(iii)* k $keyTrees$.

For each position p whose children are those at positions[2] $p0, \ldots, p(z-1)$ (with $z \geq 0$), we have:

(i) $r(p) = q$ if the following conditions hold:
   1. $t(p) = a \in \Sigma$.
   2. There exists a transition $a, E \to q$ in Δ.
   3. $r(p0) = q_0, \ldots, r(p(z-1)) = q_{z-1}$.

---

[2] The notation $p(z-1)$ indicates the position resulting from the concatenation of the position p and the integer $z-1$. If $z = 0$ the position p has no children.

4. The word $q_0 \ldots q_{z-1}$ belongs to the language generated by E.

(ii) $\$(p) = l = \langle f_1(p, concat(l_0^1, \ldots, l_{z-1}^1)), \ldots, f_n(p, concat(l_0^n, \ldots, l_{z-1}^n)) \rangle$ with $\$(p0) = l_0, \ldots, \$(p(z-1)) = l_{z-1}$ where each $l_i = \langle l_i^1, \ldots, l_i^n \rangle$ is a n-tuple.

(iii) for $(1 \leq j \leq k)$, $keyTree_{K_j}[t, p]$ is constructed using the already computed $keyTree_{K_j}[t, p0], \ldots, keyTree_{K_j}[t, p(z-1)]$, as follows:

(a) If $t(p)$ is a key label of K_j, then $keyTree_{K_j}[t, p]$ is the tree:
```
<key> t(p) = value(t, p0)</key>
```

(b) If $t(p)$ is a target label of K_j, then $keyTree_{K_j}[t, p]$ is:
```
<target pos=p refCount=0> keyTreeK_j[t, p0] ... keyTreeK_j[t, p(z-1)]
</target>
```

(c) If $t(p)$ is a context label of K_j, then $keyTree_{K_j}[t, p]$ is:
```
<context pos=p> keyTreeK_j[t, p0] ... keyTreeK_j[t, p(z-1)] </context>
```
Moreover, if $t(p)$ is a context label of a foreign key FK, then increment the attribute refCount in the corresponding $keyTree_{K_j}$.

(d) If $t(p)$ is the root label then $keyTree_{K_j}[t, p]$ is the tree:
```
<keyTree nameKey=K_j> keyTreeK_j[t, p0] ... keyTreeK_j[t, p(z-1)] </keyTree>
```

(e) In all other cases, for each key K_j, we define $keyTree_{K_j}[t, p]$ as the forest composed by all the trees $keyTree_{K_j}[t, p0] \ldots keyTree_{K_j}[t, p(z-1)]$.

Notice that, although the *keyTrees* are defined in general as forests, for the special labels mentioned in cases (a) to (d) above, we build a single tree. □

Definition 6. Validity: An XML tree t is said to be valid with respect to schema constraints if there is a successful run r, *i.e.*, $r(\epsilon) \in Q_f$. An XML tree t is said to be valid with respect to key and foreign key constraints if the lists of $\$(\epsilon)$ contain only the value *true* for each key and foreign key. □

Remark that item (ii) of Definition 5 specifies that the output for each position p in the XML tree is a tuple composed by one list for each key (or foreign key) being verified. Each list l_j in the tuple is the result of applying the output function f_j, defined for the jth key or foreign key, over the following arguments:

– p: the position in $dom(t)$.
– $concat(l_0^j, \ldots, l_{z-1}^j)$: the list formed by the information carried up from the children of p, concerning the jth key.

At the end of the run over an XML tree, each key K_j is associated to a *keyTree* K_j that respects the general schema given by Fig. 2. Attribute pos stores the target and context positions for a given key and attribute refCount indicates when a key K_j is referenced by a foreign key.

4   Incremental Validation of Updates

We consider two update operations, denoted by $insert(\mathcal{T}, p, \mathcal{T}')$ and $delete(p, \mathcal{T})$, where $\mathcal{T}$ and $\mathcal{T}'$ are XML trees and p is a position. Fig. 5 illustrates these operations on a Σ-valued tree. Only updates that preserve validity wrt the constraints are accepted.

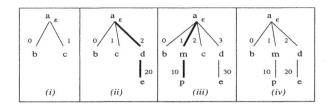

Fig. 5. (i) Initial Σ-valued tree t having labels a (position ϵ), b (position 0) and c (position 1). (ii) Insertion at $p = 2$. (iii) Insertion at $p = 1$. (iv) Deletion at $p = 2$.

4.1   Incremental Key and Foreign Key Validation

Let $\mathcal{T} = (t, type, value)$ be a valid XML tree, *i.e.*, one satisfying a collection of keys K_j $(1 \leq j \leq k)$ and foreign keys FK_j $((k+1) \leq j \leq n)$. Let $\mathcal{U} = (Q, \Sigma, \mathbf{D}, Q_f, \Delta, \Gamma)$ be a UTT specifying all the constraints that should be respected by $\mathcal{T}$. We should consider the execution of $\mathcal{U}$ over a subtree $\mathcal{T}'$ being inserted or deleted.

Given a subtree $\mathcal{T}' = (t', type, value)$, the execution of $\mathcal{U}$ over $\mathcal{T}'$ gives a tuple:

$$\langle q', \langle l_1, \ldots, l_n \rangle, \langle keyTree_{K_1}[t', \epsilon], \ldots, keyTree_{K_k}[t', \epsilon] \rangle \rangle \tag{1}$$

where q' is the state associated to the root of t', $\langle l_1, \ldots, l_n \rangle$ is a n-tuple of lists and $\langle keyTree_{K_1}[t', \epsilon], \ldots, keyTree_{K_k}[t', \epsilon] \rangle$ is a k-tuple containing the *keyTree* for each key. Notice that the n-tuple of lists has two distinct parts. Lists $l_1, \ldots, l_k$ represent keys and lists $l_{k+1}, \ldots, l_n$ represent foreign keys. Each l_j $(1 \leq j \leq n)$ is a list of pairs, *i.e.*, each l_j has the form $[c_1, \ldots, c_m]$ where each c_h is a pair containing an automaton configuration and a list of values.

When performing an insertion, we want to ensure that $\mathcal{T}'$ has no "internal" validity problems (as, for instance, duplicated values for K_j). Thus, we define $\mathcal{T}'$ as *locally valid* if the tuple (1) respects the following conditions: (A) q' is a state in Q; (B) for each list l_j $(1 \leq j \leq k)$ we have:

(i)   if the root of t' is a target position for K_j then the number of values in l_j equals the number of elements composing the key K_j;

(ii)   if the root of t' is a context position for K_j then the list l_j is $[(M_j.e, [true])]$;

(iii)   if the root of t' is a position above the context positions for K_j then the list l_j is $[c_1, \ldots, c_m]$, where each pair c_h does not contain $[false]$ as its list of values.

Notice that no condition is imposed on foreign keys. A subtree $\mathcal{T}'$ can contain tuple values referring to a key value appearing in $\mathcal{T}$ (and not in $\mathcal{T}'$).

In the following, we assume that subtrees being inserted in a valid XML tree are locally valid and we address the problem of evaluating whether an update should be accepted with respect to key and foreign key constraints. Before accepting an update, we incrementally verify whether it does not cause any constraint violation. To perform these tests, we need the context node of a key or foreign key. To this end, we define procedure *findContext* that computes:

– The context position p' for a key K_j (or a foreign key FK_j) which is an ancestor of the update position p in the tree t.

- A list l' containing the key (or foreign key) values for that context position, considering values carried up from the subtree being inserted or deleted. [3]

The tests performed for insertion operation $insert(\mathcal{T}, p, \mathcal{T}')$ are presented next. Recall that $\mathcal{T}$ is valid and $\mathcal{T}'$ is locally valid.

Algorithm 2 - Incremental tests for update operation $insert(\mathcal{T}, p, \mathcal{T}')$

1. For each list $l_j \neq [\ ]$ $(1 \leq j \leq k)$ obtained in the execution of $\mathcal{U}$ over $\mathcal{T}'$ for each key K_j do
   a) If p is under a context node of K_j then
      i. Call $findContext(p, l_j)$, that returns a context position p' and $l' = [v_1, ..., v_r]$.
      ii. For each list v in l' do
         If there exists a tuple $kval$ in $keyTree_{K_j}[t, p']$ such that $kval = v$
         then the insertion violates K_j and must be rejected
         else the insertion respects K_j.
   b) If p is the context position or it is between the root and a context node of K_j
      then the insertion respects K_j.
2. For each $l_j \neq [\ ]$ $((k+1) \leq j \leq n)$ obtained in the execution of $\mathcal{U}$ over $\mathcal{T}'$ do
   a) Call $findContext(p, l_j)$, that returns a context position p' and $l' = [v_1, ..., v_r]$.
   b) For each list v in l' do:
      If there exists a tuple $kval$ in the $keyTree_{K_i}$ such that $kval = v$
      then the insertion respects the foreign key FK_j. The reference counter that corresponds to $kval$ will be incremented at the end of the procedure, if the insertion is accepted.
      else the insertion does not respect the foreign key FK_j and must be rejected.
3. If all keys and foreign keys, together with schema constraints [5], are respected
   then accept the update and perform the modifications to $\mathcal{T}$ and all $keyTrees$.
   else reject the update.   □

Before performing an insertion, Algorithm 2 tests if we are not adding key duplicates on $\mathcal{T}$ and if the new foreign key values correspond to key values. When we refer to a tuple in a $keyTree$, this tuple is obtained by concatenating the key values found inside target tags of this $keyTree$, taking into account a context position p'. The next example illustrates an insertion operation with respect to key and foreign key constraints.

Example 5. We consider the update $insert(\mathcal{T}, 0200, \mathcal{T}')$ presented in Example 3. The execution of $\mathcal{U}$ over $\mathcal{T}'$ gives the tuple: $\langle q_{wine}, \langle [(M_1'.e_4, [Bordeaux, 1990])], [\ ] \rangle, \langle keyTree_{K_1}[t', \epsilon] \rangle \rangle$.
We see that $\mathcal{T}'$ is locally valid and that the update affects only K_1. Procedure $findContext$ returns the context position $p' = 0$ and the list $l' = [\langle Bordeaux, 1990 \rangle]$. We compare the tuples in l' with those in $keyTree_{K_1}$ (Fig. 3) for context $p' = 0$. All these tuples are distinct and thus the insertion is possible for K_1. As no other key is affected, the insertion is accepted.   □

In a similar way, we define incremental tests for the operation $delete(p, \mathcal{T})$. These tests check if the deletion of a subtree rooted at a position p does not violate constraints, before actually removing the subtree. The details are given in [1].

---

[3] Let l_j be the list of pairs obtained for K_j or FK_j by the local validity check. Procedure *findContext* executes the automaton $\overline{M}$ (composition of M_j'' and M_j') starting from the configurations in l_j and using the labels associated to the ancestors of position p [1].

5 Conclusions

This paper extends and merges our previous proposals [5,6]. In [5], we propose an incremental validation method, but only with respect to schema constraints. In [6] we just consider the validation from scratch of an XML document associated to only one key constraint. In the current paper, we deal with incremental validation of updates taking into account schema constraints together with several key and foreign key constraints. Our verification algorithm uses only synthesized values (*i.e.*, values communicated from the children to the parents of a tree), making the algorithms suitable for implementation in any parser generator, or even using SAX [14] or DOM [19]. The algorithms presented here have been implemented using the ASF+SDF meta-environment [7]. The verification of keys and foreign keys uses *KeyTrees*, which can also be used for efficiently evaluating queries based on key values.

Validity verification methods for schema constraints have been addressed by [5,10,15, 16,17,18]. The validation of updates is also treated in [10,17]. In [17], schema constraints wrt specialized DTDs are considered and incremental validation is performed in time $O(log^2(n))$, where n is the size of the document. As shown in [5], in terms of schema constraints, our incremental validation (wrt DTDs) is $O(m+1)$, where m is the number of children of the update position.

Key constraints for XML have been recently considered in the literature (for instance, in [2,4,6,8,9]) and some of their aspects are adopted in XML Schema. In our paper, the definition of integrity constraints follows the key specification introduced in [8]. As shown in [11], it is easy to produce examples of integrity constraints that no XML document (valid wrt a schema) can verify. In our work, we assume key and foreign key constraints consistent with respect to a given DTD.

In [9] a key validator which works in asymptotic linear time in the size of the document is proposed. Our algorithm also has this property. In contrast to our work, in [3,9] schema constraints are not considered and foreign keys are not treated in details. In [4] both schema and integrity constraints are considered in the process of generating XML documents from relational databases. Although some similar aspects with our approach can be observed, we place our work in a different context. In fact, we consider the evolution of XML data independently from any other database sources (in this context both validation and re-validation of XML documents can be required).

We are currently studying the following lines of research: (i) An extension of our method to deal with other schema specification, for instance XML-Schema and specialized DTDs. (ii) An implementation of an XML update language such as UpdateX [12] in which incremental constraint checking will be integrated. To this end, we shall consider a transaction including several updates and check validity of its result.

Acknowledgements. We would like to thank the anonymous referees for their suggestions to the final version of this paper.

References

1. M. A. Abrao, B. Bouchou, M. Halfeld-Ferrari, D. Laurent, and M. A. Musicante. Update validation for XML in the presence of schema, key and foreign key constraints. Technical report, Université François Rabelais Blois-Tours-Chinon, 2004 (to appear).
2. M. Arenas, W. Fan, and L. Libkin. On verifying consistency of XML specifications. In *ACM Symposium on Principles of Database System*, 2002.
3. M. Benedikt, G. Bruns, J. Gibson, R. Kuss, and A. Ng. Automated update management for XML integrity constraints. In *Programming Language Technologies for XML (PLANX02)*, 2002.
4. M. Benedikt, C-Y Chan, W. Fan, J. Freire, and R. Rastogi. Capturing both types and constraints in data integration. In ACM Press, editor, *SIGMOD, San Diego, CA*, 2003.
5. B. Bouchou and M. Halfeld Ferrari Alves. Updates and incremental validation of XML documents. In Springer, editor, *The 9th International Workshop on Database Programming Languages (DBPL)*, number 2921 in LNCS, 2003.
6. B. Bouchou, M. Halfeld Ferrari Alves, and M. A. Musicante. Tree automata to verify key constraints. In *Web and Databases (WebDB)*, San Diego, CA, USA, June 2003.
7. M. G. J. van den Brand, J. Heering, P. Klint, and P. A. Olivier. Compiling rewrite systems: The ASF+SDF compiler. *ACM, Transactions on Programming Languages and Systems*, 24, 2002.
8. P. Buneman, S. Davidson, W. Fan, C. Hara, and W. C. Tan. Keys for XML. In *WWW10, May 2-5*, 2001.
9. Y. Chen, S. B. Davidson, and Y. Zheng. XKvalidator: a constraint validator for XML. In ACM Press, editor, *Proceedings of the 11th International Conference on Information and Knowledge Management*, pages 446–452, 2002.
10. B. Chidlovskii. Using regular tree automata as XML schemas. In *Proc. IEEE Advances in Digital Libraries Conference*, May 2000.
11. W. Fan and L. Libkin. On XML integrity constraints in the presence of DTDs. *Journal of the ACM*, 49(3):368–406, 2002.
12. G. M. Gargi, J. Hammer, and J. Simeon. An XQuery-based language for processing updates in XML. In *Programming Language Technologies for XML (PLANX04)*, 2004.
13. J. E. Hopcroft, R. Motwani, and J. D. Ullman. *Introduction to Automata Theory Languages and Computation*. Addison-Wesley Publishing Company, second edition, 2001.
14. W. S. Means and M. A. Bodie. *The Book of SAX: The Simple API for XML*. No Starch Press, 2002.
15. T. Milo, D. Suciu, and V. Vianu. Typechecking for XML transformers. In *ACM Symposium on Principles of Database System*, pages 11–22, 2000.
16. M. Murata, D. Lee, and M. Mani. Taxonomy of XML schema language using formal language theory. In *Extreme Markup Language, Montreal, Canada*, 2001.
17. Y. Papakonstantinou and V. Vianu. Incremental validation of XML documents. In *Proceedings of the International Conference on Database Theory (ICDT)*, 2003.
18. L. Segoufin and V. Vianu. Validating streaming XML documents. In *ACM Symposium on Principles of Database System*, 2002.
19. L. Wood, A. Le Hors, V. Apparao, S. Byrne, M. Champion, S. Issacs, I. Jacobs, G. Nicol, J. Robie, R. Sutor, and C. Wilson. *Document Object Model (DOM) Level 1 Specification*. W3C Recommendation, http://www.w3.org/XML, 2000.

EReX: A Conceptual Model for XML

Murali Mani

Department of Computer Science
Worcester Polytechnic Institute, USA
{mmani}@cs.wpi.edu

Abstract. In the last few years, XML has been widely used as a logical
data model, and several database applications are modeled in XML. To
model a database application in XML, we should first come up with a
conceptual design for representing the application requirements, and then
translate this conceptual design to XML. Existing conceptual models
like the ER (Entity Relationship) model, UML and ORM do not have
modeling capabilities to represent main features provided by XML, such
as union types. In this work, we extend the ER model with additional
features; we call our conceptual model as EReX (ER extended for XML).
Translating an EReX design to XML enables us to make use of the
different features provided by XML. Our approach further enables us to
study a fundamental problem facing XML database community today:
what structural and constraint specification should be provided in XML
so that any generic database application can be modeled in XML.

1 Introduction

Over the last few years, XML (eXtensible Markup Language) [5] published by
W3C has established itself as a promising logical data model, that is used widely
for database applications. There are at least two good reasons for this widespread
use of XML: (a) *necessity* - XML is the lingua franca for information exchange
over the web, therefore if we need to exchange our data with web applications, we
need to model our data in XML (b) *capability* - XML provides several favorable
features often necessary for modeling present day applications such as union
types and ordered relationships. Our work focuses on the latter aspect, and we
examine how we can use these XML features effectively for database applications.

Database design process is typically done in different stages [3]. First, during
the *conceptual design phase*, the database designer represents the application
requirements as a schema in a conceptual model. Examples of conceptual models
include ER [7], UML [16], and ORM [12]. Then in the *logical design phase*, the
conceptual schema is represented as a schema in a logical model such as relational
model [8], object-relational model or XML. There is a third phase where the
logical schema is translated to a physical schema. In this work, we describe our
conceptual model called EReX, and an algorithm to translate an EReX schema
to "good" XML schemas. We do not consider the physical schema or the database
implementation, which could be in native XML databases, relational databases,
object-relational databases etc.

Z. Bellahsène et al. (Eds.): XSym 2004, LNCS 3186, pp. 128–142, 2004.

We use our work to study a fundamental problem facing XML database community today. There are different schema languages for XML; three most popular ones are DTD [5], XML-Schema [19], and RELAX-NG [15]. Each of these schema languages have different structural and constraint specification characteristics. In [14], the authors study the structural specification characteristics of the schema languages and show the following: (a) the most expressive schema languages such as RELAX-NG are closed under different set operations such as union, intersection and difference, whereas the less expressive schema languages such as DTD and XML-Schema are closed only under intersection, (b) DTD and XML-Schema guarantee unambiguous "type assignment", whereas RELAX-NG schemas may yield ambiguous type assignment. Database applications require both unambiguous type assignment as well as closure properties. XQuery approaches this problem as [18]: *we require the XML design to specify unambiguous types, but we do not place this restriction during XML query processing.* In our work, we show that XQuery's approach is good for database applications in that any generic database application can be modeled in XML using unambiguous types.

The rest of the paper is organized as follows. In the next section, we present the EReX conceptual model; we first present the ER model, mention reasons for choosing ER model, and our extensions to the ER model. In Section 3, we study different structural and constraint specification schemes for XML, and present XGrammar, a grammar based notation for XML schema languages such as DTD, XML-Schema and RELAX-NG. In Section 4, we study how to translate an EReX schema to XGrammar, and study the characteristics of the resulting XML schemas. We conclude with interesting open research problems in Section 5.

2   EReX Conceptual Model

Entity Relationship (ER) model defined by Chen in the 1970s has been widely used as a conceptual model ever since [7]. A schema is represented in the ER model using a diagrammatic notation called ER diagram. In this section, we examine the features of ER model, and our extensions.

2.1   Basic Features of ER

In the ER model, we specify structures such as *entity types, relationship types,* and *attributes*. We denote an entity type by E_i, an entity instance (also called entity, for short) of an entity type E_i as e_{i_j}, and the set of entities of an entity type in a database instance as $I(E_i)$. Figure 1 shows an entity type *Student*; $I(Student) = \{s1, s2, s3\}$. A relationship type is denoted as R_i, and it represents an association between entity types. We denote a relationship instance (also called relationship) of relationship type R_i as r_{i_j}, and the set of relationships in a database instance as $I(R_i)$. Consider a relationship type R_i between entity types $E_1, E_2, \ldots, E_n$. $I(R_i)$ defines a n-ary relation between the sets $I(E_1)$, $I(E_2), \ldots, I(E_n)$. A relationship $r \in I(R_i)$ that associates entities $e_1 \in I(E_1)$,

$e_2 \in I(E_2)$, ..., $e_n \in I(E_n)$ is also represented as $(e_1, e_2, \dots, e_n)$. Figure 1 shows a binary relationship type $AdvisedBy$ between entity types $Student$ and $Professor$. Figure 1 (c) shows $I(AdvisedBy) = \{r1, r2\}$. See that $r1 = (s1, p1)$, and $r2 = (s2, p1)$.

An entity type or a relationship type may also define attributes. Consider an attribute A of an entity type E (or relationship type R). A maps values of $I(E)$ (or $I(R)$) to "values" of A. In Figure 1, entity type $Student$ defines two attributes $snumber$ and $sname$; $snumber$ maps $s1 \to 1$, $s2 \to 2$, $s3 \to 3$; attribute $sname$ maps $s1 \to Dave$, and $s3 \to Greg$; note that $sname$ does not map $s2$ to any value. Also relationship type $AdvisedBy$ defines an attribute $project$.

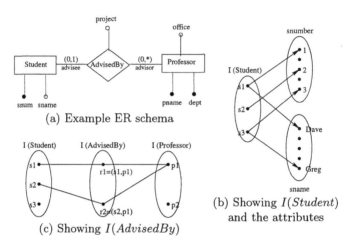

(a) Example ER schema

(c) Showing $I(AdvisedBy)$

(b) Showing $I(Student)$ and the attributes

Fig. 1. Example ER schema and a corresponding database instance fragment.

We focus on two kinds of constraints that can be specified in the ER model: *key constraints* and *cardinality constraints*. Key constraints are specified for an entity type; we say the key for an entity type E_i is its attribute A_{i_j}, if for any database instance, A_{i_j} is a one-to-one function from $I(E_i)$ to values of A_{i_j}. The key for an entity type may be composite (that is, multiple attributes). The key for an entity type E_k is the attributes $(A_{k_1}, A_{k_2}, \dots, A_{k_m})$, if for any database instance, we have a one-to-one function from $I(E_k)$ to the values in $A_{k_1} \times A_{k_2} \times \dots \times A_{k_m}$. In Figure 1 (a), we define the key for $Student$ is $(snumber)$, and the key for $Professor$ is $(pname, dept)$.

Cardinality constraints are specified for each entity type in a relationship type. We say that the cardinality constraints for an entity type E in a relationship type R is (min, max), if for any database instance, any $e \in I(E)$ must appear in at least min instances of $I(R)$, and no $e \in I(E)$ appears in more than max instances of $I(R)$. We denote unbounded cardinality by $*$. Based on the cardinality constraints, binary relationship types can be called $1:1$, $1:n$, or $m:n$ [3].

ER also has the notion of *roles*. An entity type E in a relationship type R can be said to play a *role*, denoted l. For a database instance, we define $I(l) \subseteq I(E)$ as the set of entities that appear in R in the role l. In Figure 1, *Student* plays the role of *advisee*, and *Professor* the role of *advisor* in *AdvisedBy*; $I(advisee) = \{s1, s2\}$, and $I(advisor) = \{p1\}$.

2.2 ER Model as Basis for Studying XML Requirements

There are several good reasons for studying structural and constraint specifications requirements for XML based on the ER model. First, the ER model has always been considered a representative of real world database applications. Because of this, algorithms to translate an ER schema to schemas in different logical models have been studied extensively. A simple algorithm to translate an ER schema to relational schema as given in [11] yields the relations shown in Table 1.

Table 1. Relational Instance corresponding to the ER schema in Figure 1

Student

snumber	sname
1	Dave
2	null
3	Greg

Professor

pname	dept	office
John	CS	140 FL
Dave	Math	230 FL

AdvisedBy

snumber	pname	dept	project
1	John	CS	DB1
2	John	CS	DB2

The above relational instance also shows that the ER model gives a clear interpretation of some basic concepts in database design such as nulls, compared to other models such as relational model. Another important concept in database design is normalization. Normalization can also be explained using ER model [7] as: if we assume any functional dependency $A \rightarrow B$ implies that there is an entity type with A as the key and attribute(s) B, then a "correct" ER schema and a "correct" translation algorithm will generate a relational schema guaranteed to have no redundancy (or according to [2] the entropy of any position in any instance is non-zero). In short, the resulting relational schema is in BCNF.

There has been previous work to study XML requirements from other models. In [13], the authors study in detail how a relational schema can be translated to an XML schema, and study especially the structural specification requirements for XML. However, because of the features of the relational model, the XML schemas generated have no union types, no recursive types, and is a "local tree grammar" such as DTD. Translation from UML and ORM are studied in [17] and [4]; however they also have the same issues: the resulting XML schemas do not use union types. Further, these translation algorithms are largely ad hoc and it is difficult to formalize the characteristics of the resulting XML schemas. In this work, we will study how to make use of XML features such as union types, which are important to real world applications, for example, we often need to model that an address has either a city, state or a zip.

2.3   Extensions to the ER Model

The ER model was originally influenced by the relational model, and lacks features necessary to make use of features in XML. We therefore extend the ER model, we call this extended model as EReX model. The extensions are: (a) structural specification called *categories*, (b) constraint specifications called *coverage constraints*, and *order constraints*.

Categories. Categories is a kind of relationship type similar to ISA relationship types. Given entity types $E, E_1, E_2, \ldots E_n$, we can specify $E_1, E_2, \ldots E_n$ as categories of E, if in any database instance, $I(E_i) \subseteq I(E)$, for every $1 \leq i \leq n$. We represent this in an EReX schema with arrows from the E_i's to E. This is different from ISA relationship type, as well as from the ECR model [9]: (a) ISA requires that a key constraint be specified for E (b) ECR [9] requires $I(E) \subseteq I(E_1) \cup I(E_2) \cup \ldots \cup I(E_n)$, and allows $I(E_i) \not\subseteq I(E)$. These constraints are not imposed on the categories in the EReX model. Two examples of categories are shown in Figure 2. Note that in Figure 2 (b), no key constraint is specified for *Article*; in Figure 2 (a), there can be instances of *Person* who are not instances of *PersonCity* or *PersonZip*.

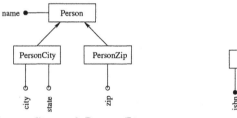

(a) *PersonCity* and *PersonZip* are categories of *Person*

(b) *Book* and *Paper* are categories of *Article*

Fig. 2. Example Categories.

Coverage Constraints. Coverage constraints are specified on entity types or roles. There are two kinds of coverage constraints (a) *total coverage*: Given entity types $E, E_1, E_2, \ldots, E_n$, where every E_i, $1 \leq i \leq n$ is a category of E, we specify that $E_1 \cup E_2 \cup \ldots E_n = E$ if for any database instance, $I(E_1) \cup I(E_2) \cup \ldots I(E_n) = I(E)$. We can specify total coverage on roles as: given entity type E, and roles $l_1, l_2, \ldots, l_n$, where every l_i, $1 \leq i \leq n$ is a role played by E in some relationship type, we specify $l_1 \cup l_2 \cup \ldots l_n = E$, if for any database instance, $I(l_1) \cup I(l_2) \cup \ldots \cup I(l_n) = I(E)$. (b) *exclusive coverage*: Given entity types E, E_1, E_2, where E_1, E_2 are categories of E, we specify $E_1 \cap E_2 = \phi$, if for any database instance, $I(E_1) \cap I(E_2) = \phi$. Similarly given entity type E, and roles l_1, l_2, where l_1, l_2 are roles played by E, we specify $l_1 \cap l_2 = \phi$, if for any database instance, $I(l_1) \cap I(l_2) = \phi$. Examples of coverage constraints are shown in Figure 3. Coverage constraints have been studied previously, in [9].

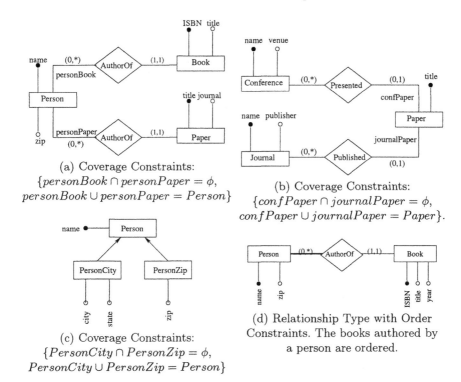

(a) Coverage Constraints:
$\{personBook \cap personPaper = \phi,$
$personBook \cup personPaper = Person\}$

(b) Coverage Constraints:
$\{confPaper \cap journalPaper = \phi,$
$confPaper \cup journalPaper = Paper\}.$

(c) Coverage Constraints:
$\{PersonCity \cap PersonZip = \phi,$
$PersonCity \cup PersonZip = Person\}$

(d) Relationship Type with Order
Constraints. The books authored by
a person are ordered.

Fig. 3. (a) and (b) show coverage constraints on roles; (c) shows coverage constraints on entity types; (d) shows order constraints.

Order Constraints. Order constraints are specified for entity types in a relationship type. Consider relationship type R between entity types $E_1, E_2, \ldots E_n$. We specify that E_i, $1 \leq i \leq n$ is ordered in R, if in any database instance the relationship instances in $I(R)$ where any $e_i \in I(E_i)$ appear is ordered. We represent this constraint in an EReX schema with a thick line between E_i and R. See figure 3 (d).

3   XGrammar

We specify an XML schema using XGrammar, a tree grammar based notation for XML schema languages such as DTD, XML-Schema and RELAX-NG, motivated by [14]. In this section, we define XGrammar and discuss different structural and constraint specification schemes for XML. We use $\mathbb{G}$ to denote a schema in XGrammar. We assume the existence of a set $\widehat{N}$ of non-terminal symbols, a set $\widehat{E}$ of element names, a set $\widehat{A}$ of attribute names, and a set $\widehat{\tau}$ of atomic data types as defined by [19], such as string, integer, ID, IDREF(S) etc. We will consider only the atomic data types ID, IDREF and IDREFS. We use the following notations for regular expressions: ϵ denotes the empty string, $+$ denotes union, "," denotes concatenation, "$a^?$" denotes "$a+\epsilon$", "a^*" denotes Kleene star, and "a^+" denotes "a, a^*".

A schema in XGrammar is denoted by a 6-tuple $\mathbb{G} = (N, E, A, S, P, \Sigma)$, where

- N is a finite set of non-terminal symbols (also called types), where $N \subseteq \widehat{N}$.
- E is a finite set of element names, where $E \subseteq \widehat{E}$.
- A is a finite set of attribute names, where $A \subseteq \widehat{A}$. We define a type $\tau \in \widehat{\tau}$ for any attribute $a \in A$.
- S is set of start symbols, where $S \subseteq N$.
- P is set of production rules of the form $X \to x$ (RE), where $X \in N$, $x \in E$, and RE is a regular expression: $RE ::= \epsilon \mid \tau \mid @a \mid Y \mid (RE + RE) \mid (RE, RE) \mid (RE)^? \mid (RE)^* \mid (RE)^+$, where $\tau \in \widehat{\tau}$, $a \in A$, $Y \in N$.
- Σ is the set of constraints, which is defined later in this section.

An example XGrammar schema and an instance document is given in Table 2. *Type assignment* (interpretation) assigns a "valid" type for each element in an instance [14]. Given an instance, we denote by $I(N_i)$, where $N_i \in N$, the set of elements in the instance that are assigned type N_i. In Table 2, we have $I(Person) = \{p1, p2\}$. We say type assignment for an instance is *unambiguous*, if it has only one possible type assignment. The type assignment for the instance in Table 2 is unambiguous.

Before we define constraints, let us define path expressions for an XGrammar schema $\mathbb{G}$. A path expression p is given by: $p ::= x \mid @a \mid parent :: x \mid p/p$, where $x \in E$, and $a \in A$. The semantics for a path expression is defined by XPath [20]. We let PE denote the set of path expressions.

We can specify three kinds of constraints in Σ for an XGrammar schema $\mathbb{G}$:

- *IDREF constraints.* Consider attribute $a \in A$. If a is of type IDREF, we define the "target type" of a as $a :: IDREF \rightsquigarrow RE_1$, where $RE_1 ::= X \mid (RE_1 + RE_1)$. If a is of type IDREFS, we define the "target types" of a as $a :: IDREFS \rightsquigarrow RE_2$, where $RE_2 ::= \epsilon \mid X \mid (RE_2 + RE_2) \mid (RE_2, RE_2) \mid (RE_2)^? \mid (RE_2)^* \mid (RE_2)^+$. Here $X \in N$. We specify the constraint if for any instance, the value of a refer to type(s) that "conform" to RE_1 (or RE_2).
- *Key constraints.* We specify a key constraint as: $key(X) = (p_1, p_2, \ldots, p_n)$; where $X \in N$, and $p_i \in PE$, $1 \le i \le n$. The semantics is as specified in [10].
- *Foreign-key constraints.* We specify a foreign key constraint as: $X(p_1, p_2, \ldots, p_n)$ REFERENCES $Y(q_1, q_2, \ldots, q_n)$, here $X, Y \in N$, and $p_i, q_i \in PE$, $1 \le i \le n$. The semantics is as specified in [10].

3.1   Structural Specification Schemes for XML

Before we study the different structural specification schemes for XML, let us define *competing non-terminal symbols* in an XGrammar schema $\mathbb{G}$. Two different non-terminal symbols $X, Y \in N$ are said to be competing if there exist two production rules in P, such that $X \to x(RE_i)$, and $Y \to x(RE_j)$, where $x \in E$. DTD is a local tree grammar and imposes the restriction that in a schema, there should be no competing non-terminal symbols. XML-Schema is a single-type tree

Table 2. Example XGrammar schema and an instance XML document

$N = \{Root, Person, Book, Paper, Review\}$
$E = \{root, person, book, paper, review\}$
$A = \{name, city, state, zip, BID, btitle,$
$\quad\quad ISBN, PID, ptitle, art, rating\}$
$S = \{Root\}$
$P = \{Root \rightarrow root \ (Person^*),$
$\quad Person \rightarrow person \ (@name,$
$\quad\quad ((@city, @state) + @zip)$
$\quad\quad (Book^+ + Paper^+), Review^+),$
$\quad Book \rightarrow book \ (@btitle, @ISBN,$
$\quad\quad @BID),$
$\quad Paper \rightarrow paper(@ptitle, @PID),$
$\quad Review \rightarrow review(@ARef, @rating)\}$
$\Sigma = $ IDREF constraints:
$\quad \{ARef::\text{IDREF}\rightsquigarrow (Book + Paper)\}$
Key constraints:
$\quad \{key(Person) = \langle @name \rangle,$
$\quad key(Book) = \langle @ISBN \rangle,$
$\quad key(Paper) = \langle @ptitle \rangle,$
$\quad key(Review) =$
$\quad\quad \langle parent :: person/@name, @ARef \rangle \}$

(a) Example XGrammar Schema

```
<root>
  <person name='N1' city='C1'
      state='S1' >
    <book btitle='T1' ISBN='I1'
        BID='B1' >
    <book btitle='T2' ISBN='I2'
        BID='B2' >
    <review ARef='P1' rating='9'>
    <review ARef='B2' rating='9'>
  </person>
  <person name='N2' zip='90095'>
    <paper ptitle='T3' PID='P1'>
    <review ARef='B1' rating='9'>
    <review ARef='B2' rating='10'>
  </person>
</root>
```

(b) Instance XML document

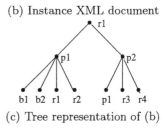

(c) Tree representation of (b)

grammar, and imposes the restriction that in any production rule $X \rightarrow x(RE)$, there are no competing non-terminal symbols in RE. RELAX-NG is regular tree grammar, and imposes no restrictions. Local and single-type tree grammars guarantee unambiguous type assignment for any instance of an XGrammar schema, whereas regular tree grammars do not give this guarantee [14].

3.2 Constraint Specification Schemes for XML

Constraint specification schemes for XML differ in whether keys and foreign keys are specified for types or path expressions. In XGrammar and in [10], they are specified for types; for XML-Schema [19], and in [6], they are specified for path expressions. If keys are specified for types, we need unambiguous type assignment; otherwise, we do not need unambiguous type assignment.

4 Translating an EReX Schema to an XGrammar Schema

In this section, we will describe an algorithm to translate an EReX schema to an XML schema in XGrammar. Compared to the translation algorithms from

ER schema to relational schema [11], we have to consider the additional features of EReX and we also have more options for representing an EReX feature in XGrammar. We will denote the input EReX schema as $\mathbb{E}$, and the output XGrammar schema as $\mathbb{G} = (N, E, A, P, S, \Sigma)$. As an example, we shall consider the EReX schema shown in Figure 4.

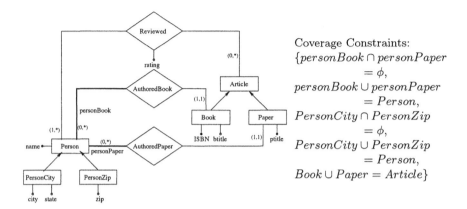

Coverage Constraints:
$\{personBook \cap personPaper$
$\qquad = \phi,$
$personBook \cup personPaper$
$\qquad = Person,$
$PersonCity \cap PersonZip$
$\qquad = \phi,$
$PersonCity \cup PersonZip$
$\qquad = Person,$
$Book \cup Paper = Article\}$

Fig. 4. Example EReX schema.

Intuition behind our algorithm. The main intuition behind our algorithm is to make use of the different coverage constraints to come up with an XML schema that has only the required number of constructs. For example, consider the coverage constraint: $personBook \cap personPaper = \phi$; this says that a person who wrote books did not write papers. If the books written by a person and papers written by a person are captured by having books and papers as "subelements" of person, then we may specify this coverage constraint as: $Person \rightarrow person(Book^* + Person^*)$. Similarly, we observe in Figure 4 that $Article$ has no attributes, so we try to see if we can come up with an XML schema with no non-terminal symbol corresponding to $Article$.

We will present our algorithm in three steps: in the first step (initialization step), we look at the entity types and their attributes, and come up with a set of non-terminal symbols, element names, attribute names, and production rules. In the second step, we look at the relationship types, and capture them. In the third step, we try to capture coverage constraints, and order constraints.

4.1   Initialization

As part of initialization, we do the following:

1. Define a non-terminal symbol in N corresponding to every entity type E_i in $\mathbb{E}$. Also define a new non-terminal symbol $Root$, which will be the start symbol. For the example in Figure 4, we get $N = \{Root, Person, PersonCity, PersonZip, Article, Book, Paper\}$.

2. Define element names as follows: define an element name *root*; define an element name corresponding to every entity type E_i that has a key constraint or that is not a category of any other entity type E_k. For Figure 4, we get $E = \{root, person, article, book, paper\}$.
   We then associate each non-terminal symbol in N with an element name in E as follows. Let function $t : N \rightarrow E$ represent this association. t is defined as: $t(Root) = root$. Let $N_i \in N$ correspond to entity type E_i in $\mathbb{E}$. If there exists $e_i \in E$ corresponding to E_i, then $t(N_i) = e_i$; otherwise $t(N_i) = t(N_j)$, where $N_j \in N$ corresponds to E_j and E_i is a category of E_j. For example, consider $PersonCity \in N$; it is a category of $Person$, and hence we will define $t(PersonCity) = person$. For Figure 4, we also get $t(Root) = root$, $t(Person) = person$, $t(PersonZip) = person$, $t(Article) = article$, $t(Book) = book$, $t(Paper) = paper$.

3. Define an attribute name in A corresponding to an attribute of any entity type or relationship type in $\mathbb{E}$. For our example, we get $A = \{name, city, state, zip, ISBN, btitle, ptitle, rating\}$.

4. Define production rules corresponding to every non-terminal symbol $N_i \in N$ as: $N_i \rightarrow n_i(RE_i)$, where $n_i = t(N_i)$, and RE_i includes the attributes in A corresponding to the attributes of E_i in $\mathbb{E}$. The production rules we obtain are shown in Table 3.

5. Define key constraints as: for every key constraint in $\mathbb{E}$ that says key for E_i is $(a_1, a_2, \ldots, a_n)$, we define a key constraint in Σ, $key(N_i) = (@a_1, @a_2, \ldots, @a_n)$. The key constraints we obtain are shown in Table 3.

Table 3. Example XGrammar after initialization

$N = \{Root, Person, PersonCity, PersonZip, Article, Book, Paper\}$
$E = \{root, person, article, book, paper\}$
$A = \{name, city, state, zip, ISBN, btitle, ptitle, rating\}$
$S = \{Root\}$
$P = \{Root \rightarrow root(\epsilon), Person \rightarrow person(@name),$
     $\quad PersonCity \rightarrow person(@city, @state), PersonZip \rightarrow person(@zip),$
     $\quad Article \rightarrow article(\epsilon), Book \rightarrow book(@ISBN, @btitle), Paper \rightarrow paper(@ptitle)\}$
$\Sigma = $ Key Constraints:
     $\quad \{key(Person) = (@name), key(Book) = (@ISBN), key(Paper) = (@ptitle)\}$

From now on, we will use the notation $N_i \in N$ corresponds to $E_i \in \mathbb{E}$, has production rule $N_i \rightarrow n_i(RE_i)$, and key constraint (if any) $key(N_i) = (p_{i_1}, p_{i_2}, \ldots, p_{i_{N_i}})$. Also for any regular expression RE, $(RE)^1$ denotes (RE).

We define a method $addID(N_i)$, to add an ID attribute for non-terminal N_i. This method checks if there exists an attribute of type ID in RE_i; if yes, then nothing is done; if no, then we set $A = A \cup N_iID$, where N_iID is of type ID; also RE_i is set as $RE_i = (RE_i, N_iID)$.

Similarly, we define a method $addRef(N_j, N_i)$, to add an IDREF attribute referring to N_i for the non-terminal N_j. This method, sets $A = A \cup N_iRef$, where N_iRef is of type IDREF; and adds an IDREF constraint to Σ as $\Sigma = \Sigma \cup N_iRef :: IDREF \rightsquigarrow N_i$.

4.2   Translating Relationship Types

Consider the relationship type R between entity types $E_1, E_2, \ldots, E_n$, with attributes $a_1, a_2, \ldots, a_m$. Such relationship types are translated as follows:

1. If R is a binary relationship type $(n = 2)$, where cardinality of one of the participating entity types, say E_2 is $(1,1)$, R is translated as:
   - If N_2 does not appear in the "right hand side" (RHS) of any production rule, then rewrite the production rule for N_1 and N_2 by setting $RE_1 = (RE_1, N_2^o)$, $RE_2 = (RE_2, @a_1, @a_2, \ldots, @a_m)$. Here o depends on the cardinality of E_1 in R: if this cardinality is $(0,1)$, $o =^?$; if $(1,1)$, $o = 1$; if $(0,*)$, $o = *$; if $(1,*)$, $o = +$.
   - If N_2 appears in the RHS of some rule, then use IDREF as: $addID(N_1)$; $addRef(N_2, N_1)$, $RE_2 = (RE_2, @N_1Ref, @a_1, @a_2, \ldots, @a_m)$.
   In Figure 4, we have two relationship types where cardinality of one of the entity types is $(1,1)$: $AuthoredBook$, and $AuthoredPaper$. These get represented as $Person \rightarrow person(@name, Book^*, Paper^*)$.
2. If R is a binary recursive relationship type $(n = 2, E_1 = E_2)$, where one of the cardinalities is $(0,1)$, translate R as: if N_1 does not appear in the RHS of any production rule, then set $RE_1 = (RE_1, N_1^o, (@a_1, @a_2, \ldots, @a_m)^?)$; here o can be $^?$ or *, depending on the other cardinality for R. If N_1 appears in RHS of some rule, then represent it as in Step 3.
3. If R is any binary relationship type $(n = 2)$, where cardinality of E_2 is $(0,1)$ and Steps 1 or 2 cannot be applied, then translate R as: $addID(N_1)$; $addRef(N_2, N_1)$; $RE_2 = (RE_2, (@N_1Ref, @a_1, @a_2, \ldots @a_m)^?)$.
4. If R is a binary relationship type, and we cannot apply Steps 1, 2 or 3, then R is a $m : n$ relationship type. This is translated as: create a new non-terminal symbol N_R, and set $N = N \cup N_R$; create a new element name e_R and set $E = E \cup e_R$; set $RE_1 = (RE_1, N_R^o)$, where o is * or $^+$; $addID(N_2)$; $addRef(N_R, N_2)$; add a new production rule $N_R \rightarrow e_R(@N_2Ref, @a_1, @a_2, \ldots, @a_m)$. The key for N_R is defined as:
   - if $key(N_1)$ is defined, then $key(N_R) = (parent :: e_1/p_{1_1}, parent :: e_1/p_{1_2}, \ldots, parent :: e_1/p_{1_{N_1}}, @N_2Ref)$.
   - if $key(N_1)$ is not defined, then $addID(N_1)$; let attribute of type ID in RE_1 be N_1ID. Now, $key(N_R) = (parent :: e_1/@N_1ID, @N_2Ref)$.
   For Figure 4, $Review$ is a $m : n$ relationship type, and we get: $Person \rightarrow person\ (@name, Book^*, Paper^*, Review^+)$, $Review \rightarrow review\ (@ARef, @rating)$, $Article \rightarrow article\ (@AID)$, $ARef :: IDREF \rightsquigarrow (Article)$, and $key(Review) = \langle parent :: person/@name, @ARef \rangle$.
5. If R is a non-binary relationship type, create a new non-terminal symbol, N_R, and a new element name e_R. Then: $RE_1 = (RE_1, N_R^o)$, $o \in \{^1, ^?, ^*, ^+\}$; $addID(N_i)$, $2 \le i \le n$; $addRef(N_R, N_i)$, $2 \le i \le n$; add a new production rule $N_R \rightarrow e_R(@N_2Ref, @N_3Ref, \ldots, @N_nRef, @a_1, @a_2, \ldots, @a_m)$. The key for N_R is defined similar to that for $m : n$ relationship types.

After translating all the relationship types for the example in Figure 4, we obtain the XGrammar as shown in Table 4.

Table 4. Example XGrammar after translating relationships

$N = \{Root, Person, PersonCity, PersonZip, Article, Book, Paper, Review\}$

$E = \{root, person, article, book, paper, review\}$

$A = \{name, city, state, zip, ISBN, btitle, ptitle, rating, AID, ARef\}$

$S = \{Root\}$

$P = \{Root \rightarrow root(\epsilon), Person \rightarrow person(@name, Book^*, Paper^*, Review^+),$
$\quad PersonCity \rightarrow person(@city, @state), PersonZip \rightarrow person(@zip),$
$\quad Article \rightarrow article(@AID), Book \rightarrow book(@ISBN, @btitle),$
$\quad Paper \rightarrow paper(@ptitle)\}, Review \rightarrow review(@ARef, @rating)$

$\Sigma = $ IDREF constraints: $ARef :: IDREF \rightsquigarrow Article$
$\quad$ Key Constraints: $\{key(Person) = (@name), key(Book) = (@ISBN),$
$\quad key(Paper) = (@ptitle), key(Review) = (parent :: person/@name, @ARef)\}$

4.3   Other EReX Features

1. Order constraints are represented as: Let R be a n-ary relationship type as in the previous subsection; let E_1 in R be ordered. R would have been represented in one of two ways: (a) N_2 (or N_R) is in the production rule of N_1 (b) N_2 (or N_R) has IDREF attribute $N_1 Ref$. In (a), order is already captured; in (b) the order is captured by: $RE_2 = (RE_2, @N_1 Order)$, or $RE_R = (RE_R, @N_1 Order)$, as the case may be. The two order constraints in Figure 4 are captured in $Person \rightarrow person(@name, Book^*, Paper^*, Review^+)$.

2. Removing unnecessary non-terminal symbols is done as:
   - Remove any non-terminal $N_i \in N$, where $RE_i = \epsilon$, and N_i does not appear on the RHS of any production rule.
   - Remove any non-terminal N_i for which $key(N_i)$ is not defined, there exists entity types $E_1, E_2, \ldots E_n$ that are categories of E_i and we have the constraint: $E_1 \cup E_2 \cup \ldots E_n = E$. Set $RE_k = (RE_k, RE_i)$, for $1 \leq k \leq n$. If N_i appears in the RHS of some production rule: if no N_k, $1 \leq k \leq n$ appears in the RHS of any production rule, then N_i is replaced with $(N_1 + N_2 + \ldots + N_n)$; otherwise, we replace N_i with a new attribute a; $A = A \cup a$; $a :: IDREF \rightsquigarrow (N_1 + N_2 + \ldots + N_n)$; $addID(N_k)$, for $1 \leq k \leq n$. If N_i appears as the target type of some IDREF attribute, then N_i is replaced with $(N_1 + N_2 + \ldots + N_n)$; $addID(N_k)$, for $1 \leq k \leq n$. For Figure 4, we remove the non-terminal $Article$, and get: $ARef ::$ $IDREF \rightsquigarrow (Book + Paper)$; $Book \rightarrow book(@ISBN, @btitle, @BID)$, $Paper \rightarrow paper(@ptitle, @PID)$.
   - Remove any non-terminal N_i for which $key(N_i)$ is not defined, N_i does not appear in the RHS of any production rule, RE_i does not have $N_i ID$, and E_i is category of E_j as: $RE_j = (RE_j, RE_i^?)$. For Figure 4, we remove $PersonCity$ and $PersonZip$ and get $Person \rightarrow person$ $(@name, (@city,$ $@state)^?, @zip^?, Book^*, Paper^*, Review^+)$.

3. All exclusive coverage constraints may not be captured in XGrammar. Represent exclusive coverage constraints as: For roles (or categories) $l_1, l_2, \ldots,$ l_n of E_k, if $l_i \cap l_j = \phi$, for $1 \leq i < j \leq n$, and $N_k \rightarrow e_k(r, Q_1^{o_1}, Q_2^{o_2},$ $\ldots, Q_n^{o_n})$, where $Q_i^{o_i}$ "corresponds" to l_i, and o_i's in $^{1,?,*,+}$, rewrite the rule as: $N_k \rightarrow e_k(r, (Q_1^{o_1} + Q_2^{o_2} + \ldots + Q_n^{o_n}))$. For Figure 4, using $PersonCity \cap PersonZip = \phi$ and using $personBook \cap personPaper = \phi$, we get $Person \rightarrow person$ (@$name$, ((@$city$, @$state)^? +$ @$zip^?$), ($Book^* + Paper^*$), $Review^+$).

4. All total coverage constraints may not be captured in XGrammar. Represent total coverage constraints as: For roles (or categories) $l_1, l_2, \ldots, l_n$ of E_k, if $l_1 \cup l_2 \cup \ldots l_n = E_k$, and $N_k \rightarrow e_k(r_1, (Q_1^{o_1} + Q_2^{o_2} + \ldots + Q_n^{o_n} + r_2))$, where $Q_i^{o_i}$ "corresponds" to l_i, and o_i's in $^{1,?,*,+}$, rewrite the rule as: $N_k \rightarrow$ $e_k(r_1, (Q_1^{o_1'} + Q_2^{o_2'} + \ldots + Q_n^{o_n'} + r_2))$. We get o_i' as: if $o_i =^?$, $o_i' =^1$; if $o_i =^*$, $o_i' =^+$; otherwise $o_i' = o_i$. For Figure 4, using $PersonCity \cup PersonZip = Person$ and using $personBook \cup personPaper = Person$, we get $Person \rightarrow person$ (@$name$, ((@$city$, @$state)$ + @zip), ($Book^+ + Paper^+$), $Review^+$).

5. Categories are related as: consider two non-terminal symbols $N_i, N_j \in N$, such that E_i is a category of E_j, call $addID(N_j)$; $addRef(N_i, N_j)$; $N_i \rightarrow$ $e_i(RE_i, @N_jRef)$.

6. Ensure that $\mathbb{G}$ is a single-type tree grammar. For this, check if any production rule has N_i and N_j where $e_i = e_j$. In this case, introduce two new non-terminal symbols N_i', N_j'; introduce two new element names $e_{i'}$, $e_{j'}$; replace N_i with N_i', and N_j with N_j', and set: $N_i' \rightarrow e_{i'}(N_i)$ and $N_j' \rightarrow e_{j'}(N_j)$.

7. Find the non-terminal symbols that do not appear on the RHS of any rule. Let they be $N_1, N_2, \ldots, N_n$. Set $Root \rightarrow root(N_1^*, N_2^*, \ldots, N_n^*)$. For Figure 4, we get $Root \rightarrow root(Person^*)$.

The final XGrammar schema from Figure 4 is given in Table 2.

4.4   Characteristics of Our Translation Algorithm

It is important to formalize the characteristics of the XGrammar resulting from our translation algorithm. We only state the characteristics; the proofs follow from our algorithm. Let us first look at information preservation. ER to relational translation loses some cardinality constraints; similarly when we use IDREF attributes in XGrammar, we could potentially lose some cardinality constraints (such as the minimum cardinality). All order constraints specified in an EReX schema are captured in XGrammar. However, not all exclusive and total coverage constraints may be captured. Also it is important to note that, XGrammar could also add some unnecessary order constraints into the schema, which were not originally present in the EReX schema. For example, the XGrammar in Table 2 adds that the reviews of a person are ordered. However, other than these, all other constraints in the EReX schema are captured in XGrammar; and no additional constraints get specified in XGrammar.

Let us examine redundancy in terms of redundancy in attribute values. We see that any attribute value that appears in the EReX instance (such as $s_1 \rightarrow$

Dave) is represented exactly once in the XGrammar instance. Therefore, if there was no redundancy in the EReX schema the resulting XGrammar schema also has no redundancy. In other words, if we assume any functional dependency $A \to B$ implies that there is an entity type with key A and attribute(s) B, then a "correct" EReX schema will produce a normalized XGrammar schema (in XNF [1]) by the above algorithm. We can show a much stronger result, that is, any update to an attribute value in EReX translates to an update of an attribute value. Similarly the insert (or deletion) of an entity or relationship translates to adding (or deleting) elements and attributes.

Let us examine other characteristics of the resulting XGrammar schemas. We see that the resulting XGrammar generates XML instances with maximal height, and it makes use of union types and recursive types. Further, we assume that any database application can be modeled in EReX. Therefore, we get our main result: *any database application can be modeled in XGrammar, where structures are specified as a single-type tree grammar, and constraints are specified on types.*

5   Conclusions and Future Work

In this work, we studied the problem of designing an XML schema for a given application, using conceptual modeling techniques. We came up with the EReX conceptual model, and studied an algorithm to translate EReX schemas to XML schemas. Our algorithm was able to make use of features such as union types and recursive types provided by XML. We further used this approach to study a fundamental problem facing the XML database community today: what structural and constraint specification schemes are needed in XML for modeling any database application. We conclude that any database application can be modeled in XML as a single-type tree grammar, with constraints specified on types.

There exist lot of open research problems in XML data models. For example, XML has the notion of document order, where all the elements are ordered; we do not have a corresponding notion in EReX schema, and do not understand what global document order means in a real world application. Another important research issue is that in order to capture the constraints in EReX omitted by XGrammar we might need a first order constraint language similar to that for relational model. Also reverse engineering XML schemas to EReX schemas is important, and it will provide a different framework for reasoning about problems such as verifying consistency of an XML schema. This problem is studied in [6,10,2]. However there exist several open problems in these areas, and our framework might be helpful to come up with a better understanding of these problems.

Acknowledgements. The author acknowledges the assistance of Prof. Antonio Badia, University of Louisville, Kentucky, and Prof. Dongwon Lee, PennState University, for their initial reviews of the paper, and insightful comments.

References

1. M. Arenas and L. Libkin. A normal form for XML documents. In *ACM Symposium on Principles of Database Systems (PODS)*, Madison, Wisconsin, June. 2002.
2. M. Arenas and L. Libkin. An information-theoretic approach to normal forms for relational and XML data. In *ACM Symposium on Principles of Database Systems (PODS)*, San Diego, CA, June. 2003.
3. C. Batini, S. Ceri, and S. B. Navathe. *"Conceptual Database Design: An Entity-Relationship Approach"*. The Benjamin/Cummings Pub., 1992.
4. L. Bird, A. Goodchild, and T. Halpin. "Object Role Modeling and XML-Schema". In *Int'l Conf. on Conceptual Modeling (ER)*, Salt Lake City, UT, Oct. 2000.
5. T. Bray, J. Paoli, and C. M. Sperberg-McQueen (Eds). "Extensible Markup Language (XML) 1.0 (2nd Edition)". W3C Recommendation, Oct. 2000. http://www.w3.org/TR/2000/REC-xml-20001006.
6. P. Buneman, S. Davidson, W. Fan, C. Hara, and W. Tan. Keys for XML. *Computer Networks*, 39(5):473–487, Aug. 2002.
7. P. P. Chen. The Entity-Relationship Model. *ACM Transactions on Database Systems (TODS)*, 1:9–36, 1976.
8. E. F. Codd. A Relational Model of Data for Large Shared Data Banks. *Communications of the ACM*, 13(6):377–387, 1970.
9. R. Elmasri, J. Weeldreyer, and A. Hevner. "The Category Concept: An Extension to the Entity-Relationship Model". *J. Data & Knowledge Engineering (DKE)*, 1(1):75–116, May 1985.
10. W. Fan, G. M. Kuper, and J. Siméon. A Unified Constraint Model for XML. *Computer Networks*, 39(5):489–505, Aug. 2002.
11. H. Garcia-Molina, J. D. Ullman, and J. Widom. *"Database Systems: The Complete Book"*. Prentice Hall, 2002.
12. T. Halpin. *Informational Modeling and Relational Databases: From Conceptual Analysis to Logical Design*. Morgan Kaufmann Pub., 2001.
13. D. Lee, M. Mani, F. Chiu, and W. W. Chu. NeT & CoT: Translating Relational Schemas to XML Schemas. In *ACM Conference on Information and Knowledge Management (CIKM)*, McLean, Virginia, Nov. 2002.
14. M. Murata, D. Lee, and M. Mani. "Taxonomy of XML Schema Languages using Formal Language Theory". In *Extreme Markup Languages*, Montreal, Canada, Aug. 2001.
15. OASIS. RELAX NG Home Page. http://www.relaxng.org.
16. OMG. OMG Unified Modeling Language Specification, Version 1.5, Mar. 2003. http://www.uml.org/.
17. N. Routledge, L. Bird, and A. Goodchild. UML and XML Schema. In *Australasian Database Conference*, Melbourne, Australia, Jan. 2002.
18. J. Simeon and P. Wadler. "The Essence of XML". In *Principles of Programming Languages*, New Orleans, LA, Jan. 2003.
19. W3C. XML-Schema Working Group. http://www.w3.org/XML/Schema.html.
20. W3C. XQuery Working Group. http://www.w3.org/XML/Query.html.

A Runtime System for XML Transformations in Java

Aske Simon Christensen, Christian Kirkegaard, and Anders Møller*

BRICS**, Department of Computer Science
University of Aarhus, Denmark
{aske,ck,amoeller}@brics.dk

Abstract. We show that it is possible to extend a general-purpose programming language with a convenient high-level data-type for manipulating XML documents while permitting (1) precise static analysis for guaranteeing validity of the constructed XML documents relative to the given DTD schemas, and (2) a runtime system where the operations can be performed efficiently. The system, named XACT, is based on a notion of immutable XML templates and uses XPath for deconstructing documents. A companion paper presents the program analysis; this paper focuses on the efficient runtime representation.

1 Introduction

There exists a variety of approaches for programming transformations of XML documents. Some work in the context of a general-purpose programming language; for example, JDOM [17], which is a popular package for Java allowing XML documents to be manipulated using a tree representation. A benefit of this approach is that the full expressive power of the Java language is directly available for defining the transformations. Another approach is to use domain-specific languages, such as XSLT [7], which is based on notions of templates and pattern matching. This approach often allows more concise programs that are easier to write and maintain, but it is difficult to combine it with more general computations, access to databases, communication with Web services, etc.

Our goal is to integrate XML into general-purpose programming languages to make development of XML transformations easier and safer to construct. We propose XACT, which integrates XML into Java through a high-level data-type representing immutable XML fragments, a runtime system that supports a number of primitive operations on such XML fragments, and a static analysis for detecting programming errors related to the XML operations.

The XML fragments in XACT are immutable for two reasons: First, immutability is always a judicious design choice (*"I would use an immutable whenever I can"*, James Gosling [26]); and second, immutability is a necessity for devising precise and efficient static analyses, in particular, of validity of dynamically constructed XML documents relative to the DTD schemas. The XACT system consists of a simple preprocessor, a runtime library, and a program analyzer. The main contribution of this paper is the description of the XACT runtime system. We present a suitable runtime representation

---

* Supported by the Carlsberg Foundation contract number ANS-1507/20.
** Basic Research in Computer Science (www.brics.dk),
   funded by the Danish National Research Foundation.

Z. Bellahsène et al. (Eds.): XSym 2004, LNCS 3186, pp. 143–157, 2004.

for XML templates that efficiently supports the operations in the XACT API. This is nontrivial mainly because of the immutability of the data type. The companion paper [20] contains a description of the static analysis of XACT programs.

We first, in Section 2, describe the design of the XACT language and motivate our design choices. Section 3 then gives a brief overview of the results from [20] about providing static guarantees for XML transformations written in XACT. Section 4 presents our runtime system and discusses time complexity of the operations. Finally, in Section 5, we evaluate the system by a number of experiments.

Related work. The most closely related work is that on JDOM [17], XSLT [18], XQuery [4], XDuce [16], Xtatic [10], CDuce [2], XOBE [19], XJ [14], Xen [22], and HaXml [27]. In comparison, the XACT language is based on a combination of the following ideas:

- XACT integrates XML processing into a *general-purpose language*, rather than being a domain-specific language as XSLT or XQuery.
- It applies a *template-based* paradigm for constructing XML values (reminiscent of that in XSLT but unlike the other systems mentioned above).
- XML values are *immutable* (in stark contrast to JDOM, XJ, and Xen).
- Deconstruction of XML values is based on the XPath language [8] (which is also used for similar purposes in XSLT, XQuery, XJ, and optionally also in JDOM).
- Static guarantees are provided through *data-flow analysis*, thereby avoiding the explicit type annotations that are required in approaches based on type systems. Such explicit types can be cumbersome to write and read, and, as noted in [14], explicit types for XML values can be too rigid since the individual steps in a sequence of operations may temporarily invalidate the data unless permitting only bottom-up construction. (JDOM and XSLT provide no similar static guarantees, and the remaining alternatives mentioned above use type systems.)

We refer to the paper [20] for a comprehensive survey of the relation between the language design of XACT and other systems. In the present paper, we focus on the relation to the runtime model of a few representative alternatives: (1) JDOM is generally considered an efficient but rather low-level platform for manipulating XML documents in Java. It provides an explicit tree representation of XML documents where nodes include parent pointers, which permits upwards traversal but prohibits sharing. (2) XSLT is a widely used XML transformation language and many implementations exist. A central part of XSLT is the use of XPath for selection and pattern matching, and much effort has been put into optimizing XPath processors for use in XSLT and other systems [12]. Our implementation of XACT uses an off-the-shelf XPath processor [21] and can hence benefit directly from such work. (3) Both Xtatic and CDuce inherit their key features— tree processing in a declarative style with regular types and patterns—from XDuce. Xtatic works in the context of C# whereas CDuce is a functional language. The paper [11] describes runtime representations for Xtatic, where the main challenges are immutability (as for XACT), efficient pattern matching (where we apply XPath instead), and DOM interoperability (using techniques that we could also apply). Since no implementation of Xtatic has been available to us, we choose the tuned implementation of CDuce as a representative for these systems for quantitative comparisons.

2   The XACT Language

Compared to other XML transformation languages, XACT is designed to be a small sublanguage that can be described in just a few pages. The XACT language introduces XML transformation facilities into the Java programming language such that XML documents, from a programmer's perspective, are first-class values on equal terms with basic values, such as booleans, integers, and strings. Programmers can thereby combine the flexibility and power of a general-purpose programming language with the ability to express XML manipulations at a high level of abstraction. This combination is convenient for many typical transformation tasks. Examples are transformations that rely on communication with databases and complex transformation tasks, which may involve advanced control-flow depending on the document structure. In these cases, one can apply XACT operations while utilizing Java libraries, for example, the sorting facilities, string manipulations, and HTTP communication. We choose to build upon Java because it is widely used and a good representative for the capabilities of modern general-purpose programming languages. Additionally, it is often used as a foundation for Web services, using for example Servlets or SOAP, which involve dynamic construction of XHTML documents or manipulation of SOAP messages.

We build XML documents from *templates* as known from the JWIG language [6]. This approach originates from MAWL [1] and <bigwig> [5], and was later refined in JWIG, where it has shown to be a powerful formalism for XHTML document construction in Web services. Our aim has been to extend the formalism to general XML transformations where both construction and deconstruction are supported.

A template is a well-formed XML fragment containing named gaps: *template gaps* occur in place of elements, and *attribute gaps* occur in place of attributes. The core notation for templates is given by xml in the following grammar:

$$
\begin{aligned}
xml :=\ & str & \text{(character data)} \\
|\ & <name\ atts>xml</name> & \text{(element)} \\
|\ & <[g]> & \text{(template gap)} \\
|\ & xml\ xml & \text{(template sequencing)} \\
atts :=\ & name="value" & \text{(attribute)} \\
|\ & name=[g] & \text{(attribute gap)} \\
|\ & \epsilon & \text{(empty sequence)} \\
|\ & atts\ atts & \text{(attribute sequencing)}
\end{aligned}
$$

Here, str denotes a string of XML character data, $name$ denotes a qualified XML name, g denotes a gap name, and $value$ denotes an XML attribute value. As an example, the following XML template, which can be useful when constructing XHTML documents, contains two template gaps named TITLE and MAIN and one attribute gap named COL:

```
<html>
  <head><title><[TITLE]></title></head>
  <body bgcolor=[COL]><[MAIN]></body>
</html>
```

Construction of a larger template from a smaller one is accomplished by *plugging* values into its gaps. The result is the template with all gaps of a given name replaced by values. This mechanism is flexible because complex templates can be built and reused

Table 1. The central methods in the XML class of XACT.

`static XML constant(String s)`	– creates a template from the constant string s
`String toString()`	– returns the textual representation of this template
`boolean equals(Object o)`	– determines equality of this template and o
`int hashCode()`	– returns the hash code of this template
`XML plug(Gap g, XML x)`	– inserts x into all g gaps in this template
`XML plug(Gap g, String s)`	– as the previous operation, but for string
`XML plug(Gap g, XML[] xs)`	– inserts the entries in xs into the g gaps in this template
`XML plug(Gap g, String[] ss)`	– as the previous operation, but for string entries
`XML[] select(XPath p)`	– returns the array of subtemplates hit by p
`XML gapify(XPath p, Gap g)`	– replaces all subtemplates hit by p by g gaps
`XML close()`	– returns this template with all gaps removed
`XML cast(DTD d)`	– runtime check for validity
`XML analyze(DTD d)`	– compile-time check for validity
`static XML smash(XML[] xs)`	– merges the entries of xs into a single template
`static XML get(String s, DTD d)`	– creates a template from a non-constant string

many times. Gaps can be plugged in any order; construction is not restricted to be bottom-up, in contrast to, for example, XDuce and XOBE.

Deconstruction of XML data is also supported in XACT. An off-the-shelf language for addressing nodes within XML trees is available, namely W3C's XPath language [8]. XPath is widely used and has despite its simplicity shown to be versatile in existing technologies, such as XSLT and XQuery. The XACT deconstruction mechanism is also based on XPath. We have identified two basic deconstruction operations, which are powerful in combination with plugging. The first is *select*, which returns the subtemplates addressed by an XPath expression. The second is *gapify*, which replaces the subtemplates addressed by an XPath expression with gaps. Select is convenient because it permits us to pick subtemplates for further processing. Gapify permits us to dynamically introduce gaps, which is important for a task such as performing minor modifications in an XML tree. Altogether, this constitute an algebra over templates, which allows typical XML manipulations to be expressed at a high level of abstraction.

We have chosen a value-based programming model as in pure functional languages. In this model, XML templates are unchangeable values and operations have no side-effects. A Java class that implements the value-based model is said to be *immutable*. Such classes are favored because their instances are safe to share, value factories can safely return the same instances multiple times, and thread-safety is guaranteed [3]. All Java value classes, such as `Integer` and `String`, are for these reasons immutable. Our templates inherit the properties and benefit by being easier to use and less prone to error than mutable frameworks, such as JDOM. Furthermore, immutability is a necessity for useful analysis, as described in Section 3.

The immutable Java class `XML`, which represents templates, has the methods shown in Table 1. All parameters of type `Gap`, `XPath`, and `DTD` are assumed to be constants and may be written as strings. The `DTD` parameters are URIs of DTDs.

XACT distinguishes between two different sources of XML data: constant templates and input data. Constant templates are part of the transformation program and are constructed using the `constant` method. The syntax for these templates is the one given by the grammar above. Input to the program is read using the `get` method, which constructs a gap-free template from a non-constant string and checks the result for validity with respect to the given DTD schema. Output from the transformation is achieved through the `toString` method, which returns the string representation of the XML template.

Templates can be combined by the `plug` method, which is overloaded to accept a template, a string, or arrays of these as second parameter. Invoking the non-array variants will plug the given string or template into all occurrences of the given gap name. The array variants will, in document order, plug all occurrences of the given gap name with entries from the given array. If the array has superfluous entries these will be ignored, and conversely, the empty string will be plugged into superfluous gaps. An exception is thrown if one attempts to plug a template into an attribute gap.

Template deconstruction is provided by the `select` and `gapify` methods. Both methods take an XPath expression as parameter, which on evaluation returns a set of nodes within the given template[1]. Invoking the `select` method gives an array containing all the subtemplates rooted at nodes in the XPath evaluation result. The `gapify` method returns a template where all subtemplates rooted at nodes in the XPath evaluation result have been replaced by gaps of the given name.

The `close` method eliminates all gaps in a template and is commonly used in combination with `toString`. The result will by construction represent a well-formed XML document. Invoking the static `smash` method concatenates the entries of the given template array into a single template[2]. The `equals` method determines equality of XML instances, and the `hashCode` method returns a consistent hash code for an XML instance. The ability to compare entire XML templates for equality permits templates to be stored in containers as values rather than as objects and can also be useful in the decision logic of transformations. In comparison, other systems either do not have an equality primitive or compare by reference instead of by value.

By placing special `analyze` methods in the code, the compile-time analyzer can be instructed to check for validity relative to the given DTDs. This is usually used in connection with the `toString` method to analyze validity of the output data. Additionally, runtime validation of a template according to a given DTD schema is provided by the `cast` method, which serves a similar purpose for the XACT analysis as the usual cast operation does for the type system of Java.

In order to integrate XACT tightly with the Java language, we provide special syntax for template constants. This relieves programmers from tedious and error-prone character escaping. A template *xml* may be written `[[`*xml*`]]`, which after character escaping is equivalent to `XML.constant("`*xml*`")`. Transformations that use this syntax are desugared by a simple preprocessor. Also, a number of useful macros, presented in [20], for commonly occurring tasks are provided. For example, the `delete` macro effectively deletes the subtrees addressed by an XPath expression by performing a `gapify` operation with a fresh gap name. Our implementation also contains a mechanism for declaring XML namespaces for constant templates and XPath expressions.

---

[1] All XPath axes are supported by XACT. Although the paper [20] focuses on the downwards axes, the program analyzer is capable of handling all axes.

[2] The paper [20] describes a more powerful operation `group` and defines `smash` as syntactic sugar. We now treat `smash` as the primitive and express `group` in terms of `smash`, `select`, and `equals` instead.

Example. We now consider a simple example, originating from [15], where an address book is filtered in order to produce a phone list. An address book here consists of an addrbook root element that contains a sequence of person elements, each having a name, an addr, and an optional tel element as children. The filtration outputs a phonelist root element that contains a sequence of person elements, where only those having a tel child remains, and with all addr elements eliminated. The following method shows how this can be implemented with XACT:

```
XML phonelist(XML book) {
  XML[] persons = book.select("/addrbook/person[tel]");
  XML list = XML.smash(persons).delete("//addr");
  return [[<phonelist><[LIST]></phonelist>]].plug("LIST",list);
}
```

We use the select operation to build an array of all person elements that have a tel child. Then, the array entries are combined into a single template, all addr elements are deleted, and the result is wrapped into a phonelist element[3].

One may additionally wish to sort the phone list alphabetically by name. Java has built-in sorting facilities for arrays, so this is accomplished by implementing a Comparator class, called PersonComparator, with the following compare method:

```
int compare(Object o1, Object o2) {
  XML x1 = (XML)o1, x2 = (XML)o2;
  String s1 = XML.smash(x1.select("/person/name/text()")).toString();
  String s2 = XML.smash(x2.select("/person/name/text()")).toString();
  return s1.compareTo(s2);
}
```

The XACT operations here simply extract the character data to be used in the comparison. The phone list can then be sorted by inserting the following line into the phonelist method (after the select operation):

```
Arrays.sort(persons, new PersonComparator());
```

The example shows how XACT integrates XML processing into Java and how a nontrivial transformation task can be intuitive to express using XACT. More example programs can be found at http://www.brics.dk/Xact/.

3   Static Guarantees

Transforming data from one XML language to another can be a quite intricate task, even if a high-level programming language is being used. In particular, it can be difficult to ensure at compile-time that the output is always valid with respect to a given DTD schema. A special property of the design of XACT is that it enables precise static analysis for guaranteeing absence of certain programming errors related to XML document manipulation. In the companion paper [20], we present a data-flow analysis that, at compile-time, checks the following correctness properties of an XACT program:

---

[3] With the notion of *code gaps*, which is included in the syntactic sugar mentioned in [20], the last operation can be written more concisely:

```
return [[<phonelist><{list}></phonelist>]];
```

output validity — that each `analyze` operation is valid in the sense that the XML template at this point is guaranteed to be valid relative to the DTD schema; and

plug consistency — that each `plug` operation is guaranteed to succeed, that is, templates are never plugged into attribute gaps.

Additionally, the analysis can detect and warn the programmer if the specified gap for a `plug` operation is never present and if an XPath expression in a `select` or `gapify` operation will never address any nodes.

Notice that XACT, in contrast to other XML transformation systems that permit static guarantees, does not require every XML variable to be explicitly typed with schema information.

The crucial property of XACT that makes the analysis feasible is that the XML templates are immutable. Analyzing programs that manipulate mutable data structures is known to be difficult [24,23], and the absence of side-effects means that we do not have to model the complex aliasing relations that otherwise may arise.

The analysis is conservative in the sense that it never misses an error, but it might report false errors. Our experiments in [20] indicate that the analysis is both precise and efficient enough to be practically useful, and that it produces helpful error messages if potential errors are detected.

4 Runtime System

We have now presented a high-level language for expressing XML transformations and briefly explained that the design permits precise static analysis. However, such a framework would be of little practical value if the operations could not be performed efficiently at runtime. In this section, we present a data structure in the form of a Java library addressing this issue.

To qualify as a suitable representation for XML templates in the XACT framework, our data structure must support the following operations:

– *Creation*: Given the textual representation of an XML template, we must build the structure representing the template.
– *Combination*: The `plug`, `close`, and `smash` operations operate directly on XML templates and must be supported directly by the data structure.
– *Navigation*: The tasks of converting a template to its textual representation, checking the template for validity according to a given schema, and evaluating an XPath expression on a template all require means for traversing the XML data in various ways. In general, we need a mechanism for pointing at a specific node in the XML tree. We call such an XML pointer a *navigator*. It must support operations for moving this pointer around the tree. To support all XPath axis evaluations, we must be able to move to the *first child* and *first attribute* of an element node, the *parent* and *next/previous sibling* of any tree node, and the *next/previous attribute* of an attribute node. We assume that this is sufficient for the XPath engine being used (for example, Jaxen [21] satisfies this).
– *Extraction*: The result of evaluating an XPath expression on the structure, using its navigation mechanism, is a set of navigators. From this set of navigators, we must be able to obtain the result of the `select` and `gapify` operations.

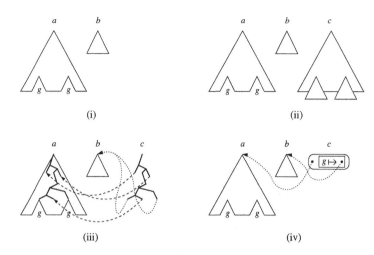

Fig. 1. The effect of performing the non-array `plug` operation, $c = a.\texttt{plug}(g, b)$. Part (i) shows the two templates, a and b, where a contains two g gaps. Part (ii) shows the naive approach for representing c, where everything has been copied. Part (iii) shows the basic approach from Section 4.1 where only the paths in a that lead to g gaps are copied and new edges are added pointing to the root of b. Part (iv) shows the lazy approach from Section 4.2 where a plug node is generated for recording the fact that b has been plugged into the g gaps of a. When the structure in (iv) is later normalized, the one in (iii) is obtained.

A naive data structure that trivially supports all of these operations is an explicit XML tree with *next_sibling*, *previous_sibling*, *first_child* and *parent* pointers in all nodes (where we encode attributes in the contents sequences). If such a data structure is used, we are forced to copy all parts of the operand structures that constitute parts of the result in order to adhere to the immutability constraint. The doubly-linked nature of the structure prohibits any sharing between individual XML values. The running times for the XACT operations on such a structure would thus be at least linear in the size of the result for each operation. As we show in the following, we can do better using a specialized data structure.

4.1   The Basic Approach

The main problem with the doubly-linked tree structure is that it prevents sharing between templates. To enable sharing, we use a singly-linked binary tree, that is, a tree with only *first_child* and *next_sibling* pointers but without the *parent* and *previous_sibling* pointers. This structure permits sharing as follows: whenever a subtree of an operand occurs as a subtree of the result, the corresponding pointer in the result simply points to the original operand subtree and thus avoids copying that subtree.

Recall that, unlike complete XML documents, an XML template does not necessarily have a single root element; rather, it can have an arbitrary sequence of elements, character data and template gaps, which we will refer to as the *top-level nodes*.

To perform a non-array `plug` operation, $a.\texttt{plug}(g, b)$, we copy just the portion of a that is not part of a subtree that will occur unmodified in the result. More precisely, this is the tree consisting of the paths from the root of a to all g gaps in a. Any pointer that branches out of these paths in the result points back to the corresponding subtree of a. If the gap has a next sibling, we will also need to copy the top-level nodes of b, since the list of successors for these nodes changes. This representation is depicted in Part (iii) of Figure 1. Note that, in general, this operation will create a DAG rather than a tree, since multiple occurrences of g in a will result in multiple pointers from the result to the root of b. The array `plug` operation is performed similarly, except that the path end pointers point to distinct templates. The `close` operation duplicates the paths to all gaps and removes the gaps from the duplicate.

To be able to find the paths to the g gaps efficiently, we must have additional information in the graph. In each node, we keep a record of which gap names occur in the subtree represented by that node. Since typical templates contain only few distinct gap names, this *gap presence* information can often be shared between many nodes and will not constitute a large overhead. Combining this information when constructing new templates is also straightforward. Now, when a `plug` operation into g traverses the graph looking for g gaps, it simply skips any branch where the gap presence information indicates that no g gaps exist. This narrows the search down to the paths from the root to the g gaps. Thus, the execution time for a `plug` operation is proportional to the number of nodes that are ancestors of g gaps in a (including preceding siblings because of our use of *first_child* and *next_sibling* pointers), plus the number of top-level nodes in b times the number of g gaps in a. For the array `plug` operation, the last term simply becomes the total number of top-level nodes in the plugged templates.

Constructing the representation of a tree from its textual representation using the `constant` operation takes time proportional to the size of the tree plus, for each node, the number of different gap names that appear in its subtree. The time for converting a template to text using `toString` is proportional to the template size.

Navigation in this structure is not as straightforward as in the doubly-linked case, since navigating backwards with *parent* or *previous sibling* requires information that is not available in the tree. We can support these directions by letting the navigators remember the entire path back to the root, and then backtrack along this path whenever a backward step is requested. In other words, we let the navigators contain all the backward pointers that the XML structure itself omits. Since navigators are always specific to one XML value, we do not restrict sharing by keeping these pointers while the navigator is used. Taking any navigator step still takes constant time.

The `select` operation simply returns a set of pointers to the nodes pointed to by the navigators that result from the XPath evaluation. Only the nodes pointed to are copied to make sure that their *next_sibling* pointers are empty. The total time for performing the `select` operation is proportional to the XPath evaluation time. The `gapify` operation first evaluates the XPath expression, resulting in a set of navigators that represent the addressed nodes. The tree from the root to these nodes is then copied, as for the `plug` operation. After that, the gap information in the nodes of the new tree is updated in a bottom-up traversal to include the new gaps. The total time for performing the `gapify` operation is proportional to the XPath evaluation time, which dominates the time for the other steps. Finally, the `smash` operation can be simulated by making a sequence of gap nodes with a fresh gap name and performing an array plug operation into these. This takes time proportional to the total number of top-level nodes in the smashed templates.

These figures may seem satisfactory; however, it turns out that this approach has some drawbacks as the following observations reveal.

- In a sequence of plug operations, each individual plug may create many nodes that will be replaced in a subsequent plug operation. If the intermediate results are not needed except as arguments for the subsequent plug operations (which is usually the case), constructing these nodes is unnecessary and wasteful. For example, a common idiom is to use a template `<li><[item]></li><[more]>` to build a list of `li` elements by repeatedly plugging the template itself into the `more` gap. Such a construction would take quadratic time in the length of the constructed list, since all preceding siblings need to be copied each time.
- Traversing the structure recursively when looking for gaps can lead to unwieldy stack sizes, since the ancestor nodes of the gaps include all preceding siblings. This problem clearly shows up in practice—the algorithm is unable to handle XML documents with more than a few thousand mutual siblings.

These observations lead us to a further refinement, as explained in the following section.

4.2   A Lazy Data Structure

We now present a modification of the basic structure that allows the operations to be performed lazily without any reconstruction taking place until explicit traversal of the tree is required. This effectively groups plug operations together in a way that permits list structures to be built in linear time.

To accomplish this, we introduce special *operation nodes* in the graph, each representing a `plug` or `close` operation (with `smash` being simulated by array `plug` as before). We call all other nodes *concrete nodes*. An operation node has one designated child node, which represents the *this* operand. There are three variants of operation nodes, corresponding to the two variants of the `plug` operation and the `close` operation, respectively: the *non-array plug node* is labeled with a gap name and has one extra edge corresponding to the value being plugged in; similarly, the *array plug node* is labeled with a gap name and an array of extra edges; and the *close node* has no extra information. Intuitively, an operation node merely records the fact that a `plug` or `close` operation has occurred without actually performing it. Part (iv) of Figure 1 illustrates this lazy variant of the plug operation.

As long as only `plug`, `close` and `smash` operations are performed, the resulting template will be represented by a DAG of operation nodes and concrete nodes, where all ancestors of operation nodes are themselves operation nodes. When the actual tree is needed, we need to unfold this structure into a DAG of only concrete nodes, so that the previously described navigation mechanism can be used. We refer to this process of eliminating operation nodes as *normalization*.

To perform normalization, we traverse the DAG depth-first while keeping track of the current *plug context*. A plug context is a map from gap names to nodes, defined by a list of operation nodes. The current plug context is always defined by the list of ancestor operation nodes of the current node. A non-array plug node maps its corresponding gap name to the root of the plugged template; an array plug node initially maps its gap name to the root of the first plugged template; and a close node maps all gap names to a special value *remove*. When more than one operation node mapping from the same gap name exist among the ancestors, the one furthest down in the DAG has precedence as it corresponds to an earlier plug operation.

Whenever we encounter a gap node with a name for which there is a mapping in the current plug context, we recursively traverse the template rooted at the node targeted by the mapping—or remove the gap node in case of the value *remove*. If the operation node is an array plug node, its mapping is changed to the next node on its list, or to the empty template if the list is exhausted. Note that the plug context in this traversal of the plugged template is defined by the operation node ancestors in the complete DAG, which includes the ones in the plugged template plus the ones created after it was plugged.

Just as for the plug operation in the basic approach, we only traverse the part of the DAG which actually needs to be duplicated. That is, we skip any branch where the gap presence information indicates that no gap exist for which there is a mapping in the current plug context. The only exception to this is the top-level nodes of plugged templates, which in general need to be duplicated, as before.

Following this strategy, we essentially perform a single traversal of the part of the final result which could not be shared with any of the constituent templates. Thus, assuming that the context lookup operations can be performed in amortized constant time (which can be accomplished by caching lookups), and assuming a constant number of distinct gap names, the running time for the entire normalization process is proportional to the number of newly created nodes. Since this is bounded by the size of the result and the result is typically traversed completely anyway, this is a satisfactory result.

To alleviate the stack requirement of the traversal, we use pointer reversal [25], which in essence uses the newly generated nodes as an explicit recursion stack. The recursion involved in the recursive unfolding of plugged templates mentioned above is done using a separate, explicit stack. Thus, with this strategy, the call stack usage is bounded by a constant, and the overall memory requirements are significantly reduced, compared to the purely recursive approach.

4.3   Java Issues

One of the prominent features of immutable data manipulation is that it works fluently in a multi-threaded environment. For this to work properly in the Java implementation, care must be taken when the internal state of a representation changes. This happens when the result of a normalization replaces the operation nodes—and this is of course properly synchronized in the implementation so that no thread will see the data structure in an inconsistent state, and no two threads will perform the same normalization simultaneously. Note also that the pointer reversal only changes newly created nodes, so another thread can traverse (and even normalize) a template sharing parts with the one being normalized without causing any problems.

A ubiquitous Java feature is the ability to compare objects using the `equals` method. This is easily (albeit not very efficiently) done for XML templates by a simple, parallel, recursive traversal. To conform to the Java guidelines, any implementation of `equals` must be consistent with the corresponding implementation of the `hashCode` method. To provide this consistency, each node includes a hash code representing the XML tree rooted at the node (including following siblings). The hash code for the entire template is then the hash code of the leftmost top-level node. This also enables a more efficient implementation of `equals`: whenever two compared subtemplates have different hash codes, their equality can be rejected right away. Furthermore, whenever two subtemplates originate from the same original subtemplate unmodified, their object identity verifies their equality.

5   Evaluation

This section describes experiments with our prototype implementation of the XACT runtime system. The main goal is to gather runtime performance measurements for a range of typical XML transformations in order to compare the performance of XACT with that of related systems. Due to the limited space, we can only provide a brief report on our evaluation results.

We have collected a suite of benchmark programs, most of which are inspired by XML transformations developed in other languages. A few programs have been developed to specifically test the worst-case behavior of our implementation. Altogether the suite covers a broad spectrum of typical XML transformation tasks.

Most of the related technologies mentioned in Section 1 are currently being developed by other research teams. Unfortunately, only a few have wished to provide an implementation, making it impossible to do a complete performance comparison of all the systems. Instead we have picked JDOM, XSLT and CDuce—for which optimized runtime systems are available—as good representatives for the different approaches. The JDOM and CDuce measurements are obtained using the latest releases (JDOM Beta 10, and CDuce 0.1.1.) The XSLT measurements are obtained using Apache Xalan 2.6, which supports the complete XSLT 1.0 language and is among the fastest Java-based implementations. For XACT, we use the lazy approach described in Section 4.2. All experiments have been executed on an 3.0 GHz Intel Pentium 4 machine with 1 GB RAM running Red Hat Linux 9.0 with Sun's Java 2 SE 1.4.2 and O'Caml 3.0.7. Since the focus of this paper is runtime performance we do not measure compilation and type checking. Furthermore, the price of parsing input XML documents says little about the relative strengths of the implementations, so this cost is excluded from measurements in order to give a fair comparison.

We start by comparing XACT with XSLT using four typical XML transformation tasks. Two transformations originate from the XSLTMark benchmark suite [9]: `Backwards` mirrors its input document by reversing the order of all node sequences; `DBOnerow` queries a person database for a single entry and transforms it into XHTML. Performance on mixed content documents is compared by `Uppercase`, which transforms all names in an address book into uppercase characters. `Phonelist` is the example from Section 2 transforming an address book into a sorted phone list. The transformations are executed on input XML documents of size 100 KB, 1 MB, and 10 MB.

	100 KB		1 MB		10 MB	
	XSLT	XACT	XSLT	XACT	XSLT	XACT
`Backwards`	551 ms	421 ms	1,615 ms	1,513 ms	15,373 ms	11,599 ms
`DBOnerow`	279 ms	160 ms	754 ms	274 ms	4,048 ms	994 ms
`Uppercase`	431 ms	246 ms	1,234 ms	634 ms	8,810 ms	5,365 ms
`Phonelist`	494 ms	423 ms	1,351 ms	1,799 ms	8,029 ms	21,834 ms

These figures indicate that the performances of the two are roughly similar. The main benefits of XACT compared to XSLT are the static guarantees and the possibility of applying the full Java language. For example, the Uppercase benchmark is only expressible in XSLT because this language contains a built-in function (translate) for mapping individual characters to other characters; more advanced character data transformations are not possible in XSLT without implementation dependent extension functions.

Next, we compare XACT with JDOM using the Linkset transformation (Example 15.8 in [13]), which extracts a set of links from an RDF feed, and the Phonelist transformation, which is described above.

	100 KB		1 MB		10 MB	
	JDOM	XACT	JDOM	XACT	JDOM	XACT
Linkset	23 ms	146 ms	128 ms	316 ms	304 ms	1,837 ms
Phonelist	80 ms	422 ms	408 ms	1,799 ms	3,212 ms	21,834 ms

These experiments indicate that the JDOM approach with mutable tree updates and purely navigational access, as one would expect, performs better than the immutable XACT approach based on XPath. However, this should be contrasted by the fact that the the XACT transformations are both shorter and more readable than the JDOM transformations. Furthermore, the XACT transformations are statically type safe in contrast to those written with JDOM.

For the comparison of XACT and CDuce we use our Phonelist transformation and the Split transformation, which is a benchmark program developed by the CDuce team and used in their performance comparisons.

	100 KB		1 MB		10 MB	
	CDuce	XACT	CDuce	XACT	CDuce	XACT
Phonelist	156 ms	422 ms	1,747 ms	1,799 ms	21,579 ms	21,834 ms
Split	94 ms	496 ms	496 ms	1,729 ms	*error*	12,897 ms

Since XACT uses Java and CDuce uses O'Caml, the performance is difficult to compare[4], but on these few benchmarks there seems to be no significant time difference for larger data sets. When running the CDuce Split transformation on the 10MB document, it runs out of memory, indicating that that the internal XML representation in XACT is more compact than the one in CDuce.

To demonstrate that the lazy approach is preferable to the basic one, we compare the two using a benchmark Logging, which extracts statistical information from a web server log file and exhibits the quadratic blowup for the basic approach:

	XACT (basic)	XACT (lazy)
Logging (100 KB)	709 ms	639 ms
Logging (1 MB)	3,189 ms	1,926 ms
Logging (3 MB)	11,227 ms	3,836 ms
Logging (10 MB)	*stack overflow*	9,011 ms

These figures show that the lazy approach can lead to significant saving in practice and how it scales smoothly to large documents.

---

[4] To exclude parsing time for CDuce, we measured the full time including parsing and then subtracted the time for performing the identity transformation.

In general, we conclude that the runtime system is sufficiently efficient. Our goal has not been to outperform the alternative XML transformation systems, but rather to be comparable in runtime performance and scalability, which complements the convenient language design and static analysis that XACT also provides.

Obviously, there are ways to improve performance further. We plan to experiment with caching of XPath parse trees, handling simple XPath expressions without involving the general XPath engine, and compiling XPath expression to basic navigation steps (as also done in the XJ project). Also, we believe that it is possible to exploit the knowledge gained from the static analysis for optimizing the evaluation of XPath expressions.

6   Conclusion

We have presented an overview of the XACT language, focusing on the runtime system. The design of XACT provides high-level primitives for programming XML transformations in the context of a general-purpose language, and, as shown in [20], it permits a precise static analysis. A special feature of the design is that the data-type is immutable, which at the same time is convenient to the programmer and a necessity for precise analysis. However, it also makes it nontrivial to construct a runtime system that efficiently supports all the XACT operations, which is the main problem being addressed in this paper. Our experiments indicate that the runtime system being proposed is sufficiently efficient to be practically useful.

Our prototype implementation, which consists of the runtime system, the desugarer, and the static analyzer supporting the full Java language, is available on the XACT home page: `http://www.brics.dk/Xact/`.

References

1. David Atkins, Thomas Ball, Glenn Bruns, and Kenneth Cox. Mawl: a domain-specific language for form-based services. *IEEE Transactions on Software Engineering*, 25(3):334–346, May/June 1999.
2. Véronique Benzaken, Giuseppe Castagna, and Alain Frisch. CDuce: An XML-centric general-purpose language. In *Proc. 8th ACM International Conference on Functional Programming, ICFP '03*, August 2003.
3. Joshua Bloch. *Effective Java Programming Language Guide*. Addison-Wesley, June 2001.
4. Scott Boag et al. XQuery 1.0: An XML query language, November 2003. W3C Working Draft. `http://www.w3.org/TR/xquery/`.
5. Claus Brabrand, Anders Møller, and Michael I. Schwartzbach. The <bigwig> project. *ACM Transactions on Internet Technology*, 2(2):79–114, 2002.
6. Aske Simon Christensen, Anders Møller, and Michael I. Schwartzbach. Extending Java for high-level Web service construction. *ACM Transactions on Programming Languages and Systems*, 25(6):814–875, November 2003.
7. James Clark. XSL transformations (XSLT) specification, November 1999. W3C Recommendation. `http://www.w3.org/TR/xslt`.
8. James Clark and Steve DeRose. XML path language, November 1999. W3C Recommendation. `http://www.w3.org/TR/xpath`.
9. DataPower. XSLTMark, 2001. `http://www.datapower.com/xmldev/xsltmark.html`.

10. Vladimir Gapayev and Benjamin C. Pierce. Regular object types. In *Proc. 17th European Conference on Object-Oriented Programming, ECOOP'03*, volume 2743 of *LNCS*. Springer-Verlag, July 2003.

11. Vladimir Gapeyev, Michael Y. Levin, Benjamin C. Pierce, and Alan Schmitt. XML goes native: Run-time representations for Xtatic, 2004.

12. Georg Gottlob, Christoph Koch, and Reinhard Pichler. XPath query evaluation: Improving time and space efficiency. In *Proc. 19th International Conference on Data Engineering, ICDE'03*. IEEE Computer Society, March 2003.

13. Elliotte Rusty Harold. *Processing XML with Java*. Addison-Wesley, November 2002.

14. Matthew Harren, Mukund Raghavachari, Oded Shmueli, Michael Burke, Vivek Sarkar, and Rajesh Bordawekar. XJ: Integration of XML processing into Java. Technical Report RC23007, IBM Research, 2003.

15. Haruo Hosoya and Benjamin C. Pierce. XDuce: A typed XML processing language. In *Proc. 3rd International Workshop on the World Wide Web and Databases, WebDB '00*, volume 1997 of *LNCS*. Springer-Verlag, May 2000.

16. Haruo Hosoya and Benjamin C. Pierce. XDuce: A statically typed XML processing language. *ACM Transactions on Internet Technology*, 3(2), 2003.

17. Jason Hunter and Brett McLaughlin. JDOM, 2004. `http://jdom.org/`.

18. Michael Kay. XSL transformations (XSLT) version 2.0, May 2003. W3C Working Draft. `http://www.w3.org/TR/xslt20/`.

19. Martin Kempa and Volker Linnemann. Type checking in XOBE. In *Proc. Datenbanksysteme für Business, Technologie und Web, BTW '03*, volume 26 of *LNI*, February 2003.

20. Christian Kirkegaard, Anders Møller, and Michael I. Schwartzbach. Static analysis of XML transformations in Java. *IEEE Transactions on Software Engineering*, 30(3):181–192, March 2004.

21. Bob McWhirter et al. Jaxen, December 2003. `http://jaxen.org/`.

22. Erik Meijer, Wolfram Schulte, and Gavin Bierman. Programming with rectangles, triangles, and circles. In *Proc. XML Conference and Exposition, XML '03*, December 2003.

23. John C. Reynolds. Intuitionistic reasoning about shared mutable data structure. In Jim Davies, Bill Roscoe, and Jim Woodcock, editors, *Millennial Perspectives in Computer Science, Proc. 1999 Oxford–Microsoft Symposium in Honour of Sir Tony Hoare*, pages 303–321. Palgrave, November 2000.

24. Shmuel Sagiv, Thomas W. Reps, and Reinhard Wilhelm. Parametric shape analysis via 3-valued logic. *ACM Transactions on Programming Languages and Systems*, 24(3):217–298, 2002.

25. H. Schorr and W. M. Waite. An efficient machine independent procedure for garbage collection in various list structures. *Communications of the ACM*, 10(8):501–506, August 1967.

26. Bill Venners. A conversation with James Gosling. JavaWorld, June 2001.

27. Malcolm Wallace and Colin Runciman. Haskell and XML: Generic combinators or type-based translation? In *Proc. 5th ACM SIGPLAN International Conference on Functional Programming, ICFP '99*, September 1999.

Teaching Relational Optimizers About XML Processing

Sihem Amer-Yahia, Yannis Kotidis, and Divesh Srivastava

AT&T Labs-Research, Florham Park NJ 07932, USA,
{sihem,kotidis,divesh}@research.att.com

Abstract. Due to their numerous benefits, relational systems play a major role in storing XML documents. XML also benefits relational systems by providing a means to publish legacy relational data. Consequently, a large volume of XML data is stored in and produced from relations. However, relational systems are not well-tuned to produce XML data efficiently. This is mainly due to the flat nature of relational data as opposed to the tree structure of XML documents. In this paper, we argue that relational query optimizers need to incorporate new optimization techniques that are better suited for XML. In particular, we explore new optimization techniques that enable computation sharing between queries that construct sibling elements in the XML tree. Such queries often have large common join expressions that can be shared through appropriate rewritings. We show experimentally that these rewritings are fundamental when building XML documents from relations.

1 Introduction

Relational systems are good for XML and XML is good for relations. On the one hand, there are mature relational systems that can be used to store the ever growing number of XML documents that are being created. On the other hand, XML is a great interface to publish and exchange legacy relational data. Consequently, most XML data today comes from and ends up in relations. Unfortunately, XML and relational data differ in their very nature. One is tree-structured, the other is flat and often normalized. Consequently, the performance of relational engines varies considerably when producing XML documents from relations. In research, several efforts explored how to build XML documents from relations efficiently [2][4][5] [7][9]. In particular, the authors in [7] argue for extending relational engines to benefit XML queries. In this work, we explore complementary *optimization* techniques that are fundamental to handle XML queries efficiently in a relational engine.

Due to the flat nature of relational data, as opposed to the nested structure of XML, generating an XML document from relations often involves evaluating multiple SQL queries (possibly as many as the number of nodes in the DTD). These queries often contain common sub-expressions in order to build the tree structure. Thus, query performance can vary considerably, necessitating a cost-based optimization of the plan for building XML documents. In [9], the authors explore rewriting-based optimizations between a query for a parent node and the queries for its children nodes in a middle-ware environment. We argue that sharing computation between queries for sibling nodes, not just between parent and children queries, is key to efficiently building XML documents

Z. Bellahsène et al. (Eds.): XSym 2004, LNCS 3186, pp. 158–172, 2004.

from relational data, both in a middle-ware environment (as in [9]) and for the query optimizer of a relational system.

Consider a publishing example where we want to build XML documents from a TPC-H database [16]. These documents conform to a DTD with Customer as a root element and its two sub-elements SuppName (for suppliers) and PartName (for parts). In order to identify the suppliers of a given customer, the TPC-H table, CUSTOMER, is joined with ORDERS and LINEITEM. This join expression needs to be joined with the SUPPLIER table to compute supplier names (i.e., element SuppName). This same join expression (between CUSTOMER, ORDERS and LINEITEM) needs to be joined with the PART table to evaluate the set of part names associated with each customer (i.e., PartName). Obviously, the sibling queries at the two elements SuppName and PartName share a large common join expression and could be merged into a single query (using an outer union) where this common join expression is factored out, enabling the relational engine to evaluate it only once. In [9], every such query merge has to go through a parent/child merge. For example, the two sibling queries at SuppName and PartName can be merged only if they are also joined with the query at Customer, resulting in a single query that is used to evaluate the whole document. If Customer is a "fat" node (containing multiple attributes such as Name, Zip and Phone), the entire customer information will be replicated with each SuppName and each PartName (because of outer-joins) which may result in higher communication costs (in a middle-ware environment) and computation costs (both in a middle-ware environment, and in a relational optimizer). Being able to merge sibling queries independently from their parent query and factor out common sub-expressions in merged queries is a key rewriting that we will explore when building XML documents from relations.

Our contributions are as follows:

- We show that sharing computation between sibling queries is a fundamental optimization for efficient building of XML documents from flat relational data.
- We describe several query rewritings that exploit shared computation between queries used to build an XML document.
- We design an optimization algorithm that applies our rewritings to find the best set of SQL queries that optimizes processing time and achieves a good compromise between processing and communication times in a middle-ware environment.
- We run experiments that compare multiple strategies of sharing common computation between sibling queries and identify their considerable performance benefits.

Section 2 describes our motivating examples and gives a formal definition of our problem. Rewriting techniques are presented in Section 3. Section 4 contains the optimization algorithm and a study of the search space. Experimental results are presented in Section 5. Related work is discussed in Section 6. Section 7 concludes.

2   Motivation and Problem Definition

2.1   Publishing Legacy Data in XML

We consider a simplified version of the relational schema of the TPC-H benchmark [16]. This schema describes parts ordered by customers and provided by suppliers.

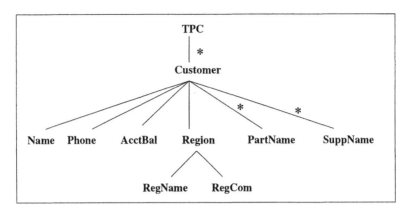

Fig. 1. Publishing Legacy Data: Example DTD

```
CUSTOMER[C_CUSTKEY,C_NAME,C_PHONE,C_ACCTBAL,C_NATIONKEY]
NATION[N_NATIONKEY,N_NAME,N_REGIONKEY]
REGION[R_REGIONKEY,R_NAME,R_COMMENT]
PART[P_PARTKEY,P_NAME]
SUPPLIER[S_SUPPKEY,S_NAME,S_NATIONKEY]
ORDERS[O_ORDERKEY,O_CUSTKEY]
LINEITEM[L_ORDERKEY,L_PARTKEY,L_SUPPKEY]
```

We want to build XML documents that conform to the DTD given in Fig. 1. To keep the exposition simple, we represent this DTD as a tree. Edges labeled with a '*' are used for repeated sub-elements. We are interested only in publishing information about customers whose account balance is lower than $5000 (predicate p). PartName contains the names of the parts ordered by a customer. SuppName contains the names of their suppliers.

It has been shown previously in [5] that it is possible to write a single SQL query (containing outer-joins and possibly outer-unions) to build an XML document for a relational database regardless of the underlying relational schema. It has also been shown in [9] that a set of SQL queries that are equivalent to the single query can be generated. In order to better explain performance issues, we examine the case where an SQL query is generated for each element in the DTD as follows (where $C = \sigma_p$ (CUSTOMER), $J1 = C \bowtie_{\text{NATIONKEY}}$ NATION $\bowtie_{\text{REGIONKEY}}$ REGION and $J2 = C \bowtie_{\text{CUSTKEY}}$ ORDERS $\bowtie_{\text{ORDERKEY}}$ LINEITEM):

$$Q_{\text{Customer}} = \pi_{\text{C\_CUSTKEY}}(C)$$
$$Q_{\text{Name}} = \pi_{\text{C\_CUSTKEY,C\_NAME}}(C)$$
$$Q_{\text{Phone}} = \pi_{\text{C\_CUSTKEY,C\_PHONE}}(C)$$
$$Q_{\text{AcctBal}} = \pi_{\text{C\_CUSTKEY,C\_ACCTBAL}}(C)$$
$$Q_{\text{Region}} = \pi_{\text{C\_CUSTKEY,R\_REGIONKEY}}(J1)$$
$$Q_{\text{RegName}} = \pi_{\text{C\_CUSTKEY,R\_REGIONKEY,R\_NAME}}(J1)$$
$$Q_{\text{RegCom}} = \pi_{\text{C\_CUSTKEY,R\_REGIONKEY,R\_COMMENT}}(J1)$$
$$Q_{\text{PartName}} = \pi_{\text{C\_CUSTKEY,P\_NAME}}(J2 \bowtie_{\text{PARTKEY}} \text{PART})$$

$$Q_{\texttt{SuppName}} = \pi_{\texttt{C\_CUSTKEY,S\_NAME}}(J2 \bowtie_{\texttt{SUPPKEY}} \texttt{SUPPLIER})$$

Several sibling queries share common expressions. The simplest example is the case of $Q_{\texttt{Name}}$, $Q_{\texttt{Phone}}$ and $Q_{\texttt{AcctBal}}$ that are all projections on the same (subset of the) CUSTOMER table. This is due to the fact that some fields in this table are used to generate sub-elements. Thus, these sibling queries could be merged into a single query Q_C. The merged query could further be merged with the parent query, $Q_{\texttt{Customer}}$, resulting in "fat" customer nodes as follows:

$$Q_C = \pi_{\texttt{C\_CUSTKEY,C\_NAME,C\_PHONE,C\_ACCTBAL}}(C)$$

The second example involves $Q_{\texttt{RegName}}$ and $Q_{\texttt{RegCom}}$ that share a common join expression $J1$. This is due to the fact that nations and regions are normalized into tables and that recovering them requires performing joins with these intermediate tables. By merging $Q_{\texttt{RegName}}$ and $Q_{\texttt{RegCom}}$ into a single query, the common expression is evaluated only once:

$$Q_{\texttt{RegNameCom}} = \pi_{\texttt{C\_CUSTKEY,R\_REGIONKEY,R\_NAME,R\_COMMENT}}(J1)$$

Furthermore, $Q_{\texttt{RegNameCom}}$ could be merged with Q_C resulting in:

$$\pi_{\texttt{C\_CUSTKEY,C\_NAME,C\_PHONE,C\_ACCTBAL,R\_REGIONKEY,R\_NAME,R\_COMMENT}}(J1)$$

The last and most interesting example is the case of the two sibling queries $Q_{\texttt{PartName}}$ and $Q_{\texttt{SuppName}}$ that share a common join expression $J2$. In order to share this join expression, the two queries could be merged. However, due to the fact that a customer has multiple parts and suppliers, merging $Q_{\texttt{PartName}}$ and $Q_{\texttt{SuppName}}$ might result in replication. Replication might slow down query processing as well as communication time. There are two ways to avoid replication in this case. Either the relational optimizer is able to optimize outer unions and the queries are rewritten using an outer-union where the common sub-expression is factored out. Or, the relational engine is forced to compute $J2$, materialize it and then use it to evaluate the two queries. The query $Q_{\texttt{PartSupp}}$ that results from the outer union is given by:

$$(\pi_{\texttt{C\_CUSTKEY,P\_NAME,NULL}}(J2 \bowtie_{\texttt{PARTKEY}} \texttt{PART})) \cup (\pi_{\texttt{C\_CUSTKEY,NULL,S\_NAME}}(J2 \bowtie_{\texttt{SUPPKEY}} \texttt{SUPPLIER}))$$

Because of the presence/absence of some indices, it might not always be the case that the merged query, $Q_{\texttt{PartSupp}}$ is cheaper than the sum of $Q_{\texttt{PartName}}$ and $Q_{\texttt{SuppName}}$. The relational optimizer could choose different plans to evaluate the common join expression in the two queries resulting in a better evaluation time than the merged query.

Finally, using an outer-join, it is possible to rewrite all of the nine queries above into a single query. That outer-join guarantees that all customers satisfying predicate p will be selected (even if they have never ordered any part). However, if all queries are merged, each customer tuple (along with its required fields) will be replicated as many times as the number of parts and suppliers for this customer. This replication is due to merging queries with their parent query and impacts computation time as well as query result size. Therefore, depending on the amount of replication generated by

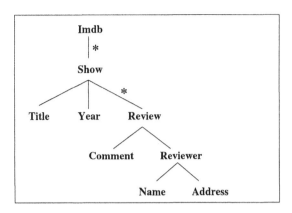

Fig. 2. Shredded XML: Example DTD

merging sibling queries with their parent query, it might be desirable to optimize queries at siblings *separately* from their parent query.

A key observation is that shared computation between sibling queries, when building XML data from relations, is often higher than shared computation between parent and children queries making sibling merges more appropriate than merging with the parent query. This is particularly true in two cases: (i) if the relational schema is highly normalized and thus, several joins involving intermediate relations are needed to compute sub-elements, and (ii) if the DTD contains repeated sub-elements that might create replication (of the parent node) when children and parent queries are merged together.

2.2   Building XML Documents from Shredded XML

There have been many efforts to explore different shredding schemas for XML into relations [1]. Most of them rely on using key/foreign key relationships to capture document structure and thus, generate sibling queries with common sub-expressions when building XML documents.

Fig. 2 contains the DTD of a document that has been shredded and stored in a relational database. The example contains information on shows such as their title and year as well as the reviews written by a reviewer who has a name and an address. We first consider the relational schema Schema1 given below:

```
SHOW[SHOW_ID,TITLE,YEAR]
REVIEW[REVIEW_ID,COMMENT,SHOW_ID]
REVIEWER[REVIEWER_ID,NAME,ADDRESS_ID,REVIEW_ID]
ADDRESS[ADDRESS_ID,ADDRESS]
```

In order to compute the Name and Address of each reviewer in a review associated with a show, the following two queries are needed (where $J = \text{REVIEW} \bowtie_{\text{REVIEW\_ID}} \text{REVIEWER}$):

$$Q_{\text{Name}} = \pi_{\text{SHOW\_ID,REVIEW\_ID,REVIEWER\_ID,NAME}}(J)$$
$$Q_{\text{Address}} = \pi_{\text{SHOW\_ID,REVIEW\_ID,REVIEWER\_ID,ADDRESS}}(J \bowtie_{\text{ADDRESS\_ID}} \text{ADDRESS})$$

These queries share a common sub-expression J. If the address of a reviewer was inlined inside a review in the relational schema, no redundant computation would have occurred. This is illustrated in Schema2 as follows:

```
SHOW[SHOW_ID,TITLE,YEAR]
REVIEW[REVIEW_ID,COMMENT,NAME,ADDRESS,SHOW_ID]
```

In this case, $Q_{\texttt{Name}}$ and $Q_{\texttt{Address}}$ correspond to simple projections on the REVIEW table and could be easily merged into a single query.

Even when a query workload is used for XML storage in relations, as in [3], our optimization techniques for SQL "publishing" queries are still useful for two reasons. First, an improved optimizer can provide more accurate cost estimates for the queries in the workload, for making cost-based shredding decisions. Second, queries that are not in the initial query workload would still need to be optimized in an ad-hoc fashion.

2.3   Problem Definition

We are interested in building XML documents from a relational store efficiently. Following the approaches used in [4][9], the structure of the resulting XML documents is abstracted as a DTD-like labeled tree structure, with element tags serving as node labels, and edge labels indicating the multiplicity of a child element under a parent element; it is important to note that multiple nodes in this DTD-like structure may have the same element tag, due to element sharing, or due to data recursion.

SQL queries are associated with nodes in this DTD-like structure, and together determine the structure and content of the resulting XML documents that are built from the relational store; the examples in Section 2.1 are illustrative. The set of SQL queries generated for a given XML document might be small. However, the amount of data that these queries manipulate can be large and thus, optimization is necessary. If we denote by S the set of all SQL queries necessary to build a document conforming to a given DTD, then the problem is formulated as follows:

find the set of SQL queries S such that $\Sigma_{s\in S}(w_p * proc(s) + w_c * comm(s))$ is minimized

where $proc$ (resp. $comm$) is a function that computes the cost of processing (resp. communicating the result of) a SQL query and w_p, w_c are weights chosen appropriately. In a centralized environment, communication cost might not be relevant in which case, it could be removed from the cost model.

3   Queries and Rewriting Rules

We explore several possible rewritings that share common computation between queries and use the relational optimizer as an oracle to optimize and estimate the cost of individual SQL queries. This technique can be used both by a middle-ware environment (as in [9]) and to extend a relational optimizer to be able to perform the optimizations we are considering.

3.1 Query Definition

In order to better explain the rewriting rules we are using, we first define the query expressions used to build a single XML document. Sorting is omitted in our queries since it does not affect our rewritings.

Definition 1 [Atomic Node] *An atomic node is a node in the DTD which has a unique instance for each distinct instance of its parent node.*

By convention, the root of the XML document is an atomic node. Examples of atomic nodes are RegName and Name (in the DTD of Fig. 1). Each customer has a single value for these nodes. Thus, given a node in the tree, there exists a functional dependency between each instance of that node and each corresponding instance of its atomic children nodes.

Definition 2 [Multiple Node] *A multiple node corresponds to a node in the DTD which may have multiple instances for each distinct instance of its parent node.*

An example of a multiple node is the PartName node.

In order to compute instances of an XML node, a unique SQL query is associated with that node. The evaluation of that query results in a set of tuples each of which is used to create an instance. There is a one-to-one correspondence between the tuples that are in the result of a SQL query at a node and the instances of that node. This semantics is similar to that of the Skolem functions used in [9]. Therefore, a key (that might be composed of attributes coming from different relations) is associated with each node in the XML document and is in the set of projected attributes at that node. Each distinct value of the key determines a distinct instance of the node to which that key is associated.

In an XML document, parent/child relationships correspond to key/foreign key joins between parent queries and children queries. Thus, in order to build the XML document tree structure, the query used at a node must always include the query at its parent node. Therefore, queries at nodes are defined as follows.

Definition 3 [Queries] *Given query $Q_p = \pi_p exp_p$ at node p (p is the key at node p) and query Q_c at node c, if c is a child of p, then Q_c is defined by one of:*

- $Q_c = \pi_{p,c} exp_p$. *Q_c is a simple projection on the expression used to evaluate the parent node p.*
- $Q_c = \pi_{p,c}(exp_p \bowtie exp_c)$. *$Q_c$ is a projection on a join expression containing the parent node expression.*

If the relational schema is highly normalized, a join expression is often necessary in computing the instances of XML nodes. In the case of a multiple node, this join is used to build a one-to-many relationship from flat relational data. If the relational schema contains an un-normalized relation, simple projections often suffice to compute node values.

In the definition given above, exp_c can be any expression that might include an arbitrary number of joins. It is necessary that the key value p used to compute the parent node p, is a subset of the keys of its children nodes. An example is the query used to evaluate atomic nodes such as Name. In this query, the customer identifier CUSTKEY is also projected out and determines the customer to which each name instance is associated. The query used to evaluate the node RegName is an example of the presence of a join expression in the child query. In fact, in this particular case, even if a join expression is used, it is guaranteed that there is a unique region name per customer. The expression at the node PartName is an example of a query used to compute a multiple node.

Given two queries corresponding to the parent and child elements or to two sibling elements, we rewrite them in two steps. First, these queries are *merged* resulting in a single SQL query. Second, *common sub-expression elimination* is applied to the merged query if it contains redundant expressions. We now define query merging and common sub-expression elimination in our context.

3.2   Query Merging

Definition 4 [Parent/child Merging] *Given a node p and its query Q_p and a node c, which is a child of p and its query Q_c, merging Q'_p and Q_c results in a query Q defined as follows:*

1. *If $Q_p = \pi_p exp_p$ and $Q_c = \pi_{p,c} exp_p$, then $Q = \pi_{p,c} exp_p$.*
2. *If $Q_p = \pi_p exp_p$ and $Q_c = \pi_{p,c}(exp_p \bowtie exp_c)$, then $Q = (\pi_p exp_p) \bar{\bowtie} (\pi_{p,c}(exp_p \bowtie exp_c))$.*

An example of the first merge is the case of merging the Customer query with the query at its child node Name. An example of the second one is the case of merging the Customer query with its child node PartName.

Definition 5 [Sibling Merging] *Given two sibling nodes c_1 and c_2 sharing a common parent p, merging their queries Q_{c_1} and Q_{c_2} results in a query Q defined as follows:*

1. *If c_1 and c_2 are both atomic nodes such that $Q_{c_1} = \pi_{p,c_1} exp$ and $Q_{c_2} = \pi_{p,c_2} exp$, then $Q = \pi_{p,c_1,c_2} exp$.*
2. *If one of c_1 or c_2 is a multiple node, then $Q = Q_{c_1} \cup Q_{c_2}$ where $\cup$ is an outer-union.*

An example of the first kind of sibling merge is the case of nodes RegName and RegCom. In this case, the expression that merges queries at those nodes has a simple union of the projection lists of the two initial queries. The second sibling merge case is more general. An example of that is the query that results from merging the queries at nodes PartName and SuppName (see Section 2).

3.3   Exploiting Common Sub-expressions

Since each query must contain its parent query, the *largest expression* a parent query shares with its children queries is itself. Thus, given two sibling queries, the *smallest expression* these queries have in common is their parent query. Sibling queries could have more in common, though. The query obtained from either the parent/child or sibling query merging will often contain redundant expressions.

The first case of parent/child merging (in Definition 4) and the first case of sibling merging (in Definition 5) rewrite the two input queries in a way that factors out the common expression between the two queries. The two remaining cases, in the same definitions, are the cases that will be discussed in this section.

Definition 6 [Parent/child Sharing] *The merged query is* $Q = (\pi_p exp_p) \bar{\bowtie}$ $(\pi_{p,c}(exp_p \bowtie exp_c))$, *where* $(\pi_p exp_p)$ *is the parent expression, which can be factored out as follows:* $Q = \pi_{p,c}(exp_p \bar{\bowtie} exp_c)$.

One might think that it is always a good idea to factor out the common parent expression after a parent/child merge. Our experiments, in Section 5, show that this choice might not always be the best depending on the presence of selection predicates in the expressions.

Definition 7 [Sibling Sharing] *Given two sibling queries* Q_{c_1} *and* Q_{c_2}, *where* c_2 *is a multiple node, depending on* c_1 *being atomic or multiple, the merged query* Q *is defined by:*

1. $Q = (\pi_{p,c_1} exp_p) \cup (\pi_{p,c_2}(exp_p \bowtie exp_{c_2}))$.
2. $Q = (\pi_{p,c_1}(exp_p \bowtie exp_{c_1})) \cup (\pi_{p,c_2}(exp_p \bowtie exp_{c_2}))$.

The query in the second sibling sharing case is the one that deserves most attention. Let us consider the example of merging PartName and SuppName (in the DTD of Fig. 1) and write the corresponding queries in SQL.

Below, we give three versions of the query that merges $Q_{\texttt{PartName}}$ and $Q_{\texttt{SuppName}}$. Q, MaxQ and MinQ are three equivalent queries where common sub-expressions are treated differently.

```
Q
select  Q.ckey, Q.sname, Q.pname
from
((select distinct 1 as L, C_CUSTKEY as ckey, S_SUPPKEY as skey, S_NAME as sname,
                NULL as pkey, NULL as pname
   from   CUSTOMER,SUPPLIER,LINEITEM,ORDERS
   where  S_SUPPKEY=L_SUPPKEY and L_ORDERKEY=O_ORDERKEY
   and    C_CUSTKEY = O_CUSTKEY and C_ACCTBAL < 5000 )
UNION ALL
 (select distinct 2 as L, C_CUSTKEY as ckey,
                NULL as skey, NULL as sname,
                P_PARTKEY as pkey, P_NAME as pname
   from   CUSTOMER,PART,LINEITEM,ORDERS
   where  P_PARTKEY=L_PARTKEY and L_ORDERKEY=O_ORDERKEY
   and    C_CUSTKEY = O_CUSTKEY and C_ACCTBAL < 5000)
 ) Q
order by Q.ckey,L;
```

Q is the "naive" query where $Q_{\texttt{PartName}}$ and $Q_{\texttt{SuppName}}$ are merged using an outer-union. No common expression elimination is applied to it. Dummy field L is introduced to separate parts and suppliers for each customer (for the purpose of building the final XML document).

```
MaxQ
select distinct C_CUSTKEY as ckey, Q.sname,Q.pname
from   ORDERS, CUSTOMER, LINEITEM
((select 1 as L, S_SUPPKEY as skey,
        S_NAME as sname, NULL as pkey, NULL as pname
   from   SUPPLIER)
```

```
UNION ALL
(select 2 as L, NULL as skey, NULL as sname,
       P_PARTKEY as pkey, P_NAME as pname
  from   PART)
) Q
where C_ACCTBAL < 5000 and C_CUSTKEY = O_CUSTKEY
and   L_ORDERKEY = O_ORDERKEY and (Q.skey = L_SUPPKEY or Q.pkey = L_PARTKEY)
order by C_CUSTKEY,L;
```

MaxQ is a rewriting of Q where the common join between ORDERS, CUSTOMER and LINEITEM is factored out. This join is the *largest shared expression* between the two siblings. The disjunctive condition (Q.skey = L_SUPPKEY or Q.pkey = L_PARTKEY), results from the fact that the common join expression needs to be joined with suppliers using Q.skey = L_SUPPKEY and with parts using Q.pkey = L_PARTKEY. The outer-union operation now computes all suppliers and parts.[1]

```
MinQ
select distinct C_CUSTKEY as ckey, Q.sname, Q.pname
from   ORDERS, CUSTOMER,
((select  1 as L, L_ORDERKEY, S_NAME as sname, NULL as pname
  from    SUPPLIER,LINEITEM
  where   S_SUPPKEY=L_SUPPKEY)
  UNION ALL
(select  2 as L, L_ORDERKEY, NULL as sname, P_NAME as pname
  from    PART, LINEITEM
  where   P_PARTKEY=L_PARTKEY)
) Q
where C_ACCTBAL< 5000
and   C_CUSTKEY = O_CUSTKEY and Q.L_ORDERKEY = O_ORDERKEY
order by C_CUSTKEY,Q.L;
```

MinQ is a variant of MaxQ where the main goal is to avoid disjunctive join conditions and cope with current day relational optimizers which are unable to deal with disjunctive predicates efficiently. However, since MinQ replicates a portion of the common join condition (in the example, the one with the LINEITEM table), it might not always perform better than MaxQ. Therefore, we explore both rewritings: *complete common sub-expression elimination* which results in unions and may introduce disjunctive conditions and *partial common sub-expression elimination* which results in unions and has only conjunctive predicates.

4   Optimization

We designed two greedy algorithms: OptimizeSiblings() and OptimizeAll(). OptimizeSiblings() explores merges and computation sharing between sibling queries only while OptimizeAll() interleaves merging of sibling queries and merging of parent/child queries.

4.1   Sibling Optimization

OptimizeSiblings(), given in Algorithm 2, explores the benefits of sibling merging for each pair of sibling nodes. The benefit of merging two sibling queries can be either

---

[1] This may not be the case if additional predicates on parts and/or suppliers are used.

Algorithm 1 compute_benefit() Algorithm

Require: x, y

1: #define cost(q) (w_p*proc(q)+w_c*comm(q))
2: c_before_merge = cost(x) + cost(y)
3: c_after_merge = min(cost(Q(x,y)), cost(MaxQ(x,y)), cost(MinQ(x,y))){pick best sibling merge}
4: benefit(x,y) = c_before_merge − c_after_merge

Algorithm 2 OptimizeSiblings() Algorithm

Require: $Tree$

1: **while** not_empty(s_list) **do**
2:     pick (x,y): max(benefit(x,y)) in s_list {Pick most beneficial siblings to merge}
3:     **stop if** benefit(x,y)<0
4:     sibling_merge_rewrite(x,y) {replace x, y with merged query}
5:     children(x)+=children(y) {y-subtree is attached to x}
6:     remove(y,*) from s_list
7:     remove(*,y) from s_list
8:     compute_benefit(x,*) in s_list
9:     compute_benefit(*,x) in s_list
10: **end while**

---

positive or negative. It is computed as the difference between the processing and communication costs of the two queries at nodes x and y and the rewritten query (where both queries are merged) (see Algorithm 1).

Candidate pairs are stored in a list s_list. At each step in the optimization algorithm, the sibling pair that offers the best benefit (say (x,y)) is selected to be rewritten. The query at node x now contains the merged expression between x and y. The query at node y no longer exists. Thus, all pairs of the form (y,*) and (*,y) are removed from the candidate sibling merges s_list. This includes (x,y), which is no longer a candidate pair. Finally, since the query expression at node x has been modified, the algorithm recomputes the benefit of all candidate sibling merges that involve node x (i.e., (x,*) and (*,x)).

Once two sibling queries are merged, OptimizeSiblings() rewrites them to eliminate common computation. The algorithm chooses the best of Q, MaxQ and MinQ using compute_benefits().

If two sibling queries are merged, their children queries become siblings and could be considered for additional sibling merges. However, the potential for these new sibling queries to share large common sub-expressions reduces. In addition, considering these queries for sibling merging would increase the search space size. Therefore, as a heuristic, the only candidate sibling pairs (x,y) we consider are the ones where x and y are siblings in the initial set of queries.

4.2 Combined Optimization

OptimizeAll() is given in Algorithm 3. Once a parent/child or a sibling merge has been performed, the difference between OptimizeAll() and OptimizeSiblings()

Algorithm 3 OptimizeAll() Algorithm

Require: Tree
  1: **while** not_empty(list=union(s_list,pc_list)) **do**
  2:    pick (x,y): max(benefit(x,y)) in list
  3:    **stop if** benefit(x,y)<0
  4:    **if** (x,y) in s_list **then**
  5:      sibling_merge_rewrite(x,y)
  6:    **else**
  7:      pc_merge_rewrite(x,y)
  8:    **end if**
  9:    children(x)+=children(y)
10:    remove (y,*) and (*,y) from s_list
11:    compute_benefit(x,*) in s_list
12:    compute_benefit(*,x) in s_list
13:    remove(parent(y),y) from pc_list
14:    compute_benefit(parent(x),x) in pc_list
15:    compute_benefit(x,*) in pc_list
16: **end while**

---

is the impact on pc_list, the candidate parent/child merges list. Since node y does not exist anymore, (parent(y),y) needs to be removed from pc_list. In addition, since the query at node x now contains the merged query, the benefits of (parent(x),x) and of (x,*) are recomputed. In order to remain within good complexity bounds, the same assumption as for OptimizeSiblings() is made on sibling merges. In addition, this assumption is also made for parent/child merges. When a parent/child merge (x,y) is performed, the subtree rooted at y becomes directly related to x. In this case, we do not consider the new children of x as candidate merges.

4.3 Cost Analysis

Given $|\mathcal{S}|$ queries, the maximal initial size of pc_list is $|\mathcal{S}|\text{-}1=O(|\mathcal{S}|)$ and the maximal initial size of s_list is $\Sigma_{q\in\mathcal{S}}(f(q)(f(q)-1)/2) = O(|S|^2)$, where $f(q)$ is the fanout of query q (number of children queries) in the XML tree. The initialization of the two lists needs $O(|S|^2)$ time and space. At each step where a pair (x,y) is selected, we remove at least one element from pc_list. For each node q whose children are in s_list there can be at most $f(q)$ sibling merges each taking at most $O(f(q))$ time. Therefore, the number of iterations is linear in the number of queries and each takes linear time. Thus, the number of steps required is linear in the number of queries: $O(|S|)$ where the initial number of elements in s_list is at most $O(|S|^2)$.

5 Experiments

Due to space constraints, we only present a short set of experiments that evaluate sibling rewritings against the rewriting techniques of [9] and [15]. These experiments were carried on a 500Mhz Pentium III PC with 256MB of main memory and refer to

Table 1. Execution Times (secs)

	Q1	Q2	Q3	Q12	Q13	Q23	Q123
	Small-Doc						
Q	2.91	154.46	200.30	242.86	316.29	568.88	849.07
MaxQ	-	-	-	1034.70	1332.63	473.48	3338.18
MinQ	-	-	-	-	-	349.11	3136.87
	Large-Doc						
Q	11.51	1193.03	1439.83	1396.97	1695.97	3626.64	5897.71
MaxQ	-	-	-	1352.12	1650.23	2366.28	5794.31
MinQ	-	-	-	-	-	2175.90	5586.54

an instance of the TPC-R [16] dataset using scaling factor 0.2. We used a commercial RDBMS for storing the data. All tables have indices on primary and foreign keys.

5.1 Data

Our documents conform to a simpler version of the DTD in Fig. 1 with only the Customer, PartName and SuppName nodes. There are three basic queries corresponding to the nodes of this DTD. Query Q1 instantiates the Customer node, Q2 the PartName node and Q3 the SuppName node.

We used the field C_CUSTKEY of the CUSTOMER table to control the size of the documents we build. For the case denoted as "Small-Doc", we instantiated the document for customers with C_CUSTKEY less than 5000 (i.e., 5000 tuples). The document denoted as "Large-Doc" is generated with no restrictions on C_CUSTKEY. The Customer node for both documents is "fat", i.e. all fields from table CUSTOMER are published as attributes of Customer. Table 1 summarizes the execution times of all possible parent-child/sibling merges as well as the queries corresponding to each node in the DTD. Qij denotes the merged result of queries Qi and Qj. For example Q12 is the result of a parent/child merge of Q1 and Q2, while Q23 stands for the sibling merge of Q2 and Q3. The second and third rows of the table are the modified queries (MaxQ for complete subexpression elimination and MinQ for partial subexpression elimination). Note that common subexpression elimination is not defined for all queries (e.g. Q1).

5.2 Results

Looking at the execution times for the Small-Doc case, a first observation is that extensive common subexpression elimination in some cases results in substantially worse performance. The reason for this effect is twofold. The first is that common subexpression elimination might generate disjunctive predicates that are hard to optimize (see query MaxQ in Section 3.3). The second reason is that often common expressions are helpful for preserving selections. For instance, both Q12 and Q13 make use of the selection on C_CUSTKEY through the repeated join with the CUSTOMER table. Partial common expression elimination (MinQ23 and MinQ123 in this example) is better than complete subexpression elimination but (in the case of Q123) no better than no common subexpression elimination. In comparison with the complete common subexpression elimination rewriting, the partial one maintains the join of table PART (resp. SUPPLIER) with table LINEITEM in the rewriting for Q2 (resp. Q3) in Q23 (same for Q123). This is necessary to avoid generating a disjunctive predicate (see MinQ in Section 3.3).

In the Large-Doc case, common expression elimination pays off in all cases compared to executing Q1, Q2 and Q3 independently. This is because the common expression in each merged case is expensive and should be evaluated a minimal number of times. Furthermore, partial elimination of the common subexpression benefits both queries Q23 and Q123 as in the previous case.

Looking at the complete times for producing the pieces of the document in the relational engine for all meaningful combinations of the aforementioned queries: [Q1, Q2 and Q3], [Q12 (parent/child merge) and Q3], [Q2 and Q13 (parent/child merge)], [Q1 and Q23 (sibling merge)], [Q123 (single query)], plan Q1+Q23 is marginally faster than plan Q1+Q2+Q3 in the Small-Doc case, while it is about 18% faster in the Large-Doc case.

6 Related Work

Since we are optimizing common sub-expressions among multiple queries, our work share similarities with multi-query optimization (see, e.g., [13]). It is well known that multi query optimization is exponential [13]. Our work benefits from application-dependent information (building XML trees) to optimize sibling queries instead of attempting to optimize an arbitrary subset of queries. This reduces the complexity of the optimization.

In [7], the authors extend relational query engines with a new operator that processes sets of tuples. They define new rewriting rules that involve that operator and show how to integrate that operator in a relational optimizer. This work motivates the necessity to extend relational optimizers. In our work, we do not introduce a new operator, rather, we explore new rewriting rules.

In [9], the authors focus on merging parent and children queries. The rewritings we propose are more general than the ones in [9] and explore an additional dimension that has been proven to result in better efficiency. In [15], the authors provide an extension to SQL to express XML views of relations and carry an experimental study of publishing relational data in XML. This work has not adopted an optimization approach to this problem.

Finally, in [4], the authors present ROLEX, a system that extends the capabilities of relational engines to deliver efficiently navigable XML views of relational data via a virtual DOM interface. DOM operations are translated into an execution plan in order to explore lazy materialization. The query optimizer uses a characterization of the navigation behavior of an application to minimize the expected cost of that navigation. This work could benefit from our new optimizations if they are integrated into a relational system.

7   Conclusion

We discussed the problem of efficiently building XML documents from relations and showed that exploring common computation between sibling queries is a fundamental algebraic rewriting when optimizing SQL queries used to build XML documents. In particular, we showed that in the case where an element has both unique and repeated children, sibling merging combined with partial common sub-expression elimination, enables computation sharing without replicating data. This strategy can be used both inside and outside a relational engine.

References

1. S. Amer-Yahia, M. Fernández. Techniques for Storing XML. Tutorial. ICDE 2002.
2. M. Benedikt, C.Y. Chan, W. Fan, R. Rastogi, S. Zheng, A. Zhou. DTD-Directed Publishing with Attribute Translation Grammars. VLDB 2002.
3. P. Bohannon, J. Freire, P. Roy, J. Siméon. From XML Schema to Relations: A Cost-based Approach to XML Storage. ICDE 2002.
4. P. Bohannon, S. Ganguly, H. F. Korth, P. P. S. Narayan, P. Shenoy. Optimizing View Queries in ROLEX to Support Navigable Result Trees. VLDB 2002.
5. M. J. Carey, J. Kiernan, J. Shanmugasundaram, E. J. Shekita, S. N. Subramanian. XPERAN-TO: Middleware for Publishing Object-Relational Data as XML Documents. VLDB 2000.
6. D. Chamberlin, J. Clark, D. Florescu, J. Robie, J. Simeon, M. Stefanescu XQuery 1.0: An XML Query Language. http://www.w3.org/TR/query-datamodel/.
7. S. Chaudhuri, R. Kaushik, J. F. Naughton. On Relational Support for XML Publishing: Beyond Sorting and Tagging. SIGMOD Conference 2003.
8. J. M. Cheng, J. Xu. XML and DB2. ICDE 2000.
9. M. Fernandez, A. Morishima, D. Suciu. Efficient Evaluation of XML Middle-ware Queries. SIGMOD 2001.
10. D. Florescu, D. Kossmann. A Performance Evaluation of Alternative Mapping Schemes for Storing XML in a Relational Database. IEEE, DE Bulletin 1999.
11. Y. Ioannidis. Query Optimization. ACM Computing Surveys, symposium issue on the 50th Anniversary of ACM. Vol. 28, No. 1, March 1996, pp. 121-123.
12. C.C. Kanne, G. Moerkotte. Efficient Storage of XML Data. ICDE 2000.
13. P. Roy, S. Seshadri, S. Sudarshan, S. Bhobe. Efficient and Extensible Algorithms for Multi Query Optimization. SIGMOD 2000.
14. J. Shanmugasundaram, J. Kiernan, E. J. Shekita, C. Fan, J. Funderburk. Querying XML Views of Relational Data. VLDB 2001.
15. J. Shanmugasundaram, E.J. Shekita, R. Barr, M.J. Carey, B.G. Lindsay, H. Pirahesh, B. Reinwald. Efficiently publishing relational data as XML documents. VLDB Journal 10(2-3): 133-154 (2001).
16. Transaction Processing Performance Council. TPC-H Benchmark: Decision Support for Ad-Hoc queries. http://www.tpc.org/.

Adjustable Transaction Isolation in XML Database Management Systems

Michael P. Haustein and Theo Härder

University of Kaiserslautern
Dept. of Comp. Science, Database and Information Systems,
D-67653 Kaiserslautern, Germany.
{haustein | haerder}@informatik.uni-kl.de.

Abstract. Processing XML documents in multi-user database management environments requires a suitable storage model of XML data, support of typical XML document processing (XDP) interfaces, and concurrency control (CC) mechanisms tailored to the XML data model. In this paper, we sketch the architecture and interfaces of our prototype native XML database management system which can be connected to any existing relational DBMS and provides for declarative and navigational data access of concurrent transactions. We describe the fine-grained CC mechanisms implemented in our system and give a first impression of the so achieved benefits for concurrent transaction processing in native XML database management systems.

1   Introduction

Run an experiment on available DBMSs with collaboratively used XML documents [16] and you will experience a "performance catastrophe" meaning that all transactional operations are processed in strict serial order. Storing XML documents into relational DBMSs forces the developers to use simple CLOBs or to choose among an innumerable number of algorithms mapping the semi-structured documents to tables and columns (the so-called *shredding*). In any case, there are no specific provisions to process concurrent transactions guaranteeing the ACID properties and using typical XDP interfaces like SAX [2], DOM [16], and XQuery [16] simultaneously. Especially isolation in relational DBMS does not take the properties of the semi-structured XML data model into account and causes disastrous locking behavior by blocking entire CLOBs or tables.

Native XML database systems often use mature storage engines tailored to relational structures [13]. Because their XML document mapping is usually based on *fixed numbering* schemes used to identify XML elements, they primarily support efficient document retrieval and query evaluation. Frequently concurrent and transaction-safe modifications would lead to renumeration of large document parts which could cause unacceptable reorganization overhead and degrade XML processing in performance-critical workload situations. As a rare example of an update-oriented system, Natix [5] is designed to support concurrent transaction processing, but accomplishes alternative solutions for data storage and transaction isolation as compared to our proposal.

Our approach aims at the adequate support of all known types of XDP interfaces (event-based like SAX, navigational like DOM, and declarative like XQuery) and pro-

Z. Bellahsène et al. (Eds.): XSym 2004, LNCS 3186, pp. 173–188, 2004.

vides the well-known ACID properties [7] for their concurrent execution. We have implemented the XML *Transaction Coordinator* (XTC) [9], an (O)RDBMS-connectable DBMS for XML documents, called XDBMS for short, as a testbed for empirical transaction processing on XML documents. Here, we present its advantages for concurrent transaction processing in a native XDBMS achieved by a storage model and CC mechanisms tailored to the XML data model. This specific CC improves not only collaborative XDP but also SQL applications when "ROX: Relational Over XML" [8] becomes true.

An overview of the XTC architecture and their XDP interfaces is sketched in Section 2. Concurrent data access is supported by locks tailored to the taDOM tree [10]—a data model which extends the DOM tree—as outlined in sections 3 and 4, thereby providing tunable, fine-grained lock granularity and lock escalation as well as navigational transaction path locking inside an XML document. In Section 5, we give a first impression of concurrent transaction processing gains, before we wrap up with conclusions and some aspects of future work in Section 6.

2   System Architecture and XDP Interfaces

Our XTC database engine (*XTCserver*) adheres to the widely used five-layer DBMS architecture [11]. In Figure 1, we concentrate on the representation and mapping of XML documents. Processing of relational data is not a focus of this paper.

The *file-services* layer operates on the bit pattern stored on external, non-volatile storage devices. In collaboration with the OS file system, the *i/o managers* store the physical data into extensible *container files*; their uniform block length is configurable to the characteristics of the XML documents to be stored. A *buffer manager* per container file handles fixing and unfixing of pages in main memory and provides a replacement algorithm for them which can be optimized to the anticipated reference locality inherent in the respective XDP applications. Using pages as basic storage units, the *record, index*, and *catalog managers* form the *access services*. The record manager maintains in a set of pages the tree-connected nodes of XML documents as physically adjacent records. Each record is addressed by a unique life-time ID managed within a B-tree by the index manager [9]. This is essential to allow for fine-grained concurrency control which requires lock acquisition on unique identifiable nodes (see Section 4). The catalog manager provides for the database metadata. The *node manager* implementing the navigational access layer transforms the records from their internal physical into an external representation, thereby managing the lock acquisition to isolate the concurrent transactions. The *XML-services* layer contains the *XML manager* responsible for declarative document access, e. g., evaluation of XPath queries or XSLT transformations [16].

At the top of our architecture, the agents of the *interface layer* make the functionality of the XML and node services available to common internet browsers, ftp clients, and the *XTCdriver* thereby achieving declarative / set-oriented as well as navigational / node-oriented interfaces. The XTCdriver linked to client-side applications provides for methods to execute XPath-like queries and to manipulate documents via the SAX or DOM API. Each API accesses the stored documents within a transaction to be started by the XTCdriver. Transactions can be processed in the well-known isolation levels *uncommitted, committed, repeatable*, and *serializable* [1].

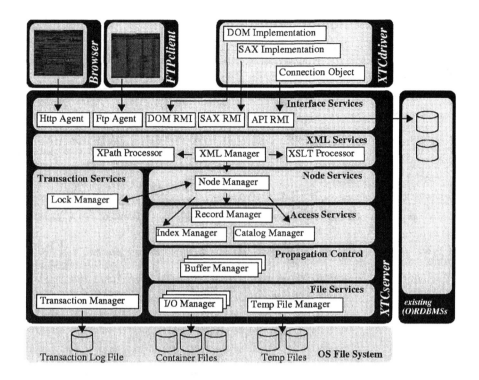

Fig. 1. XTC architecture overview

3   Storage Model

Efficient and effective synchronization of concurrent XDP is greatly facilitated if we use a specialized internal representation which enables fine-granular locking. For this reason, we will introduce two new node types: *attributeRoot* and *string*. This representational enhancement does not influence the user operations and their semantics on the XML document, but is solely exploited by the lock manager to achieve certain kinds of optimizations when an XML document is modified in a cooperative environment. As a running example, we, therefore, refer to an XML document which is slightly enhanced for our purpose to a so-called *taDOM tree* [10], as shown in Figure 2.

AttributeRoot separates the various attribute nodes from their element node. Instead of locking all attribute nodes separately when the DOM method *getAttributes()* is invoked, the lock manager obtains the same effect by a single lock on attributeRoot. Hence, such a lock does not affect parallelism, but leads to more effective lock handling and, thus, potentially to better performance. A string node, in contrast, is attached to the respective text or attribute node and exclusively contains the value of this node. Because reference to that value requires an explicit invocation of *getValue()* with a preceding lock request, a simple existence test on a text or attribute node avoids locking such nodes. Hence, a transaction only navigating across such nodes will not be blocked, although a concurrent transaction may have modified them and may still hold exclusive locks on them.

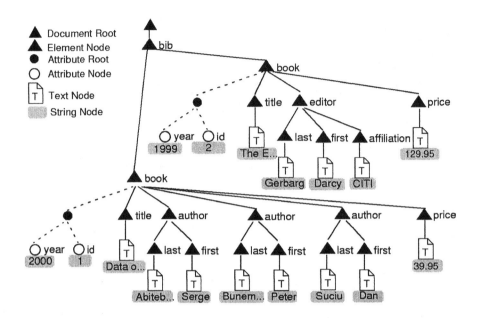

Fig. 2. A sample taDOM tree

It is essential for the locking performance to provide a suitable storage structure for ta- DOM trees which supports a flexible storage layout that allows a distinguishable (separate) node representation of all node types to achieve fine-grained locking. Therefore, we have implemented various container types which enable effective storage of very large and very small attribute and element nodes as well as combinations thereof [9]. Furthermore, fast access to and identification of all nodes of an XML document is mandatory to enable efficient processing of direct-access methods, navigational methods, and lock management. For this reason, our record manager assigns to each node a unique node ID (rapidly accessible via a B-tree) and stores the node as a record in a data page. The tree order of the XML nodes is preserved by the physical order of the records within logically consecutive pages (chained by next/previous page pointers) together with a so-called level indicator per record.

4   Concurrency Control

So far, we have explained the newly introduced node types and how fast and selective access to all nodes of an XML document can be guaranteed. In a concurrent environment, the various types of XML operations have to be synchronized using appropriate protocols entirely transparent to the different XDP interfaces supported. Hence, a lock manager is responsible for the acquisition and maintenance of locks, processing of the quite complex locking protocols and their adherence to correctness criteria, as well as optimization issues such as adequate lock granularity and lock escalation.

Because the DOM API not only supports navigation starting from the document root, but also allows jumps "out of the blue" to an arbitrary node within the document, locks must be *automatically*, that is, by the lock manager, acquired in either case for the path of ancestor nodes. The currently accessed node is called *context node* in the following.

This up-to-the-root locking procedure is performed as follows: If such an ancestor path is traversed the first time and if the IDs of the ancestors are not present in the so-called parent index (on-demand indexing of structural relationships [9]) for this path, the record manager is invoked to access stored records thereby searching all ancestor records. The IDs of these records are saved in the parent index. Hence, future traversals of this ancestor path can be processed via the parent index only. Navigational locking of children or siblings is optimized by such structural indexes in a similar way.

The lock modes depend on the type of access to be performed, for which we have tailored the *node lock* compatibilities and defined the rules for lock conversion as outlined in Section 4.1 and Section 4.2. To achieve optimal parallelism, we discuss means to tune lock granularities and lock escalation in Section 4.3. When an XML document has to be traversed by navigational methods, then the actual navigation paths also need strict synchronization. This means, a sequence of method calls must always obtain the same sequence of result nodes. To support this demand, we present so-called *navigation locks* in Section 4.4. Furthermore, query access methods also need strict synchronization to accomplish the well-known *repeatable read* property and, in addition, the prevention of *phantoms* in rare cases. Our specific solution is outlined in Section 4.5.

4.1   Node Locks

While traversing or modifying an XML document, a transaction has to acquire a lock in an adequate mode for each node before accessing it. Because the nodes in an XML document are organized by a tree structure, the principles of multi-granularity locking schemes can be applied. The method calls of the different XDP interfaces used by an application are interpreted by the lock manager to select the appropriate lock modes for the entire ancestor path. Such tree locking is similar to multi-granularity locking in relational environments (SQL) where intention locks communicate a transaction's processing needs to concurrent transactions. In particular, they prevent a subtree s from being locked in a mode incompatible to locks already granted to s or subtrees of s. However, there is a major difference, because the nodes in an ancestor path are part of the document and carry user data, whereas, in a relational DB, user data is exclusively stored in the leaves (records) of the tree (DAG) whose higher-level nodes are formed by organizational concepts (e. g., table, segment, DB). For example, it makes perfect sense to lock an intermediate XML node n for reads, while in the subtree of n another transaction may perform updates. For this and other reasons, we differentiate the read and write operations thereby replacing the well-known (IR, R) and (IX, X) lock modes with (NR, LR, SR) and (IX, CX, X) modes, respectively. As in the multi-granularity scheme, the U mode plays a special role because it permits lock conversion. Figure 3a contains the compatibility matrix for our lock modes whose effects are described now:

- An NR lock mode (node read) is requested for reading the context node. To isolate such a read access, an NR lock has to be acquired for each node in the ancestor path. Note, the NR mode takes over the role of IR together with a specialized R, because it only locks the specified node, but not any descendant nodes.

- An IX lock mode (intention exclusive) indicates the intent to perform write operations somewhere in the subtree (similar to the multi-granularity locking approach), but not on a direct-child node of the node being locked (see CX lock).

- An LR lock mode (level read) locks the context node together with its direct-child nodes for shared access. For example, the method *getChildNodes()* only requires an LR lock on the context node and not individual NR locks for all child nodes. Similarly, an LR lock, requested for an attributeRoot node, locks all its attributes implicitly (to save lock requests for the *getAttributes()* method).

- An SR lock mode (subtree read) is requested for the context node c as the root of subtree s to perform read operations on all nodes belonging to s. Hence, the entire subtree is granted for shared access. An SR lock on c is typically used if s is completely reconstructed to be printed out as an XML fragment.

- A CX lock mode (child exclusive) on context node c indicates the existence of an X lock on some direct-child node and prohibits inconsistent locking states by preventing LR and SR lock modes. In contrast, it does not prohibit other CX locks on c, because separate direct-child nodes of c may be exclusively locked by concurrent transactions.

- A U lock mode (update option) supports a read operation on context node c with the option to convert the mode for subsequent write access. It can be either converted back to a read lock if the inspection of c shows that no update action is needed or to an X lock after all existing read locks on c are released. Note, the asymmetry in the compatibility definition among U and (NR, IX, LR, SR, CX) which prevents granting further read locks on c, thereby enhancing protocol fairness, that is, avoiding transaction starvation.

- To modify the context node c (updating its contents or deleting c and its entire subtree), an X lock mode (exclusive) is needed for c. It implies a CX lock for its parent node and an IX lock for all other ancestors up to the document root.

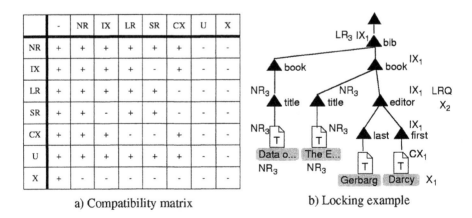

-	NR	IX	LR	SR	CX	U	X
NR	+	+	+	+	+	+	-	-
IX	+	+	+	+	-	+	-	-
LR	+	+	+	+	+	-	-	-
SR	+	+	-	+	+	-	-	-
CX	+	+	+	-	-	+	-	-
U	+	+	+	+	+	+	-	-
X	+	-	-	-	-	-	-	-

a) Compatibility matrix   b) Locking example

Fig. 3. Node locking for the taDOM tree

Note again, this differing behavior of CX and IX locks is needed to enable compatibility of IX and LR locks and to enforce incompatibility of CX and LR locks.

Figure 3b represents a cutout of the taDOM tree depicted in Figure 2 and illustrates the result of the following example: Transaction T_1 starts modifying the value *Darcy* and, therefore, acquires an X lock for the corresponding string node. The lock manager complements this action by accessing all ancestors and by acquiring a CX lock for the parent and IX locks for all further ancestors. Simultaneously, transaction T_2 wants to delete the entire $< editor >$ node including the string *Gerbag* for which T_2 must acquire an X lock. This lock request, however, cannot be immediately granted because of the existing IX lock of T_1. Hence, T_2-placing its request in the lock request queue (LRQ: X_2) – must synchronously wait for the release of the IX lock of T_1 on the $< editor >$ node. Meanwhile, transaction T_3 is generating a list of all book titles and has, therefore, requested an LR lock for the $< bib >$ node to obtain read access to all direct-child nodes thereby using the level-read optimization. To access the title strings for each $< book >$ node, the paths downwards to them are locked by NR locks. Note, LR_3 on $< bib >$ implicitly locks the $< book >$ nodes in shared mode and does not prohibit updates somewhere deeper in the tree. If X_2 is eventually granted for the $< editor >$ node, T_2 gets its CX lock on the $< book >$ node and its IX locks granted up to the root.

4.2 Node Lock Conversion

The compatibility matrix shown in Figure 3a describes the compatibility of locks acquired on the same node by separate transactions. If a transaction T already holds a lock and requests a lock in a more restrictive or incomparable mode on the same node, we would have to keep two locks for T on this node. In general, k locks per transaction and node are conceivable. This proceeding would require longer lists of granted locks per node and a more complex run-time inspection algorithm checking for lock compatibility. Therefore, we replace all locks of a transaction per node with a single lock in a mode giving sufficient isolation. The corresponding rules are specified by the *lock conversion matrix* in Figure 4, which determines the resulting lock for context node c, if a transaction already holds a lock (matrix header row) and requests a further lock (matrix header column) on c. A lock l_1 specified by an additional subscripted lock l2 (e. g., CX_{NR}) means that l_1 has to be acquired on c and l_2 has to be acquired on each direct-child node of c. An example for this procedure is given in the now following paragraph.

Assume, a user starts a transaction requesting all child nodes of c which results in acquiring an LR lock on c. LR mode locks c and all direct-child nodes in shared mode. After that, the user wants to delete one of the previously determined child nodes. Therefore, the transaction acquires an X lock on the corresponding child node and—applying the locking protocol—this requires the acquisition of a CX lock on c which already holds the LR lock. Using rule CX_{NR} specified in Figure 4, the transaction has to convert the existing LR

	-	NR	IX	LR	SR	CX	U	X
NR	NR	-	IX	LR	SR	CX	NR	X
IX	IX	IX	-	IX$_{NR}$	IX$_{SR}$	CX	IX	X
LR	LR	LR	IX$_{NR}$	-	SR	CX$_{NR}$	LR	X
SR	SR	SR	IX$_{SR}$	SR	-	CX$_{SR}$	SR	X
CX	CX	CX	CX	CX$_{NR}$	CX$_{SR}$	-	CX	X
U	U	U	U	U	U	U	-	X
X	X	X	X	X	X	X	X	-

Fig. 4. Lock conversion matrix

lock on c to a CX lock and to acquire an NR lock on each direct-child node of c (except the child node which is already locked for deletion by an X lock).

4.3 Tunable Node Lock Granularity and Lock Escalation

Entire subtrees in the taDOM tree can be locked by both SR locks enabling shared access or X locks granting exclusive access. In either case, we want to improve flexibility, efficiency, and potential parallelism of our locking protocols by enabling tunable lock granularity and lock escalation. The combined use of them increases operational throughput because, due to lock escalation, the number of lock requests can be reduced enormously and, due to fine-tuned lock granularity, higher concurrency may be gained.

To tune the lock granularity of nodes for each transaction separately, the parameter *lock depth* ($ld \geq 0$) is introduced. Parameter ld describes the lock granularity by means of the number of node levels (from document root) on which locks are to be held. If a lock is requested for context node c whose path length to the document root element is greater than ld, only an SR lock for the ancestor node belonging to the lock-depth level is requested. In this way, nodes at deeper levels than indicated by ld are locked in shared mode using an SR lock on the node at level ld, that is, entire subtrees are locked starting at the specified lock-depth level of the requesting transaction. As a corollary, $ld = 0$ provides document locks, e.g., locks on the $< bib >$ node in Figure 5. This allows the traversal of a large document fragment in read mode without acquiring any additional node locks. In the same way, several X locks can be replaced with a single X lock at a chosen document level $l \leq ld$.

Figure 5 shows the taDOM-tree cutout of Figure 3b illustrating the effect of the lockdepth parameter. With $ld = 2$, the NR locks of transaction T_3 on the $< title >$ and $< editor >$ nodes are replaced with SR locks for the $< title >$ nodes. The IX, CX, and X locks of T_1 on the $< editor >$ node and its descendants are replaced by a single X lock on the $< editor >$ node. As a prerequisite, it requires CX and IX locks on the ancestor nodes $< book >$ and $< bib >$, respectively. Transaction T_2 is again in a wait state, because the requested X lock is not compatible to the existing X lock of T_1.

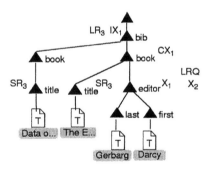

Fig. 5. Coarse-grained node locks with lock depth 2

In a similar way, lock escalation can be achieved. To tune lock escalation, we introduce two parameters, the *escalation threshold* (*et*) and the *escalation depth (ed)*. The lock manager scans the taDOM tree at prespecified intervals. If the manager detects a subtree in which the number of locked nodes of a transaction exceeds the percentage threshold value defined by *et*, the locks held are replaced by an adequate lock at the subtree root, if possible (i. e., no conflicting locks are encountered). Read and write locks are replaced by SR and X locks. The parameter *ed* defines the maximal subtree depth starting from the leaves of a taDOM tree up to the scanned subtree root. Obviously, there is certainly a trade-off to be observed for lock escalation which decreases concurrency of read and write transactions, but, in turn, a reduction of the number of held locks and of lock acquisitions is achieved saving lock management overhead. Its empirical evaluation remains a future task.

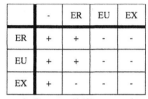

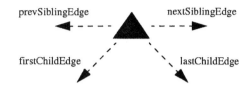

a) Compatibility matrix

b) Virtual navigation edges on an element-node

Fig. 6. Locking navigational operations in a taDOM tree

4.4 Navigation Locks

So far, we have discussed optimization issues for locks where the node to be accessed was specified by its unique ID. In addition, the DOM API also provides for ($\sim$ 20) methods which enable the traversal of XML documents where access is specified relative to the context node. In such cases, synchronizing a navigation path means that a sequence of navigational method calls or modification (IUD) operations—starting at a known node within the taDOM tree—must always yield the same sequence of result nodes within a transaction. Hence, a path of nodes within the document evaluated by a transaction must be protected against modifications of concurrent transactions. Assume in Figure 2, a transaction T navigates through all or a range of < *book* > nodes and wants to be isolated from concurrent inserts of new < *book* >

nodes. Of course, we have already introduced some lock modes which enable in this situation perfect, but (too) expensive isolation caused by (too) large lock granules. For example, if we acquire an LR lock on the < *bib* > node, all < *book* > nodes are implicitly granted in shared mode. An SR lock on < *bib* > would even prohibit updates on the entire document. We, however, want to support a solution only using minimal lock granules, that is, node locks of mode NR. Therefore, we introduce *virtual navigation edges* for element and text nodes within the taDOM tree (Figure 6b) which are locked in addition to their confining nodes.

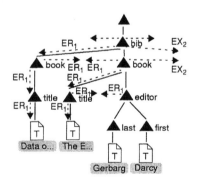

Fig. 7. Use of navigation locks

While navigating through an XML document and traversing the navigation edges, a transaction has to request a lock for each edge, in addition to the node locks (NR) for the nodes visited. Note, these edges are logical objects which are not materialized but embodied by their confining nodes. Because each navigation step only performs local operations (first/last, next/previous) to a sibling or child of the context node c, the

R/U/ X locks known from relational records or tables are sufficient. Traversal operations between nodes need bidirectional isolation: For example, if *getNetxtSibling()* is invoked on node c and delivers node n, then, as a first step, the next-sibling edge of c is locked. In addition, we must lock the previous-sibling edge of n to prohibit path modifications between n and c through another transaction via node n. To support such traversals efficiently, we offer the ER, EU, and EX lock modes corresponding to R/U/X. Their use observing the compatibilities shown in Figure 6a can be summarized as follows:

- An ER lock mode (edge read) is needed for an edge traversal in read mode, e. g., by calling the *getNextSibling()* or *getFirstChild()* DOM method for the nextSiblingEdge or firstChildEdge, respectively.
- An EX lock mode (edge exclusive) enables an edge to be modified which may be needed when nodes are deleted or inserted. For all edges, affected by the modification operation, EX locks are acquired, before the navigation edges are redirected to their new target nodes.
- The EU lock mode (edge update) eases the starvation problem of write transactions (see lock mode U in Section 4.1).

Figure 7 illustrates navigation locks on virtual navigation edges. To keep Figure 7 comprehensible, we do not show the node locks, e.g., NR or CX. Transaction T_1 starts at the $< bib >$ node and reads three times the first-child node (that is, the node sequence $< bib >$, $< book >$, $< title >$, $< text >$) to get the string value (Data o . . .) of the first book title. Then T_1 refers to the next-sibling node of the current <book> node and repeats twice the first-child method to get the title of the second book. At this point, the requested book is located, and T_1 finally gets the next sibling of the current $< title >$ node which is the $< editor >$ node. Apparently, our protocol allows concurrent transaction T_2 to append a new book by acquiring EX locks for the next-sibling edge of the last $< book >$ node and for the last-child edge of the $< bib >$ node. Of course, T_2 has to protect its ancestor path in a sufficient mode – its CX lock on $< bib >$ is compatible with the NR lock of T_1.

4.5   Prevention of Phantoms

As outlined so far, our protocols enable fine-grained solutions for *repeatable read* and even *serializable* when record-oriented operations are used, i. e., direct as well as navigational access to sequences of document nodes. Note, "gaps" between nodes can be protected by edge locks which prohibit a newly inserted document node to appear as a phantom.

But how do we solve the phantom problem in XML documents for set-oriented access? If we are willing to lock larger granules and thereby potentially sacrifice some parallelism, we can use the same trick known from multi-granularity locking: we just acquire an exclusive lock one level above the working node, that is, on its direct ancestor, and prevent the transaction from being confused by phantom inserts. Obviously, this straightforward approach also increases blocking and deadlock probability. For example, if the *getElementsByTagName()* method of the DOM API is invoked on an arbitrary node n, all its sibling nodes and their subtrees are locked, because the parent node of n holds the phantom-preventing lock. Hence, this approach may turn out to be too coarse.

Because we may not guarantee "serializability" in the strict sense when fine-grained lock protocols are used for set-oriented access, we currently support the so-called consistency level 2.99 [7] in such situations. Our mechanism described in [10] is based on the concept of precision locks [14]. Because our empirical experiments outlined in Section 5 do not critically rely on effective phantom protection, we will not refine it here. While it is path oriented and can, therefore, be also exploited for (simple) declarative interfaces, phantom prevention for the full expressiveness of XQuery is subject of our future research.

5   Performance Evaluation

In our first experiment, we consider the basic cost of lock management described so far. For this purpose, we use the *xmlgen* tool of the XMark XML benchmark project [15] to generate a variety of XML documents consisting of 5,000 up to 25,000 individual XML nodes. The documents are stored in our native XDBMS [9] and accessed by a client-side DOM application requesting every node by a separate RMI call. To reveal lock management overhead, each XML document is reconstructed by a consecutive traversal in depth-first order under isolation levels *committed* and *repeatable read*. Isolation level *committed* certainly provides higher degrees of concurrency with (potentially) lesser degrees of consistency of shared documents; when used, the programmer accepts a responsibility to achieve full consistency. Depending on the position of the node to be locked, it may cause much more overhead, because each individual node access requires short read locks along its ancestor path. In contrast, isolation level *repeatable read* sets long locks until transaction commit and, hence, does not need to repetitively lock ancestor nodes. In fact, they are already locked due to the depth-first traversal.

These expectations are confirmed by the results of this first experiment as depicted in Figure 8. The potential performance gain of the reduced isolation level *committed* is contrasted by the dramatically increasing lock management overhead due to repeated locking and releasing of locks along the entire ancestor path. Hence, substantial lock processing time is consumed in *committed* mode (>300% of the recon-

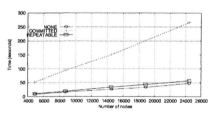

Fig. 8. Document reconstruction time

struction time under isolation level *none*, i. e., without locking overhead), whereas the overhead for *repeatable read* is acceptable ($\sim 25\%$). To guarantee highly consistent documents, *repeatable read* should be used for concurrent transactions. However, its penalty of longer lock durations has to be compensated by effective and fine-granular lock modes which coincides with the objectives of our proposal.

The second experiment illustrates the benefits for transaction throughput depending on the chosen isolation level and lock-depth value. For this purpose, we extend the sample document of Figure 2 to a library database by grouping the books into specific topics and adding a persons' directory. The DataGuide describing the resulting XML document is depicted in Figure 9. We created the library document with 500 persons and 25,000 books grouped into 50 specific topics. The resulting document (requiring approximately 6,4 MB) consists of 483,317 XML nodes and is stored in our XDBMS [9].

We apply different transaction types simulating typical read/write access to XML documents. Transaction T_B is searching for a book with a randomly selected title. This simulates a query of a library visitor. The activities of the library employees are represented by transactions T_P, T_L, and T_R. Transaction T_P is searching for a randomly chosen person by his/her last name. Transactions T_L and T_R are simulating the lending of books. Transaction T_L randomly locates a person and a book to be lent; then it adds a new child node containing the person's id to the $< history >$ element within the located $< book >$ subtree. Transaction T_R "returns" the book by setting the return attribute of the corresponding $< lend >$ element to the current system date.

Ten clients with read transactions of type T_B and one client with a read transaction of type T_P are continuously executing for ten minutes on the library document to provide a base load on the XDBMS. Two clients are executing write transactions of type T_L and T_R making a total of 13 concurrent transactions in the system. A deadlock detector is scanning the wait-for graph of the transactions every five seconds. The XDBMS is running on an *IBM eServer xSeries 235* with two *Intel Xeon-A* 2.4GHz processors. The server

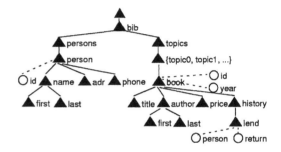

Fig. 9. DataGuide of the library document

machine executes *Microsoft Windows Server 2003 Enterprise Edition*, whereas the clients are running on an *IBM R32 Think-Pad*, connected with a 100Mbps network to the server.

To explore transaction throughput in two different processing modes, we run this experiment in batch mode (no human interaction while a transaction is running) and with human interaction. The latter case is simulated by a delay of 5 seconds by which the duration of *long locks* is extended in each transaction, before they are released at transaction commit. At least in relational environments, everybody would expect a decrease of transaction throughput with increasing isolation levels: *none, uncommitted, committed, repeatable read, serializable,* where in our experiments both isolation levels *repeatable read* and *serializable* produce identical results. On the other dimension, with increasing lock depth—if facilitated by the element position processed in the tree— growing transaction throughput is anticipated because of shrinking lock granules.

Without surprise, maximum transaction throughput is reached for isolation level *uncommitted* in all experiments, because read locks are abandoned. Write locks, in turn, seriously interfere with concurrent transactions only at lock depth 0 and 1 (see Figure 10a and 11a), whereas they hardly affect them at lock depths 2 to 7.

5.1   Batched Transaction Processing

As the most striking observation, conducting our experiment in batch-processing mode revealed in all cases a higher throughput at isolation level *repeatable read* than at *com-*

mitted, because the long read locks avoid the subsequent traversals of ancestor paths for lock acquisitions in most cases. The curves of committed write transactions (depending on the lock depth) are similar at all isolation levels (see Figure 10a). Most of the conflicts (waiting cycles or deadlocks) are occurring at lock depth 0 resp. 1, because transactions T_B, T_L, and T_R are locking the $< bib >$ resp. the $< topics >$ nodes. Hence, all isolation levels nearly yield the same throughput of write transactions.

Enhancing the lock depth value from 1 to 2, much more write transactions commit, because most of them are executed concurrently (only those accessing the same topic have to be serialized). The number of successful write transactions is slightly increasing from lock depth 2 to 7, because the transactions are keeping long locks which avoid a repeated traversal of complete ancestor paths in most cases when additional locks are requested. But surprisingly, a higher degree of isolation also enables higher throughput of write transactions, which can be explained by the following observation: *Repeatable read* yields shorter transaction processing times than *committed* because the read operations of the write transactions T_L and T_B do not acquire and immediately release (a set of) short read locks for each node access.

The number of committed transactions (Figure 10b) is primarily depending on the commits of the readers T_B and T_P, because, compared to the writers T_L and T_R, they contain less operations and are executed by more client threads in parallel. Because of the short read locks, the throughput for *committed* behaves even worse than for *repeatable read*. The peak at lock depth 1 is caused by transaction T_P which is executed without interference while T_B, T_L, and T_R are frequently blocking each other. This peak number of commits (mainly due to T_P) decreases from lock depth 1 to 4, because more and more transactions of type T_B, T_L, and T_R successfully finish thereby increasing lock and transaction management overhead. At lock depth 4, locking conflicts of transactions T_L and T_R do not affect T_B anymore. Hence, from lock depths 4 to 7, the XDBMS seems to be in a kind of steady state and achieves stable transaction throughput.

5.2   "Interactive" Transaction Processing

Transactions interrupted by human interactions "the human is in the loop") or performing complex operations may exhibit drastically increased lock duration times. While the average transaction response time and lock duration was far less than a second in batch-processing mode, now the average lock duration was "artificially" increased probably by more than a factor of 10. As a consequence, the finer granularity of locks and the duration of *short read locks* gained in importance on transaction throughput while the relative effect of lock management overhead was essentially scaled down. Longer lock durations and, in turn, blocking times reduced the number of successful commits (write and overall transactions) to about 50% and 10% as shown in Figure 11a and b and caused a relative performance behavior as anticipated in relational environments.

In general, transaction throughput can be increased by decreasing the level of isolation (from *repeatable read* down to *uncommitted*) or increasing the lock depth (if possible). As observed at lock depths 4 to 7 in Section 5.1, all transactions can be executed in parallel and our XDBMS approaches stable transaction throughput in this experiment.

For future benchmarks, we expect the gap between *uncommitted* and *committed* to grow larger for "deeper" XML documents (longer paths from the root to the leaves).

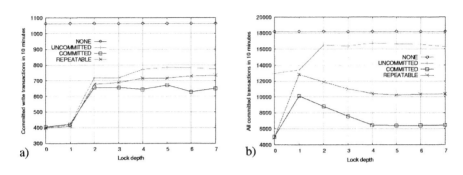

Fig. 10. Successful batch-processed transactions

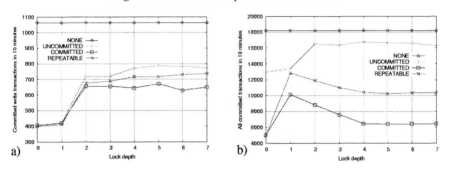

Fig. 11. Successful transactions with human interaction

Similarly, the gap between *committed* and *repeatable read* widens with an increasing percentage of write transactions (causing more waiting cycles).

6   Related Work, Conclusions, and Future Work

So far, only a few papers deal with fine-grained CC in XML documents. DGLOCK [6] explores a *path-oriented protocol* for semantic locking on DataGuides. It is running in a layer on top of a commercial DBMS and can, therefore, not reach the fine granularity and flexibility of our approach. In particular, it cannot support ID-based access and position-based predicates. Another path-oriented protocol is proposed in [3, 4] which also seems to be limited as far as the full expressiveness of XPath predicates and direct jumps into subtrees are concerned. To our knowledge, the only competing approach which is also navigation oriented comes from the locking protocols designed for Natix [12]. They are also tailored to typical APIs for XDP. While the proposed lock modes are different to ours, the entire protocol behavior should be compared. Currently, we have the advantage that we do not need to simulate our protocols, but we can measure their performance on existing benchmarks and get real numbers.

    In this paper, we have primarily explored transaction isolation issues for collaborative XML document processing. We first sketched the design and implementation of our native XML database management system. For concurrent transaction processing, we have introduced our concepts enabling fine-granular concurrency control on taDOM trees representing our natively stored XML documents. As the key part, we have described the locking protocols for direct and navigational access to individual nodes of a taDOM tree, thereby supporting different isolation levels. The performance evaluation has revealed the locking overhead of our complex protocols, but, on the other hand, has confirmed the viability, effectiveness, and benefits of our approach. As a striking observation, lower isolation levels on XML documents do not necessarily guarantee better transaction throughput, because the potentially higher transaction parallelism may be (over-)compensated by higher lock management overhead. There are many other issues that wait to be resolved: For example, we did not say much about the usefulness of optimization features offered. Effective phantom control needs to be implemented and evaluated (thereby providing for isolation level *serializable*), based on the ideas we described. Then, we can start to systematically evaluate the huge parameter space available for collaborative XML processing (fan-out and depth of XML trees, mix of transactional operations, benchmarks for specific application domains, degree of application concurrency, optimization of protocols, etc.).

Acknowledgements. The anonymous referees who pestered us with many questions helped to improve the final version of this paper.

References

[1] American National Standard for Information Technology. Database Languages - SQL - Part 2: Foundation (1999)
[2] D. Brownell. SAX2. O'Reilly (2002)
[3] S. Dekeyser, J. Hidders. Path Locks for XML Document Collaboration. Proc. 3rd Conf. on Web Information Systems Engineering (WISE), Singapore, 105-114 (2002)
[4] S. Dekeyser, J. Hidders, J. Paredaens. A Transaction Model for XML Databases. World Wide Web Journal 7(2): 29-57 (2004)
[5] T. Fiebig, S. Helmer, C.-C. Kanne, G. Moerkotte, J. Neumann, R. Schiele, T. Westmann. Natix: A Technology Overview. A.B. Chaudri et al. (Eds.): Web, Web Services, and Database Systems, NODe 2002, Erfurt, Germany, LNCS 2593, Springer, 12-33 (2003)
[6] T. Grabs, K. Böhm, H.-J. Schek: XMLTM: Efficient Transaction Management for XML Documents. Proc. ACM CIKM Conf., McLean, VA, 142-152 (2002)
[7] J. Gray, A. Reuter. Transaction Processing: Concepts and Techniques. Morgan Kaufmann (1993)
[8] A. Halverson, V. Josifovski, G. Lohman, H. Pirahesh, M. Mörschel. ROX: Relational Over XML. Proc. 30th VLDB Conf., Toronto (2004)
[9] M. Haustein, T. Härder. Fine-Grained Management of Natively Stored XML Documents, submitted (2004)
[10] M. Haustein, T. Härder. taDOM: A Tailored Synchronization Concept with Tunable Lock Granularity for the DOM API. Proc. 7th ADBIS Conf., Dresden, Germany, 88-102 (2003)
[11] T. Härder, A. Reuter. Concepts for Implementing a Centralized Database Management System. Proc. Computing Symposium on Application Systems Development, Nürnberg, Germany, 28-60 (1983)
[12] S. Helmer, C.-C. Kanne, G. Moerkotte. Evaluating Lock-Based Protocols for Cooperation on XML Documents. SIGMOD Record 33(1): 58-63 (2004)

[13] H. V. Jagadish, S. Al-Khalifa, A. Chapman. TIMBER: A Native XML Database. The VLDB Journal 11(4): 274-291 (2002)

[14] J. R. Jordan, J. Banerjee, R. B. Batman: Precision Locks. Proc. ACM SIGMOD Conf., Ann Arbor, Michigan, 143-147 (1981)

[15] A. Schmidt, F. Waas, M. Kersten. XMark: A Benchmark for XML Data Management. Proc. 28th VLDB Conf., Hong Kong, China, 974-985 (2002)

[16] W3C Recommendations. http://www.w3c.org (2004)

Fractional XSKETCH Synopses for XML Databases

Natasha Drukh[1], Neoklis Polyzotis[2], Minos Garofalakis[3], and Yossi Matias[1]

[1] School of Computer Science, Tel Aviv University, Tel Aviv 69978, Israel,
kreimern@post.tau.ac.il, matias@cs.tau.ac.il
[2] Dept. of Computer Science, Univ. of California - Santa Cruz, Santa Cruz, CA 95064, USA,
alkis@cs.ucsc.edu
[3] Bell Labs, Lucent Technologies, Murray Hill, NJ 07974, USA,
minos@research.bell-labs.com

Abstract. A key step in the optimization of declarative queries over XML data is estimating the selectivity of path expressions, i.e., the number of elements reached by a specific navigation pattern through the XML data graph. Recent studies have introduced XSKETCH structural graph synopses as an effective, space-efficient tool for the compile-time estimation of complex path-expression selectivities over graph-structured, schema-less XML data. Briefly, XSKETCHes exploit localized graph stability and well-founded statistical assumptions to accurately approximate the path and branching distribution in the underlying XML data graph. Empirical results have demonstrated the effectiveness of XSKETCH summaries over real-life and synthetic data sets, and for a variety of path-expression workloads. In this paper, we introduce fractional XSKETCHes (fXSKETCHES) a simple, yet intuitive and very effective generalization of the basic XSKETCH summarization mechanism. In a nutshell, our fXSKETCH synopsis extends the conventional notion of binary stability (employed in XSKETCHes) with that of *fractional stability*, essentially recording more detailed path/branching distribution information on individual synopsis edges. As we demonstrate, this natural extension results in several key benefits over conventional XSKETCHes, including (a) a simplified estimation framework, (b) reduced run-time complexity for the synopsis-construction algorithm, and (c) lifting the need for critical uniformity assumptions during estimation (thus resulting in more accurate estimates). Results from an extensive experimental study show that our fXSKETCH synopses yield significantly better selectivity estimates than conventional XSKETCHes, especially in the context of complex path expressions with branching predicates.

1 Introduction

XML has rapidly evolved from a mark-up language to a de-facto standard for data exchange and integration over the web. A testament to this is the increasing volume of published XML data, together with the concurrent development of XML query processors that will allow users to tap into the vast amount of XML data available on the Internet. The successful deployment of such query processors depends crucially on the existence of high-level declarative query languages. There exist numerous proposals that cover a wide range of paradigms, but a common characteristic among all XML-language proposals is the use of *path expressions* as the basic method to access and retrieve specific

Z. Bellahsène et al. (Eds.): XSym 2004, LNCS 3186, pp. 189–203, 2004.

elements from the XML database. A path expression essentially defines a complex navigational path, which can be predicated on the existence of sibling paths or on constraints on the values of visited elements. As a concrete example, in a bibliography database, the path expression //author[book]/paper/sigmod/title (which adheres to the syntax of the standard XPath language [1]) selects the set of all title data elements discovered by the label path //author/paper/sigmod/title, but only for author elements that have *at least one* book child (a condition specified by the author[book] branch).

Similar to relational optimization, optimizing XML queries with complex path expressions depends crucially on the existence of concise summaries that can provide effective compile-time estimates for the selectivity of these expressions over the underlying (large) graph-structured XML database. This problem has recently attracted the attention of the database research community, and several techniques [2,3,4,5,6,7, 8] have been proposed targeting different aspects of the problem. XSKETCH structural graph synopses [5,6] have recently been introduced as an effective data-reduction tool that enables accurate selectivity estimates for branching path expressions. In a nutshell, XSKETCH synopses exploit localized graph stability and well-founded statistical assumptions to accurately approximate the path and branching distribution in the underlying XML data graph; furthermore, XSKETCHes can be augmented with summary information on data-value distributions to handle path expressions with value predicates [6]. Compared to previously proposed techniques, the XSKETCH synopsis mechanism targets the most general version of the estimation problem: XPath expressions with branching and value predicates, over graph-structured, schema-less XML databases. Experimental results with a variety of query workloads on different data sets have demonstrated the effectiveness of XSKETCHes as concise summaries of XML data.

In this paper, we introduce *fractional* XSKETCHes (fXSKETCHES) a simple, yet intuitive and very effective generalization of the basic XSKETCH synopses based on the concept of *fractional edge stabilities*. Briefly, instead of simply recording whether a synopsis edge is stable or not (i.e., the conventional "binary" notion of stability employed in the XSKETCH model), our fXSKETCH synopses record the *degree of stability* for each edge as a *fraction* between 0 ("no-connection") and 1 ("fully stable"). As we demonstrate, this natural generalization has a direct positive impact on the underlying estimation framework. First, it simplifies the expressions for query-selectivity estimates, thus allowing for faster estimation. Second, and perhaps most importantly, it lifts the need for certain critical uniformity assumptions during basic XSKETCH estimation, thus resulting in significantly more robust and accurate estimates. Furthermore, the removal of such uniformity assumptions also reduces the search space (and, therefore, the time complexity) of the synopsis-construction algorithm, since it effectively obviates the need for specialized synopsis-refinement operations to address regions of non-uniformity. These observations are backed up by an extensive experimental study which evaluates the performance of our generalized fXSKETCH synopses on a variety of XML data sets and query workloads. Our results clearly indicate that fXSKETCHES yield significant improvements in accuracy when compared to original XSKETCH summaries. These improvements are more apparent in the case of complex path expressions with branching predicates, where the uniformity assumptions of the original XSKETCH model can introduce large errors;

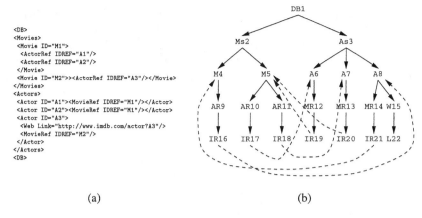

```
<DB>
 <Movies>
  <Movie ID="M1">
   <ActorRef IDREF="A1"/>
   <ActorRef IDREF="A2"/>
  </Movie>
  <Movie ID="M2">><ActorRef IDREF="A3"/></Movie>
 </Movies>
 <Actors>
  <Actor ID="A1"><MovieRef IDREF="M1"/></Actor>
  <Actor ID="A2"><MovieRef IDREF="M1"/></Actor>
  <Actor ID="A3">
   <Web Link="http://www.imdb.com/actor?A3"/>
   <MovieRef IDREF="M2"/>
  </Actor>
 </Actors>
<DB>
```

(a)   (b)

Fig. 1. Example XML document (a) and XML data graph (b).

fractional stabilities, on the other hand, lift the need for such assumptions thus resulting in significantly better fXSKETCH-based selectivity estimates.

The remainder of this paper is organized as follows. Section 2 covers some preliminary material on XML and path expressions, while Section 3 provides a short overview of the original XSKETCH model [5,6]. Our generalized fXSKETCH synopsis model is described in Section 4, where we discuss the definition of fractional stabilities and their implications on the estimation framework and the synopsis-construction process. Section 5 presents the results of our experimental study, while Section 6 gives some concluding remarks and our plans for future work.

2   Preliminaries

XML Data Model. Following previous work on XML and semistructured data [9,10], we model an XML database as a large, directed, node-labeled *data graph* $G = (V_G, E_G)$. Each node in V_G corresponds to an XML element in the database and is characterized by a *unique object identifier (oid)* and a *label* (assigned from some alphabet of string literals) that captures the semantics of the element. (We use $\texttt{label}(v)$ to denote the label of node $v \in V_G$.) Edges in E_G are used to capture both the element-subelement relationships (i.e., element nesting) and the explicit element references (i.e., id/idref attributes or XLink constructs [11,12,9,13]). Note that non-tree edges, such as those implemented through id/idref constructs, are an essential component and a "first-class citizen" of XML data that can be directly queried in complex path expressions, such as those allowed by the XQuery standard specification [14]. We, therefore, focus on the most general case of XML data *graphs* (rather than just trees) in what follows.

Example 1. Figures 1(a,b) show an example XML document and its corresponding data graph. The document is modeled after the Internet Movie Database (IMDB) XML data set (www.imdb.com), showing two movies and three actors. The graph node corresponding to a data element is named with an abbreviation of the element's label and a unique id number. Note that we use dashed lines to show graph edges that correspond to id-idref relationships.

XPath Expressions. Abstractly, an XML path expression $\bar{l}$ (e.g., in XQuery [14]) defines a navigational path over the XML data graph, specifying conditions on the labels and (possibly) the value(s) of data elements. Following the XPath standard [1], a *simple path expression* is of the form $l_1/l_2/\ldots/l_n$, where the l_i's are document labels. The result of the path expression includes all elements u_n for which there exists a document path $u_1/u_2/\ldots/u_n$ with $\text{label}(u_i) = l_i$. A *branching path expression* has the form $\bar{l} = l_1[\bar{l}^1]/\ldots/l_n[\bar{l}^n]$, where the l_i's are labels and each $\bar{l}^i$ is a (possibly empty) label path specifying a branching path predicate at location i. Thus, a branching path expression is formed from a simple path expression $l_1/l_2/\ldots/l_n$ by attaching (one or more) branching predicates $[\bar{l}^i]$ at specific nodes in the path. Each $[\bar{l}^i]$ clause represents an existential condition, requiring that there exists *at least one* $\bar{l}^i$ label branch attached at point i of the expression. For example, consider the document graph of Figure 1 and the simple path expression `Actor/MovieRef/IDREF/Movie` that retrieves elements with ids 4 and 5; if we add a [Link] branch on `Actor`, then the new path expression `Actor-[Link]/MovieRef/IDREF/Movie` only retrieves element 4. Note that if all branch predicates are empty, a branching path expression degenerates to a simple path expression $l_1/\cdots/l_n$.

It is possible to extend branching path expressions with predicates on the *values* of traversed elements. As an example, the XPath expression `Actor[/MovieRef/IDREF/-Movie/Title=''Snatch'']` retrieves all actors that have starred in a movie with title "Snatch". In the interest of space, we ignore element values when we discuss the specifics of our fXSKETCH synopses, focusing primarily on the label path and branching structure of the underlying database – the necessary extensions to handle values and value predicates follow along similar lines as the analogous extensions for basic XSKETCHes [6].

3   A Review of XSKETCH Synopses

Synopsis Model. The XSKETCH synopsis mechanism [5,6] relies on a generic graph-summary model that captures the basic path structure of the input XML tree. Formally, given a data tree $G = (V_G, E_G)$, a graph synopsis $\mathcal{S}(G) = (V_S, E_S)$ is a directed node-labeled graph, where (1) each node $v \in V_S$ corresponds to a subset of element (or, attribute) nodes in V_G (termed the *extent* of v – $\text{extent}(v)$) that have the *same label*, and (2) an edge in $(u, v) \in E_G$ is represented in E_S as an edge between the synopsis nodes whose extents contain the two endpoints u and v. Each synopsis node u stores the (common) label $\text{label}(u)$ of all elements in its extent, and an element-count field $|u| = |\text{extent}(u)|$ (we use u and $\text{extent}(u)$ interchangeably in what follows). Figure 2(a) shows a graph synopsis for the document of Figure 1, where elements are partitioned according to their label (synopsis nodes are named with the first letter of their label in upper case).

XSKETCH synopses [5,6] are specific instantiations of the graph-synopsis model described above. In order to cover key properties of the path and branching distribution, the basic synopsis is augmented with edge labels that capture localized *backward- and forward-stability* [15] conditions across synopsis nodes. An edge $u \rightarrow v$ is **B**ackward (resp., **F**orward) stable, if all elements in the extent of v (resp., u) have at least one parent (resp., child) element in the extent of u (resp., v). As an example, Figure 2(b) shows the XSKETCH summary for the graph synopsis of Figure 2(a). Note that edge A→MR is both

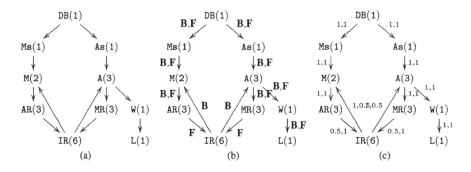

Fig. 2. (a) Graph Synopsis, (b) XSKETCH Synopsis, (c) fXSKETCH Synopsis.

backward and forward stable since all MovieRefs have an Actor parent, and all Actors have at least one MovieRef child. As a result, |MR| = 3 is an accurate selectivity estimate for path expression A/MR, while |A| = 3 is an accurate estimate for A[/MR]. As shown in [5,6], such *localized* stability information can be combined to effectively capture key properties of the *global* path structure, and provide accurate estimates on the selectivity of XPath expressions over the original XML document graph.

Estimation Framework. The XSKETCH framework uses the concept of *path embeddings* in order to estimate the selectivity of any branching path expression. In short, a synopsis path $u_1/\ldots/u_k$ is called an embedding of the simple path expression $l_1/\ldots/l_k$, if $\text{label}(u_i) = l_i$ for each $1 \leq i \leq k$. Similarly, a synopsis twig $\bar{u} = u_1[\bar{u}^1]/\ldots/u_k[\bar{u}^k]$, where $\bar{u}^i$ is a synopsis path, is called an embedding of the branching path expression $\bar{l} = l_1[\bar{1}^1]/\ldots/l_k[\bar{1}^k]$, if $u_1/\ldots/u_k$ is an embedding of $l_1/\ldots/l_k$ and $\bar{u}^i$ is an embedding of $\bar{1}^i$, for each $1 \leq i \leq k$. The selectivity of an XPath expression can be estimated as the sum of selectivities of its unique embeddings, and the problem is thus reduced to estimating the selectivity of a single embedding.

To estimate the selectivity of a single embedding, the XSKETCH estimation algorithms identify sub-components comprising only stable edges (for which accurate estimates can be given based on edge stability), and then apply statistical (uniformity and independence) assumptions at the "breaking" points of the stability chain(s). A detailed description of the estimation framework can be found in [5,6]; here, we use a simple example to illustrate the basic concepts. Consider the synopsis of Figure 2(b) and the path embedding M/AR/IR[/A/MR]. We express the selectivity of the embedding as $|IR| \cdot f(M/AR/IR[/A/MR])$, where the $f()$ term denotes the fraction of elements in IR that are reached by the embedding. Using the *Chain Rule* from probability theory, this fraction can be written as follows:

$$f(M/AR/IR[/A/MR]) = f(M/AR) \cdot f(AR/IR \mid M/AR) \cdot f(IR[/A/MR] \mid M/AR/IR)$$
$$= f(M/AR) \cdot f(AR/IR \mid M/AR) \cdot f(IR[/A] \mid M/AR/IR) \cdot$$
$$f(A[/MR] \mid M/AR/IR[/A]).$$

We observe that, by virtue of **B**-stability, the term $f(M/AR)$ is equal to 1 (all elements in IR have a parent in AR); similarly, by virtue of **F**-stability, the term $f(A[/MR] \mid M/AR/IR[/A])$ is also equal to 1 (all elements in A have at least one child in MR).

The remaining two terms, however, cannot be computed based solely on available stability annotations. To compensate for this lack of path-distribution information, the XS-KETCH estimation framework applies an *independence assumption*, that de-correlates the needed fractions from incoming or outgoing paths as follows: $f(AR/IR \mid M/AR) \approx f(AR/IR)$, $f(IR[/A] \mid M/AR/IR) \approx f(IR[/A])$. Thus, our selectivity expression is written as:

$$f(M/AR/IR[/A/MR]) = f(AR/IR) \cdot f(IR[/A]).$$

To approximate the required fractions, the XSKETCH estimation algorithm applies two *uniformity assumptions* based on the stored node counts. Since these assumptions are central in the theme of this paper, we define them formally below.

A1 [Backward-Edge Uniformity Assumption]. Given an XSKETCH node v, the incoming edges to v from all parent nodes u of v such that v is *not* **B**-stable with respect to u are *uniformly distributed* across all such parents in proportion to their element counts.

A2 [Forward-Edge Uniformity Assumption]. Given an XSKETCH node v, the outgoing edges from v to all children u of v such that v is *not* **F**-stable with respect to u are *uniformly distributed* across all such children in proportion to their element counts, and the total number of such edges is *at most* equal to the total of these element counts.

Returning to our example, Assumption **A1** provides the approximation $f(AR/IR) \approx |AR|/(|AR| + |MR|) = 3/6$, while Assumption **A2** yields $f(\exists\ IR/A) \approx |A|/\max\{|A| + |M|, |IR|\} = 3/6$. Thus, the estimate of the fraction is 0.25, and the overall path-expression selectivity can be approximated as $|IR| * 0.25 = 1.5$

Overall, the XSKETCH estimation framework uses stabilities in order to identify fully-stable subpath embeddings (for which accurate estimates can be given), and resorts to statistical assumptions to compensate for the lack of detailed path-distribution information in the synopsis. Clearly, the validity of these assumptions directly affects the accuracy of the resulting estimates. As we discuss next, the XSKETCH framework addresses this issue during the construction phase, where the goal is to find a "good" partitioning of elements into synopsis nodes such that the underlying estimation assumptions are valid [5,6].

XSKETCH **Construction.** At an abstract level, the XSKETCH construction problem can be defined as follows: Given a document graph G and a space budget S, build an XSKETCH synopsis of G that requires at most S storage of units, while minimizing the estimation error. Given the specifics of the XSKETCH model, this can be re-stated as follows: Compute a partitioning of data elements into synopsis nodes, such that the resulting XSKETCH (a) needs at most S units of storage, and (b) maximizes the validity of the estimation assumptions, thus minimizing error. Given that finding an optimal solution is typically an $\mathcal{NP}$-hard problem [5], the proposed XSKETCH construction algorithm (termed BUILDXSKETCH [5]) employs a heuristics-based, greedy search strategy in order to construct an effective, concise summary. In what follows, we provide a brief description of the key concepts behind the BUILDXSKETCH algorithm (more details can be found in [5]).

BUILDXSKETCH constructs an XSKETCH summary by incrementally refining a coarse synopsis, until it exhausts the available space budget. The starting summary assigns elements to synopsis nodes based solely on their label and, thus, represents a very coarse partitioning of the input document graph. At each step, this coarse partitioning is refined by applying one of three types of *refinement operations*, namely b-stabilize, f-stabilize, and b-split, on a specific synopsis node. Such refinement operations split the synopsis node (according to a specific criterion), resulting in a more refined partitioning. The split criterion is directly tied to the estimation assumptions that the refinement targets. For instance, the b-stabilize operation splits the node so that one of the two new nodes becomes **B**-stable with respect to a particular parent; in this manner, **B**-stability is now guaranteed along the new edge and the new summary is expected to have better estimates in the refined area. To select one of the possible refinements at each step, the BUILDXSKETCH algorithm employs a *marginal-gains* strategy: the refinement that yields the largest increase in accuracy per unit of additional required storage is chosen. Intuitively, this strategy leads to a summary which is more refined where correlations are stronger (and, thus, estimation assumptions are less valid), and less refined where the independence and uniformity assumptions provide good estimates of the true selectivities.

4   The fXSKETCH Model

As discussed in Section 3, the basic XSKETCH model employs the conventional, "binary" form of edge stabilities [15] in order to capture the key properties of the underlying path and branching structure. If stability is present (i.e., a value of 1), then there are strong guarantees on the connectivity between elements of edge-connected synopsis nodes; if, on the other hand, it is absent (i.e., a value of 0), then the XSKETCH estimation framework needs to apply independence and uniformity in order to approximate the true selectivity of the corresponding edge condition. In this section, we propose a simple, yet powerful generalization of the basic XSKETCH model based on a novel, more flexible notion of *fractional stabilities*. In a nutshell, instead of treating edge stability as a binary attribute, our new synopsis model uses a real number which reflects the *degree of stability* for each synopsis edge. In this manner, the synopsis stores distribution information at a finer level of detail, thus increasing the accuracy of the overall approximation.

Before describing our proposed synopsis mechanism in more detail, we present a simple example that illustrates the motivation behind fractional stabilities. Consider the sample document of Figure 3(a), where the numbers along edges denote the numbers of child elements. Figure 3(b) shows the coarsest XSKETCH synopsis, which groups together elements according to their tags (for simplicity, we omit **F**-stabilities from the figure). Note that the basic XSKETCH estimation framework has to apply a backward-edge uniformity assumption (**A1**) in order to estimate the number of f elements at the end of a path expression. Considering the skew in element counts, however, this assumption obviously introduces large errors in the estimate; as an example, the selectivity fraction of the embedding B/F is estimated as $f(B/F) = 1/(1 + 1 + 1 + 1) = 0.25$, while its true value is only 10^{-4}! In order to capture such skew, the XSKETCH construction algorithm would have to apply successive stabilization operations, in order to separate the f elements according to their incoming path. This, however, would lead to a finer partitioning, thus inevitably increasing the storage requirements of the synopsis. In addition, stabilization operations mainly target independence assumptions and it is not clear if the greedy construction algorithm can actually discover their relation to an invalid uniformity assumption (in the sample document, for example, independence is in fact valid). Note that, although we focused our example on backward uniformity, a similar argument can be made for forward-edges as well (Assumption **A2**).

As a solution to this shortcoming of the original XSKETCH model, we propose to store more detailed information along the edges of the graph synopsis in the form of *fractional stabilities*. More formally, these are defined as follows.

Definition 1. *Let $S(G) = (V_S, E_S)$ be a graph synopsis and $(u, v) \in E_S$ be a synopsis edge. The fractional **B**-stability of (u, v), denoted as $\mathbf{B}_q(u, v)$, is the fraction of elements in v that have at least one parent in u. The fractional **F**-stability of (u, v), denoted as $\mathbf{F}_q(u, v)$, is the fraction of elements in u that have at least one child in v.*

Clearly, our new model of fractional edge stabilities subsumes conventional, binary stabilities. More specifically, an edge (u, v) is **B**-stable (resp., **F**-stable) if and only if $\mathbf{B}_q(u, v) = 1$ (resp., $\mathbf{F}_q(u, v) = 1$), and unstable otherwise. Moreover, it is interesting to note that, by definition, fractional stabilities always provide *zero-error estimates* for path embeddings of length 2. For instance, the selectivity of an embedding u/v can be accurately estimated as $|v| \cdot \mathbf{B}_q(u, v)$, while for the length-2 branch $u[v]$, the selectivity is simply equal to $|u| \cdot \mathbf{F}_q(u, v)$. At this point, we can formally define our novel synopsis model of *fractional* XSKETCHes *(f*XSKETCHES*)* as follows.

Definition 2. *An fXSKETCH summary $S(G) = (V_S, E_S)$ of a document graph G is a graph synopsis of G that records the fractional stabilities $\mathbf{B}_q(u, v)$ and $\mathbf{F}_q(u, v)$ for each edge $(u, v) \in E_S$.*

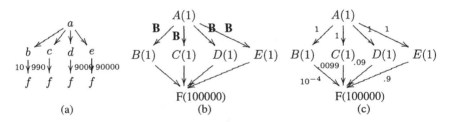

Fig. 3. (a) XML Document, (b) XSKETCH, (c) fXSKETCH.

Figure 3(c) depicts an example fXSKETCH for the document of Figure 3(a) (the edges are annotated with fractional **B**-stabilities only, since all fractional **F**-stabilities are equal to 1). Obviously, assuming a fixed synopsis-graph structure, an fXSKETCH has increased storage requirements when compared against the corresponding XSKETCH: instead of storing only two bits per edge (to denote absence or presence of **B/F**-stability), each fXSKETCH edge needs to record two real numbers (i.e., the new fractional stabilities). This finer level of detail, however, allows a concise fXSKETCH summary to capture richer information in limited space, without resorting to a finer partitioning of elements to synopsis nodes. Returning to the example of Figure 3, we observe that the fXSKETCH contains accurate information for all paths of length up to 2, while maintaining the coarsest partitioning of elements to synopsis nodes; the XSKETCH, on the other hand, will exhibit high estimation errors due to an inaccurate uniformity assumption and, as mentioned earlier, can capture skew only by resorting to a much finer partitioning of elements. This intuitive advantage of fractional stabilities is corroborated by our experimental findings, where our fXSKETCH synopses consistently return significantly more accurate selectivity estimates for the same synopsis space budget (Section 5).

We now discuss how our new fractional stabilities are integrated in the general XSKETCH framework for path-expression selectivity estimation. Once again, the key observation here is that fractional stabilities essentially provide *zero-error estimates* for the selectivities of single-edge path embeddings. More formally, if (u, v) is any edge in the fXSKETCH synopsis, then the selectivity fractions $f(u/v)$ and $f(u[v])$ are simply defined as $f(u/v) = \mathbf{B}_q(u, v)$ and $f(u[v]) = \mathbf{F}_q(u, v)$. Thus, instead of applying uniformity assumptions to approximate such terms (possibly incurring large estimation errors), our fXSKETCH estimation algorithm can retrieve the accurate information directly from the stored fractional stabilities. As an example, consider again the embedding M/AR/IR[A/MR] over the synopsis of Figure 2(b). After applying the Chain Rule and independence assumptions, the selectivity is expressed as $f(M/AR/IR[A/MR]) \approx f(AR/IR) \cdot f(IR[/A])$, where AR/IR and IR/A are the non-stable edges of the embedding. An XSKETCH summary would now employ Assumptions **A1** and **A2** to approximate the needed fraction terms; on the other hand, an fXSKETCH makes use of the corresponding fractional stabilities, arriving at the result $f(M/AR/IR[A/MR]) \approx \mathbf{B}_q(AR, IR) \cdot \mathbf{F}_q(IR, A)$. Note that fractional stabilities are at least as accurate as XSKETCH uniformity assumptions and, thus, assuming a fixed synopsis graph, the fXSKETCH estimate is guaranteed to be at least as accurate as the XSKETCH estimate (provided that independence is a valid assumption). Of course, for a fixed space budget, the fXSKETCH synopsis graph is typically smaller (see discussion above); nevertheless, our experimental results clearly show that, even in this case, our notion of fractional stabilities is a consistent winner.

Overall, the use of fractional stabilities simplifies the estimation framework by lifting the assumptions on backward- and forward-edge uniformity. In essence, the only assumptions needed by our selectivity-estimation algorithm are basic independence assumptions that de-correlate a selectivity fraction from other parts of the path embedding. The advantage of not applying uniformity assumptions is two-fold. First, estimates become more accurate since the required selectivity fractions are stored explicitly as fractional stabilities and need not be estimated (with potentially large errors). Second, the estimation process becomes faster, as applying uniformity typically entails scanning the parent (or, child) nodes of a synopsis node and computing sums of element counts.

The removal of the uniformity assumptions has a positive impact on the *synopsis-construction algorithm* as well. In essence, the BUILDXSKETCH algorithm is simplified since it only needs to consider b-stabilize and f-stabilize operations; the b-split refinement, which specifically targeted uniformity assumptions, becomes redundant and can be safely ignored. The end result is that the number of possible refinements per step is reduced, thus leading to faster synopsis-construction times.

5 Experimental Study

In this section, we present the results of an extensive experimental study on the performance of the new fXSKETCH model. The goal of this study is two-fold: (a) to evaluate the effectiveness of fXSKETCHES as concise summaries for graph-structured XML data, and (b) to compare the accuracy of the new summarization model against the original XSKETCH framework. We have conducted experiments on real-life and synthetic XML data, using a variety of query workloads. Our key findings can be summarized as follows:

- The fXSKETCH synopses are effective summaries of graph-structured XML data, enabling accurate estimates for the selectivity of complex path expressions. The experiments show that, an XMark fXSKETCH synopsis achieves an average estimation error of 0.8%, with storage requirements that amount to 0.1% of the data size.
- fXSKETCHES perform consistently better than XSKETCHes in terms of estimation error. More specifically, higher accuracy is obtained for the same synopsis size, and a smaller size is achieved for the same accuracy. For instance, a 5KB fXSKETCH synopsis of the XMark data set has a 10 fold improvement in accuracy when compared to an XSKETCH synopsis of the same size. In addition, the fXSKETCH framework is more robust with respect to workloads that contain numerous branching predicates. For instance, the estimation error of a 5 KB XSKETCH synopsis for the IMDB data set can vary of up to 100%, between path expressions with and without branching predicates; on the other hand, an fXSKETCH of the same size has a variation of up to 15%.
- fXSKETCHES compute relatively accurate estimates even for the coarsest synopsis. With XMark data set, the use of fractional stabilities in the coarsest summary have reduced the estimation error to 9% (compared to 27% for the coarsest XSKETCH synopsis).
- fXSKETCHES have reduced requirements in terms of construction time. Given a specific space budget, an fXSKETCH is both more efficient to construct and more accurate compared to a XSKETCH. In addition, fXSKETCHES provide accurate estimates even for low space budgets, thus leading to shorter construction times.

Overall, our experimental findings verify the effectiveness of the fXSKETCH framework and demonstrate its benefits over the original XSKETCH proposal.

5.1 Experimental Methodology

Implementation. We implemented a prototype of the proposed fXSKETCH framework over the existing XSKETCH code-base. Our implementation encodes fractional stabilities in the standard float representation, so each non **B**- of **F**-stable edge contributes an additional 4 bytes to the synopsis size. Note that XSKETCH and fXSKETCH synopses of the same size are different in the size of the synopes graphs - an fXSKETCH will always be the smaller graph (less nodes and edges).

The parameters of the build algorithm were set to V=10% and P=200 for both fXSKETCH and XSKETCH construction (details on the construction algorithm can be found in the XSKETCH studies [5,6]). In the results that we report, the maximum size of the computed synopses was limited to 2% of the underlying XML data size.

Data Sets. We use two graph-structured data sets[1] in our experiments: IMDB, a real-life data set from the Internet Movie Database (www.imdb.com), and XMark, a synthetic data set that records the activities of an on-line auction site. Table 1 summarizes the main characteristics of the data sets in terms of the file size, and the sizes of the corresponding perfect and coarsest synopsis. The coarsest summary, termed the *label-split graph*, partitions elements to nodes based solely on their label. The perfect summary, termed the *B/F-Bisimilar graph*, partitions elements so that all the edges of the resulting synopsis are **B**- and **F**-stable (i.e., their fractional stabilities are equal to 1). This property guarantees that the selectivity estimate for any branching path expression has zero error. Overall, both data sets have large perfect summaries thus motivating the need for concise synopses. Note that the sizes reported do not include the space needed to store the actual text of the element labels; each label is hashed to a unique integer and the mapping is stored in a separate structure that is not part of the summary.

Table 1. Characteristics of the three data sets

	IMDB	XMark
File Size	3 MB	10 MB
Number of elements	102,755	206,131
Nodes in Label-Split Graph	123	84
Nodes in B/F-Bisimilar Graph	49,181	197,508
Size of Label-Split Graph	3.4 KB	2.1 KB
Size of B/F-Bisimilar Graph	1.1 MB	4.5 MB

Table 2. Average result sizes

	IMDB	XMark
Simple	484	1125
Light-Branching	1351	1773
Heavy-Branching	1331	2420

Query Workload. We evaluate the accuracy of the generated summaries against three different workloads, each one consisting of 1000 path expressions: (a) *Simple Paths*, which contains simple path expressions only, (b) *Heavy Branching Paths*, in which 90% of path expressions have branching predicates and (c) *Light Branching Paths*, in which 40% of path expressions have branching predicates. In each case, all path expressions are positive, i.e., they have non-zero selectivity, and are generated by sampling paths from the corresponding perfect synopsis. Except for branching predicates, which comprise of one or two steps, the length of the sampled paths is distributed between 2 and 5 and the sample is biased toward high counts in the perfect synopsis. As a result, the generated path expressions follow the distribution of the data, with high-count labels being referenced more frequently in the query set. Table 2 shows the average result size (in terms of the number of elements) for the path queries in each workload.

We have also experimented with *negative* workloads, i.e., path expressions that do not discover any elements in the data graph. Our results have shown that both XSKETCH

---

[1] We use the same data sets as the original XSKETCH study [5]

and fXSKETCH summaries consistently produce close to zero estimates with negligible error and therefore we omit this workload from our presentation.

Evaluation Metric. As in the original XSKETCH study [5], we quantify the accuracy of both XSKETCHes and fXSKETCHes based on the average absolute relative error of result estimates over path expressions in our workload. Given a path expression p with true result size c, the absolute relative error of the estimated count e is computed as $|e - c| / max(c, s)$. Parameter s represents a sanity bound that essentially equates all zero or low counts with a default count s and thus avoids inordinately high contributions from low-count path expressions. We set this bound to the 10-percentile of the true counts in the workload (i.e., 90% of the path expressions in the workload have a true result size $\geq s$).

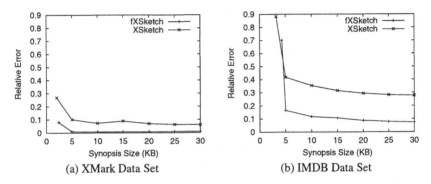

(a) XMark Data Set   (b) IMDB Data Set

Fig. 4. XSKETCH and the fXSKETCH estimation error for Heavy Branching Paths

5.2   Experimental Results

fXSKETCH **Performance for Branching Paths.** In this experiment, we evaluate the performance of our fXSKETCH synopses for the heavy-branching paths workload. Figure 4 depicts the estimation error of fXSKETCHes and XSKETCHes as a function of the synopsis size, for the IMDB and XMark data sets. Note that, in all the graphs that we present, the estimation error at the smallest summary size corresponds to the label-split graph synopsis (i.e., the coarsest summary). Overall, the results indicate that fXSKETCHes are effective summaries that enable accurate estimates for the selectivity of branching path expressions. In the case of XMark, for instance, the estimation error is reduced below 1% after a few refinements and it remains stable thereafter. For the more irregular IMDB data set, the estimation error stabilizes at 7% for a space budget of 25KB, which represents a very small fraction of the original data size. Compared to XSKETCHes, it is evident that the new fXSKETCH synopses perform consistently better. For the IMDB data set, for instance, a 25KB fXSKETCH has an average error of 7%, compared to 28% for the XSKETCH of the same size - a 4 fold improvement. It is interesting to note that the fXSKETCH-computed estimates are significantly more accurate even for the case of the coarsest synopsis. For the XMark data set, for instance, the average error for the coarsest fXSKETCH is 8% (2.5KB of storage), while the error for the coarsest XSKETCH is more than 25% (2.1KB of storage).

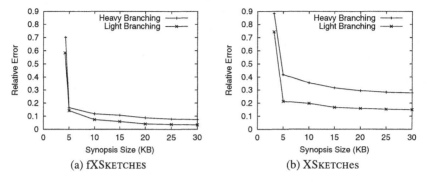

Fig. 5. Estimation accuracy for different branching worklads: (a) fXSKETCHES, (b) XSKETCHes.

Workload Comparison. Figure 5 depicts the estimation error for XSKETCH and fXSKETCH synopses respectively, for the two different types of branching workloads (we note that the numbers for the Heavy Branching workload are identical to Figure 4). We report the results for the IMDB data set only, as its structure is more irregular than that of the XMARK data set. The plot indicates that fXSKETCHES are more robust in terms of their performance than XSKETCHes. As shown in Figure 5(b), the fXSKETCH error follows a similar pattern in both types of workload, with the error of Heavy Branching being slightly increased (as expected). XSKETCHes, on the other hand, exhibit significantly different errors depending on the workload type (Figure 5(a)). The increased error for Heavy Branching suggests that the forward-edge uniformity assumption is not valid in the underlying data graph, thus leading to significant errors as the number of branches increases. fXSKETCH estimation, on the other hand, relies on fractional stabilities in order to capture accurately the distribution of document edges along each non-stable synopsis edge; as a result, an fXSKETCH summary provides better approximations for smaller budget sizes.

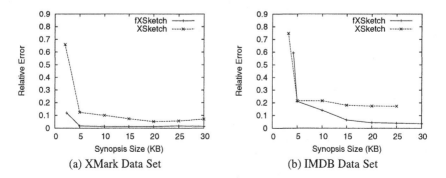

Fig. 6. XSKETCH and the fXSKETCH estimation error for Simple Paths

fXSKETCH **Performance for Simple Paths**. In this experiment, we evaluate the performance of fXSKETCHES for simple path expressions. Figure 6 depicts the estimation error of fXSKETCHES and XSKETCHes as a function of the synopsis size, for the IMDB and XMark data sets. Similar to the previous experiment, fXSKETCHES provide more accurate estimates compared to XSKETCHes. For the XMark data set, the estimation error for fXSKETCHES stabilizes at 1.7% (5KB of storage), while for XSKETCHes it remains at a considerably higher 7% (20KB of storage). The results follow a similar trend for the IMDB data set, where the error for fXSKETCHES is reduced to 4% for the 20KB synopsis, while the XSKETCH error stabilizes at 17% for the same space budget. In both data sets, and in accordance to our findings in previous experiments, we observe an improvement in accuracy for the coarsest summaries. The difference is more notable in the XMark data set - 12% vs. 66% - and comes at a very small increase in the storage requirements of the summaries: 2450 bytes for the fXSKETCH vs. 2100 bytes for the XSKETCH.

6   Conclusions and Future Work

Estimating the selectivity of complex path expressions is a key step in the optimization of declarative queries over XML data. In this paper, we have proposed the fXSKETCH model, a generalization of the original XSKETCH framework to the new concept of fractional stabilities. Intuitively, fractional stabilities capture the degree of stability of synopsis edges, and essentially free the estimation framework from the, potentially, erroneous, uniformity assumptions. The net result is a simplified estimation framework that can provide more accurate estimates with less computation. Results from an extensive experimental study have verified the effectiveness of the new model in providing low-error selectivity estimates for complex path expressions and have demonstrated its benefits over the original XSKETCH synopses.

In our future work, we plan to fine-tune certain aspects of the proposed framework. More specifically, the current storage overhead of fractional stabilities can reach up to 30-45% of the total synopsis size, depending on the data set. We intend to investigate techniques of reducing this overhead, by selectively choosing which fractional stabilities to materialize. In essence, this would allow a hybrid model where both fractional stabilities and the uniformity assumptions are used during estimation. A second direction that we intend to explore is the incremental maintenance of fXSKETCH synopses in the presence of data updates, or the refinement of summaries based on query feedback (self-tuning synopses). We believe that fractional stabilities are a suitable model for such techniques since they record distribution information at a finer level of detail and can thus track more reliably the statistical characteristics of the underlying data.

References

1. Clark, J., DeRose, S.: "XML Path Language (XPath), Version 1.0". W3C Recommendation (available from http://www.w3.org/TR/xpath/) (1999)
2. Aboulnaga, A., Alameldeen, A.R., Naughton, J.F.: "Estimating the Selectivity of XML Path Expressions for Internet Scale Applications". In: Proceedings of the 27th Intl. Conf. on Very Large Data Bases. (2001)

3. Freire, J., Haritsa, J.R., Ramanath, M., Roy, P., Siméon, J.: "StatiX: Making XML Count". In: Proceedings of the 2002 ACM SIGMOD Intl. Conf. on Management of Data. (2002)

4. Lim, L., Wang, M., Padmanabhan, S., Vitter, J., Parr, R.: XPathLearner: An On-Line Self-Tuning Markov Histogram for XML Path Selectivity Estimation. In: Proceedings of the 28th Intl. Conf. on Very Large Data Bases. (2002)

5. Polyzotis, N., Garofalakis, M.: "Statistical Synopses for Graph Structured XML Databases". In: Proceedings of the 2002 ACM SIGMOD Intl. Conf. on Management of Data. (2002)

6. Polyzotis, N., Garofalakis, M.: "Structure and Value Synopses for XML Data Graphs". In: Proceedings of the 28th Intl. Conf. on Very Large Data Bases. (2002)

7. Wang, W., Jiang, H., Lu, H., Yu, J.X.: Containment join size estimation: Models and methods. In: Proceedings of the 2003 ACM SIGMOD Intl. Conf. on Management of Data. (2003)

8. Wu, Y., Patel, J.M., Jagadish, H.: "Estimating Answer Sizes for XML Queries". In: Proceedings of the 8th Intl. Conf. on Extending Database Technology (EDBT'02). (2002)

9. Kaushik, R., Shenoy, P., Bohannon, P., Gudes, E.: "Exploiting Local Similarity for Efficient Indexing of Paths in Graph Structured Data". In: Proceedings of the Eighteenth Intl. Conf. on Data Engineering, San Jose, California (2002)

10. Milo, T., Suciu, D.: "Index structures for Path Expressions". In: Proceedings of the Seventh International Conference on Database Theory (ICDT'99), Jerusalem, Israel (1999)

11. Bray, T., Paoli, J., Sperberg-McQueen, C.M., Maler, E.: "Extensible Markup Language (XML) 1.0 (Second Edition)". W3C Recommendation (available from http://www.w3.org/TR/REC-xml/) (2000)

12. DeRose, S., Maler, E., Orchard, D.: "XML Linking Language (XLink), Version 1.0". W3C Recommendation (available from http://www.w3.org/TR/xlink/) (2001)

13. McHugh, J., Widom, J.: "Query Optimization for XML". In: Proceedings of the 25th Intl. Conf. on Very Large Data Bases. (1999)

14. Chamberlin, D., Clark, J., Florescu, D., Robie, J., Siméon, J., Stefanescu, M.: "XQuery 1.0: An XML Query Language". W3C Working Draft 07 (available from http://www.w3.org/TR/xquery/) (2001)

15. Paige, R., Tarjan, R.E.: "Three Partition Refinement Algorithms". SIAM Journal on Computing **16** (1987)

Flexible Workload-Aware Clustering of XML Documents

Rajesh Bordawekar[1] and Oded Shmueli[2]

[1] IBM T. J. Watson Research Center
Hawthorne, NY 10532, U.S.A.
bordaw@us.ibm.com
[2] Computer Science Department, Technion
Haifa 32000, Israel
oshmu@cs.technion.ac.il

Abstract. We investigate workload-directed physical data clustering in native XML database and repository systems. We present a practical algorithm for clustering XML documents, called XC, which is based on Lukes' tree partitioning algorithm. XC carefully approximates certain aspects of Lukes' algorithm so as to substantially reduce memory and time usage. XC can operate with varying degrees of precision, even in memory constrained environments. Experimental results indicate that XC is a superior clustering algorithm in terms of partition quality, with only a slight overhead in performance when compared to a workload-directed depth-first scan and store scheme. We demonstrate that XC is substantially faster than the exact Lukes' algorithm, with only a minimal loss in clustering quality. Results also indicate that XC can exploit application workload information to generate XML clustering solutions that lead to major reduction in page faults for the workload under consideration.

1 Introduction

Current database and repository systems use two main approaches for storing XML documents. The first approach maps an XML document into one or more relational tables [4,1]. Stored XML documents are then processed via traditional relational operators. The second approach, *Native XML Storage*, views the document as an XML tree. It partitions the XML tree into distinct records containing disjoint connected subtrees [8,3,11]. XML records are then stored in disk pages, either in an unparsed, textual form, or using some internal representation. In this paper, we concentrate on the native XML storage approach.

Unlike relational databases where data is queried using *value-dependant* select-project-join (SPJ) queries, XML document processing is dominated by *path-dependant navigational* XPath queries. In practice, such navigational traversals are often aided by path indices that reduce the number of path navigations across stored XML records. However, *index-only* processing cannot completely eliminate such path traversals as XML query patterns are often complex and it is impractical to maintain multiple path indices to cover all possible paths

Z. Bellahsène et al. (Eds.): XSym 2004, LNCS 3186, pp. 204–218, 2004.
© Springer-Verlag Berlin Heidelberg 2004

of the entire XML document. In reality, disk-resident XPath processors employ a *mixed*, i.e., part navigational, part indexed, processing model.

Physical *co-location* or *clustering* of data items has been extensively used in database systems for exploiting common data access patterns to improve query performance. Data clustering was shown to be particularly effective when the underlying data model is hierarchical in nature and supports queries whose execution path traversals remain relatively stable (e.g., IBM's IMS [10]). In native XML database systems, XPath operations result in navigations across stored XML records, which are similar to those in hierarchical or object-oriented databases. Clustering techniques could also be applied for storing XML documents in native XML databases, where *related* XML nodes can be clustered and stored in the same disk page. Here, two XML nodes are *related* if they are connected via a link and examining one of them is likely to soon lead to examining the other. As disk pages have limited capacity, not all related XML nodes can fit in a single disk page. Therefore, one needs to decide how to assign related XML nodes to disk pages. This paper investigates the following **XML clustering problem**: Given *a static* XML document[1], *mixed* XPath processing model, and associated navigational workload information, identify related XML nodes and efficiently cluster them to disk pages.

We formulate the XML clustering problem as a tree partitioning problem. The tree to be partitioned is a *clustering tree*, namely an XML tree augmented with node and edge weights. We then propose XC, a new tree partitioning algorithm that can operate with varying degrees of precision under space and time constraints. XC is based on LUKES, Lukes' tree partitioning algorithm [9]. While LUKES is an exact algorithm, XC is an approximate algorithm.

The main contribution of this work is a practical solution to the XML clustering problem using a tree partitioning approach which uses XML navigational behavior to direct its partitioning decisions. A key contribution of this work is XC, which has the following advantages over LUKES:

- First, XC exploits intrinsic structural regularities in Lukes' dynamic programming algorithm, namely, *ready* clusters (Section 3), to improve its memory consumption and running time, *without affecting its precision*. With this optimization, XC acts as an efficient version of the precise LUKES algorithm.
- Second, XC implements a parametric approximation of the dynamic programming procedure that allows it to tradeoff precision for time. This enables XC to exhibit linear-time behavior without significant degradation in quality over the precise solution.
- Third, under memory constraints, XC *continuously, on-the-fly* adapts its precision by selectively eliminating dynamic programming options such that the memory limitations are not violated. This allows XC to tradeoff precision for memory.

The other significant contribution of the paper is the experimental validation of XC using a prototype XML clustering system, **XCS**. We used **XCS** to compare

---

[1] We don't consider inter-document clustering.

XC against an alternative XML partitioning scheme, workload-directed depth-first scan & storage (WDFS). The experiments evaluate the quality of tree partitioning and measure the number of page faults for various XPath query workloads under different paging scenarios using the mixed XPath processing model with prefix path indexes. Experimental results demonstrate that XC computed *approximate* partitions were closer in value to the *optimal* partition computed by the precise Lukes' algorithm, at a fraction of the runtime costs. Similarly, XC computed higher valued partitions than WDFS, with a slight overhead in performance. When clustering using workloads consisting of XPath queries, XC was able to compute a partition that matched the XPath navigation behavior. The physical layout generated by XC caused fewer page faults, sometimes by more than an order of magnitude, than WDFS. XC's ability to use different degrees of approximation in practically linear time, its ability to execute under severe memory constraints and its ability to capture workload features, even in presence of indexes, make it a highly suitable candidate for enabling workload-directed XML clustering for both online and offline scenarios.

The rest of the paper is organized as follows. The tree partitioning problem is formalized in Section 2. LUKES is reviewed in Section 2, and in Section 3, we present XC. The experiments are detailed in Section 4. Related work is summarized in Section 5. Section 6 presents conclusions and future work directions.

2   The Tree Partitioning Problem

Consider a rooted tree $T = (V, E)$, where V is a set of *nodes* and $E \subseteq V \times V$ is a set of *edges*. A *cluster over* T is a non-empty subset of V. When no confusion arises, we simply use the term *cluster*. A *partition of* T, P^T, is a set of pairwise disjoint clusters over T whose union equals V, that is $P^T = \{c_1, \ldots, c_k\}$, $k \geq 1$, such that $\bigcup_{i=1}^{k} c_i = V$, and $c_i \cap c_j = \emptyset$, for all $i \neq j$. Each edge (i, j) of T is associated with a non-negative integer *value*, v_{ij}. The *size* of a cluster c, $size(c)$, is the sum of the weights of its nodes; formally, $size(c) = \Sigma_{i \in c}\, w_i$. The *value* of a cluster c, $value(c)$, is the sum of the values of its edges; formally, $value(c) = \Sigma_{(i,j) \in E\, \wedge i \in c\, \wedge j \in c}\, v_{ij}$. The *value* of a partition P^T, $value(P^T)$, is the sum of the values of its clusters; formally, $value(P^T) = \Sigma_{c \in P^T}\, value(c)$. Let W, the *cluster weight bound*, be a positive integer. The *tree partitioning problem* is formulated thus: Find a highest value partition, P^T_{opt}, among all the possible partitions of T, such that the size of each cluster in P^T_{opt} does not exceed W. P^T_{opt} is said to be an *optimal partition* of T.[2] So, $P^T_{opt} = \{c_1, \ldots, c_k\}$ such that $size(c_i) \leq W$, for $i = 1, \ldots, k$, and $value(P^T_{opt}) = Max\{value(P^T)$ $\mid P^T$ *is partition of* T and $\forall c \in P^T$, $size(c) \leq W\}$.

Lukes' Tree Partitioning Algorithm (LUKES): Lukes' algorithm, LUKES, addresses the tree partitioning problem. LUKES operates on a tree in a bottom-up manner; it considers a node only after all the node's children have been considered. Consider a partition $P^{T'}$ of a subtree T' (of T) rooted at node x.

---

[2] In general, there may be more than one optimal partition.

The unique cluster in $P^{T'}$ which contains x is called the *pivot cluster* of $P^{T'}$. The weight of a partition $P^{T'}$ is the size of its pivot cluster. LUKES uses dynamic programming on the partition weights as follows: For each subtree, say rooted at a node x, and for each feasible total cluster size U (i.e., $w_x \leq U \leq W$), LUKES constructs, if possible, an optimal subtree partition in which the pivot cluster is of size U. So, LUKES associates with node x a *set* of partitions, each optimal under the constraint that the pivot cluster size is U. When considering a node x, the partitions that are associated with each child node of x are used to update the collection of partitions, one per each feasible total cluster size, for x. Once the tree root node is processed, the final result, P^T_{opt}, is the highest value partition associated with the root; as Lukes showed, P^T_{opt} has the maximum partition value among all possible partitions of the tree.

LUKES: Lukes' algorithm consists of the following steps:

1. For each leaf node u with weight $w = w_u$, form the partition P_w, with value 0, consisting of a single pivot cluster containing the node u ($P_w = \{\{u\}\}$). Mark this partition as the optimal partition for u. For all internal non-leaf nodes v, form similar initial partitions, each containing a single cluster with value 0 and weight $w = w_v$.

2. Arbitrarily choose some node x with weight $w = w_x$, such that all of x's children are now leaf nodes. For the subtree rooted at node x, compute for $w' = w, w + 1, \cdots, W$, the optimal partition, if one exists, in which the cluster containing x (i.e., the pivot) has weight w' (recall that W is the weight bound). To find these optimal partitions, perform the following steps:

   a) Let node i be the first child of node x.

   b) For each partition P of node x and for each partition Q of node i, generate intermediate partitions I_1 and I_2 as follows:

      i. Let c_x be the pivot cluster of P (containing x) and let c_i be the pivot cluster of Q (containing i).

      ii. **Merging:** If $size(c_x) + size(c_i) \leq W$, then create a new cluster, $c_m = c_x \bigcup c_i$, i.e., merge the two respective pivot clusters. Create a new partition, $I_1 = \{c_m\} \bigcup (P - \{c_x\}) \bigcup (Q - \{c_i\})$, i.e., by "gluing" c_m and the remaining clusters from partitions P and Q.

      iii. **Concatenation:** If Q is marked as the optimal partition for node i, create a new partition $I_2 = P \bigcup Q$, i.e., concatenate clusters from partitions P and Q to form a new partition. Else, $I_2 = \{\{ \}\}$, with value 0.

   c) Update the intermediate partitions associated with node x. Let a (resp., b) be the weight of the cluster containing node x in I_1 (resp., node i in I_2). If the current partition of weight a associated with x, P_a, is such that $value(P_a) < value(I_1)$ then discard P_a and replace it with I_1. Then, if the current partition of weight b associated with x, P_b, is such that $value(P_b) < value(I_2)$ then discard P_b and replace it with I_2. If i is the last child of node x, proceed to Step 3, otherwise, let i be the next child of x and go to Step 2b.

3. Mark a partition, with the maximum value among the intermediate partitions associated with node x, as the *optimal* partition, P_{opt}^x, for the subtree
with root x. Delete the children of node x from tree T. Node x is now a
leaf. If node x is the root then P_{opt}^x is the computed *optimal* partition of T.
Otherwise, go to Step 2.

The inner loop (Step 2) is executed for every internal node in the tree. This
loop involves combining partitions of the internal node with the partitions of
its children (Step 2b). In the worst case, a parent may possess W intermediate
partitions after processing its first child (Step 2c); these W partitions can then
be combined with W partitions of every remaining child. For an n-node tree,
Step 2b can be invoked at most $n - 1$ times, leading to an $O(n\ W^2)$ running
time.

3   XC: An Approximate Tree Clustering Algorithm

We now present a new approximate tree partitioning algorithm, XC, tailored for
clustering large XML documents. Both LUKES and XC recursively partition a
clustering tree. Recall that the *clustering tree* is the XML tree augmented with
node and edge weights, both integers. Node weights are the (text) sizes of the
XML nodes. Edge weights model the importance of putting the nodes into the
same cluster. Once a subtree of the clustering tree is completely partitioned, we
call it a *processed subtree* (and its root a *processed node*). XC provides following
improvements over LUKES:

Identification of Ready Clusters: While partitioning a clustering tree,
LUKES creates new partitions by merging and concatenating clusters from partitions of its processed subtrees. As a result, LUKES retains and propagates a
larger number of partitions and clusters until the final successful partition is
computed, leading to excessive memory usage and runtime costs. XC addresses
this problem by aggressively detecting those clusters that are **guaranteed** to be
part of *any* final partition. Such clusters are called, *ready clusters*. A cluster in a
partition associated with a processed node x is *ready* iff it satisfies the following
conditions:

1. It does not contain node x and hence it cannot be involved in any future
cluster merge operations, and
2. It is a member of **every** intermediate partition, including the *optimal* partition, associated with node x.

According to condition (1), since the ready cluster is not a pivot cluster of
any intermediate partition of a processed subtree, it can not be modified via the
merging operation (Step 2b:ii). Condition (2) guarantees that every future generated partition using the intermediate partitions will contain the ready cluster.
Hence, the ready cluster can be safely removed from the intermediate partitions
of the processed subtree without affecting the correctness of the final solution.
XC detects ready clusters as soon as the subtree rooted at node x is processed

and forwards it (along with its XML data) for further processing (e.g., the page assignment sub-system, see Section 4.1, Figure 1). Once the page assignment sub-system assigns a ready cluster to a page, the XML nodes, contained in the cluster, can be deleted along with their XML data. This can lead to significant reduction in memory usage and consequently improves the running time. With only this optimization, XC behaves like an *optimized* version of the *exact* LUKES.

Approximate Dynamic Programming using Weight Intervals: Since LUKES is an exact algorithm, it explores *all* possible relevant alternatives before producing an optimal partition. For a tree with n nodes, for every node n', with weight $w \geq 1$, LUKES examines all possible partitions with weights from w to the weight bound, W. This results in $O(nW)$ space and $O(nW^2)$ time complexities. To address this problem, XC partitions the $(1, W)$ weight range into equal sized *weight intervals* and retains only one partition for each weight interval. The number of the weight intervals is specified by the application using the *chunk_size* parameter. The value of *chunk_size* can vary from 1 to W and is a divisor of W. The chosen partition of each weight interval has the *maximum value* among the partitions whose weights fall in that interval. So, for XC, following internal node processing, (LUKES, Step 2) there are at most $W_c = \frac{W}{chunk\_size}$ intermediate partitions associated with the node. Similarly, the inner loop (LUKES, Step 2b) iterates over the weight intervals from 1 to W_c. These modifications reduce the space complexity to $O(n\ W_c)$ and time complexity to $O(n\ W_c^2)$. This weight interval approximation technique is used only for *assigning* intermediate partitions in the proper interval. The decision whether to merge clusters (LUKES, Step 2b) is still based on *actual* cluster weights (rather than the interval to which the partition containing the cluster belongs). When *chunk_size* = 1, XC operates exactly as LUKES; it also finds an optimal partition. When *chunk_size* = W, only one intermediate partition is produced per each node. In other words, when *chunk_size* = W, XC operates as a simple greedy algorithm. In general, by changing the chunk_size, one can control the precision of XC's approximate tree partitioning algorithm.

Handling Memory Constraints: In spite of the memory reduction techniques employed by XC, its memory consumption can still be very large, particularly for large XML documents and for smaller chunk_size values. We now describe the technique employed by XC which uses *ready sub-partitions*, to work effectively subject to a memory limit. A *ready sub-partition* is a partition that is associated with the root of an already processed subtree (of the clustering tree), which is a *subset* of the computed best approximate partition for the *whole* clustering tree. If one could identify a ready sub-partition, then the sub-partition's clusters can be forwarded for further processing and the memory of associated data structures could be reclaimed immediately. Observe that the elimination of partitions also *reduces the number of options for future dynamic programming considerations*; further reducing the computation and memory usage. XC uses the following mechanism to choose a partition as the next ready sub-partition. Once a subtree is processed, its intermediate partitions are retained until its parent node is processed. XC maintains a bounded-length (a parameter k, e.g., $k = 8$) list, HL, of the current up to k highest value partitions that are associated with processed nodes (i.e., roots of processed subtrees whose parents are not yet processed). Given a memory limit M, XC computes *high* and *low* "water marks" for managing memory usage (e.g., $low = 0.7M < high = 0.9M < M$). When memory usage crosses the high water mark, corrective actions are triggered. Once it reaches the low water mark, normal operation resumes. Upon crossing the high water mark, XC chooses a partition, P, with the highest value from HL. XC then marks this partition as a ready sub-partition, forwards its clusters to the page assignment sub-system, and then reclaims the memory of the associated data structures. Observe that P will also form a subset of the final result partition. XC then removes the XML node v_P with which P is associated (i.e., a root of a processed subtree) and discards v_P's link to its parent. This process of eliminating highest value partitions from HL proceeds *continuously* until either the memory usage falls below the low water mark or the optimal partition list is empty. If the memory-usage violation persists and the optimal partition list is empty, then, as soon as any subtree is processed, its optimal partition is immediately marked as ready and is eliminated, in the process described above.

4   Experimental Evaluation

We ran XC with different degrees of precision and compared it against WDFS, a workload-directed depth-first scan and store scheme [12].[3] WDFS is a natural clustering algorithm that scans an XML document in depth-first manner. In a greedy fashion, it produces XML nodes and uses the workload information (i.e., the edge weights) to store nodes connected by edges with higher weights in the same cluster. The cluster is mapped into disk pages as soon as it is full. A major advantage of WDFS is that it places together XML nodes whose processing completes in temporal closeness. Another advantage of WDFS is that it is ideal for implementation in an online single-pass environment.

4.1   XCS: A Prototype XML Clustering System

For experimental purposes, we partitioned several XML documents from the University of Washington XML repository using **XCS** (Figure 1). **XCS** is a prototype XML clustering system that scans an XML document, partitions it into clusters and assigns the clusters to (disk) pages, all in a single pass. It consists of three distinct sub-systems: edge-weight assigner, tree partitioner and page assigner.

Edge-weight Assigner: **XCS**'s edge-weight assigner uses application workload information to assign weights to the clustering tree edges. Currently, the workload information consists of a list of XPath queries and their relative weights.

---

[3] Interested reader is referred to [2] for complete experimental results.

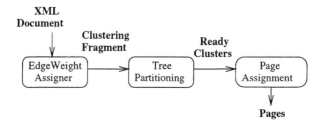

Fig. 1. XCS Architecture.

These weights capture relevant workload features such as the frequency or importance of specific XPath queries. **XCS**'s edge-weight assigner uses a simulator that mimics execution of a hypothetical XPath processor using the mixed XPath processing model. Currently, in addition to the traditional navigational approach, the simulator also supports XPath processing using **prefix path indexes** on a query's sub-path.[4] While executing an XPath query, those edges covered by the path indexes, the simulator assigns the weight 0 (which mimics the index-directed "jumping over" operation), the remaining edges, which are used in navigation, are assigned the corresponding relative weight. Intuitively, the assigned weight models the fact that the nodes connected by that edge are traversed in (temporal) succession by the XPath processor, and using that edge. The edge weights represent cumulative weight increments generated by traversals for the XPath queries in the workload. The higher is the edge weight, higher is the traversal affinity between the connected nodes.

Tree Partitioner and Page Assigner: Once the edge-weight assigner assigns the edge weights, the memory resident portion of the clustering tree is handled by the tree partitioning system (which can use either XC or WDFS). As soon as the tree partitioner identifies clusters suitable for storage, such clusters are forwarded to the page-assignment sub-system which maps them to pages. When XC is used as the tree partitioner, the page assignment sub-system uses an online bin-packing algorithm that makes page assignment decisions solely on the basis of weights of the currently available ready clusters (Section 3). The WDFS uses a greedy strategy to map clusters to pages.

4.2   Evaluation of XC

We first investigate the effect of chunk_size on the quality (in terms of the partition value) and performance of XC. Recall that XC uses dynamic programming over weight intervals rather than over the entire weight range (see Section 3). In XC, the weight interval is determined by the chunk_size parameter (which determines the number of dynamic programming intervals). Table 1 illustrates the effects of the chunk_size parameter on the final partition value and the total

---

[4] It could be easily extended to support generalized path indexes and text indexes.

execution time. In this experiment, an XML file, `xmark.xml` of size 110 KB, and containing 2647 XML nodes, is clustered with a weight bound, W=1 KB. The chunk_size, c, is varied from 1024 to 1. Clustering tree edges are randomly assigned weights. As illustrated in Table 1, as chunk_size decreases, the value of the final partition solution increases. As the chunk_size decreases, the number of weight intervals used, $\frac{W}{c}$, increases and XC becomes more precise. However, as XC's precision increases, the amount of computation grows (recall that the time complexity of XC is $O(n \ (\frac{W}{c})^2)$), leading to an increase in memory usage and running time. When the chunk_size is 1, XC behaved like the *exact* LUKES, and the required running time was more than 7 hours. The difference in solution values for the chunk_sizes of 1024 and 1, is very small ($< 2\%$), but the execution times varied drastically (432 ms. for 1024 vs. more than 7 hours for 1). This indicates that XC's strategy of dynamic programming over weight intervals and retaining the highest valued partition per weight interval, works well in practice. As the results demonstrate, XC with chunk_size of 1 (equivalently, LUKES), exhibits unrealistic memory and runtime requirements and for varying chunk_sizes, XC obtains good solutions with reasonable memory and runtime usage.

Table 1. Effect of Dynamic Programming over Weight Intervals on XC using xmark.xml of size 110 KB. The weight bound was 1 KB and the chunk_size is varied from 1024 to 1. When the chunk_size was 1, XC acted as an optimized version of LUKES.

chunk_size	Value	Memory Usage (bytes)	Time (ms)
1024	20244	49904	432
512	20355	62581	423
256	20430	85603	590
128	20442	116393	1171
64	20460	176740	3040
32	20460	289407	10687
16	20460	523074	44974
8	20460	1012078	195832
4	20460	1910695	960775
1 (LUKES)	20460	7625395	28610786

We measured the impact of identifying ready clusters on the quality of results. We clustered 5 XML documents with and without using the ready clusters. The edges were assigned random weight. We found that for all 5 documents, the memory usage increased when the ready clusters were not identified. In many cases, that resulted in a significant degradation in the overall running time. For example, while partitioning `mondial.xml` of size 1.97 MB, XC used 2227547 bytes and needed 41.1 sec when ready clusters were identified; without the ready-cluster identification, the same document used 6059854 bytes and required 156.91 sec. Ready cluster identification reduces the number of data structures that need to be retained and propagated during the clustering process. It doesn't reduce the number of iterations (which is determined by the chunk_size) but it reduces the amount of work per iteration as the amount of data to be handled decreases, and improves overall memory behavior by reducing memory usage and memory footprints of key data structures. It should be noted that for all cases, regardless of the ready cluster identification, the final solution value was the same.

We also ran an experiment where we clustered an XML document using a clustering tree that didn't store the XML data values. We found that the overall running time was similar to when the clustering tree stored the data values. As stated earlier, XC uses an incremental garbage collector to detect and remove dead objects quickly. This, along with the ready cluster identification, makes the clustering application computationally bound. Hence, once the ready cluster identification is used, the number of iterations has the most impact on the overall running time.

Table 2. Evaluating Memory-Constrained Execution of XC using chunk_size of 4 KB on mondial.xml. As the available memory is reduced, maximum memory utilization and running time improve without significant changing the final solution value.

Memory Limit (bytes)	Memory Usage (bytes)	Value	Time (ms)
∞	1425850	8388200	32511
1000000	900576	8353100	37305
500000	452095	8207900	32070
100000	91264	8138600	17794
50000	47247	7996000	13164
30000	25815	7817300	9049

Table 2 presents the behavior of XC under various specified memory usage limits. We clustered an XML file, mondial.xml, of size 1.97 MB and containing 154855 nodes, using random edge weights. We used the weight bound of 4 KB and ran the experiment, first using a chunk_size of 4096 and without any memory limits. We then repeated the experiment with smaller memory limits (we varied the amount of available memory from 1 MB to 30 KB). The results demonstrate that XC performs well even under extreme memory constraints. Furthermore, as the amount of available memory is reduced, XC degrades gracefully (values of the resultant partitions for the two extreme cases only differ from the best approximate solution by 6%). With tighter memory limits, execution time drops from 32.5 seconds to 9.049 seconds.

The next experiment compares the effectiveness of XC with that of another tree partitioning algorithm, WDFS. We first describe clustering results obtained based on workload-based edge weight assignment. In this experiment, we consider the extreme case in which the workload consists of a single XPath query on mondial.xml:

Table 3. Partitioning mondial.xml using workload-based edge weights. XC computes better partitions than WDFS, but at a higher runtime cost.

chunk_size (bytes)	Value	Time (ms)
WDFS		
4096	279000	11540
XC		
4096	410500	15233
1024	412800	17608
512	415600	21124
256	423700	30640
128	423800	53818
64	432900	132149
32	423900	534455

/mondial/country/province/city. We considered the execution of this query by a hypothetical XPath processor. The edges of the XML tree that would be traversed during such an execution were assigned weight 100. The document was then partitioned by WDFS and XC using various chunk_sizes. The results are illustrated in Table 3. In all cases, we see a clear advantage for XC over WDFS in terms of partition values.

4.3   Evaluating Using the Prototype Clustering System, XCS

While the previous experiments examine XC's usefulness as a clustering algorithm which produces high value partitions in reasonable space and time, this sub-section investigates the usefulness of the resulting clustering for applications. To this end, we tested how the resulting page layouts affect query processing.

The testing was performed in the context of the prototype clustering system, **XCS** (Section 4.1). For these tests, we considered the following query workload on mondial.xml, consisting of four XPath queries:

(Q1) /mondial/country/province[2]/city   150
(Q2) /mondial/country[//enthicgroups]   100
(Q3) /mondial/country/province/city[longitude or lattitude]   150
(Q4) /mondial/organization/members   100

Queries Q1 and Q3 were assigned the weight, 150, and queries Q2 and Q4 were assigned the weight, 100. Queries Q1 and Q2 were executed using a prefix path index on /mondial/country and the query Q3 was executed using another prefix path index on /mondial/country/province. We clustered mondial.xml in **XCS** using XC and WDFS as the tree partitioning algorithms. We first used the combined workload consisting of 4 queries and then repeated the experiments for individual workloads consisting of a single query. We used a weight bound of 4 KB for all experiments and for XC, we used a chunk_size of 1 KB.

We simulated the execution of each query using the mixed XPath processing model under different clustering scenarios. We generated traces of XML nodes traversed while executing the XPath queries with and without path indices. These traces, along with the page layouts for different clusterings, were used for evaluating the paging behavior. We modified two important parameters to vary the paging scenarios. The first, *buffer size* is the number of disk pages that can be held in memory. The second, *prefetch quantity*, is the number of contiguous disk pages that are fetched in a single disk access (starting at the page addressed and including consecutive pages). The first scenario used a buffer size of 1 page with a 1 page prefetch (denoted by 1/1); the second scenario considered infinite buffer size (i.e., a fetched page is retained in memory for the duration of the execution) and 1 page prefetch (denoted by Inf/1); the final scenario simulated a realistic situation of using a buffer with 64 pages with a 2 page prefetch (denoted by 64/2). This scenario used a simple LRU scheme for discarding in-memory pages. In all cases, we assumed a page size of 4 KB.

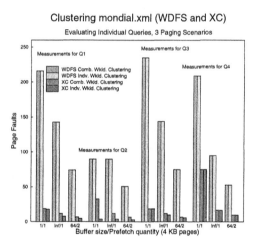

Fig. 2. Page faults for WDFS- and XC-based Clustering for combined and individual query workloads. The weight bound was 4 KB and the chunk_size was 1 KB. Execution of queries Q1, Q2, and Q3 used prefix path indexes. Query Q4 used navigation over parent-child edges.

Figure 2 represents the page fault measurements for WDFS- and XC-based clustering using combined (namely, the clustering was based on all four queries) and individual (namely, the clustering was based on a single query) workloads. As demonstrated by the results, in all cases, XC caused fewer page faults than WDFS. While WDFS was able to exploit local parent-child traversal affinities, XC was able capture and exploit traversal affinities over *paths* of the abstract XML tree. Although the best paging performance was observed when the document was clustered solely based on the single workload query, the paging performance of individual queries didn't degrade substantially when the document was clustered using the combined query workload. The biggest gain was observed for the query, Q2, which was assigned the weight 100. When the combined workload was used, XC generated a clustering that favored the queries Q1 and Q2, which had heavier weights. In contrast, query Q4 exhibited no improvement when the individual query workload was used. Query Q4 did not traverse the same region as the remaining three queries and hence, it solely determined the partitioning of its region, even under the combined workload. This result demonstrated that XC was able to compute the final solution that matched both the *combined* traversal pattern and *individual* traversal patterns.

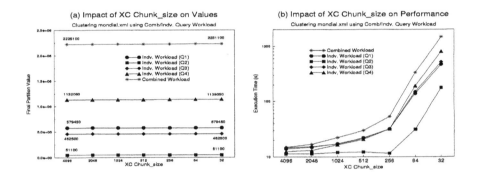

Fig. 3. Impact of XC's chunk_size of the final partition value (a) and the overall execution time (b). `mondial.xml` was partitioned using the combined and individual workloads. The weight bound was 4 KB. Execution of queries Q1, Q2, and Q3 used prefix path indexes. Query Q4 used navigation over parent-child edges.

We also studied the impact of XC's precision on the clustering behavior. We clustered `mondial.xml` using the combined workload with the weight bound, W= 4 KB, and reran the experiment by varying the chunk_size from 4096 to 32. We found that 32 was the smallest chunk_size for `mondial.xml` for which XC could compute the final solution in a reasonable amount of time. Figures 3(a) and (b) illustrate the impact of XC's chunk_size on the final partition value and the overall execution time. As Figure 3(a) shows, apart from the combined and individual Q4 workloads, the chunk_size had no effect on the final partition value. The query Q4, `/mondial/organization/members`, traverses a region of the XML tree that is closer to the root. Since XC is a bottom-up algorithm, subtrees closer to the root are processed in the later stages of the algorithm. Hence, a more precise version of XC is needed to exploit local affinities in those subtrees that could be processed later in the algorithm. As shown in Figure 3(a), the difference in values corresponding to the maximum and minimum chunk_sizes (i.e., 4096 and 32) was extremely small ($< 1\%$). However, as the chunk_size was reduced, XC's running time increased by an order of magnitude (Figure 3(b)). These results illustrate that for smaller chunk_sizes (i.e., at higher precision), XC can compute a better final partition (as shown for the query Q4), but at higher precision, XC always requires large running times. These results also indicate that clustering at higher precision may not always lead to an improvement in the number of page faults.

5   Related Work

Determining if there exists a tree partition with a value at least v is NP-complete in the ordinary sense (Problem ND15, acyclic partitioning) [5]. Johnson and Niemi propose two algorithms for this problem [7]. Both exhibit higher running times than LUKES.

Since early days of database development, physical clustering of related data items has been examined for exploiting data access patterns. An early reported application of clustering for physical database design was in hierarchical databases [10]. Object-oriented databases (OODBs) have used clustering of logically related objects for achieving better physical object placement [12,6]. Object clustering in OODBs has not been widely accepted primarily due to the complexities of object-oriented programming (e.g., dynamically changing object access patterns) and problems with effectively partitioning the resultant object graph. OODBs traditionally use graph partitioning algorithms for partitioning a clustering graph whose node weights represent object sizes and edge weights denote access behavior. Such algorithms exhibit large space and time requirements. Furthermore, these graph partitioning techniques are not suitable for partitioning trees as they can't exploit structural aspects of trees for making partitioning decisions. Also, these algorithms assume the entire graph to be generated before partitioning and need *multiple in-memory* passes over the generated graph. Interestingly, [6] uses Lukes' tree partitioning algorithm when the clustering graph is a tree and concludes that it is not useful in real applications due to its large memory usage.

In [3], Fiebig et al. describe Natix, a native XML system that splits XML documents into multiple subtrees (records) such that each subtree record can fit into a page. Their splitting algorithm uses a split matrix to determine which nodes that should be always stored together. We believe a schema-agnostic workload-directed clustering algorithm like XC can be used to generate tree partitions and these partitions could be then integrated into the Natix-like record structure.

6   Conclusions and Future Work

In this work, we presented XC, a new approximate tree partitioning algorithm, that is tailored for clustering static XML documents. We showed that XC improves on Lukes' tree partitioning algorithm. XC is an approximate tree partitioning algorithm, exhibiting running time that is linear in the size of the input file. XC can even operate within a memory limit. XC can be used in varying degrees of precision; higher precision could potentially compute better solutions, although with higher memory and runtime costs. Extensive experimental evaluation demonstrated that workload-directed clustering of XML document works well in practice. Furthermore, clustering of XML documents using XC is superior to clustering based on the WDFS, an alternative workload-directed clustering scheme. This validates our formulation of the XML clustering problem as a tree partitioning problem. XC was able to capture and exploit XML navigational workload affinities over paths of the abstract XML tree. Our current work involves extending these techniques for clustering XML documents in scenarios where either the workload is changing dynamically or the XML document is structurally updated. We also plan to investigate extensions to XC to exploit affinities across sibling edges.

References

1. P. Bohannon, J. Freire, P. Roy, and J. Simeon. From XML Schema to Relations: A Cost-Based Approach to XML Storage. In *Proceedings of the 18th IEEE International Conference on Data Engineering*, pages 64–80, 2002.
2. R. Bordawekar and O. Shmueli. Flexible Workload-aware Clustering of XML Documents. Technical report, IBM T. J. Watson Research Center, May 2004.
3. T. Fiebig, S. Helmer, C. Kanne, J. Mildenberger, G. Moerkotte, R. Schiele, and T. Westmann. Anatomy of a Native XML Database System. Technical Report, University of Mannheim, 2002.
4. D. Florescu and D. Kossmann. Storing and Querying XML Data using an RDBMS. *IEEE Data Engineering Bulletin*, 22(3):27–34, 1999.
5. M. S. Garey and D. S. Johnson. *Computers and Intractability*. W. H. Freeman and Co., 1979.
6. C. A. Gerlhof, A. Kemper, C. Kilger, and G. Moerkotte. Partition-Based Clustering in Object Bases: From Theory to Practice. In *Proceedings of the Foundations of Data Organization and Algorithms, FODO'93*, pages 301–316, 1993.
7. D. S. Johnson and K. A. Niemi. On Knapsacks, Partitions, and a New Dynamic Programming Technique for Trees. *Mathematics of Operations Research*, 8(1), 1983.
8. C. Kanne and G. Moerkotte. Efficient Storage of XML Data. In *Proceedings of the 16th International Conference on Data Engineering*. IEEE Computer Society, March 2000.
9. J. A. Lukes. Efficient Algorithm for the Partitioning of Trees. *IBM Journal of Research and Development*, 13(2):163–178, 1974.
10. M. Schkolnick. A Clustering Algorithm for Hierarchical Structures. *Transactions on Database Systems*, 2(1):27–44, 1977.
11. H. Schoning and J. Wasch. Tamino - An Internet Database System. In *Advances in Database Technology – EDBT'00*, pages 383–387, 2000.
12. M. M. Tsangaris and J. F. Naughton. On the Performance of Object Clustering Techniques. In *Proceedings of the 1992 ACM SIGMOD International Conference on Management of Data*, pages 144–153. ACM Press, 1992.

XIST: An XML Index Selection Tool

Kanda Runapongsa[1], Jignesh M. Patel[2], Rajesh Bordawekar[3], and
Sriram Padmanabhan[4]

[1] Khon Kaen University, Khon Kaen 40002, Thailand, krunapon@kku.ac.th
[2] University of Michigan, Ann Arbor MI 48105, USA, jignesh@eecs.umich.edu
[3] IBM T.J. Watson Research Center, Hawthorne NY 10532, USA, bordaw@us.ibm.com
[4] IBM Sillicon Valley Lab, San Jose CA 95134, USA, srp@us.ibm.com

Abstract. XML indices are essential for efficiently processing XML queries
which typically have predicates on both structures and values. Since the number of all possible structural and value indices is large even for a small XML
document with a simple structure, XML DBMSs must carefully choose which
indices to build. In this paper, we propose a tool, called XIST, that can be used by
an XML DBMS as an index selection tool. XIST exploits XML structural information, data statistics, and query workload to select the most beneficial indices.
XIST employs a technique that organizes paths that evaluate to the same result
into *structure equivalence groups* and uses this concept to reduce the number
of paths considered as candidates for indexing. XIST selects a set of candidate
paths and evaluates the benefit of an index for each candidate path on the basis of
performance gains for non-update queries and penalty for update queries. XIST
also recognizes that an index on a path can influence the benefit of an index on
another path and accounts for such index interactions. We present an experimental
evaluation of XIST and current XML index selection techniques, and show that the
indices selected by XIST result in greater overall improvements in query response
times.

1   Introduction

An XML document is usually modeled as a directed graph in which each edge represents a parent-child relationship and each node corresponds to an element or an attribute.
XML processing often involves navigating this graph hierarchy using regular path expressions and selecting those nodes that satisfy certain conditions. A naïve exhaustive
traversal of the entire XML data to evaluate path expressions is expensive, particularly in
large documents. Structural join algorithms [1,8,27] can improve the evaluation of path
expressions, but as in the relational world, join evaluation consumes a large portion of
the query evaluation time. Indices on XML data can provide a significant performance
improvement for path expressions and predicates that match the index. However, an
index degrades the performane of update operations and requires additional disk space.
As a result, determining which set of indices to build is a critical administrative task.
These considerations for building indices are not new, and have been investigated extensively for relational databases[24,3]. However, index selection for XML databases

Z. Bellahsène et al. (Eds.): XSym 2004, LNCS 3186, pp. 219–234, 2004.
© Springer-Verlag Berlin Heidelberg 2004

is more complex due to the flexibility of XML data and the complexity of its structure. The XML model mixes structural tags and values inside data. This extends the domain of indexing to the combination of tag names and element content values. In contrast, relational database systems mostly consider only attribute value domains for indexing. Moreover, the natural emergence of path expression query languages, such as XPath, further suggests the need for *path indices*. Path indices have been proposed in the past for object-oriented databases and even as join indices [23] in relational databases. Unlike relational and object-oriented databases, XML data does not require a schema. Even when XML documents have associated schemas, the schemas can be complex. An XML schema can specify optional, repetitive, recursive elements, and complex element hierarchies with variable depths. In addition, a path expression can also be constrained by the content values of different elements on the path. Hence, selecting indices to speed up the evaluation of XML path expressions is challenging.

This paper describes XIST, a prototype XML index selection tool that uses an integrated cost/benefit-driven approach. The cost models used in this paper are developed for a prototype native XML DBMS that we are building. As in other native XML systems, this system stores XML data as individual nodes [27,17,12,7,14], and also uses stack-based join algorithms [1,8,2] for evaluating path expressions. However, the general framework of XIST can be adapted to systems with other cost models by modifying the cost equations that are presented in this paper.

1.1   Contributions

Our work makes the following contributions:

- We propose a cost-benefit model for computing the effectiveness of a set of XML indices. In this cost-benefit analysis, we account for the index update costs and also consider the interaction effect of an index on the benefit of other indices. By carefully reasoning about index interactions, we can eliminate redundancy computations in the index selection tool.
- When the XML schema is available, XIST uses a concept of *structure equivalence groups*, which results in a dramatic reduction in the number of candidate indices.
- We develop a *flexible* tool that can recommend candidate indices even when only some input sources are available. In particular, the availability of only either the schema or the user workload is sufficient for the tool.
- Our experimental results indicate that XIST can produce index recommendations that are more efficient than those suggested by current index selection techniques. Moreover, the quality of the indices selected by XIST increases as more information and/or more disk space is available.

The remainder of this paper is organized as follows. Section 2 presents data models, assumptions, and terminologies used in this work. In Section 3, we describe the overview of the XIST algorithm. Sections 4, 5, and 6 describe the individual components of XIST in detail. Experimental results are presented in Section 7, and the related work is described in Section 8. Finally, Section 9 contains our concluding remarks and directions for future work.

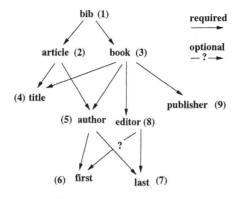

Fig. 1. Sample XML Schema

2 Background

In this section, we describe the XML data models, terminologies, and assumptions that we use in this paper.

2.1 Models of XML Data, Schema, and Queries

We model XML data as a tree. We encode the nodes of the tree using Dietz's numbering scheme [11,10]. Each node is labeled with a pair of numbers representing its positions on preorder and postorder traversals. Using Dietz's proposition, node x is an ancestor of node y if and only if the preorder number of node x is less than that of node y and the postorder number of node x is greater than that of node y. This basic numbering scheme can be extended to include an additional number that encodes the level of the node in the XML data tree. This numbering scheme is used in our cost models when performing the structural joins [27,8,1] between parents and children or between ancestors and descendants. We need the additional level information of a node to differentiate between parent-child and ancestor-descendant relationships.

We model an XML schema as a directed label graph. An XML schema is written in the W3C XML Schema Definition Language which describes and constrains the content of XML documents. It allows the definition of groups of elements and attributes. We can group elements sequentially, or choose some elements to appear and others to disappear, or define an unordered set of elements. An edge between each node in the XML Schema graph here is the edge between a parent element and a child element while child elements are grouped sequentially. The required edge from node A to node B refers that the minimum number of occurrences of B that appear inside node A is at least one; on the other hand, the optional edge refers that the minimum number of occurrences of B that appear inside node A is zero. Figure 1 shows the schema of a sample bibliography database that we use as a running example throughout this paper.

2.2 Terminologies and Assumptions

We now define terminologies for paths and path indices that are used in this paper.

A *label path* p (referred to as a path as well) is a sequence of labels $l_1/l_2/.../l_k$ where the length of the path is k. We assume that the returned result of path p is the ending node of path p. Path p_d is dependent on path p if p is a subpath of p_d. For example, path $l_1/l_2/.../l_k$ is dependent on path l_1/l_2.

A *path index (PI)* on path p is an index that has p as a key and returns the node IDs (NIDs) of the nodes that matched p. (As discussed in Section 2.1, an NID is simply a triplet encoding the begin, end, and level information.)

An *element index (EI)* is a special type of a path index. Since an element "path" consists of only one node, the element index stores only the NIDs of the nodes matched by the element name.

A *candidate path (CP)* is a path on which XIST considers as a candidate for building an index. The corresponding index on the candidate path is called a *candidate path index (CPI)*.

In our work, we consider the following types of indices as candidates: (i) structural indices on individual elements, (ii) structural indices on simple paths as defined above, and (iii) value indices on the content of elements and attribute values. It is possible to extend our models to include other types of indices, such as an index on a twig query, in the future.

3 The XIST Algorithm

In making its recommendations for a set of indices, XIST is designed to work flexibly with the availability of a schema, a workload, and data characteristics of an XML data set. Figure 2 shows an overview of XIST, which consists of four modules that adapt to a given set of input configuration. The first module is the *candidate path selection* module, which eliminates a large number of potentially irrelevant path indices. It uses the following two techniques: (i) If the query workload is available, this module eliminates paths that are not in the query workload, and (ii) If the schema is available, the tool identifies and prunes equivalent paths that can be evaluated using a common index.

To compute the benefits of indices on candidate paths, we use either the *cost-based benefit computation* module or the *heuristic-based benefit computation* module, depending on the availability of data statistics. When data statistics are available, the cost-based benefit computation module is employed. When data statistics are not available, the heuristic-based benefit computation module is operated instead. (The computation carried out by the benefit computation modules may be present in many optimizers, and these modules could be shared by the query optimizer.)

The last module is *configuration enumeration*, which in each iteration chooses an index from the candidate index set that yields the maximum benefit. The configuration enumeration module continues selecting indices until a space constraint, such as a limit on the available disk space, is met.

Figure 3 presents the overview of the XIST algorithm. In the following sections, we describe in detail the steps shown in this figure. The first phase, the selection of candidate paths (CPs), is presented in Section 4. Section 5 discusses the benefit computations for the indices on the selected CPs (CPIs). Finally, Section 6 describes the re-computation for the benefits of CPIs that have not been chosen (line 9).

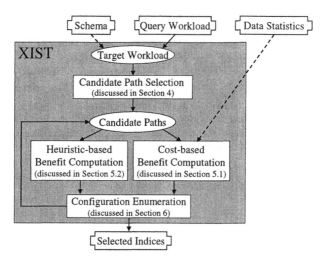

Fig. 2. The XIST Architecture

4   Candidate Path Selection

In this section, we address the important issue of selecting candidate paths (CPs). Since the total number of candidate paths for an XML schema instance can be very large, for efficiency purposes, it is desirable to identify a subset of the candidate paths that can be safely dropped from consideration without reducing the effectiveness of the index selection tool. The candidate path selection module in XIST employs a novel technique to achieve this goal.

Our strategy for reducing the number of CPs is to share an index among multiple paths. Our approach for grouping similar paths involves identifying paths that share the same ending nodes. Since the ending nodes of these paths are the same, the index on a single path of the paths in this group returns the same set of nodes that other paths will (assume that the returned nodes of the path are only the ending nodes of the path).

Definition 1. *A path p_u, $n_1/n_2/.../n_k$, is a unique path if there is one and only one incoming required edge to n_i and there is one and only one incoming required edge to node n_i which must be exclusively from node n_{i-1} for $i = 2$ to k.*

Definition 2. *Path p_1 and path p_2 are in the same structure equivalence group if 1) p_1 and p_2 share the same suffix subpath, 2) the starting node of the shared suffix subpath must have only one incoming edge, and 3) the non-suffix subpath is a unique path.*

We refer to a group of paths that share the same ending nodes as a *Structure Equivalence Group (SEG)*. As an example of an SEG consider the schema shown in Figure 1. A sample SEG in this schema is the set containing the following paths: bib/book/publisher, book/publisher, and publisher. For brevity, we refer to the paths using the concatenation of the first letter of each element on the path (for

Inputs: An index space constraint k (which can be the available disk space [default], or the number of indices), an XML schema, a query workload, and optional data statistics. The algorithm requires at least the schema or the workload.

Output: A set of recommended path indices, S

XIST()

// Phase 1: Candidate Path Selection

1. use the XML schema or the query workload to compute the target workload W.
2. choose paths and subpaths in the target workload W to form the set of candidate paths (CPs).

// Phase 2: Benefit Computation

3. for each CP p, compute the benefit of the corresponding CPI: I_p. The benefit is $B(I_p)$

// Phase 3: Configuration Enumeration

4. initialize the set of selected indices, S to I_E where I_E is the set of element indices.
5. **while** ($|S| < k$)
6.   select $p \in CP$ and $I_p \notin S$ such that $B(I_p)$ is the maximum.
7. $CP = CP - p$
8. $S = S \cup I_p$
9. $\exists p \in CP$, recompute the benefits of candidate path indices, $B(I_p)$
10. **endwhile**

Fig. 3. The XIST Algorithm

example, we refer to bib/book/publisher as bbp). As shown in the schema graph in Figure 1, bbp is a unique path as p has only one parent, and each of its ancestors also has only one parent. Nodes that match bbp are the same as nodes that match the suffix paths of bbp which are bp and p. Thus, these paths are in the same SEG. However, suppose that if publisher has two parents: book and article. Then, bib/book/publisher, book/publisher and publisher do not form a SEG since we cannot assume that publisher is the publisher of the book (book/publisher). The publisher can also be the publisher of the article (book/article). On the other hand, book/publisher and /bib/book/publisher form a SEG. In this SEG, the shared suffix subpath is book/publisher

Instead of building indices on each path in an SEG, XIST only builds an index on the shortest path in each SEG. We choose the shortest path because the space and access time of indices in SEGs can often be reduced. This is because the shortest path can simply be a single element. In such an index, we only need to store three integers *(begin, end, level)* per index entry, whereas in indices on longer paths require storing six integers per index entry.

Since structure equivalence groups are determined based only on the XML schema, these groups are valid for all XML documents conforming to the XML schema. The SEGs cannot be determined by using data statistics because statistics do not indicate whether a node is contained in only one element type. Since some elements in XML data can be optional, they may not appear in XML document instances and thus may not appear in data statistics as well.

5   Index Benefit Computation

In this section, we describe the internal benefit models used by the XIST algorithm to compute the benefits of candidate path indices (CPIs). The total benefit of an index

Inputs: A set of existing indices S, a target workload W, and a CPI on path p, I_p
Output: The benefit of I_p, $B(I_p)$
ComputeIndexBenefit()
// F_E and F_D are functions for benefit computation
1. $B_E = 0$
2.   **for** path $p_e \in EQ(p)$ and $p_e \in W$
3. $B_e = F_E(p, p_e, S)$
4. $B_E = B_E + B_e$
5.   **endfor**
6. $B_D = 0$
7.   **for** path p_d with p as a subpath and $p_d \in W$
8. $B_d = F_D(p, p_d, S)$
9. $B_D = B_D + B_d$
10. **endfor**
11. if data statistics are available
12. $B(I_p) = B_E + B_D - U(I_p)$
13. else
14. $B(I_p) = B_E + B_D$

Fig. 4. The Index Benefit Computation Algorithm for CPI I_p

I_p, $B(I_p)$, is computed as the sum of: (i) B_E, which is the benefit of using I_p for answering queries on the equivalent paths of p (recall that all paths in an EQ share the same path index), and (ii) B_D, which is the benefit of using I_p for answering queries on the dependent paths of p. Figure 4 presents an algorithm for computing the total benefit of I_p, $B(I_p)$.

5.1 Cost-Based Benefit Computation

When data statistics are available, XIST can estimate the cost of evaluating paths more accurately. The collected data statistics consist of a sequence of tuples, each representing a path expression and the cardinality of the node set that matches the path (also called the cardinality of a path expression). XIST uses the path cardinality to predict path evaluation costs. In reality, however, these costs depend largely on the native storage implementation and the optimizer features of an XML engine. To address this issue, we approximate the path evaluation costs via abstract cost models based on our experimental native XML DBMS.

Computing Evaluation Costs. The cost of evaluating a path with the index on the path is estimated to be proportional to the cardinality of the path since the path index is implemented using a hash index and the hash index access cost is proportional to the number of items retrieved from the hash index. Let $C(p_1/p_2, S \cup I_{p_1/p_2})$ be the cost of evaluating p_1/p_2. Then,

$$C(p_1/p_2, S \cup I_{p_1/p_2}) \approx K_I \times (|p_1/p_2|) \tag{1}$$

where K_I is a constant and $|p_1/p_2|$ is the cardinality of the nodes matched by p_1/p_2.

If an index on a path does not exist, XIST splits the path into two subpaths and then recursively evaluates them. When splitting the path, XIST needs to determine the join order of subpaths to minimize the join cost. The chosen pair has the minimal sum of the cardinalities of subpaths. Subpaths are recursively split until they can be answered using existing indices. After subpaths are evaluated, their results are recursively joined to answer the entire path. Finding an optimal join order is not the focus of this paper, but it has been recently proposed [26].

When XIST joins a path of two indexed subpaths, it uses a structural join algorithm [1], which guarantees that the worst case join cost is linear in the sum of sizes of the sorted input lists and the final result list. Let S be the set of indices which exclude the index on p_1/p_2, and $C(p_1/p_2, S)$ be the cost of joining between path p_1 and path p_2. Then,

$$C(p_1/p_2, S) \approx K_J \times (|p_1| + |p_2| + |p_1/p_2|) \tag{2}$$

where K_J is the constant and $|p_i|$ is the estimated cardinality of the nodes that match p_i. The estimated cardinality of the nodes that match the paths are given as an input of the XIST tool (by the XML estimation module in the system).

Since the maintenance cost for an index can be very expensive, XIST also considers the maintenance cost in the index benefit computation. The actual cost for updating a path index is very much dependent on the system implementation details, and different systems are likely to have different costs for index updates. In this paper, for simplicity, we use an update cost model in which the update cost for a given path index is proportional to the the number of entries being updated in the path index. (This cost model can be adapted in a fairly straightforward manner if the cost needs to include a log-based factor, which is a characteristic for tree-based indices.)

Let $U(I_{p_1/p_2})$ be the cost of updating the index on path p_1/p_2, then

$$U(I_{p_1/p_2}) \approx K_U \times (|p_1/p_2|) \tag{3}$$

where K_U is the constant and $|p_1/p_2|$ is the cardinality of the nodes that match p_1/p_2.

Using Cost Models for Computing Benefits. Now we describe how the cost models are used to compute the total benefit of an index when data statistics are available. The benefit function $F_E(p, p_e, S)$ is the function to compute the benefit of using I_p to completely evaluate a path in the structure equivalence group of p (p_e), assuming the set of indices S exists. The benefit function $F_D(p, p_d, S)$ is the function to compute the benefit of using I_p to partially answer a dependent path of p (p_d), assuming the set of indices S exists.

$$
\begin{array}{ll}
F_E(p, p_e, S) & = C(p_e, S) - C(p, S \cup I_p) \\
F_D(p, p_d, S) & = C(p_d, S) - C(p_d, S \cup I_p)
\end{array}
$$

Fig. 5. F_E and F_D for I_p (with Statistics)

5.2   Heuristic-Based Benefit Computation

When data statistics are not available, XIST estimates the benefit of the index by using the lengths of queries and the length of the candidate path (CP). The benefit of a candidate path index (CPI) is estimated based on: a) the number of joins required to answer queries with and without the CPI, and b) the use of a CPI to completely or partially evaluate a query.

In the following paragraphs, we use the following notations: p is a CP, I_p is a CPI, p_e is an equivalent path of p (a path that I_p can completely answer), and p_d is a dependent path of p (a path that I_p can partially answer).

We first consider the benefit of I_p when it can completely answer a query. This benefit is computed by the F_E function, which estimates the number of joins needed as the length of the shortest unindexed subpath of p. Let $L(p)$ be the length of path p, S be the set of existing indices, and $L'(p, S)$ be the length of the shortest unindexed subpath in p. $L'(p, S)$ is the difference between the length of p and that of the longest indexed subpath of p.

Next, we consider the benefit of I_p when it can partially answer a query. This benefit is computed by the F_D function. Like F_E, F_D estimates the number of joins needed to answer the query. However, in this case, the number of joins needed is more than just the length of an unindexed subpath of the query. The closer the length of p to the length of unindexed subpath of the query, the higher benefit of I_p is. We use the difference between the length of p and that of the query as the number of the joins that the index cannot answer. The benefit functions F_E and F_D are shown in Figure 6.

$$
\begin{aligned}
F_E(p, p_e, S) \;&=\; L'(p_e, S) \\
F_D(p, p_d, S) \;&=\; L'(p_d, S) - (L(p_d) - L(p)) \\
&=\; L'(p_d, S) - L(p_d) + L(p)
\end{aligned}
$$

Fig. 6. F_E and F_D for I_p (Without Statistics)

6   Configuration Enumeration

After the benefit of each CPI is computed using F_E and F_D in the index benefit algorithm (Figure 4), the first two phases of the XIST algorithm (Figure 3) are completed. In the third phase, XIST first selects the CPI with the highest benefit to the set of chosen indices S. Since XIST takes the index interaction into account, it needs to recompute the benefits of CPIs that have not been chosen. The key idea in efficiently recomputing the benefits of CPIs is to recompute only the benefits of the indices on paths that are affected by the chosen indices. A naïve algorithm would recompute the benefit of each CPI that has not been selected. In contrast, XIST employs a more efficient strategy no matter whether it uses the heuristic-based benefit computation or cost-based benefit computation. The strategy is briefly described below.

XIST considers three types of paths that are affected by a selected index on path p: (a) subqueries that have not been evaluated and that contain p as a subpath, (b) paths that are subpaths of p, and (c) paths that are not subpaths of p but are subpaths of paths in (a).

Using these relationships between selected paths and other unselected paths, we can reduce the number of benefit re-computations for the unselected indices. We need to re-compute the benefits of unselected indices because the benefits of these indices depend on the existence of selected indices. The situation in which the benefits of one index depends on the existence of other indices is called *index interaction*.

If we did not find such relationships between the selected indices and the unselected indices, we could spend an excessive amount of time in computing the benefits of many remaining unselected indices.

7   Experimental Evaluation

In this section, we present the results from an extensive experimental evaluation of XIST, and compare it with current index selection techniques.

7.1   Experimental Setup

The XIST tool that we implemented is a stand-alone C++ application. It uses the Apache Xerces C++ version 2.0 [20] to parse an XML schema. It also implements the selection and benefit evaluation of candidate indices, and the configuration enumeration. We then used the indices recommended by the XIST toolkit as an input to an native XML DBMS that we are currently developing. This system implements stack-based structural join algorithms [1]. It uses B+tree to implement the value index, and uses a hash indexing mechanism to implement the path indices. It evaluates XML queries as follows: if a path query matches an indexed pathname, the nodes matching the path are retrieved from the path index. If there is no match, the DBMS uses the structural join algorithm [1] to join indexed subpaths. Queries on long paths are evaluated using a pipeline of structural join operators. The operators are ordered by the estimated cardinality of each join result, with the pair resulting in the smallest intermediate result being scheduled first. A query with a value-based predicate is executed by evaluating the value predicate first.

In all our experiments, the DBMS was configured to use a 32 MB buffer pool. All experiments were performed on an 1.70 GHz Intel Xeon processor, running Debian Linux version 2.4.13.

7.2   Data Sets and Queries

We used the following four commonly used XML data sets: DBLP [18], Mondial [25], Shakespeare Plays [13], and XMark benchmark [22]. For each data set, we generated a workload of ten queries. These queries were generated using a query generator which takes the set of all distinct paths in the input XML documents as input. The detail of the generation method can be found in the full-length version of the paper [21].

As an example, using the generation method, some of the queries on the Plays data set are as follow: FM/P and /PLAY/ACT/EPILOGUE/SPEECH[SPEAKER="KING"].

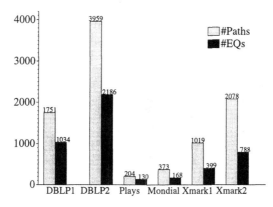

Fig. 7. Number of Paths and Structure Equivalence Groups

7.3   Experimental Results

We now present experimental results that evaluate various aspects of the XIST toolkit. First, we demonstrate the effectiveness of the path structure equivalence group (SEG) in reducing the number of candidate paths. Then, we compare the performance of XIST with the performance of a number of alternative index selection schemes. We also performed the experiments to access the impact of the different types of inputs (namely query workload, XML schema and statistics) on the behavior of the XIST toolkit. In addition, we also analyzed the performance of all the index selection schemes when the workload changes over time. However, due to the space limitation, only partial experimental results of the impact of different types of inputs are presented here; more experimental results are presented in the full-length version of this paper [21].

The execution time numbers presented or analyzed in this paper are cold numbers, i.e., the queries do not benefit from having any pages cached in the buffer pool from a previous run of the system.

Effectiveness of Structure Equivalence Groups. Paths in an structure equivalence group are represented by a single unique path which is the smallest path pointing to the same destination node. Therefore, the number of structure equivalence groups denotes the number of such unique paths.

Figure 7 plots the number of paths and the number of structure equivalence groups for all the data sets used in this experimental evaluation. In this figure, DBLP1 and XMark1 represent those paths from DBLP and XMark with lengths up to five, and DBLP2 and XMark2 represent those paths with lengths up to ten. As shown in Figure 7, the number of structure equivalence groups is fewer than the number of total paths by 35%-60%. *This result validates our hypothesis that the number of candidate paths can be reduced significantly using the XML schema to exploit structural similarities.*

Comparison of Different Indexing Schemes. We compare the performance of the following sets of indices: indices on elements (*Elem*), indices on paths with length up to two (*SP*), indices suggested by XIST (*XIST*), and indices on the full path query

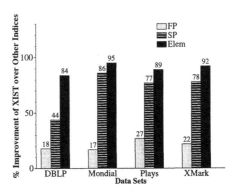

Fig. 8. Performance Improvement of *XIST*

definitions (*FP*). The *Elem* index selection strategy is interesting because it is a minimal set of indices to answer any path query. *SP* is a set of indices on short paths. *XIST* is a set of indices chosen by the XIST tool with given all input information (schema, statistics, and query workload). *FP* is a set of indices that requires no join when evaluating paths without value-based predicates.

All indexing schemes (*Elem*, *SP*, *XIST*, and *FP*) only build indices on paths without value-based predicates. To evaluate paths with value-based predicates, a join operation is used between the nodes returned from indices and the nodes that match the value predicates. We choose to separate the value indices from a path indices to avoid having an excessive number of indices – one for each possible different value-predicate. In our experimental setup, all indexing schemes share the same value indices to evaluate paths with value-based predicates.

Figure 8 shows the performance improvement of *XIST* over other indices for the four experimental data sets. The results shown in Figure 8 illustrate that *XIST* consistently outperforms all other index selection methods for all the data sets. *XIST* is better than *Elem* and *SP* because *XIST* requires fewer joins for evaluating the queries. *XIST* performs better than *FP* largely because the use of structure equivalence groups (SEGs) while evaluating path queries. In many cases, long path queries without value predicates are equivalent to queries on a single element. In such cases, if the size of the element index is smaller than the size of the path index, XIST recommends using the element index to retrieve answer. On the other hand, *FP* needs to access the larger path index. Another reason for the improved performance with *XIST* is that for some data sets the total size of *XIST* indices (including element indices and path indices) is smaller than that of *FP* indices (including element indices and path indices). The total size of *XIST* indices is smaller because it shares a single index among the equivalent paths. Note that the equivalent paths cannot be determined when using *FP* since *FP* does not take a schema as an input information. *FP* takes only query workload as an input information. Table 1 presents the sizes of data sets and indices for all data sets.

Table 1. Sizes of Data Sets and Indices

Data Set	Size (MB)	Index Size (MB)			
		Elem	*SP*	*FP*	*XIST*
DBLP	117	91	117	110	101
Mondial	2	2	3	3	3
Plays	8	80	86	85	81
XMark	11	27	27	27	27

7.4 Impact of Input Information on XIST

In this section, we compared the execution times when using indices suggested by XIST with indices selected by other index selection strategies.

Due to space limitations, in this paper we only present the results for DBLP and XMark when the workload information is available. DBLP represents a shallow data set (short paths), and XMark represents a deep data set (long paths). The experimental results for these two data sets are representative of the results for the other two data sets.

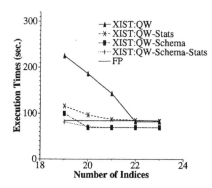

Fig. 9. Performance on DBLP

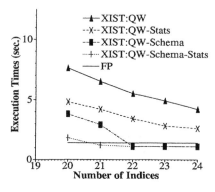

Fig. 10. Performance on Xmark

When the workload information is available, *FP* and *XIST* exploit the information to build indices that can cover most of the queries. *FP* indices cover all paths without value-based predicates in the workload. Thus, its index selection is close to optimal (without any join). When using *FP*, the only joins that the database needs are the joins between the returned nodes from the path index and the nodes that satisfy the value predicates. In Figures 9-10, the number of *FP* indices is used to assign the initial number of indices that the XIST tool generates.

As opposed to the heuristic-based benefit function, the cost-based benefit function guarantees that the more useful indices are chosen before the less useful indices. The execution times of *XIST* with QW-Stats (QW-Schema-Stats) gradually decrease as opposed to the execution times of *XIST* with QW (QW-Schema). This is particularly noticeable in Figure 10.

8   Related Work

In the 1-index [19], data nodes that are bisimilar from the root node stored in the same node in the index graph. The size of the 1-index can be very large compared to the data size, thus A(k)-index [16] has been proposed to make a trade off between the index performance and the index size. While k-bisimilarity [16] is determined by using XML data, the SEGs in this paper are determined by using an XML schema. Recently, D(k)-index [6], which is also based on the concept of bisimilarity, has been proposed as an adaptive structural summary. Like XIST, D(k) also takes the query workload as an input. However, XIST also takes the XML schema into account while D(k) does not. Although both k-bisimilarity and SEGs group paths that lead to the nodes with the same label, SEGs group paths in an XML schema but k-bisimilarity group paths in XML data.

Chung et al. have proposed APEX [9], an adaptive path index for XML documents. Like APEX, XIST exploits the query workload to find indices that are most likely to be useful. On the other hand, APEX does not distinguish the benefit of indices on two paths with same frequencies, but XIST does. In addition, APEX does not exploit data statistics and XML schema in index selection as opposed to XIST.

Recently, Kaushik et al. have proposed F&B-indexes that use the structural features of the input XML documents [15]. F&B indexes are forward-and-backward indices for answering branching path queries. Some heuristics in choosing indices, such as prioritizing short path indices over long path indices are proposed [15]. On the other hand, XIST takes many additional parameters, such as the information from a schema or a query workload.

Many commercial relational database systems employ index selection features in their query optimizers. IBM's DB2 Advisor [24] recommends candidate indices based on the analysis of workload of SQL queries and models the index selection problem as a variation of the knapsack problem. The Microsoft SQL Server [3,4] uses simpler single-column indices in an iterative manner to recommend multi-column indices. XIST groups a set of paths (a set of multiple-columns) that can share the index.

Our work is closest to the index selection schemes proposed by Chawathe et al. [5] for object oriented databases. Both the index selection schemes [5] and XIST find the index interaction through the relationships between subpath indices and queries. However, XIST exploits the structural information to reduce the number of candidate indices and optimize the query processing of XML queries while [5] only looks at the query workload to choose candidate indices for evaluating object-oriented queries.

9   Conclusions

In this paper, we have described XIST, an XML index selection tool, which recommends a set of path indices given a combination of a query workload, a schema, and data statistics. By exploiting structural summaries from schema descriptions, the number of candidate indices can be substantially reduced for most XML data sets and workloads. XIST incorporates a robust benefit analysis technique using cost models or a simplified heuristic. It also models the ability of an index to effectively evaluate sub-paths of a path expression. Our experimental evaluation demonstrates that the indices selected by XIST perform better compared to existing methods.   In our experimental evaluation, we had to tailor the cost model used in XIST to accurately model the techniques that are implemented in our native XML system. However, we believe that the general framework of XIST, with its use of structure equivalence groups and efficient benefit recomputation methods, can be adapted for use with other DBMSs with different implementation and query evaluation algorithms. To adapt this general framework to other systems, accurate cost models equations are required that account for the system-specific details. Within the scope of this paper, we have chosen to focus on the general framework and algorithms of an XML index selection tool, and have demonstrated that its effectiveness for our native XML DBMS.

In the future, we plan on extending XIST to include additional types of path indices, such as indices on regular path expressions and on twig queries.

References

1. S. Al-Khalifa, H. Jagadish, N. Koudas, J. Patel, D. Srivastava, and Y. Wu. Structural Joins: A Primitive for Efficient XML Query Pattern Matching. In *ICDE*, San Jose, CA, February 2002.
2. N. Bruno, N. Koudas, and D. Srivastava. Holistic Twig Joins: Optimal XML Pattern Matching. In *SIGMOD*, pages 310–321, Madison, Wisconsin, June 2002.
3. S. Chaudhuri and V. Narasayya. An Efficient, Cost-Driven Index Selection Tool for Microsoft SQL Server. In *VLDB*, pages 146–155, Athens, Greece, September 1997.
4. S. Chaudhuri and V. Narasayya. Auto Admin "What-If" Index Analysis Utitlity. In *SIGMOD*, pages 367–378, Seattle, Washington, June 1998.
5. S. Chawathe, M. Chen, and P. S. Yu. On Index Selection Schemes for Nested Object Hierarchies. In *VLDB*, pages 331–341, Santiago, Chile, September 1994.
6. Q. Chen, A. Lim, and K. W. Ong. D(K)-Index:An Adaptive Structural Summary for Graph-Structured Data. In *SIGMOD*, pages 134–144, San Diego, CA, June 2003.
7. S.-Y. Chien, V. J. Tsotras, C. Zaniolo, and D. Zhang. Efficient Complex Query Support for Multiversion XML Documents. In *EDBT*, pages 161–178, Prague, Czech Republic, 2002.
8. S.-Y. Chien, Z. Vagena, D. Zhang, V. J. Tsotras, and C. Zaniolo. Efficient Structural Joins on Indexed XML Documents. In *VLDB*, pages 263–274, Hong Kong, China, 2002.
9. C. Chung, J. Min, and K. Shim. APEX:An Adaptive Path Index for XML Data. In *SIGMOD*, pages 121–132, Madison, WI, June 2002.
10. P. Dietz and D. Sleator. Two Algorithms for Maintaining Order in a List. In *Proc. 19th Annual ACM Symp. on Theory of Computing (STOC'87)*, pages 365–372, San Francisco, California, 1987.
11. P. F. Dietz. Maintaining Order in a Linked List. In *Proceedings of the Fourtheenth Annual ACM Symposium of Theory of Computing*, pages 122–127, San Francisco, California, May 1982.
12. T. Grust. Accelerating XPath Location Steps. In *SIGMOD*, pages 109–120, Madison, Wisconsin, 2002.
13. J. Bosak. The Plays of Shakespeare in XML.
    http://metalab.unc.edu/bosak/xml/eg/shaks200.zip.
14. H. V. Jagadish, S. Al-Khalifa, A. Chapman, L. V. S. Lakshmanan, A. Nierman, S. Paparizos, J. M. Patel, N. Niwatwattana, D. Srivastava, Y. Wu, and C. Yu. TIMBER: A Native XML Database. *The VLDB Journal*, 11(4):274–291, 2002.
15. R. Kaushik, P. Bohannon, J. F. Naughton, and H. F. Korth. Covering Indexes for Branching Path Expressions. In *SIGMOD*, pages 133–144, Madison, WI, May 2002.

16. R. Kaushik, P. Shenoy, P. Bohannon, and E. Gudes. Exploiting Local Similarity for Efficient Indexing of Paths in Graph Structured Data. In *ICDE*, pages 129–140, San Jose, CA, February 2002.

17. Q. Li and B. Moon. Indexing and Querying XML Data for Regular Path Expressions. In *VLDB*, pages 361–370, Roma, Italy, September 2001.

18. M. Ley. The DBLP Bibliography Server. http://dblp.uni-trier.de/xml/.

19. T. Milo and D. Suciu. Index Structures for Path Expressions. In *Proceedings of the International Conference on Database Teorey*, pages 277–295, Jerusalem, Israel, January 1999.

20. T. A. X. Project. Xerces C++ Parser. http://xml.apache.org/xerces-c/index.html.

21. K. Runapongsa, J. M. Patel, R. Bordawekar, and S. Padmanabhan. XIST:An XML Index Selection Tool. http://gear.kku.ac.th/~krunapon/research/xist.pdf.

22. A. Schmidt, F. Wass, M. Kersten, D. Florescu, I. Manolescu, M. Carey, and R. Busse. An XML Benchmark Project. Technical report, CWI, Amsterdam, The Netherlands, 2001. http://monetdb.cwi.nl/xml/index.html.

23. P. Valduriez. Join indices. *ACM Trans. Database Syst.*, 12(2):218–246, 1987.

24. G. Valentin, M. Zuliani, D. Zilio, G. Lohman, and A. Skelley. DB2 Advisor:An Optimizer Smart Enough to Recommend its Own Indexes. In *ICDE*, pages 101–110, 2000.

25. W. May. The Mondial Database in XML. http://www.informatik.uni-freiburg.de/~may/Mondial/.

26. Y. Wu, J. Patel, and H. Jagadish. Structural Join Order Selection for XML Query Optimization. In *ICDE*, pages 443–454, Bangalore, India, 2003.

27. C. Zhang, J. Naughton, D. DeWitt, Q. Luo, and G. Lohman. On Supporting Containment Queries in Relational Database Managment Systems. In *SIGMOD*, Santa Barbara, California, May 2001.

Author Index

Lecture Notes in Computer Science

For information about Vols. 1–3072

please contact your bookseller or Springer